Carl H. Rinne
The University of Michigan — Flint

Consulting Editor
Ellis Evans
University of Washington

ATTENTION
The Fundamentals of Classroom Control

Charles E. Merrill Publishing Company
A Bell & Howell Company
Columbus Toronto London Sydney

This book is dedicated to my parents
Carl H. Rinne, Sr.
Maxine Murray Rinne

Published by Charles E. Merrill Publishing Company
A Bell & Howell Company
Columbus, Ohio 43216

Cover Designer: Tony Faiola
Text Designer: Cynthia Brunk
Production Editor: Molly Kyle

Photo Credits: p. 72, top, Northshore Publishing Co., Bothell, Washington; bottom, Strix Pix; p. 73, top, Strix Pix; bottom, Paul Conklin.

Library of Congress Catalog Card Number: 83-62011
International Standard Book Number: 0-675-20044-X
1 2 3 4 5 6—90 89 88 87 86 85 84
Printed in the United States of America

This book is written for several different audiences, each of which has a vested interest in classroom control: experienced teachers of all age levels and subject areas, in all instructional settings, to help them improve their skills of classroom control; new teachers, student teachers, and intern teachers at all grade levels to help answer their never-ending questions ("What should I do to control my classes? What else could I do? Why should I do that?"); teacher educators who want to help teachers make classroom control an applied science as well as a challenging art; and administrators and other school officials who have long searched for an objective way to evaluate classroom control.

Attention: The Fundamentals of Classroom Control is a logical text for courses on classroom management and discipline, on education foundations and student or practice teaching, and for general teaching methods courses. It is also a practical supplementary text for educational psychology and educational sociology.

This book explains hundreds of teacher control techniques and offers three basic principles to help you know which technique to use when and how. Conventional books on classroom control tell you to stop student misbehavior first, then focus student attention on lesson content — a two-step process.

PREFACE

But effective teachers know how to focus attention automatically, in one step. You can use this text in preservice or inservice teacher education courses, and in your classroom as a basic reference. The Taxonomy of Classroom Controls is comprehensive and helpful to both new and experienced teachers.

Chapter 1 provides a brief introduction to some of the notable "systems" that have been developed in recent years for classroom control, including the theories of Bloom, Glasser, Gordon, Dreikurs, Berne, Kounin, Skinner, and Alschuler.

Chapter 2 demonstrates that the teacher's first responsibility is to keep student attention focused on lesson content. It explains and illustrates visual cues to student attention, and introduces the concept of low profile classroom control which is fundamental to effective teaching. This chapter contains the comprehensive Taxonomy of Classroom Controls, along with principles to govern its use.

Chapters 3 through 19 describe hundreds of techniques of classroom control and occasions when each technique may be appropriate. Most of these chapters contain exercises in low profile techniques, to help you build skills and thus increase confidence and competence.

Chapter 20 analyzes some of the infamous games students play to bait teachers, evade work, and attract attention, and suggests ways to stop these games. Chapter 21 examines some of the games teachers play when they lose control of student attention, and suggests techniques for regaining control. Chapter 22 explains effective techniques for negotiating the noninstructional problems, disagreements, and conflicts that inevitably arise in classrooms.

We see in the Epilogue that teaching is a universal enterprise, and that the fundamental skills of teaching in one country are fundamental to teaching in other countries as well, with supporting evidence from a study of elementary and secondary schools in Japan. Appendix A cites several research studies that directly relate student attention to learning outcomes, and Appendix B, written primarily for administrators, supervisors, and teacher educators, gives specific, practical criteria for evaluating teacher effectiveness in classroom control.

Most chapters contain practical training exercises with complete, class-tested directions for instructor and students. These exercises are essential to skill mastery; if you do them with reasonable care, you will be able to measure your growing competence. Most exercises provide either for the instructor's direct observation of each person's skill or for written peer monitoring of the skill according to clearly stated criteria.

ACKNOWLEDGEMENTS

During its development over ten years, this book has been funded, aided, and influenced by many people. My earlier work on patterned transactions between teachers and students was funded by a Faculty Grant from the Horace Rackham School of Graduate Studies at The University of Michigan. The University of Michigan-Flint Faculty Development Committee supported my preliminary studies in classroom culture and a portion of my later observational work in Japanese classrooms. The Regents of The University of Michigan supported my 1979 sabbatical to Japan. The Kyoto University Faculty of Education provided me with visiting scholar status and logistical and administrative support during my five months of research in Japan. For this support and to these boards and faculties, I am grateful indeed.

I thank the many principals and teachers in the American elementary and secondary schools which I and my project staff members visited between 1974 and 1977 to observe predictable patterns of teacher-student interaction. I also thank the many principals and teachers in the elementary and secondary schools of the Kansai area of Japan for permitting me to visit their schools for interviews and classroom observations, and the English Club of Kyoto University whose members translated questionnaires for me.

I am grateful to Professor Tetsuya Kobayashi for sponsoring my stay in Japan and my affiliation with Kyoto University; to Mr. Yoshitaka Goda and Miss Kayoko Murata who gave extraordinary time and energy to my project; to Dr. Shusuke Nakajima and his wife Noriko who provided their lovely home and hospitality to me and my family during our stay in Kyoto; and to Bridget Cooper, who not only arranged the Japan Project, but served as able interpreter and administrative assistant during the entire venture.

I appreciate the support of my colleagues at The University of Michigan-Flint, particularly Dr. Thomas Filson, Dr. E. E. Sullivan, Dr. Harold Stahly, Dean James Yankovick, Dean Wesley Rae, Provost Gregory O'Brien, Dr. Ellis Perlman, Dr. Mary Cooper, and Dr. Carol Anselm. Various portions of the manuscript were typed by Mrs. Miriam Filpansik, Ms. Sally Johnson, Mrs. Hallie Taylor, Ms. Rebecca Greber, Mrs. Donna Usitalo, and Ms. Ellen Prokopow.

My students continue to teach me. Without them, this book would not have been conceived or written. A number of student research assistants at The University of Michigan were of great help in gathering classroom data: Judy Darnton, Sue McCarty, Sheila Evans, Michelle Scherer, Ralph Mott, Debbie Bohn, Kenny Feiner, Steve Menken, Carole Cummings, Debbie Urick, Ronda Thorpe, Tom Ketner, Ann Mason, Cynthia Peyton, Vickie Lanning, Lee Clark, Lois Alexander, and Janet Middleton.

In particular, I am grateful to Michael Lerner, who served as Principal Research Assistant for the major pilot study in classroom culture; to Reva Hawke, who coordinated the processing of the Japan Study data and tried hard to keep me on schedule; and to Robert Wainright, who provided statistical analysis for the classroom culture study.

Early portions of this book were read and criticized by many of my students at The University of Michigan-Flint and by Wilma Longstreet, Cary Cherniss, Steven Bossert, Doris Orr, Sue McCarty, Reva Hawke, Carolyn Pelton, Richard Plourde, Kathleen Smith, and Dolores Dawson. I am grateful to all of these friends for their advice and encouragement.

I am especially indebted to Professor Joyce Putnam and her colleagues and students at Michigan State University both for class testing earlier versions of this book and for influencing my thinking during the final stages of rewriting the manuscript.

Harriet Feldlaufer helped me with literature search and documentation for Chapters 3 through 19; in addition, she brought an alert mind and critical eye to the entire project. Her judgment was invaluable, her dedication extraordinary.

I also wish to thank Bill Burgard for his help with the book's creative art.

And finally to my family who have endured this book and its author through trying times: I am grateful for their patience and their hope.

CONTENTS

ATTENTION
The Fundamentals of Classroom Control

CURRENT SYSTEMS
OF CLASSROOM CONTROL

1

Should a teacher adopt one system of classroom control and use it constantly, or borrow parts of various systems and use them appropriately? No currently known "system" is sufficient to anticipate and provide for all situations of classroom control, but several systems offer valuable insights into the nature and means of control, and their various parts can be immensely useful to teachers. The most notable are:

- "Behavior modification," described by several authors and based on principles of operant conditioning devised by B. F. Skinner.
- "Reality Therapy," developed and described by William Glasser.
- "Discipline Without Tears," developed and described by Rudolf Dreikurs and others.
- "Teacher Effectiveness Training," developed by Thomas Gordon.
- "Transactional Analysis," developed by Eric Berne and elaborated by Thomas Harris and others.
- "Social Literacy," developed and described by Alfred Alschuler and Paulo Freire.
- "Discipline and Group Management," research studies on classroom discipline by Jacob Kounin and others.
- "Mastery Learning," developed by Benjamin Bloom and others.
- "Eclectic Discipline," developed by Charles Wolfgang and Carl Glickman.

This list contains two surprises: Kounin's work is not a formal system, but rather a report of research, while Bloom's Mastery Learning has no formal link with classroom discipline. Yet Kounin's work describes effective teaching in considerable detail, and Mastery Learning is in every way an important proposal for classroom control through careful organization of content and instruction and through continuous evaluation of learning.

BEHAVIOR MODIFICATION: SKINNER ET AL.

In 1953, Professor B. F. Skinner of Harvard University published *Science and Human Behavior,* the first major statement of the principles of operant conditioning. Operant conditioning occurs when a person's spontaneous behavior is encouraged—through rewards or praise or other reinforcement—with the result that the behavior becomes stronger and more habitual. In other words, a teacher can influence a student's behavior by skillfully encouraging or discouraging that behavior. Every teacher behavior, whether overt or covert (that is, external or internal), has a potential influence on student behavior (see Method Z). In fact, one might define teaching as the art of applying principles of operant conditioning by creating conditions that make certain desired student behaviors appear, then encouraging only those desired behaviors and withholding encouragement from all others.

Most people today think of Professor Skinner's influence on education in terms of behavior modification. Skinner's Programmed Learning applies behavior modification principles to written teaching materials.

CONTINGENT REINFORCEMENT

Behavior modification urges the teacher to reward acceptable student behavior and ignore unacceptable behavior. Most studies show this technique of contingent attention, that is, teacher attention contingent upon acceptable behavior, to be a powerful force in learning. For example, Madsen, Becker, and Thomas (1968) varied teacher techniques in an experimental study and found that rules alone affected student behavior very little but that a combination of selective rewarding-ignoring was "very effective" (p. 148).

The technique of reward is simply to watch those students who are most often off-task, and when a student behaves appropriately, make comments such as:

"I like the way you are..."

"You're doing a good job on..."

"You got the first one right..."

Nonverbal praise, such as nodding, smiling, or patting on the head or back, can be just as effective as verbal. The important principle is to praise what the student does, not the student himself.

"Ignoring" is an important teacher skill because it avoids the possibility that teacher attention of any kind, positive or negative, might strengthen the very student behavior the teacher is trying to diminish or eliminate.

REINFORCERS

A teacher can use many different kinds of rewards or "reinforcers"; for example:

1   Primary reinforcer—An item or event that directly satisfies a student's human needs (candy, a drink of water, a cookie).

2   Secondary reinforcers—Tradable or symbolic rewards for purchasing or attracting other rewards (tokens such as money or chips or points can be used to obtain desired goods and services; grades, stars, and awards can attract later praise and approval). Teacher praise and peer approval are considered secondary reinforcers.

Reinforcers may be positive (the reinforcer itself is desirable) or negative (the student tries to escape an unpleasant reinforcer). For example, a student works harder to avoid getting low grades on quizzes, thereby avoiding a negative reinforcer and gaining a positive one.

PUNISHMENT

Punishment imposes consequences on undesirable student behavior after the behavior is over. Most behavior modification authorities do not advocate punishment. There is some evidence, however, that punishment can work if it is quick, severe but not too severe, and always preceded by a warning so the student can choose to avoid the punishment (Gage & Berliner, 1979, p. 297).

PREMACK PRINCIPLE

The Premack Principle is the technique of using high probability behaviors (activities students are likely to engage in because they like them) as rewards for low probability behaviors (activities students don't want to do); in other words, privileges:

> "OK, you kids can sign yearbooks as soon as you finish your map worksheets."

Notice the difference between that statement and this nonreinforcing one:

> "OK, you kids should be working on your map worksheets now instead of signing yearbooks."

SCHEDULE OF REINFORCEMENT

A key skill in behavior modification is reinforcing early behavior immediately after it occurs—within seconds. Then, after the early behavior is established, the teacher can schedule later reinforcement on the basis of *ratio* (reinforcing every instance, then every other instance, then every third instance, etc.) or *interval* (reinforcing every 10 seconds, 30 seconds, 60 seconds, etc.).

REINFORCEMENT OF INCOMPATIBLE BEHAVIORS

Incompatible behaviors are those that are difficult for students to perform simultaneously with the undesired behaviors. Here are some examples:

- Some students are off-task, some are on. The teacher praises the students who are on-task.
- Suzy goofs off 60 percent of her seatwork time; the teacher rewards her during the other 40 percent.
- The student talks off-task during class. The teacher gives him a token during the various times he is not talking off-task.

SHAPING AND CHAINING

This teacher technique employs a sequence of events (see Buckley & Walker, 1970, p. 91):

1. The teacher selects the student behavior or skill to be acquired and breaks it down into small steps to be learned in sequence. For example:
   Hold pen correctly in hand.
   Hold pen close to paper.
   Touch pen to paper.
   Hold pen at proper angle.
   Make a generally circular shape for letter "0."
   Make circle increasingly circular and increasingly smaller.

2. The teacher rewards each step as it occurs in the sequence. The teacher does not wait until the student has successfully drawn an "0" before praising; praise begins immediately.

3. When the whole task is complex, each small component is taught and rewarded separately, then all components are linked together; this is *chaining*. For example, "Push in the clutch, release the brake, look both ways and ahead, release the clutch as you press easily on the accelerator—now put them all together as you start the car moving forward."

EXTINCTION

Extinction is the withholding of reinforcement that had previously been given for a certain behavior.

A teacher can unwittingly extinguish a desired student behavior. If the teacher had encouraged Pearl to volunteer by calling on Pearl whenever she raised her hand, the teacher might inadvertently extinguish Pearl's volunteering by no longer calling on her.

But most teachers would want to extinguish Wendy's habit of interrupting other students. If the teacher found that he had unwittingly been reinforcing Wendy's interrupting by scolding her — giving her attention — at each interruption, he might begin to extinguish the interruptions by ignoring Wendy when she interrupts, and calling on her at other times when she raised her hand.

TIME OUT

Time out differs from extinction, and for some teachers, it also differs from punishment. Time out refers to removing the student to a neutral and remote space, devoid of interesting objects, for periods usually no longer than ten minutes. During time out, the student does not talk, play, or work on academic assignments; time out is a cooling-off period, a time for reflection.

REINFORCER SATIATION

When the teacher uses a reinforcement so frequently that it is no longer effective, a new reinforcer is needed.

SIMPLE STIMULUS CHANGE

Teachers can easily change most students' behavior — without using any of the foregoing techniques — simply by changing the conditions under which the behavior occurs. For example, when a teacher paces the lesson quickly, most student off-task behaviors automatically correct themselves as students adjust to meet the new conditions. (This is the basic principle behind Method H, Varying Student Activities, chapter 7.)

REALITY THERAPY: GLASSER

Each student needs success, says Glasser. Failure does not help people develop and learn; only success does.

In his classic *Schools Without Failure* (1969), Glasser insists that a school wastes its time using specialists to work with individual students who are failing in school. Students' problems so often originate in the school system that it is the system that should change the conditions under which students fail. Glasser says schools cannot blame the home or other influences for students' failure in school.

At the same time today's schools breed failure through their values and practices, students are still responsible for their own needs, behavior, and their own bad choices when they get into trouble and fail. They are often unequipped to make better choices, however, unless someone takes an interest in helping them learn to make judgments; that person is most logically their teacher.

People who rely on emotion are more likely to fail; people who succeed rely on reason and logic. So the teacher has to help the failing student to think and succeed. To help a failing student succeed, the teacher must:

1   Ask the student, without reproach or preaching, "What are you doing?" and elicit an honest response.
2   Get the student to make a value judgment about how his actions are contributing to his failure (e.g., "Yeah, I'm really messing myself up doing this, I know.").
3   Ask the student to select a better course (the teacher can make suggestions, if needed).
4   Require the student to make a plan for changing his behavior. (Glasser uses the term "commitment" in place of "plan.")
5   Hold the student responsible for following through on the plan, and accept no excuses.
6   Let natural consequences follow misbehavior, even when those consequences are painful, but do not punish; that is, do not add extra pain. Punishment only creates another failure.
7   If necessary, isolate the student who continually violates his plans, but do not punish him.
8   Stay with the student as long as he needs help. Insist that he make and fulfill a new plan every time he fails.

Glasser is a great advocate of class meetings; like Dreikurs, Gordon, and Alschuler, Glasser sees class meetings as an arena for students and teacher to talk with one another as persons in equal standing, posing and answering questions and posing and solving problems, for the purpose of producing consensus—rather than unilateral pronouncement—about how people should behave in the classroom and why.

DISCIPLINE WITHOUT TEARS: DREIKURS AND ASSOCIATES

Rudolf Dreikurs considers teachers and students equal in the sense that they are all human beings with human needs, who should not be cruel to each other in any way but, rather, should try to understand and support each other as members of the class group (1972).

Students misbehave because they are human, hence social, hence eager to find their rightful places in the class group. Every action a student takes, whether appropriate or inappropriate, is an effort to belong, to be recognized as a group member. When a student does not receive recognition, he becomes discouraged, and uses destructive behavior to gain that recognition. "We should realize," says Dreikurs, "that a misbehaving child is only a discouraged child trying to find his place; he is acting on the faulty logic that his misbehaviour will give him the social acceptance which he desires" (1972, p. 32).

The misbehaving child may be pursuing any one or more of four goals of student misbehavior:

1 *Getting attention.* This is the most common initial goal of student misbehavior.
2 *Getting power.* To achieve this goal, the student uses all kinds of power-seeking techniques. He may be stubborn, argumentative, deceitful, and he may throw temper tantrums—all techniques for establishing a recognized place for himself in the group.
3 *Getting revenge.* When the student feels beaten down in his struggle for power, he may retaliate, seeking revenge for the hurt he feels others have done to him. He may be sullen, defiant, or violent.
4 *Displaying inadequacy.* The student who has failed to get attention may become so discouraged that he expects only failure and defeat—or so he may pretend.

These four goals of misbehavior are actually "mistaken goals," says Dreikurs, goals the erring student may pursue without even being aware he is doing so.

TEACHER ACTION TO CORRECT MISBEHAVIOR

Dreikurs' first step is to confront the student with the several possible goals of his misbehavior, without criticism or anger, to permit the student to better understand his own intentions. The conversation may go like this:

TEACHER: Do you know why you did...?
STUDENT: No. (And he may be quite right.)
TEACHER: Would you like to know? I have some ideas...Would you be willing to listen?
STUDENT: OK. (Children usually will say yes.)
TEACHER: (In a nonjudgmental and unemotional way, the teacher poses four questions, letting the student respond to one at a time)
Could it be that you want special attention?
Could it be that you want your own way and hope to be boss?
Could it be that you want to hurt others because you feel hurt by them?
Could it be that you want to be left alone?

The teacher must ask all four questions, because the student may be pursuing more than one goal at a time. The teacher attends to nonverbal as well as verbal cues when trying to diagnose the student's underlying problem.

The next step is to take appropriate action, depending upon the student's inappropriate goals:

1 Getting attention:
Ignore the misbehaving student.
Be firm, not annoyed.
Give lots of attention at other times.
2 Getting power:
Admit that the student has power. ("Of course I can't *make* you do this.")

Ask for his aid. ("I really need your help in this. I hope you *will* help.")
Make an agreement.

3   Getting revenge:
Apply natural consequences.
Do the unexpected.
Try to convince the student that he is liked.

4   Displaying inadequacy:
Encourage the student when she tries.
Avoid supporting the student's feelings of inferiority.
Offer constructive approaches.

In general, Dreikurs urges strongly supportive measures to control student misbehavior. He advocates the use of class meetings or discussion periods, during which
students may raise problems and propose solutions, to promote cooperative problem solving rather than conflict and power struggles.

Every student needs encouragement, not praise, to help motivate his
efforts; encouragement acknowledges what the student does, while praise merely
rewards the person himself and directs his attention to himself rather than to what
he is doing.

Dreikurs urges natural consequences rather than rewards and punishment. Rewards, he argues, are actually bribes that ultimately discourage student
self-reliance and responsibility, while punishment invites retaliation. Natural consequences, on the other hand, occur in the natural course of events and therefore
are the most legitimate instructive forces for learning to live in a democratic society.

TEACHER EFFECTIVENESS TRAINING: GORDON

When a student has a problem, the teacher's principal technique in Thomas
Gordon's T. E. T. (1974) system is "active listening" or "feedback," by which Gordon
means the paraphrase and reflecting skills discussed in Method O (chapter 12).[1]
Other listening skills, such as "passive listening," "acknowledgment," and "door
openers" also help communicate the teacher's acceptance of the student, which is
the goal of all T. E. T. techniques.

Active Listening: "You're feeling that he's picking on you?"
Passive Listening: Silence with eye contact.
Acknowledgment: Nodding, leaning forward, "I see what you mean," and "Uh
huh."
Door Opener: "I see you guys are fighting a lot lately. Want to talk about it?"

Gordon's prime concern is that teachers and students talk with one another, person
to person, rather than exert power over each other. A teacher should not take
responsibility for problems that belong to a student (e.g., the student is not doing
his homework or is having trouble concentrating in class) but should help the
student solve his own problem. Gordon's active listening/feedback can be used

with students who resist the teacher's requests or depend on the teacher to solve their problems; feedback can also be effective with students who are troubled — angry, resentful, fearful, or offended. The goal is to help a student be able to say, verbally or nonverbally, "I really feel better now that I've talked to you; I think I understand now."

TEACHER: ...and you think they are cutting you out of the action?
STUDENT: Yeah, they're mad at me.
TEACHER: They're mad?
STUDENT: Well, I kicked the ball over the fence.
TEACHER: You think they're mad at you because you stopped the game.
STUDENT: Yeah.
TEACHER: And you think they're going to stay mad at you.
STUDENT: Maybe I could tell them I'm sorry.

When the teacher "owns the problem," such as feelings of annoyance, frustration, anger, resentment, or physical sensations of tension, headache, or jumpiness, the principal technique is the "I-message," a simple and honest report of the teacher's condition without intimations of blame or accusations: "When paper is left on the floor, I feel mad, because I live here, and I don't like people littering up the place where I live, and I resent having to go around picking up other people's messes, and I don't think it's fair." The successful I-message has three parts:

1 The specific behaviors that occur with the teacher's problem (e.g., "When paper is left on the floor");
2 The tangible or concrete effects of the behavior (e.g., "I have to go around picking up...");
3 The teacher's own feelings in the matter ("I feel mad," "I don't like," "I resent").

After the teacher sends an I-message, the student has a problem, so the teacher must immediately shift back into active listening.

Gordon is a strong proponent of modifying the classroom environment, by rearranging, systematizing, enriching, simplifying, etc., to remove conditions that cause problems for teachers and students.

He is also a leading proponent of the Win–Win method of resolving conflicts between teachers and students (Gordon calls it "Method III") in which teachers resist their natural impulses to use power-authority (which usually forces students to rebel, resist, defy, retaliate, lie, sneak, tattle, cheat, bully, summon allies, submit out of fear, apple polish insincerely, avoid taking risks, withdraw and drop out, fantasize, and regress) and instead use the I-message active-listening procedure in a six-step problem-solving process.[2] At the end of this process, everyone "wins"; no one loses:

1 Define the problem according to the perceptions of both sides, then agree on exactly what it is that both parties want solved.

2 Generate possible solutions through a brainstorming process in which no possibilities are eliminated, but instead are all kept "on the table" for later examination.

3 Evaluate the solutions by crossing out any solution that is objectionable to either party; use active listening and I-messages to make sure each party's position is made known throughout the process. Emerge with several solutions tolerable to both parties.

4 Make the decision by choosing the best solution through consensus, but *do not vote.*

5 Decide who will implement the decision by assigning clear responsibilities.

6 Assess the success of the solution by asking such questions as "Was this a good decision?" and "Has our problem been resolved?" and "Are we happy with what we did?"

Gordon urges teachers to use class meetings to establish rules that all will follow, as opposed to making up rules and dictating them to students.

TRANSACTIONAL ANALYSIS: BERNE ET AL.

Eric Berne, a California psychiatrist, wanted to translate the basic principles of Freudian psychology into practical terms the lay public could understand and use. His work has spurred the writing of many publications, some of which are oriented specifically to classroom teaching.

The first purpose of Transactional Analysis (TA) is to help the teacher understand that each person, teacher or student, is actually a composite of at least three different people, three different states of being that control one's behavior and one's style of interacting with others. The three states that exist simultaneously are parent, adult, and child.

Parent The "parent" state in each of us is the vast collection of memories we have of all the *external* authority figures in our lives — parents, teachers, and other "big people" — whose behaviors we internalize and automatically tend to accept as right, correct, and proper. The parent part of us records all the admonitions, rules, laws, and "how to's" of authority, including nonverbal expressions and tones of voice, as well as the nurturing behaviors, including warm reassurances and supportive, loving, and caring behaviors, both verbal and nonverbal.

Child Our "child" state is the vast collection of all the *internal* experiences — feelings, impulses, and responses — of our early years. One part of our child records all the negative feelings of guilt, rage, fear, and unhappiness that make us conclude "I'm not OK"; the other part of the child contains and records the vast store of our positive feelings, including delight and joy, creativity and curiosity, and the good feelings of response to nurturing and love.

Adult Our "adult" state is the capacity to reason and think, to gather and store objective data, and process that data in a way not automatically determined by our "parent," on the basis of unquestioned authority, or by our "child," on the basis of unexamined feelings or impulse.

Any of the three states, parent, adult, or child, can produce either a functional or dysfunctional response to instructional situations. Imagine, for example, that the teacher is giving a homework assignment. Functional student responses might sound like these:

> **PARENT:** The way I see it, if your teacher tells you to do this homework, then you should do it.
> **ADULT:** I think I can do this homework in about half an hour if I hurry.
> **CHILD:** This is going to be interesting—I like decimals.

Dysfunctional student responses, on the other hand, might resemble these:

> **PARENT:** Even though we didn't do any homework the last two nights, this is going to take two hours, and the school policy is one hour of homework per night.
> **ADULT:** This homework won't count on my grade, so why should I do it?
> **CHILD:** Blah—I hate decimals.

The teacher can use his knowledge of TA to help students respond functionally rather than dysfunctionally. When the teacher speaks from his own critical "parent," for example, he is most likely to elicit a Not–OK Child response from the student:

> **TEACHER:** I told you before, Jenny, I want you to quit fooling around. Now why can't you pay attention?
> **STUDENT:** Oh, all right. Hmph.

If the teacher wants the student to be a self-motivated and self-controlled worker on lesson activities, the teacher's strategy should be to target some part of the student other than his Not–OK child:

> **TEACHER:** I know this is not fun for you right now, but when you learn how to do it, it *will* be fun—and you *can* do it. OK, now try . . .

Here, the teacher's pep talk (see Method W) is, according to TA terminology, "stroking" the "Not-OK Child," that is, soothing or reassuring or comforting the Not-OK feelings to make it easier for the student to shift from his "Not-OK Child" state into his "Adult" state, where he can think and reason and learn.

The teacher can also use TA to control student game playing. The purpose of most student games is to get "strokes" from the teacher, in the form of attention or recognition. If the student cannot get positive strokes (praise, encouragement, rewards), he will go after negative strokes (reprimands, punishment), for both positive and negative strokes represent teacher time and attention. Ken Ernst's *Games Students Play* (1972) lists many such games, as does Herbert Foster's excellent book on inner-city black student culture, *Ribbin', Jivin', and Playin' the Dozens* (1974). (In this text, see chapter 20.)

SOCIAL LITERACY: ALSCHULER/FREIRE

Alfred Alschuler (1980) bases his control model on the work of Paulo Freire, an educational innovator who developed a method for teaching literacy to Brazilian adults in just thirty hours. To use Alschuler's system, the teacher must develop a different approach—"an alternative mind set"—from two common approaches which Alschuler calls *magical-conforming* and *naive-reforming*.

In the magical-conforming approach, people either fail to recognize a problem, or resign themselves to it. This attitude reveals itself in phrases such as "Just one of those things, you know?"; "That's the way these kids are"; and "Why bother? You'll accomplish nothing and just end up hurting yourself." The problem is "magical" because it seems to arise for no apparent reason, and one meets the problem by adjusting to it, or by ignoring it.

In the naive-reforming approach, people ascribe a problem to individuals, and assume that solving the problem requires changing the individuals. This attitude appears in phrases such as "If the principal of this school were on the ball, everything would be better," or "If I could just kick that kid out, all my worries would be over."

Alschuler recommends a *critical-transforming* approach to change the system rather than the individuals who function within it.

> The goals of Social Literacy training are to change oppressive roles, not role inhabitants; oppressive goals, not those who advocate them; oppressive rules, not the rule enforcers; oppressive practices, not the practitioners; oppressive policies, not the policy makers; oppressive norms, not the normal people who act them out. (Alschuler, 1980, p. 38)

Alschuler offers "socially literate methods" for redirecting blame from individuals to the system:

First, resolve discipline conflicts through dialogue. "Dialogue" refers to a real exchange of views between teacher and student, not a one-way teacher monologue. The teacher must hear what the student says as well as speak clearly herself. Second, speak true words about conflicts. "True words" are those that focus on the problem, without attacking or blaming people, and that show one's willingness to work cooperatively to resolve the conflict. Third, raise consciousness. After identifying the problem, or the aspect of the system that is oppressive, those who have been responsible for perpetuating the system must change their behavior. Alschuler and Freire apparently assume that almost anyone can accomplish this goal once the basic conflict is revealed. Fourth, use the nuclear problem-solving process. This group-discussion process (two or more persons) consists of four simple steps:

Step 1   The problem poser describes for the group, without interruption, a conflict incident.

Step 2   The group takes five minutes to list as many patterns (repeated events or repeated behaviors) as possible that the reported incident illustrates or samples.

Step 3   Group members brainstorm ways to change the rules or roles that cause people to behave in the problem pattern(s).

Step 4 Group members agree upon a first step in resolving the conflict pattern, anticipating the obstacles and planning how to overcome them.

Alschuler's book gives detailed instructions for using the process in classrooms, and provides considerable evidence of the success his methods have enjoyed in Springfield, Massachusetts; Hartford, Connecticut; and elsewhere in the United States where school systems have been transformed in highly positive ways by adopting social literacy methods.

DISCIPLINE AND GROUP MANAGEMENT: KOUNIN

Jacob Kounin does not actually propose a "system" of classroom control; he simply reports the results of investigations he and his colleagues conducted (Kounin, 1970) to discover the difference between teachers with successful classroom control and teachers with major and continuing behavior and attention problems among their students.

In his initial research, Kounin asked whether successful teachers react to and treat student disruptions differently than less successful teachers. In the study, they did not—both groups used "desist" techniques that generally had insignificant and even counterproductive effects on student behavior.

Kounin's later research turned to other characteristics of successful and less successful classrooms, and here a number of distinct differences emerged.[3]

Withitness This term refers to the practice among successful teachers of continually monitoring and being aware of what is going on in their classrooms, then taking prompt action to solve problems before they grow to larger proportions. In other words, these teachers control larger problems by preventing them; they control disruptions while they are minor. Successful teachers do not make mistakes about where misbehavior originates or wait too long to correct it.

Less successful teachers tend to focus attention on one part of the room or on an individual or single group of students, seemingly unaware of what goes on elsewhere.

Overlapping Overlapping refers to the ability of successful teachers to attend to more than one matter at a time without becoming frustrated or confused or ineffective. The successful teacher tends to student problems more quickly than does the less successful teacher, who can only concentrate on one matter at a time.

Smooth Transitions The successful teachers in Kounin's study trained their students to follow routines efficiently and automatically, without distracting others in the class. Transitions were quick and quiet.

Less successful teachers seemed unprepared for transitions, as did their students. Interruptions, distractions, and delays were obvious in these classrooms.

Momentum Successful teachers paced their instruction quickly and effectively, without distraction, interruptions, and delays.

Group Alerting   The successful teachers used a variety of techniques to keep students attentive and active; less successful teachers lacked these techniques.

Accountability   The successful teachers in Kounin's study used a wide variety of techniques to keep themselves informed of student learning and attention: recitations, student comments, showing of answers, and volunteering to participate. Successful teachers also used many techniques to activate and monitor student performance.

Ripple Effects   One of the most important observations Kounin reported is the ripple effect, the effect on the audience of teacher "desist" actions directed toward a particular student. Kounin found that "task-focused desists ('You can't learn if you play with paper clips') produced more favorable ripple effects than approval-focused techniques ('I don't like children who play with paper clips')" (1980, p. 142). In other words, the teacher's actions toward one student not only affect other students but affect them differently, depending upon the task-orientation of the actions.

When we consider Kounin's work in its entirety, we begin to see a coherent picture emerge of careful teacher planning and alert teacher execution of plans. As much as any other writer in this field, Kounin is describing a "system" of effective teaching.

MASTERY LEARNING: BLOOM

You may be surprised to find Mastery Learning considered as a system of classroom control, for mastery learning has almost nothing to do with conventional notions of classroom discipline. Yet Bloom's principles of content design and instructional methodology are a superb example of an effective classroom control system at work.

Benjamin Bloom (1968) proposes that schools should expect up to 90 percent of their students to master all aspects of the curriculum; the schools should provide every student with enough time and assistance to attain mastery. Bloom's system is derived from a model of instruction proposed by John Carroll (1963); Carroll says the degree of learning for any student is a function of the time allowed for learning, the student's motivation to learn, the time the student *needs* to learn, the quality of instruction, and the student's ability to understand instruction. If the quality of instruction is poor or if the student's ability is low, the student will need more time to master the curriculum.

Mastery learning allows each student to demonstrate mastery at any time; hence, every student moves at his own pace through the curriculum. We might suspect that students would become impossibly spread apart in mastery as the faster students shoot ahead, but Bloom insists that exactly the opposite occurs. As formerly "slow" students gain genuine mastery of the material, they begin to move ahead more rapidly, and the range of student abilities begins to narrow. Students become motivated by their successes, their self-concepts improve, and their later learning requires less time than their earlier learning. Mastery learning reduces the range of student achievement in a classroom rather than increases it.

Instructional aids for students are widely diverse and highly individualized—tutorial aides, small group instruction, varied texts and teaching approaches (if one approach does not work, try another), workbooks, programmed instruction, instructional drills and games—all are used as appropriate.

Although evaluation studies do not often show that 90 percent of students attain mastery, mastery learning classrooms nevertheless produce impressive results compared with conventional classrooms, where teachers move all students through the curriculum whether the students are ready or not. Burns (1979) interprets current research studies on mastery learning as showing that 50 percent of mastery-taught students learn as well or better than the top 20 percent of nonmastery students; that is, mastery-learning techniques have the power to move a typical student from the 50th to the 80th percentile of a nonmastery group (p. 112). Ironically, despite the fact that they are sensible and successful, mastery learning procedures are slow to seize the fancy of American educators.[4]

ECLECTIC DISCIPLINE: WOLFGANG AND GLICKMAN

Wolfgang and Glickman's *Solving Discipline Problems* (1980) has so far been the most comprehensive of all books on conventional classroom control in America. The authors examine the whole spectrum of classroom discipline systems and try to help teachers choose from among the many options.

The Eclectic Discipline System is built on a "Teacher Behavior Continuum" (TBC), representing varying power relationships between teacher and student. At the left end, the student has greatest control over his own behavior; at the right end, the teacher exercises complete power over the student's behavior (Wolfgang & Glickman, 1980, p. 17).

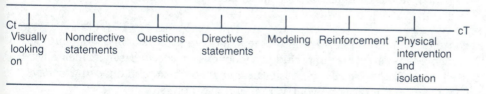

FIGURE 1.1 Teacher Behavior Continuum (Wolfgang and Glickman)

Wolfgang and Glickman describe and analyze nine major systems of classroom discipline, placing them appropriately on the TBC, and offering suggestions as to how the teacher might choose among the various options (1980, p. 18).

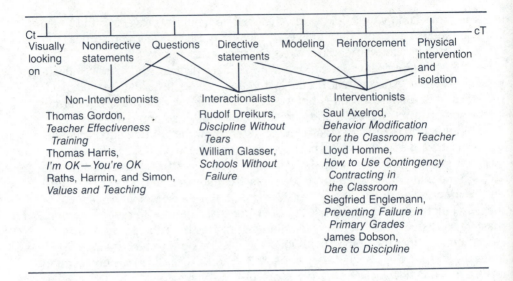

FIGURE 1.2   TBC and Teacher Options (Wolfgang and Glickman)

The teacher can choose his discipline actions according to any of the following criteria.

1   The teacher's own philosophical/psychological beliefs about how children develop (whether from "an inner unfolding of potential" or from the impact of external conditions or from the interaction of inner and outer forces);

2   The teacher's own feelings and subjective preferences (e.g., "I simply do not like treating students as if they were animals to be manipulated");

3   The teacher's own values and beliefs concerning student and teacher power (e.g., "The best way is to give students power immediately but then gradually take it away if they do not use it properly");

4   The teacher's perception of each individual student's social development (e.g., "I think it would be unrealistic to expect three-year-old Suzy to explain why she acted that way").

Because of their strong conviction that teachers are professionals, Wolfgang and Glickman adamantly refuse to prejudge a teacher's choice. In essence, their advice to teachers is: "Here are all the possibilities; now go ahead and choose whichever one you like on the basis of whatever criterion you prefer."

SUMMARY

Most of the systems reviewed in this chapter are conventional systems of classroom control whose immediate purpose is to control student misbehavior. In the chapters to follow, you will be studying a different system of classroom control based on fundamental principles whose immediate purpose is to focus student attention on lesson content.

Yet each of these conventional systems is important because it develops one or more specific techniques of classroom control and shows what the teacher can accomplish when he uses those techniques well. The question then becomes: when should the teacher use one technique, and when another? The conventional answer to this question, so well expressed by Wolfgang and Glickman, is to base classroom control decisions on the teacher's subjective preferences, judgments, and feelings. In contrast, the fundamental principles we will discuss in chapter 2 insist that classroom control should be based *first* on principles, *then* on the teacher's judgment and intuition.

NOTES

1   Gordon disagrees with the use of what I call Thought-test questions (see Method O) in cases in which students have problems; he calls them "roadblocks" to effective student thinking and problem solving.

2   You might notice the similarity between Gordon's procedure and that of "Choice Counseling" decision making; see Method CC (chapter 22), based on a model by Simon et al. If you are interested in Gordon's procedures for Win–Win negotiation, you may wish to refer to similar statements in Fisher and Ury's *Getting to Yes* (1981).

3   In short, Kounin's observations of effective teaching are actually observations of Low Profile controls; seen together as a group of techniques, they complement one another and also comprise a major portion of the Taxonomy's Level 1 techniques:

	Bf1	Ja1	Na1	Td1
Ba1		Jb1	S1	
Bc1			Ta1	V1
Bd1	Gb1	L1	Tb1	Xa1
Be1	H1	Ma1	Tc1	

A final note on Kounin's initial research: the "desist" orders that Kounin studied are not only high profile, according to the Taxonomy of this book, but have also been found to be nonproductive or counterproductive in many other research studies, particularly those in behavior modification (see Method Z). The careful lesson preparation and design that Kounin exalts are defined in this book as low profile teacher controls. It seems reasonable to believe that, while Kounin's successful teachers had mastered many low profile control techniques, they had not mastered them all. In particular, had any of the observed teachers exhibited the techniques of Methods Q1, R1, U1, Xb1, Xb2, and Ya1 rather than "desist" orders, I assume a significant difference would have appeared between successful and less successful teachers. Since these low profile methods are not yet well known or widely practiced among teachers, it is not surprising that even Kounin's successful teachers were forced to use ineffective "desists."

4   On the Taxonomy, we can locate the techniques that characterize the mastery learning system:
High expectations of student learning: Aa1
Teacher confidence in student learning: Ab1
Continuous evaluation of instruction: Ac1
Selected content objectives: Ba1

Operationally stated objectives: Bbl
Carefully paced objectives: Bcl
Evaluation standards are published before instruction: Bdl
Continuous monitoring: Bel
Immediate, specific feedback: Bfl
Flexible grouping: El
Individually paced activities: Gal
Automatic transitions: Gbl
Varied activities according to need: Hl
High participation and practice rate: Ia1
In short, each basic characteristic of mastery learning is a low profile classroom control.

REFERENCES

ALSCHULER, A., & SHEA, J. The discipline game: Playing without losers. *Learning,* 1974, *3,* 80–86.

ALSCHULER, A. *School discipline.* New York: McGraw-Hill, 1980.

BERNE, E. *Games people play.* New York: Grove Press, 1964.

BLOCK, J. *Mastery learning: Theory and practice.* New York: Holt, Rinehart and Winston, 1971.

BLOOM, B. *Human characteristics and school learning.* New York: McGraw-Hill, 1976.

BLOOM, B. *All our children learning.* New York: McGraw-Hill, 1981.

BUCKLEY, N., & WALKER, H. *Modifying classroom behavior: A manual of procedures for classroom teachers.* Champaign, Ill.: Research Press, 1970.

BURNS, R. Mastery learning: Does it work? *Educational Leadership,* November 1979, *37,* 110–113.

CARROLL, J. A model of school learning. *Teachers College Record,* 1963, *64,* 723–733.

CHAPMAN, A. *The games children play.* New York: Berkley, 1971.

DREIKURS, R., & GREY, L. *A new approach to discipline: Logical consequences.* New York: Hawthorn Books, 1968.

DREIKURS, R., & CASSEL, P. *Discipline without tears.* New York: Hawthorn Books, 1972.

DREIKURS, R., GRUNWALD, B., & PEPPER, F. *Maintaining sanity in the classroom: Classroom management techniques.* New York: Harper and Row, 1982.

ERNST, K. *Games students play (and what to do about them).* Millbrae, Calif.: Celestial Arts, 1972.

FISHER, R., & URY, W. *Getting to yes: Negotiating agreement without giving in.* Boston: Houghton Mifflin, 1981.

FOSTER, H. *Ribbin', jivin', and playin' the dozens.* Cambridge, Mass.: Ballinger, 1974.

FREIRE, P. *Pedagogy of the oppressed.* New York: Seabury Press, 1970.

GAGE, N., & BERLINER, D. *Educational psychology.* Chicago: Rand McNally, 1979.

GLASSER, W. *Reality therapy.* New York: Harper and Row, 1965.

GLASSER, W. *Schools without failure.* New York: Harper and Row, 1969.

GORDON, T. *T.E.T. Teacher effectiveness training.* New York: David McKay, 1974.

HARRIS, T. *I'm OK — You're OK.* New York: Harper and Row, 1969.

JAMES, M., & YONGWARD, D. *Born to win: Transactional analysis with gestalt experiments.* Menlo Park, Calif.; Addison-Wesley: 1971.

KOUNIN, J. *Discipline and group management in classrooms.* New York: Holt, Rinehart and Winston, 1970.

MADSEN, C., BECKER, W., & THOMAS, D. Rules, praise, and ignoring: Effects of classroom control. *Journal of Applied Behavioral Analysis, 1968, 1,* 139–150.

SKINNER, B. F. *Science and human behavior.* New York: Macmillan, 1953.

SKINNER, B. F. *The technology of teaching.* New York: Appleton-Century-Crofts, 1968.

WOLFGANG, C., & GLICKMAN, C. *Solving discipline problems.* Boston: Allyn and Bacon, 1980.

THE FIRST FUNDAMENTAL: ATTENTION TO LESSON CONTENT

2

The primary purpose of the school is to help students learn lesson content. Content is the knowledge, skills, awareness, relationships, and whatever else students are sent to school to learn. Since considerable research evidence, as well as common sense, tells us that the more attention a student pays to a lesson, the more likely he is to learn it (see Appendix A), teachers should help every student pay attention to lesson content and avoid distracting any student's attention unnecessarily.

When true instruction is occurring, the student's mind is focused on lesson content only, not on the teacher or the teacher's methods, or on any other peripheral thoughts. The teacher's first task in instruction is to guide each student's attention to the lesson content and keep it there for a necessary and appropriate period of time. If the student does not pay attention to the lesson, instruction does not take place.

FIGURE 2.1   The Problem of Attention

Many people worry so much about student inattention in the classroom that they are satisfied if students simply pay attention to the teacher; some people even believe that students are performing well when they sit noiselessly in their seats looking at the teacher. This is absurd, since as Thorndike said many years ago, "It is not enough simply to have attention; it must be attention to the right thing" (1911, p. 106). Learning does not come from attention to the teacher, but rather from attention to lesson content.

ATTENTION TO LESSON CONTENT

Attention to lesson content is called by many names: student attention, attending behavior, student engaged time, time-on-task, academic learning time, and other similar terms (James, 1890; Flanders, 1966; Berliner, 1979). Regardless of what they call it, most educators would agree on this definition of "attention to lesson content": the student's mind is focused either on lesson content or on applying lesson content to other matters appropriate to the lesson. (The teacher judges what is appropriate to the lesson.)

VISUAL CUES OF ATTENTION

The first cues to student attention are visual: a glance, a shrug, a smile, a hand wave, a shift of body position, visual cues noticeable to the teacher from some distance away. Seizing upon one or more of these, the teacher may then look for confirmation of attention: a correct body motion, a written sign, or a spoken word. Little wonder that the oldest and wisest advice in teaching is "Keep your eyes open," because the teacher's first cue to student attention is usually seen, not heard.

Prospective teachers should begin their training by memorizing the visual cues of student attention, since these cues are the teacher's most basic diagnostic tool. Practice watching students in classes, and classify their probable attention; notice how cues change, indicating that students are continually slipping into and out of attention.

Some descriptions will help you understand Figure 2.2.

ATTENTION CUES[1]

A student who shows any of these cues during instruction probably has his mind on lesson content. No one cue is 100 percent conclusive, but any combination of two or more cues should make the teacher confident of attention.

Eye Movement The student's eyes move appropriately for the lesson: from teacher to notes to teacher during a lecture; from text to paper to text during seatwork; from speaker to speaker during class discussion. When a student's eyes stop moving, do not assume he is paying attention; assume now that he is in *unknown* attention.

Body Tension The student sits on the edge of his chair in clear response to the lesson, or leans forward, cocks his head, holds his hand up, rises up out of his seat,

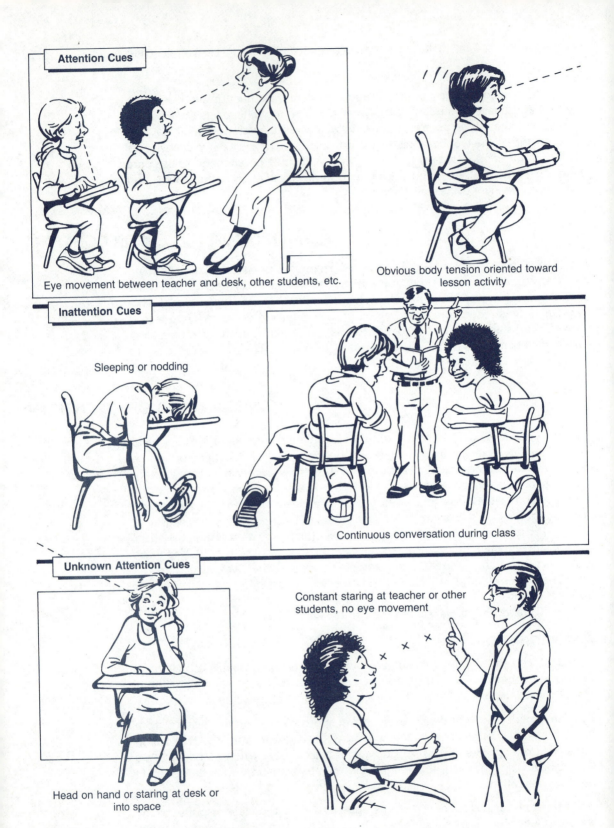

FIGURE 2.2 Visual Cues of Student Attention

24

Active participation of any kind: notetaking, seatwork, etc.

Obvious lesson-oriented responses to teacher or to other students

Continuous looking out the window, etc.

Skylarking, horseplay

Occasional conversation during class

Any reading, marking, or other activity not observable by teacher

holds a paper or book up off the table, or even draws his feet up underneath his chair (Morrison, 1931, p. 124) — all of these lesson-responsive positions or movements are cues of attention, and the teacher can usually trust them. If these cues are not clearly responsive to the lesson, the teacher should assume either unknown attention or inattention.

Active Participation   The student writes notes or does seatwork that the teacher can see, participates in group discussions, asks questions (whether apt or not), or otherwise participates appropriately in the lesson activity.

Responses   The student frowns, smiles, or otherwise changes facial expression when the teacher or another student makes a content-oriented statement; shifts position in his seat when a tense moment arrives in the lesson; or gives a nonverbal response to a lesson event.

The teacher must be careful not to confuse paying attention with knowing the right answer. A student who has his mind on lesson content but gives a wrong answer might provoke a reprimand ("You must not have been paying attention") that would be neither accurate nor fair.

INATTENTION CUES

Inattention cues include sleeping or nodding, continuous conversation with a classmate, steady gazing out the window, and horseplay or other generally disruptive or distracting activity. When a student shows any one of these behaviors during instruction, his mind is probably not on the lesson content. Any combination of visual inattention cues makes inattention almost certain.

UNKNOWN ATTENTION CUES

Many new teachers and some experienced teachers misinterpret unknown attention cues. "Unknown" means the teacher cannot use the cues reliably to judge student attention, because the probabilities are too close to chance that the student's mind is on or off the lesson. Yet some teachers use the cues anyway; for example:

Head on Hand   Sometimes teachers assume this cue means daydreaming, a risky interpretation.

Constant Staring   Many teachers assume the student who stares at her while she is talking is paying close attention, despite some students' skill at daydreaming behind glazed eyes.

Occasional Conversation   Some teachers assume occasional talkers are not paying attention to the lesson; others assume they are discussing the lesson. Both assumptions are risky; most teachers cannot make reliable judgments from this cue.

Unobserved Activity   When students are apparently reading or writing or engaged in other activity the teacher cannot directly observe, their attention is always unknown. Every student knows the comic-book-inside-the-textbook routine, and young students doodle on their notes as frequently as do adults. The only way a teacher can judge whether a student's activity is on-task or off-task is to monitor the activity. (See Method B in chapter 4.)

Is there a foolproof method of determining which Unknown Attention students are actually paying attention? Yes; it is to assume that no student is paying attention unless he gives clear visual attention cues. For this the teacher requires accuracy and speed. The teacher's observations must be accurate to avoid wishful thinking and fast to avoid wasted time. In a classroom of twenty to fifty students, there is no time for long scientific studies of which students are and are not paying attention. Visual attention cues, properly used, are fast and foolproof.

THE PROFESSIONAL TEACHER'S FUNDAMENTAL RESPONSIBILITY

The professional teacher's fundamental responsibility in classroom control is to change all inattention and unknown attention behaviors into attention behaviors during instruction; that is, to strive for 100 percent attention in the classroom at all times during instruction.

While it is true that few teachers can maintain constant 100 percent attention, the most effective teachers usually come very close. They start, stop, and maintain lessons in such a way that inattention almost never appears, and unknown attention is relatively infrequent. Effective teachers can and do control student attention through skillful use of professional techniques.

Many of us remember a teacher who was able to make a subject come alive for us. We were captivated by what we were to learn, and everything the teacher said and did focused our attention and energies on the subject matter. That teacher never stopped the lesson to say "Pay attention" or "Stop talking!" The teacher captured our attention and instructed us, all at the same time.

Indeed, our best teachers today do not have to tell students to pay attention; their students just do. These teachers seem magical: they use techniques that automatically focus student attention on lesson content. They rarely use conventional high profile classroom controls.

HIGH PROFILE CLASSROOM CONTROL

Most conventional classroom control techniques require two steps to focus student attention on lesson content. First, the teacher calls the student's attention to the teacher; then the teacher strives to *shift* the student's attention to lesson content. Teacher X (giving an assignment to the class) illustrates this conventional two-step approach: "Now on page 26, you should do the problems [notices Johnny looking out the window]...Johnny? Now *you* turn around and pay attention. Now everybody look at the bottom of page 26, at the graph which shows that...."

Figure 2.3 shows Teacher X's two distinct steps in control. Notice how every example of this conventional approach to classroom control first distracts the

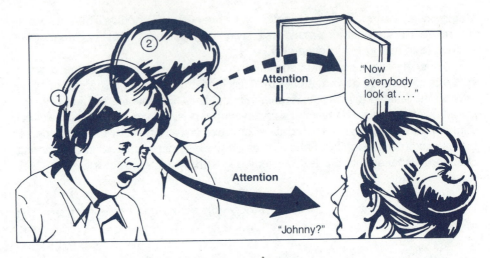

FIGURE 2.3 High Profile Classroom Control (Two-step)

student's attention *away* from the lesson in the hope of inducing the student to pay attention later:

> "All right, may I have your attention please?"
> "I want to see all eyes up here."
> "We will simply have to wait until we have everyone's attention."
> "I want it *quiet* in here!"
> "Why aren't you paying attention?"
> "Why are you talking instead of listening?"
> "Stop fooling around and get to work!"
> "Sit up straight and pay attention!"
> (Turns lights out as signal for order.)
> (Claps hands for attention.)
> (Puts inattentive students' names on the chalkboard.)

These conventional control techniques are all high profile—they are clearly seen and heard; they attract attention to themselves. While Teacher X might be considered firm or no-nonsense according to conventional wisdom, Teacher X has unfortunately distracted the attention of the entire class away from lesson content (some students will even wonder just what Johnny was looking at); in addition, Teacher X has incurred a great risk of distracting Johnny's attention too. After hearing the teacher's commands, Johnny might easily focus on his embarrassment, fear, or resentment. He will turn his eyes to page 26, but his thoughts will likely be elsewhere.

LOW PROFILE CLASSROOM CONTROL

As you might guess, low profile controls are hard to detect; in fact, they are almost invisible to an untrained observer. Here is Teacher Y (giving an assignment to the class) using a low profile approach: "Now on page 26, you should do the problems. [Notices Johnny looking out the window.] All of you, including Annie, Johnny, Brucie, and Sarah, can look at the graph at the bottom of page 26, which shows..."

The goal of low profile classroom control is to direct or guide student attention to the content of the lesson without intervening steps or distractions; it is an automatic, one-step process.

Teacher Y demonstrates that a high profile approach is probably not necessary in Johnny's case. In fact, most normal classroom situations can be controlled adequately and efficiently with low profile techniques. Teacher Y illustrates one such technique. Avoiding Teacher X's habit of using student names in reprimands, Teacher Y occasionally inserts students' names at random into the lesson content directions, in the belief that where each student's name appears, his attention usually follows. Teacher Y's students are accustomed to hearing their names in the lesson — they do not flinch or snicker when they hear them — so this teacher is able to continue the lesson smoothly with no distraction or interruption for discipline. Most remarkably, Johnny, the target of control, is probably not aware he is being controlled! Johnny has no reason to feel embarrassed or resentful, and since his attention is likely to be attracted by the sound of his name, he will probably shift his attention to the lesson. If Teacher Y's control does not succeed, she can use another low profile technique, easily and quickly, and has lost nothing in using the first.

A third category of controls, mid profile, may distract one or a few students, but not the whole class. Here are some basic definitions of controls.

In classroom control, *profile* is the degree to which student attention is diverted from lesson content to a distracting person or event. *High profile control* diverts most students' attention, directly or indirectly, to the teacher ("Look at me!"), to a distracting student or act ("What are you doing back there?"), or to some other non-lesson factor before shifting student attention to lesson content. *Low profile control* techniques do not divert any student's attention, but instead automatically focus all students' attention on lesson content. *Mid profile control* techniques divert

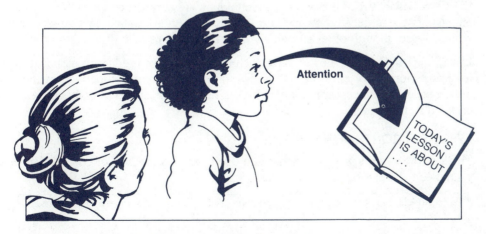

FIGURE 2.4 Low Profile Classroom Control (One-step)

one or a few students' attention from the lesson before shifting attention to lesson content.

Many levels or degrees of profile are possible within our three major categories; an arbitrary but useful number of profile levels is seven.

Low Profile		Mid Profile			High Profile	
Level 1	Level 2	Level 3	Level 4	Level 5	Level 6	Level 7

FIGURE 2.5   Levels of Profile in Classroom Control

LEVEL 1 (LOW PROFILE)   These control techniques allow almost no risk or probability of distracting any student's attention from the lesson content, including the target student.*

LEVEL 2 (LOW PROFILE)   These techniques offer a little risk that the target student's attention may be distracted from the lesson by the control technique, but the risk or probability of distraction is quite low for the target student and zero for everyone else.

LEVEL 3 (MID PROFILE)   These techniques run some moderate risk or probability that the control will distract the target student's attention from the lesson; however, no one else's attention is distracted.

LEVEL 4 (MID PROFILE)   These techniques run high probability of diverting the target student's attention from the lesson, perhaps completely; however, no one else's attention is distracted.

LEVEL 5 (MID PROFILE)   These techniques are almost certain to distract the attention of the target student from the lesson and perhaps distract some other students as well.

LEVEL 6 (HIGH PROFILE)   These techniques are almost certain to distract the attention of the target student from the lesson and rather significantly distract other students also, though other students will probably not remain distracted for long.

LEVEL 7 (HIGH PROFILE)   These techniques interrupt the lesson significantly for a large number of students in the class, including the target student. Some time and energy (not necessarily observable) is needed for students to become re-oriented to the lesson.

EYES AS A CONTROL METHOD

Think of the various ways a teacher can use eyes as a method of control. These examples illustrate the several profile levels.

---

*"Target student" refers to the particular student the teacher wants to control at a given moment.

LEVEL 1 You are talking to your class about plants. To ensure that everyone is paying attention and also to reassure every student that you are talking to *him*, you constantly keep your eyes moving around the room, making eye contact with every student at least once every 30 seconds as you talk. You include Jake and Jo (who are whispering to each other) in your regular round of eye contacts.

LEVEL 2 You continue to talk about plants, keeping your eyes moving around the room but coming back briefly now and then to Jake and Jo, who are whispering to each other. You make eye contact with them as you do with everyone else.

LEVEL 3 You continue to talk about plants, keeping your eyes moving around the room but looking often at Jake and Jo, who are whispering to each other. You make eye contact with them as well as with everyone else.

LEVEL 4 You continue to talk about plants to your class, but you keep your eyes steadily on Jake and Jo, who are whispering to each other. You try to maintain steady eye contact with them.

LEVEL 5 You continue to talk about plants to your class, but you keep your eyes steadily on Jake and Jo, who are whispering to each other; when they look at you, you give them an eye-blink signal, which means "cool it." Other students notice your signal.

LEVEL 6 You continue to talk about plants, then pause and glare briefly at Jake and Jo, who are whispering to each other. Most other students notice your glare, and some exchange sly smiles with one another.

LEVEL 7 You continue to talk about plants, then stop and fix a long, icy stare at Jake and Jo, who are whispering to each other. The other students in the class look from you to Jake to Jo, then back to you again—and now no one is thinking about plants.

THE TAXONOMY OF CLASSROOM CONTROL

Every technique of classroom control can be classified in terms of its probable distraction to students. Table 2-1 presents a large number of professional techniques, in what we shall call a Taxonomy of classroom control. (You will notice that eye control appears in the Taxonomy as Method L.) Each Taxonomy method is explained in chapters 3 through 19.

PURPOSE OF THE TAXONOMY

The purpose of the Taxonomy is not to establish absolute categories of classroom control, but rather to compare categories. In many cases, the Taxonomy classifications are supported by empirical research studies, particularly the low and high profile techniques. In other cases, particularly the mid profile, the classifications are supported primarily by logic; in these cases, we must wait for investigators to provide empirical data to support or refute these classifications.

TABLE 2.1   Taxonomy of Classroom Control

A Taxonomy of Classroom Controls

METHOD	LOW PROFILE		
	Level 1	Level 2	Level 3
A. Expectation			
a. Student Educability	Expect that all students can learn	Expect that all students can learn, some with difficulty	
b. Teacher Confidence	Expect that teacher can teach everyone	Expect the need to use special methods for many students	Expect the need to use special methods for a few students
c. Teacher Self-evaluation	Evaluate own teaching automatically and use results	Evaluate own teaching occasionally and use results	
B. Content and Evaluation			
a. Selecting Content Objectives	Students can master next step with moderate effort	Students can master next step with ease	Students can master next step with some difficulty
b. Stating Content Objectives	Stated in specific learning terms		Stated in general learning terms
c. Pacing Content Objectives	Next skill is immediately available	Next skill is immediately ready to be prepared	Next skill ready after short wait for a few students
d. Evaluation of Learning	Reveal continuous, objective standards before performance	Reveal periodic, objective standards before performance	Subjective, continuous, arranged before performance
e. Monitoring	Continuously train students in self-evaluation	Continuously observe and question students to appraise their learning	Monitor student learning through frequent quizzes, tests, drills
f. Feedback to Students	Immediate, specific feedback to every student	Immediate, general feedback to every student	Delayed, specific feedback to every student
C. Instructional Strategies			
a. Expository	Give clear advance organizers followed by relevant examples	Demonstrate concepts or skills to be learned, followed by practice or examples	Give examples first, the concept after delay

MID PROFILE		HIGH PROFILE	
Level 4	Level 5	Level 6	Level 7
Expect that all students can learn, except one or two		Expect that several students cannot learn	Expect that most students cannot learn
	Expect difficulty succeeding with one or two students	Expect difficulty succeeding with several students	Expect difficulty succeeding with most students
Submit to evaluation when required and sometimes use results	Accept positive feedback, reject negative	Ignore all feedback information on own teaching	Resist evaluation of teaching
Students can master next step with great difficulty	Students have already recently mastered next step in content	Students cannot master next step in content in near future	Students have already mastered next step in content long ago
Announced to most students but not all	Stated in specific activity terms	Stated in general activity terms	Never announced
Next skill pressed on a few students before previous one mastered	Next skill ready for a few students after long delay	Class pressed into next skill before previous skill mastered	Class given long delay until next skill presented
Subjective, sporadic, arranged before performance	Objective; standards revealed after performance	Evaluation premature or nonexistent	Evaluation results inaccurate
Monitor student learning through infrequent tests and examinations	Monitor student learning through standardized tests	Monitor through nonspecific third-party reports	Make assumptions instead of monitoring
Delayed, general feedback to every student	Feedback to some, none to others	No feedback to anyone	Incorrect feedback to several students
Give examples in an illogical or incorrect sequence	Give insufficient examples to support the concept	Give inappropriate or irrelevant examples	Give incorrect information

TABLE 2.1   continued

C. Instructional Strategies	Level 1	Level 2	Level 3
b. Discovery	Provide intriguing problems/examples, urge students to resolve/explain	Urge efficient hypothesis-testing, present subsequent examples strategically	Discourage non-strategic questions and experiments
D. Media and Materials	Total environment, simulation	Moderate use of variety of media	Media used for novelty or variation in routine
E. Grouping Students	Establish ad hoc groups for needs of lesson and students	Establish permanent groups for specific learning tasks	Group students for peer tutoring
F. Organizing Space			
a. Low Achievers	Mix high and low achieving students	Place students close to teacher	
b. Seatwork/ Laboratory	Separate study positions		Seat students around large tables
c. Small Groups	Cluster chairs facing center	Cluster desks facing one another	Seats around ends of large tables
d. Lecture/ Presentation	Desks auditorium-style	Seats auditorium-style	Seats in one large circle, square, or U-shape
e. Recitation/Class Discussion	One large circle/square	One or more pairs of rows opposite one another	Seats/desks auditorium style
f. Learning Centers/Laboratory	Separate, self-contained, remote location for each station	Two or more subject-matter stations together	
g. Resources	Ready at learning stations	Close to learning stations	Resources to pairs of students
G. Controlling Time			
a. Pacing Activities	Next activity or step immediately available	Next activity or step immediately ready to be prepared	Few students wait briefly for next activity or segment
b. Transitions	Fast, automatic, initiated by students when needed	Fast, automatic, according to schedules and routines	Supervised by student monitors according to routines
H. Varying Student Activities	Vary activities according to lesson content	Adjust activities according to student attention and needs	Students vary own activities within prescribed control limits

Level 4	Level 5	Level 6	Level 7
Give hints	Provide inadequate examples or ask students to guess	Tell correct answer, structure lesson to "rediscover" that answer	Assume students can solve/discover without structure or previous experience
Media without integration or explanation	Constant use of only one medium	Awkward use of media: time delays, mistakes	Media that do not work or are irrelevant
Rely exclusively on large group	Permanent homogeneous small groups in all subject areas	Permanent homogeneous small groups in each subject area	Any group used for inappropriate or undefined purposes
		Place students remote from teacher	Group problem students together
Pair student desks in parallel	Cluster small desks facing one another	Pair student desks facing each other	
Arrange seats auditorium-style	Odd-man-out seating	Split-groups seating	Split groups with shared members
One or more pairs of rows opposite one another	Seats around large tables	Cluster desks in groups	Paired desks facing each other
Odd-man-out seating in room	Seats around large tables	Cluster desks in groups	Paired desks facing each other
	Stations in unmonitored location		Stations in central traffic areas of classroom
Resources to small groups	Resources in subareas	Multiple resources, central	Single resources, central
Few students forced into new activity prematurely	Few students forced into long delay for next activity	Entire class forced into new activity prematurely	Entire class forced into long delay for next activity
Teacher cue with teacher instructions at the time	Incomplete, resulting in false starts	Announcements to some students disturb other students	Lengthy or haphazard
Vary activities according to preset pattern or schedule	Students vary own activities within non-content limits	Continue the same activity indefinitely	Vary activities without purpose or continuity or stop all activity

TABLE 2.1   continued

	Level 1	Level 2	Level 3
I. Activating Students			
a. Inducing Group Activity	Organize for high content participation and practice	Adapt activities for high content participation	Organize for peer teaching and tutoring
b. Inviting Passive Students	Name-dropping, eye contact, and open body position	Direct address of several students, in content, without pause	Give student a content-oriented task during lesson
J. Supervision and Management			
a. Student Self-control	Pretrain students in general principles of classroom management	Assume rules and observe without formal announcement or training	Establish routines: pretrain for particular occasions or for teacher cue
b. Supervision	Directly supervise students at all times	Pretrain students to use self-monitoring	
c. Participatory Management	Joint planning/ management of limited aspects of instruction	Students advise teacher on policies and procedures	Joint planning/ management of all aspects of instruction
K. Voice			
a. Volume	Change voice volume for content effects	Silent pauses for content effects	Content-word voice-overs to mask small distractions
b. Pitch	Vary voice pitch		Monotone for content effect
L. Eyes	Look at all students as lesson goes on	Look at target students slightly longer than others	Look at target students more frequently than others
M. Gestures			
a. Pointing	Point or nod to lesson object/prop	Use gestures to emphasize topical point	
b. Touching	Physically guide elementary student re: content	Physically comfort or reward elementary students re: content	Physically guide secondary student re: content
N. Location			
a. Teacher	Change position in room periodically	Move into area of target students as lesson continues	Pass by target students as lesson continues

Level 4	Level 5	Level 6	Level 7
Assign extra content work activities	Assign extra non-content work activities	Allow any activity students desire	Assign non-content activities during instruction
	Direct address, wait for response	Public signal of nonparticipation	Public rebuke for nonparticipation
Post rules in the classroom	Remind target students of rules privately during lesson	Briefly remind class of rules during lesson	Stop lesson to announce rules, train students, or hold class meeting
	Random, occasional, direct supervision	Regular but occasional direct supervision	No provision for supervision of learning activities
Teacher changes prior agreements for clearly stated reasons	Teacher jointly plans with some students, not others	Teacher ignores student opinions for no apparent reason	Teacher changes prior agreements for no apparent reason
Exaggerated volume changes	Loud volume throughout the entire lesson	Brief silence to wait for order	Prolonged silence or shouts to restore order
Exaggerated change of voice pitch	Monotone voice	Whining tones	Voice disability
Look at target students constantly, occasionally check other students	Look at target students constantly, signal with eyes	Look at students with brief glare	Look at students with long glare
Remove student's distracting object privately		Remove student's distracting object publicly	Point at distracting student or make irrelevant gestures
	Touch arm or shoulder of target students in inattention	Physically comfort or reward secondary student during instruction	Physically restrain or punish student during instruction
	Stand next to target student as lesson continues	Remain continuously stationary during lesson	Move continually and constantly during lesson

TABLE 2.1   continued

	Level 1	Level 2	Level 3
b. Students	Seats designated before lesson	Shift in and out of buzz groups	Students choose own positions before lesson begins
O. Active Listening	Acknowledgment, parroting, paraphrase, inquiry regarding content	Reflecting or thought-test regarding content	Long paraphrase questions during instruction
P. Conversation Control	Brief paraphrase	Acknowledgment or parroting	Reflecting or extended paraphrase
Q. Control Speaker Role	Conversation control (paraphrase), invite new speaker on same topic	Conversation control (reflecting), invite new speaker on same topic	Conversation control (parroting), invite new speaker on same topic
R. Control Topic	Use conversation control (paraphrase), change topic	Use conversation control (reflecting), change topic	Use conversation control (parroting), change topic
S. Control Group Discussion	Induce total group participation and effort	Assign responsibilities to group members and train them	Monitor all group interaction
T. Instructional Questions			
a. Standard Procedures	Ask question, wait, call on volunteer, wait	Ask question, wait, call on nonvolunteer, wait	Ask question, wait for answer, repeat question to another student
b. Question Types	Ask lower level, closed, convergent questions on content	Ask higher level questions on content	Ask open questions about personal experiences that relate to content
c. Wrong Answers	Identify source of error automatically, ask again	Probe	Prompt
d. Diagnosis	Ask step-by-step questions about prerequisite knowledge and skills	Request student to demonstrate problem situation	
U. Names	Use name dropping of all students in content of lesson	Include target student's name, with others, in content of lesson	Use target student's name alone in content of lesson

Level 4	Level 5	Level 6	Level 7
Move furniture to form small groups (adjacent)		Move target student's position during instruction	Stop lesson to move target student's position
Continual message check with target students	Continual message check with cue words	Active listening to maintain non-content talk during instruction	Active listening to maintain off-lesson topics during instruction
Continual message check	Override speaker	Interrupt speaker with support	Interrupt speaker with contradiction
Acknowledge or silent wait, invite new speaker	Interrupt, override, or shift topic/speaker simultaneously	Signal an interruption, invite original speaker	Reprimand speaker, then invite another speaker
Acknowledge the speaker, then change topic	Interrupt/override speaker with new topic; change topic and speaker simultaneously	Signal that prior topic is not favored, then change topic	Denigrate speaker's topic, then change topic
Permit some members to be passive or absent	Dismiss or exclude one or more group members	Use the group as a vehicle or sounding board for own ideas	Permit group to operate without leadership
Call student name before asking question	Ask question, then quickly switch to another student	Direct no-cue question to inattentive or unknown attention students	Interrupt student answers with own answers
Ask affective-oriented questions which relate to content	Use vague language, overly lengthy or complex questions, rephrase several times	Ask questions of no apparent purpose, direction, relevance	Ask questions inappropriate to lesson purpose
Ask why student answered, identify source of error, ask again	Correct wrong answer	Ignore wrong answer	Accept wrong answer as if it were correct
Ask student why he is having the problem	Ask questions that have already been answered	Stop diagnosis before completion	Ask same diagnostic question many times
	Non-content name dropping or direct address without pause during lesson	Non-content name dropping or direct address with pause during lesson	Use target student's name in reprimand

TABLE 2.1   continued

	Level 1	Level 2	Level 3
V. Directions	Public directions to attend to specific lesson content/objects	Public or private directions for how to observe/ponder lesson content, etc.	Public directions to individual during instruction
W. Pep Talks	Pep talk to class on content learning	Pep talk to students in private on content learning	Pep talk to student publicly on content learning
X. Control of Distractions			
a. Anticipating	Anticipate problems, solve automatically	Anticipate problems, solve in orientation	Observe and meet problems during instruction
b. Acting	Ignore minor distraction or divert attention	Incorporate distraction into lesson content	Content word voice-overs to mask small distractions
Y. Criticism			
a. Balanced	Specific, content-oriented, balanced criticism to class	Specific, content-oriented, balanced criticism to target students	
b. Praise	Specific, content-oriented praise to class	Specific, content-oriented praise to target students in private	General, content-oriented praise to target students in private
c. Rebuke/ Reprimand	Specific, content-oriented request to student		Specific, content-oriented disvalue to target students in private
Z. Rewards and Punishments	Provide intrinsic rewards in learning materials and activities	Reward on-task or near-task behaviors, ignore off-task behaviors	Wait for on-task behavior, reward it with a token

Level 4	Level 5	Level 6	Level 7
Private, non-content directions to individual		Non-content directions to individual students in public	Non-content directions to entire class
Pep talk to student privately on non-content behavior		Pep talk to target students in public on non-content behavior	Pep talk to class on non-content behavior
Stop a student's work to correct a procedure		Stop lesson to answer questions on procedure	Stop lesson to change procedures or hold class meeting
Remove distracting object as lesson goes on	Verbal/nonverbal "desist" in private during instruction	Verbal/nonverbal "desist" in public during instruction	Remove distractor from group
Unclear or unlinked content-oriented, balanced criticism to target students privately		Unclear or unlinked, content-oriented, overgeneralized criticism to class	Non-content criticism to students during instruction
Non-content praise in private		Continuous praise to target students in public	Non-content praise to class or target students in public
A non-content disvalue (desist) to target student privately		Non-content disvalue or request to students in public	Lights out, heads down, loud noise, dramatic public reprimands
Withhold rewards from target student, provide to others; reward non-content behavior	Use nonphysical punishments	Isolate target student	Administer physical punishment other than isolation

USING THE TAXONOMY

Building Awareness   The Taxonomy is a comprehensive list of all the professional tools available for classroom control. In learning his professional tools, therefore, the novice teacher might conceivably be expected to learn the Taxonomy well enough to demonstrate these two skills:

1   "If someone asks me about any control method, such as Pep Talk (Method W), I can describe a low profile, a mid profile, and a high profile example."
2   "If someone asks me to name all the available low profile techniques, I can recite and explain at least 80 without looking at the Taxonomy."

You might read and refer to the higher profile levels, 3 through 7, as to an encyclopedia; few teachers need training in mid and high profile techniques, but most teachers need greater awareness of and training in low profile skills.

Diagnosing Teaching Practices[2]   If a teacher finds his present control methods and techniques do not effectively control student attention, he can use the Taxonomy as a diagnostic tool, with these simple steps:

1   Beginning with Method Aa, examine the first line of the Taxonomy and find your current expectations on that line according to Steps 2 and 3.
2   Think about your so-called best days in the classroom. What is your predominant expectation on such days? Mark it with a solid circle.
3   Now think about your worst days in the classroom. What is your predominant expectation then? If different from (2), mark it with a dotted circle.
4   Repeat Steps 2 and 3 for Method Ab and each line thereafter.
5   Now ask yourself, "Am I using higher profile controls than I need, and thus incurring greater risk of student inattention?"

Once you know the Taxonomy, the next step is to practice using it to exercise effective classroom control in any instructional setting according to the fundamental principles of classroom control.

THE FUNDAMENTAL PRINCIPLES OF CLASSROOM CONTROL

Principle No. 1 — Attention   Keep the student's attention on the lesson content. Avoid distracting the target of control; avoid distracting the rest of the class.

Principle No. 2 — Lowest Profile   Use the lowest profile control technique possible and feasible in any case of classroom control. Do not rely exclusively or primarily on high profile control.

Principle No. 3 — Sequence   When a low profile technique does not work, begin a sequence: repeat the technique, try another low profile technique, or use several low profile techniques simultaneously before going to a higher profile technique. Do not leapfrog control levels.

FUNDAMENTAL PRINCIPLES IN ACTION

Imagine that you are a novice teacher during your first class. You notice Leslie making a paper airplane while you are talking. Recalling fundamental principle no. 1 (attention), you think, "Here is a clear case of inattention, and I should take action." You continue the lesson smoothly and follow fundamental principle no. 2 (lowest profile) as you move in Leslie's direction, looking at her occasionally as you do so. She persists. Following fundamental principle no. 3 (sequence), you continue your lesson smoothly and begin a control sequence. Remaining at Level 1, you change your voice to a loud whisper (with no effect on Leslie), then continue moving to Leslie's vicinity, looking at her more frequently as you carry on the lesson, then pause beside her. She stops and pays attention—you think. You ask a question of another student, then name-drop the second student's name along with Leslie's name, then ask an open question of the class, and notice Leslie's hand go up in response. In 30 seconds, you have Leslie's active participation—she has volunteered—with no distraction to any other student.

While all the fundamental principles are important, principle no. 3 (sequence) is basic to teacher morale and confidence. The teacher uses skills expecting them to work, but also expecting to act if they do not. The truly effective teacher is almost never at a loss, no matter what students do, and is never more distractive in control techniques than absolutely necessary.

THE TAXONOMY IN THE SCIENCE AND ART OF TEACHING

For the moment, assume that when we use the fundamentals of classroom control to choose a profile level for any situation, we engage in the science of teaching. Definite rules operate, and we make limited choices on the basis of clear principles. This is the science of classroom control. We move left to right across the columns of the Taxonomy in accordance with our fundamental principles. In classroom control, the seven profile levels are limited and discrete; moreover, the three fundamental principles are also limited and discrete. Therefore, the professional teacher's first decision in classroom control—which profile level to choose according to the fundamental principles—is a scientific decision.

When we reach the proper column, however, we have literally millions of different combinations of techniques in that column from which to choose, and our choices are no longer based on simple principles. We are now in the realm of teacher discretion, of style, of personal preference, all of which are elements of art. This indeed is the art of classroom control: we move up and down each column of the Taxonomy, selecting techniques we consider appropriate.

No teacher or researcher or writer can prescribe a single technique at any level of control that is logical or sensible for all classroom situations. That is why there are so many different books available on classroom discipline, management, and control. A useful guide for thinking about artistic questions of control is Wolfgang and Glickman's *Solving Discipline Problems* (1980).

The problem in American classroom control is not that teachers lack resources for artistic decisions—we have almost more artistic advice and inspiration than we can use. The problem is that we too often ignore the scientific principles that should determine the first step in any teaching decision. One solution is to install in our heads a small steady voice to remind us whenever we violate one of our fundamentals: "Careful, Mr. Smith, you just leaped to high profile control." A better solution is to train ourselves to make classroom control decisions scientifically: precede every artistic decision in control (selection of technique) with a scientific decision (selection of profile level) according to the fundamental principles of classroom control. This guideline is a working definition of balance between science and art in teaching.

In the chapters to follow, you can explore some of the most effective, most powerful methods and techniques of classroom control available. These methods are not new; they have always been used by effective teachers. But they are used well by only a few teachers, so you may find many of them new, or even a bit strange, so different are they from common teaching practice. You may not have been lucky enough to watch or work with a truly effective, truly fine teacher before you entered your teacher training program; nevertheless, you have a professional responsibility to join the ranks of effective teachers and increase their numbers.

EXERCISE: IDENTIFYING LOW PROFILE TEACHER CONTROLS

The Problems High profile classroom controls are easy to recognize by almost anyone, regardless of professional training.

Low profile classroom controls are usually difficult to recognize by untrained observers.

The Skills Recognize selected examples of high profile and low profile classroom controls.

Develop facility in classifying high and low profile controls — verbal and nonverbal, organizational and behavioral — as you observe instruction.

PREPARATION FOR CLASS EXERCISE Read the following observations from a real classroom situation and categorize each teacher control as high, mid, or low profile according to the definitions below.

High The control may distract the attention of large numbers of students away from lesson content.

Mid The control may distract the attention of just one student (the target) or a small number of students away from lesson content.

Low The control will probably not distract anyone's attention from lesson content.

The teacher:

_____ (a) To get students' attention, raises voice while introducing lesson content terminology.

_____ (b) Gives time deadlines for seatwork assignments — talks slowly and clearly.

_____ (c) Uses eye contact to check comprehension (visual cues).

_____ (d) Tells students to begin work on... (specific content terms).

_____ (e) Changes position in room as students begin seatwork.

_____ (f) Quiet verbal reprimand to student for not having her book open yet.

_____ (g) Yells at a group of students who are still talking.

_____ (h) Circulates in room, helping with individual problems.

_____ (i) Uses eye contact to check rest of class while helping individuals.

_____ (j) Interrupts class to make announcement about the class paper drive.

_____ (k) Calls out individuals' names to get their attention before resuming the lesson.

_____ (l) Prolonged silence, waiting for attention.

_____ (m) Urges students to work on the paper drive because the class needs money.

_____ (n) Class back to seatwork assignment; teacher looks around the room.

_____ (o) Leans over and glares at individual who is working on another assignment. No one else notices.

_____ (p) Points to a content word in the text.

_____ (q) Students smile as they do their seatwork assignment.

_____ (r) Student stops work, raises his hand to find out what to do next, then looks again at his paper and resumes work.

Check your classifications with mine. (a) As long as the teacher is talking about the lesson content during an introduction, I consider the control low profile. But if the teacher raises her voice to dwell on the mechanics or the procedures of the lesson rather than the content to be learned, I assume the students' minds are not on content, and I call the control high. Here, the control is low. (b) Lesson content words seem to be missing here, so it is high profile. There are many ways to get students to think about lesson content while also giving them administrative mechanics (see Method V). (c) Low profile. (d) No content words—high. (e) Low. (f) Mid. (g) High. (h) Low. (i) Low. (j) High. (k) High. (This is the kind of unconscious teacher practice that makes kids flinch or jump when they hear their names in the classroom. "What's wrong?" they think; "What did I do?") (l) High (A traditional, conventional, generally approved waste of time) (m) High (Off-content) (n) Low. (o) Mid. (p) Low. (q) Low. (r) Low. If I were to graph my observations of this teacher, the graph would look like Figure 2.6.

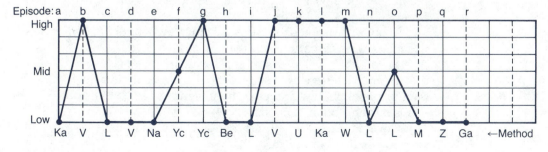

FIGURE 2.6 Graphing a Teacher Profile

Now read the following script of a demonstration class. Read through the entire script, then go back and categorize the teacher control devices as low, mid, or high profile. You may copy the Sample Observation Form on a separate sheet. (Notice that the lines on the script are numbered for your convenience; note line numbers on your observation form. Your form should provide space for at least 20 entries.)

TEACHER OBSERVATION FORM (DEMONSTRATION SCRIPT)

Read through the Demonstration Script. When you notice a classroom control technique, classify it—with a circle—as Low, Mid, or High Profile, and note briefly what the teacher does or says. Afterwards, turn to the Taxonomy and classify the level of each technique.

Example: ▶ LOW MID HIGH		LEVEL _____
Line: _____ LOW MID HIGH		LEVEL _____
_____ LOW MID HIGH		LEVEL _____
_____ LOW MID HIGH		LEVEL _____
_____ LOW MID HIGH		LEVEL _____
_____ LOW MID HIGH		LEVEL _____
_____ LOW MID HIGH		LEVEL _____

⋮   ⋮   ⋮   ⋮   ⋮   ⋮

PROFILE: When so directed, transfer each Level rating above to the graph below and put a *heavy dot* (see example) on the graph. Join the dots.

DEMONSTRATION SCRIPT: CLASSROOM CONTROLS

T: This lesson is about what I call the Conversation Control   1
Technique, which lets *you* control a conversation while someone   2
else is talking. S₁, you look puzzled.   3
S₁: Yeah, when someone *else* is talking, *they* control the con-   4
versation. At least, that's what *I* think.   5
T: So you don't feel in control unless you're the talker, right?   6
S₁: Right, because when I am talking, I can talk about what I   7
want to talk about and that puts *me* in control, see, and nobody   8
else is talking, so I'm in control...   9
T: [Break in] So when *you* set the topic, *you* control the con-   10
versation; is *that* your point?   11
S₁: Yeah.   12

T: [Quickly] S_2, you're nodding your head. Does that mean you 13
agree? 14
$S_{3,4,5,6}$: [Mumble out loud, giggle, etc.] 15
S_2: Well, kind of. 16
T: OK, now if you'll all look here at this chart, this is how con- 17
versation control works. S_1 could use it, S_2, you can do it too, and 18
so could S_3 and S_4 and S_7. The first thing you do is break in when 19
somebody else is talking, and then you paraphrase what they are 20
saying, and then you wait for them to agree. 21
S_8: What do you mean, "paraphrase?" 22
$S_{9,10}$: [Argue — "You *give* me that, it's mine!" "No, it isn't, be- 23
cause I..." etc.] 24
T: What's going on back there? Whatever...whatever you people 25
are doing back there, I want it to stop right now, do you under- 26
stand me? You're interrupting the whole class, S_9 — you sit up and 27
pay attention, do you hear me? (Pause) OK, now where were we? 28
Oh yeah — "paraphrase" means that you repeat back in your own 29
words what somebody else has said. Do you understand what I 30
mean? S_{10}, turn around. 31
[**All S**]: [General mumble, conversation with one another.] 32
T: Now I want you all to try this technique, S_{11}, S_{12}, S_{13}, every- 33
body. I am going to say something to you, and I want you all to 34
paraphrase it out loud in chorus, even if your paraphrase is differ- 35
ent from someone else's. OK? Here we go: 36
  "The temperature is 55°F in this room." [Hand signal] 37
[**All S**]: [Paraphrase out loud in chorus] 38
T: Another statement: 39
  "I like history more than any other subject." 40
[**All S**]: [Paraphrase out loud in chorus] 41
T: Now another statement, and this time turn to your neighbor 42
and check one another to see if your neighbor agrees that your 43
paraphrase is correct. Ready? Here's the statement: 44
  "Conversation control is not hard at all." 45
[**All S**]: [Check your paraphrase with your neighbor.] 46
T: [Override the class noise.] Now look again here at this chart. 47
I'm moving so you all can see how the paraphrase and agreement 48
begin with "breaking in." What do you think "breaking in" means? 49
Anyone? 50
S_{14}: [Loud] Steal something! [All S laugh] 51
T: [Long drawl] Right — just the way you're stealing my lesson 52
away from me, right S_{14}? 53
S_{14}: [Long drawl] Right.... [All S laugh] 54
T: Now S_{14}, tell me, is it rude to interrupt someone when he or 55
she is talking? 56
S_{14}: Well, sure, uh, you're not supposed to talk when somebody 57
else is talking...[Fade out] 58

After you have completed "observing" the Demonstration Script class and have classified each teacher technique, use the Taxonomy to help you determine Levels, and transfer your Level ratings to the profile graph at the bottom of the sheet, making large dots as shown in the earlier example. You are now ready for class exercises.

EXERCISE 1 (about 30 minutes)

1   In class, meet with a small group of four to six people and produce one rating sheet, upon which everyone agrees, for the entire group. Again, make a graph of the group's ratings.
2   Present your group's observations to the rest of the class, perhaps by posting your graph and explaining it orally. Try to reach a class concensus through open discussion.

Conclusion   The purpose of this exercise is to familiarize you with what low, mid, and high profile controls actually look and sound like — if you have never thought about these kinds of things before — and to build your skills in observing and judging teacher controls during instruction, in the heat of battle.

EXERCISE 2 (about 15 minutes)

Before doing this class exercise, review the three fundamental principles of classroom control.

In class, with the help of your instructor, compare your profile of the Demonstration Script Teacher with each of the following patterns.

A teacher who is in the habit of throwing little distractions — perhaps brief public and private reprimands — into the middle of a lesson would exhibit Pattern A. There's good low profile here too, but the effective low profile may be spoiled by all the distractions.

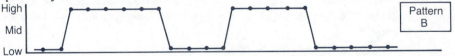

Pattern B is that of a teacher who gets up there and stays, perhaps by using long lectures on classroom rules or proper conduct during the time that has been planned for reading or math. Again, the effects of low profile here may be spoiled by the high.

Pattern C of classroom control is extremely effective. This teacher may be working with a class that is absolutely bananas, perhaps on the day before Halloween or Christmas vacation, or the hour just before or after lunch. You cannot judge this teacher's professionalism by the students' behavior; you need look only at the *teacher's* behavior, and Pattern C suggests that the teacher's profile of control is no higher than necessary at any moment. When increasing profile, the Pattern C teacher does it gradually and slowly — in sequence — to distract students as little as possible.

How effective is Pattern D? We cannot say without knowing the attention level of the students. For example, if the kids are in high attention, this teacher must be considered effective. If the kids are in low attention, the teacher either is oblivious to the problem or doesn't know how to go higher.

How effective is pattern E? This teacher has not prepared a lesson, is not teaching at the moment, or both. The class may be taking a break, or they may be getting ready for a new lesson. This appears to be a noninstructional period; there are no signs of classroom control of instruction in evidence.

Notice the importance here of a qualified observer. An untrained observer could look at a beautifully controlled class of Low Profile Pattern D and perhaps think it was E. So train your observer, whether colleague, supervisor, administrator, or instructor, to be aware of your Low Profile professional control skills.

EXERCISE 3 (about 15 minutes)

Your instructor will "teach" a lesson for 3 minutes. (Any subject matter will do; for example, read aloud and explain the assignment at the end of this chapter.) During this lesson, you will not only be a student, but also an observer. Use the Teacher Profile Observation Sheet below, and follow its directions exactly. You will find the pace of this activity extremely fast, so take only brief notes. It will help if your instructor can give you examples of high, mid, and low profile techniques; the lesson should not be an example of fine teaching, but rather a display of different control techniques.

At some time during the lesson, you should select one of the student behaviors below and do it; watch the instructor out of the corner of your eye so you can continue your observation without any interruption of your notetaking.

- Put your head down on your desk and keep it there until the instructor controls your attention in some manner.
- Turn around and face toward another group member; stay that way until the instructor controls your attention in some manner.

■ Hum quietly to yourself until the instructor controls your attention. (Don't hum while someone else is humming; wait till the other person finishes, or choose another behavior.)

Conclusion   In open class discussion, compare observations, ratings, teacher actions, and results. If you have time, do the exercise again; you will be more proficient after more practice.

Assignment   Observe three different teachers, each for a 10-minute segment, using a regular Teacher Profile Observation Sheet similar to the one in Appendix B. Record your observations every 15 seconds in exactly the same way we are doing Exercise 3.

If you cannot observe three different teachers, you may observe one teacher on three different occasions. Your assignment will consist of three completed Observation Sheets.

As you observe teachers using control techniques, remember: the mind of the student is the key factor, not the style of the teacher. For example, a teacher may shout to direct students' minds in two different ways:

High profile shout: "Sit down right now!"
Low profile shout: "That can't be true, right? Why? Because the vapor has already escaped, see? Sure!"

At the end of your report, ponder and criticize the following claims:

When you see students growing restless and fooling around and not paying attention, you usually see, at the same time, a lack of low profile controls.

High profile control techniques often create problems for the teachers who use them. High profile control assumes that students whose attention has been fastened on the teacher in Step 1 will indeed shift to lesson content in Step 2, but this is a risky assumption. A lot can happen between Steps 1 and 2; for example, another student could distract the target student's attention by giggling, the target student could perform for his audience, or the teacher could unconsciously create another distraction.

CLASSROOM CONTROL: TEACHER PROFILE OBSERVATION SHEET
(TRAINING VERSION)*

Teacher:_____   Observer:_____

Date:_____ Time Started:_____ Class Size:_____

Directions to Observer: At every 15-second interval, note the specific control technique the teacher is using. Then later, mark on the graph, with a heavy dot, the approximate level of control in use at each interval.

Minutes	0			1			2			3	
	·		·		·		·		·		7
High	·		·		·		·		·		6
	·		·		·		·		·		5
	·		·		·		·		·		4
Mid	·		·		·		·		·		3
	·		·		·		·		·		2
Low	·		·		·		·		·		1

. . .

— —

1—

. . .

— —

2—

. . .

— —

3—

*Copies of this form may be duplicated from this text.

NOTES

1   These visual cues are consistent with cues postulated by Lahaderne (1968), Cobb (1972), Samuels and Turnure (1974), Good and Brophy (1978), and others.

2   The reader who likes to fit all classroom controls into a Create-Maintain-Restore model might read the Taxonomy this way:

Create: Some of the Taxonomy's classroom controls appear to create productive conditions for learning: by controlling our expectations, lesson content, activities, and grouping of students, and by setting goals and insisting on accountability, we create conditions that enhance student attention and student achievement; we also prevent classroom control problems before they start. (See Methods A through J, also Z.)

Maintain: Some of the Taxonomy's classroom controls appear to maintain student attention and on-task behavior: eye contact, body gestures, and using student names, all help keep student attention on-task. (See Methods G through Z.)

Restore: Some of the Taxonomy's classroom controls appear most clearly to restore student attention that has been lost: pep talks, criticism, and control of distractions seem most clearly to be corrective measures in classroom control. (See Methods J, K, M, N, Q, R, T, U through Z.)

The problem with create-maintain-restore models is that the functions they categorize are not discrete. For example: if you, as the teacher, move Suzie's seat because she continually talks with her neighbor, you are not only restoring Suzie's attention, but are also helping other students to maintain their own attention to the lesson; in addition, you are creating more favorable learning conditions for Suzie in the future.

Another way to read the Taxonomy is in terms of proactive and reactive controls. Some experts argue, logically, that the best teacher control occurs before the lesson starts (proactive):

The key to classroom management success lies in the things the teacher does ahead of time to create a good learning environment and a low potential for trouble. (Good and Brophy, 1978, p. 166).

Other experts cite important teacher behaviors during instruction, which we might call reactive: Kounin, for example, discusses "withitness" (the teacher knows what is going on), "overlapping" (the teacher can attend to two or more issues simultaneously), "group alerting" (the teacher maintains a group focus during recitation rather than becoming focused on a single student), and others (Kounin, 1970, p. 144).

The taxonomy techniques most clearly proactive are the Low Profile techniques of Methods A through I, also Xa and Z; the techniques most clearly reactive include K through Y. Method J is difficult to classify.

Most experts agree that both proactive and reactive controls are required in effective teaching, but it is often difficult to distinguish between the two categories. For example, when you see that your carefully planned lesson is dragging—your students are getting restless and inattentive—you might either speed up your tempo or shift the activity in some way. Your purpose is to eliminate student inattention now (reactive) and enhance student attention three to five minutes from now (proactive), at the same time.

REFERENCES

BERLINER, D. Tempus educare. In P. Peterson & H. Walberg (Eds.), *Research on teaching: Concepts, findings, and implications.* Berkeley, Calif., McCutchan, 1979.

COBB, J. Relationship of discrete classroom behaviors to fourth-grade academic achievement. *Journal of Educational Psychology,* 1972, *63,* 74–80.

FLANDERS, N. Interaction analysis in the classroom: A manual for observers. Ann Arbor, Mich.: School of Education, University of Michigan, 1966.

GOOD, T., & BROPHY, J. *Looking in classrooms.* Harper & Row, 1978.

JAMES, W. *The principles of psychology* (Vol. 1). New York: Henry Holt, 1890.

MORRISON, H. *The Practice of Teaching in the Secondary School.* Chicago: The University of Chicago Press, 1931.

ROSENSHINE, B. Content, time, and direct instruction. In P. Peterson and H. Walberg (Eds.), *Research on teaching: Concepts, findings, and implications.* Berkeley, Calif.: McCutchan, 1979.

SAMUELS, S., & TURNURE, J. Attention and reading achievement in first grade boys and girls. *Journal of Educational Psychology,* 1974, *66,* 29–32.

THORNDIKE, E. *The principles of teaching.* New York: A. G. Seiler, 1911.

WOLFGANG, C., & GLICKMAN, C. *Solving discipline problems.* Boston: Allyn and Bacon, 1980.

CONTROL OF EXPECTATIONS (METHOD A)

3

This chapter examines how teachers expect certain things to happen in classrooms. Some teacher expectations appear to help student learning; others appear to hinder it. In other words, even teacher attitudes are low and high profile.

METHOD Aa
Student Educability: Does the teacher expect that students can learn?

American girls were long told, or told themselves, that mathematics is not a proper study for them because it is technical and better suited to boys. Researchers claim these adverse expectations made girls perform less well in mathematics than boys, and caused them to withdraw from mathematics studies (Jacobs, 1978; Fennema and Sherman, 1978).

How much of the power of expectation (also called "self-fulfilling prophecy" and "Pygmalion Effect") is folklore, and how much is true? Scholars debate the validity of research on the power of expectation to shape human behavior (Elashoff and Snow, 1971; Brophy & Good, 1974; Cooper, 1979; Brophy, 1982), but there are compelling reasons for teachers to believe that their attitudes of expectation help or hinder students.

LEVEL 1: The teacher expects that all students in the class can learn.

Ronald Edmonds (1981) has studied the differences between more effective schools ("improving") and less effective schools ("declining"). One difference is teacher expectation for student learning:

> There is a clear contrast in the evaluations that teachers and principals make of the students in the improving and declining schools. The staffs of the improving schools tend to believe that *all* of their students can master the basic objectives...while the declining schools' teachers project the belief that students' ability levels are low and, therefore, they cannot master even these objectives. The staffs of the improving schools hold decidedly higher and apparently increasing levels of expectations with regard to the educational accomplishments of their students. In contrast, staff of the declining schools are much less likely to believe that their students will complete high school or college. (p. 6)

LEVEL 2: The teacher expects that all students in the class can learn, some with difficulty.

Effective teachers plan for individual differences, then teach to those differences with low profile techniques (see Methods Bal, Bcl, Bel, El, Fal, H2, Tcl, Tdl).

The risk in this expectation comes when the teacher begins to treat students differently in ways that are not beneficial; for example, a number of studies claim that, under ordinary circumstances, teachers treat low achievers in ways that tend to keep them low achievers (Rist, 1970; Rosenthal and Jacobson, 1968; Brophy and Good, 1974; Taylor, 1979; Brophy, 1982). Student self-image, social behavior, and achievement appear to be affected by the classifications and labels teachers give them, and teachers' attitudes can be conditioned by student self-reports. When the little boy says, "I can't do this — I'm too dumb," the word "dumb" can stick with the teacher and shape her future judgment of and behavior toward that boy (Darley and Fazio, 1980, discuss the power of attribution).

LEVEL 3: (None.)

LEVEL 4: The teacher expects that all students in the class except one or two can learn.

This is the classic problem of "the dumb kid" in class whom the teacher may politely call "slow," but from whom she actually expects little or no learning, and actually "gives up" on the student.

Teacher statements such as "This kid can't learn math" or "This kid is just no good in English" or "This kid will never learn good manners" are never justified. Somewhere there are fine teachers who know how to teach that kid math, English, and manners:

> If something is not learned the first time through, they will teach it again.... These [effective] teachers treat student failure as a challenge; they do not write off certain youngsters as unteachable because they lack ability or experiential background.... They believe that the students are capable of learning and that they are capable of teaching them successfully. (Brophy, 1980, p. 527)

Brophy and Good (1974) list several teacher behaviors that appear to communicate low expectations to students; the list is probably familiar to you:

1 Waiting less time for low achievers to answer than for high achievers;
2 In response to incorrect answers, giving high achievers clues to answers, repeated questions, or new questions, but giving low achievers the correct answer directly or calling on another student to respond;
3 Praising marginal or inaccurate answers from low achievers (in some studies);
4 Criticizing low achievers disproportionately more than high achievers;
5 Praising low achievers disproportionately less than high achievers;
6 Not acknowledging low achievers' answers, even when correct;
7 Paying less attention to low achievers, looking more at high achievers;
8 Calling on low achievers less often;
9 Seating low achievers farther from the teacher;
10 Demanding less academic work of low achievers and making fewer systematic efforts to improve their performance;
11 Penalizing low achievers for behavior ignored in high achievers.

The Level 4 expectation is not always dysfunctional; when worded in a particular way, the expectation may be justified: "Given this lesson or this task, this student just can't learn" is a sensible judgment when a physical, intellectual, or emotional disability or lack of development prevents a student's learning and promotes frustration; in such cases, the teacher should create more suitable learning experiences for the student or make a professional referral. At the same time we justify this expectation, however, we need to remember the education of Helen Keller and other extraordinary handicapped persons who defy sensible people's expectations.

LEVEL 5: (None.)

LEVEL 6: The teacher expects that several students in the class cannot learn.

Sometimes this expectation arises from frustration, when one has tried everything but failed to control several students' attention and learning. Sometimes the expectation arises from racial, cultural, or sexual stereotypes (Rist, 1970; Brophy & Good, 1974; Persell, 1977; Brookover et al., 1979; Edmonds, 1979; Taylor, 1979). The probability of low morale and general distraction is high for a classroom whose teacher holds this expectation, whether or not it is justified.

This expectation may be justified when lesson demands are beyond the students' physical or intellectual development; for example; "Given this lesson, these kids just can't learn" or "These five-year-olds just can't learn to shoot basketball jump shots."

LEVEL 7: The teacher expects that most students in the class cannot learn.

(See discussion under Levels 4 and 6.)

EXERCISES: CONTROLLING TEACHER EXPECTATIONS OF STUDENTS (OBSERVATION VS. INFERENCE)

Almost everyone reads into situations something that is not really there. Our impressions of the world often have little to do with reality, even when that reality is right before us to see, hear, or feel. In everyday language, we call our distorted impressions "biases," "stereotypes," "prejudices," and "predetermined judgments." Sometimes we try to deny them, thus fooling ourselves even more, but they are always with us.

Preparation for Class Exercises   First read this sentence:

Finished files are the result of years of scientific study combined with the experience of many years.

Now go back and count the F's in the sentence—count them only once, and then write the number here. _____

It is possible that you counted six F's, because that is the correct number. However, because the "F" in "of" sounds like a "V," it seems to disappear, and most adults count only three F's in the sentence.

It is remarkable how frequently we fail to perceive things as they actually are, and even more remarkable how other people tend to act according to our perceptions. A student "overachieves" in one class because the teacher thinks the student is great, but "underachieves" in another teacher's class because she considers him slow or unmotivated or ill mannered.

Now read these definitions:

Objective statement: The person tells what he or she actually saw or heard or touched.

Subjective statement: The person tells what he or she judges, infers, believes, concludes, feels, thinks.

Classify each of the following statements with an "O" if objective, an "S" if subjective:

(1) _____ They smiled as they wrote in their lab manuals.
(2) _____ They enjoyed writing in their lab manuals.
(3) _____ You are very tall.
(4) _____ You are taller than anyone else in the class.
(5) _____ The room was in chaos.
(6) _____ Students were talking out loud during the seatwork period.

The statements are paired as follows:

(1) and (2): (1) is what the teacher saw, hence objective; (2) is the teacher's subjective inference.

(3) and (4): (3) is the teacher's subjective judgment or conclusion, based on personal experience and beliefs about tallness. (4) is an objective statement whose truth can be tested by anyone.

(5) and (6): (5) is the teacher's subjective conclusion, judgment, feeling, or belief about the students in the room that is objectively described in (6).

Read the following suggestions for countering the automatic and natural tendency to use prior information, value judgments, and thinking habits.

STRATEGIES FOR POSTPONING JUDGMENTS

When you first hear or read prior information about a student (another teacher's coffee lounge report, for example, or an entry in the student's school file):

- If the report is subjective, remind yourself that the report is telling you less about the student and more about the reporter.
- If the information seems to be objective, remind yourself that the information is already biased by another person's perception and therefore may be as subjective as your own "objective" report of the F's in the "Finished Files" sentence.
- Tell yourself that what you are hearing is only an hypothesis, not a fact; wait to test the hypothesis later.

When you encounter the student for the first or the five-hundredth time:

- Look for visual, objective cues and patterns of behavior.
- Treat most of your judgments as hypotheses to be proved or disproved later, not as facts.

EXERCISE 1 (15–20 minutes)

1   Join a small group of four or five members.

2   In your group, assume that you are a teacher starting a new school year and receiving reports from your students' previous teachers. Your problem is not whether to hear each report, but rather what to do after you hear it.* Apply the strategies for postponing judgment to each teacher statement; decide with your group which parts of each statement are objective and subjective; then decide exactly how you should think about each part according to the strategies.

3   Returning to your all-class group, report your decisions (your instructor will act as moderator).

Teacher Statements:
    Sylvia is an able student.
    Glen is a daydreamer — he needs a lot of prodding and reminding.
    Becky can't seem to stay out of trouble — she's constantly bickering with the other girls.
    Stafford always completes his work on time, and the quality is satisfactory.

Conclusion   Some tasks seem impossible before we try them. In the following exercises, you will practice exactly those skills of observation and postponed judgment the strategies endorse.

EXERCISE 2   CONTROLLING STUDENTS' EXPECTATIONS OF THE TEACHER (FIRST IMPRESSIONS)

Researchers report, to no experienced teacher's surprise, that the first day and first week of school are very important to the students' perceptions and behavior for the rest of the year.[1] Think, then, about what students are most likely to notice about you. Do they hear what you say, or does your appearance catch their attention? Can you control what they notice, or do you feel that what they look at or hear is beyond your control?

The fact is that you can control what other people notice about you and where they direct their attention. Every successful cosmetologist knows how, as does a successful politician, magician, actor, actress, trial lawyer, or advertiser. Every teacher should know how, too. The following exercises are actually experiments. You will appear before some other people, and they will tell you what they noticed most about you; the question is, do they notice what you want them to notice?

The key to success in these exercises is your ability to distinguish between objective and subjective experiences.

Objective experience: You actually see or hear or touch something. You *notice* it.

---

*The teacher who decides beforehand what information he will choose to hear and not hear risks insularity and bigotry (see Method Ac5).

Subjective experience: You make a judgment or inference, or are aware of a feeling. You *believe* or *conclude* or *feel* something.

1   Fold an 8½ × 11 sheet of paper three times to form eight sections. Separate the sections by tearing. You now have eight slips of paper; keep them for this and the next two exercises.
2   At a signal, your instructor reads out loud the definitions of objective experience and subjective experience, adding to or elaborating as he wishes.
3   During the reading, be aware of what you notice about your instructor. What is making an impression on you?
4   At the end of the reading, write your instructor's name on one slip; on the other side of the slip, write three things (six words or fewer) that you notice about your instructor during the reading. Do not sign the slip. Be sure to follow this rule: your statements must report an objective experience only, not subjective.
5   Your instructor then collects the slips and quickly reads them out loud, one by one, stating whether each statement is or is not objective. If you are not sure why any statement is or is not objective, ask.

Conclusion   This exercise focuses your attention on one of the most basic teaching skills. A teacher who confuses her own feelings, attitudes, or beliefs with a student's actual behavior is a teacher who cannot correctly diagnose learning problems. For example, a student frowns at the teacher's assignment, and the teacher thinks, "He must not like what I said" (then unconsciously avoids the student, not looking at him or moving near him). If the frown actually means the student doesn't understand the assignment, the teacher's feelings will prevent student learning. Or, if a student "fools around," pushing and punching other students, the teacher may think, "He's got a bad temper. I'd better scold him for it." If the pushing and punching are a response to savage baiting and teasing by other students, the teacher's scolding may exacerbate an already difficult situation. Other examples are the teacher who takes everything personally, or one who favors students of one race because he is convinced they are more able, or one who clings to nonproductive routines because she thinks her students are happier that way — these teachers confuse feelings and facts; they cannot be effective observers and decision makers in the classroom. In short, a teacher must avoid reading into the situation something that isn't there. Perhaps the best book on this subject for teachers is Brophy and Good's *Teacher-Student Relationships* (1974); also see Rosenthal and Jacobson, *Pygmalion in the Classroom* (1968).

EXERCISE 3 (10–20 minutes)

What is a first impression? A first impression is composed of two different experiences, one's observation, then an inference. The first experience your students have when they meet you is always objective; they notice things about you — your hair or glasses or clothes, facial expressions, tone of voice, and sometimes the words you say. Something strikes their senses. Strangely, however, they may not be aware

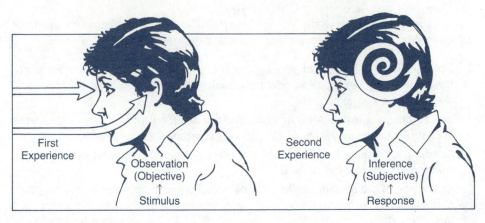

FIGURE 3.1   The First Impression

of what they notice because of their second experience, typically subjective, that is often so rapid, so automatic, that it obliterates the first experience:

S_1: What do you think of your new teacher?

S_2: She's nice.

S_1: Nice? What makes you think that?

S_2: Oh, I don't know. Maybe because she's so friendly.

S_1: What gave you that impression?

S_2: Oh, I don't know. She just is!

S_1: Now think for a minute. What did she do or say that you thought was friendly?

S_2: Well, she smiled at me once.

Notice how S_1 keeps trying to get S_2 back to the original, or first, experience, and how hard it is! Human nature often makes us confuse what we observe with what we feel. But that first experience is always there, nevertheless. So the point is that your students' subjective responses, in first impressions, are completely out of your control. You can do nothing at your first meeting about a student's memory, personal history, and beliefs and attitudes. The only student experience you can control at first meeting is what he sees, hears, and touches; that experience you can control to a surprisingly high degree. Try your skill in this next exercise.

1   You will meet in a small group of three or four persons. In that meeting, each person will talk to the group for one minute explaining his feelings about the following topic:

When the teacher tries to control students' first impressions of her, she runs a risk of appearing unnatural and phony.

During each person's talk, the other members of the group will be aware of what they notice about the speaker: what they see or hear, not what they infer, judge, or feel. Then they will report their observations to the speaker.

2   On one slip of paper, write your name, circle it, then turn the slip over and write three things (six words or fewer) that you want your audience to notice about you during your talk. Be sure to follow this rule: your statements must be *objective,* not subjective. For example, perhaps during your talk you want your audience to notice your right elbow; on your slip you write:

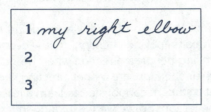

At the same time you think quickly about how to direct their attention to your right elbow: perhaps you could point to it, look at it, or even point it toward them. (This example is really given only in jest; you will benefit more from the exercise if your statements are absolutely legitimate.) As another example, you may want your audience to notice what you say (a reasonable hope for a teacher):

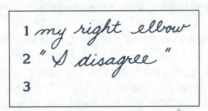

Put your words in quotation marks, because you want your audience to notice the exact words.

Conceal your three statements from the others.

3   On signal, begin your meeting. One person, the speaker, gives his name and speaks for one minute (timed by another group member, who announces when the time is up). In the next minute, the other group members write the speaker's name on a slip, turn the slip over, and write three things they noticed about the speaker; these statements must follow the rule, and quotations should bear quotation marks.

All group members keep their slips, and move quickly to the next speaker, then the next, until all have spoken. (The instructor may wish to control the time of each segment to maintain a reasonable pace.)

4   After the presentations, collect all your slips and compare the actual impressions with your intended impressions. What impressed your audience? The group might discuss these and offer suggestions, at your request, about what you could do to control an audience's attention more effectively. Ignore any statement that violates the rule of objectivity. Subjective statements are not helpful here because they do not tell what you did or said that was noticed; they only report the listener's state of mind.

5 Put a check mark beside each reported observation that matches one of your own.

Conclusion How many persons checked at least 50 percent of the reported observations given to them? Now, how did you do it? (Those with fewer than 50 percent would like to know!) Was it merely luck? Or did certain techniques really seem to work?

Now think about the logic of what we are doing here. Is it not true that "noticing something" means "paying attention" to it — even if ever so slightly? If so, are we not then controlling people's attention when we control what they notice? And when we control their attention, are we not directing and focusing their minds? Most people agree that a student cannot start to learn a lesson, whatever it may be, until his mind is on the lesson. So we were exploring in Exercise 3 some ways to control where a student's mind is focused.

METHOD Ab
Teacher Confidence: Is the teacher confident that the student will learn?

Does teacher self-confidence directly relate to student attention? That is, if the teacher feels he can teach well and his students will learn, are his students more likely to pay attention to lesson content? Our discussion must be largely speculative because we do not have data to make strong claims; the structure of the following profile levels is consistent with logic, not empirical evidence available to us now.[2]

LEVEL 1: The teacher expects that every student in the class will learn.

The work of Ronald Edmonds and others appears to support the claim that high student performance, requiring attention to lesson content, goes hand in hand with the teacher's confidence that she can teach every student without exception (Edmonds, 1979).

Marva Collins, a black teacher on Chicago's West Side, runs a private inner-city school in which she teaches every student Shakespeare — and they love it. She knows she can teach them, and she does. (Collins, 1982. Also see Good and Brophy, 1978; Brophy and Good, 1974.)

LEVEL 2: The teacher expects that many students in the class will need individualized instruction.

The teacher's expectation does not label students; it simply anticipates different kinds of services for different students.

LEVEL 3: The teacher expects that one or two students will need individualized instruction.

Individualized instruction is normally a sensible approach to teaching, even when it benefits only one or two students, but it incurs the risk that other students will label the one or two students who are given special treatment "teacher's pet" or "dummy." To individualize instruction without alienating the target student, the teacher must exercise considerable care. (See Methods Aal, Bal, Bel, El, Fal, Tcl, Tdl, and Xal.)

LEVEL 4: (None.)

LEVEL 5: The teacher expects difficulty in succeeding with one or two students.

Unlike Levels 2 and 3, this attitude predicts both teacher action and unsuccessful student performance. Words like these express this attitude: "I don't know if I can work with those two kids. I know they're smart enough and all that, but they're so different from the other kids, you know? I just don't know if I can teach them."

The risk is that "those two kids" and their close friends, as well, may sense the teacher's attitude. The most effective antidotes to the risks here are to search for alternative strategies and spend extra time setting them up. Then take extra time orienting the target students to your new or special program. You can also look for other resources to help you work effectively with the target students in your own room—parent tutorial aides or special materials, for example.

Your goal is to behave in such a way that your attitude automatically changes to Level 3 or Level 1, a "magical" notion of self-control but nevertheless effective.

LEVEL 6: The teacher expects difficulty succeeding with several students.

The risk of student inattention increases when a teacher loses self-confidence because something goes wrong during the lesson. At least one student is likely to detect the teacher's panic, and general restlessness can easily follow. But remember that general restlessness does not necessarily spell disaster; it simply means the students' minds are probably drifting away from lesson content.

There are several effective ways to manage loss of confidence during a lesson. For example, you can admit your misgivings to yourself and change the class activity to one with which you feel more confident. (Prior planning of alternatives is essential; see the example of alternative lesson plans in Morine-Dershimer [1977, pp. 62–64]; also see Yinger [1980].)

Or, tell yourself you are experimenting to see whether this particular lesson can succeed: "I am striving to *make* it succeed, but if it does not, I will find out why—I will ask my students later to help me." Then proceed with your lesson. If the lesson does indeed turn sour, follow through with your students' feedback: "Look, this lesson we just did, it didn't turn out the way I wanted it to. What do you think the problem was?" Your students will almost always be helpful and enthusiastic consultants; they are sometimes flattered to be asked, and will usually be impressed with you. Keep this session short; it is noninstructional time, and your students may grow weary of it after a minute or so. (Also see Method Jc2.)

LEVEL 7: The teacher expects difficulty succeeding with most students.

Some teachers live with this expectation all year; a few realize they are in the wrong profession and decide, wisely, to leave teaching; a few others resolve to acquire the skills they need and seek help; a few stay on the job, do nothing to improve themselves, but protest that they have a right to teach and must do so because they need the paycheck.

EXERCISES: BUILDING TEACHER CONFIDENCE

In this group of exercises, you will teach in situations of increasing difficulty and challenge. Your task is to think about how effective teaching depends on feedback from students. The more aware you are of what your students think and do, the better teacher you are. Your confidence in your teaching abilities will increase as your awareness and control increase.

PREPARATION FOR CLASS EXERCISES

1 Tear two 8½ × 11 blank sheets of paper in half to make four 8½ × 5½ sheets.
2 Using only the particular geometric shapes and objects below, in whatever configuration you wish, draw a design or picture or random objects on one of the sheets. Be as clever or prosaic as you wish.

3 Use only these shapes, in only the number given here, to make your design. You must use all the shapes.
4 Do not show your design to anyone else.

EXERCISE 1 (15 minutes)

1 To begin the exercise, sit back-to-back with another member of your class so you cannot see that person's face or paper.
2 At your instructor's signal, you, as teacher, begin to give "an assignment"—in the blind—to your student. To do this, tell the person exactly what to draw so as to duplicate your design on one of his blank sheets. Do not look at him or at his sheet; he may not make any sound during your teaching, nor may he look at you or your sheet.
3 At the end of five minutes, your instructor will signal for you to reverse roles, without checking your success yet, so you will now be the student and your partner will be your teacher for five minutes. Repeat Steps 1 and 2.

Conclusion   Hold your original and your student's tracing together up to the light and compare your student's performance with your original "assignment." In this exercise, you as teacher were limited to using only your expectations of your student's success and your assumptions about how well you were teaching.

EXERCISE 2 (15 minutes)

Change partners. This exercise is exactly like Exercise 1, except that now the teacher may look at the student's face and talk freely with him; you may not look at his drawing, and he may not look at yours. To begin the exercise, sit face-to-face with your partner (a different partner from Exercise 1) and place a large book or other shield to prevent your both seeing each other's papers. Use all your student's visual and auditory cues to improve your teaching.

Conclusion   Again, compare your student's performance with your original assignment. In this exercise, you as teacher were aided not only by your expectations of your student's success but also by your partial awareness of how your student was learning. Did you benefit? Did your student benefit also?

EXERCISE 3 (15 minutes)

Change partners. This exercise is exactly like Exercise 1, except that now the teacher and student may talk freely with one another, and the teacher may look at the student's paper while giving the assignment in this classroom simulation. However, the student may not see the teacher's paper.

Conclusion   The point of the exercise is that teachers need to check their assumptions continually about how well they are teaching. We must not rely only on intuition or prior judgments; rather, we must look for feedback. With feedback, we have an objective and legitimate right to be confident in our teaching; without feedback, we can only make a subjective assumption.

METHOD Ac
Teacher Self-Evaluation: Does the teacher evaluate his or her own teaching performance?

How do teachers go about measuring, comparing, and judging their performance? There are Low Profile ways that enhance student attention and achievement, and High Profile ways that inhibit student learning.

Because the teaching profession does not encourage systematic evaluation of its members, and because local school district evaluation is often perfunctory at best, most teachers must rely on self-evaluation to improve their performance.

LEVEL 1: The teacher evaluates own teaching continuously, and automatically utilizes results.

Effective teachers are self-evaluators (Good and Brophy, 1978; Good and Brophy, 1980, chapter 21); they are not afraid to look hard at their performance and say, "I did this part well, but this part was lousy."

What evaluation techniques can the teacher use? Of the hundreds available, a few are: monitoring student attention, asking diagnostic questions, evaluating student tests and quizzes, and discussing their learning with the students.

For example, you can monitor your students' attention cues continuously during instruction and ask yourself, "Is what I am doing now helping my students or not? Should I try something else?"[3] Look at content — is it stated in the proper language for your students, and does it present appropriate images? Examine your objectives — are they low profile or high? Look at the time interval between the start of an instructional control and the moment at which a target student begins giving you attention cues. You can organize small buzz groups; do the buzz groups begin talk immediately upon forming — or even before they are properly seated — or do they sit about awkwardly for a while before they begin? Or, when you see Cindy in unknown attention (staring at the wall), modify your lecture with choral responses; how long before Cindy actively responds?

You can ask diagnostic questions (see Method Td), and use the answers to measure the effectiveness of your previous instruction. You can also use every test, quiz, or other evaluation of student learning to measure the effectiveness of your own instruction. (Contrast this technique with the occasional teacher attitude, "If the kid doesn't learn, it's the kid's fault — I'm doing all I can.") Evaluation of actual learning can suggest how effectively certain topics or skills were taught, as well as indicate what should be taught next.

You can also evaluate your teaching by asking your students, after each small unit or block of study, what you did or said during the unit that they felt was most helpful to their learning and what was least helpful.

Students can give valid and valuable information about what they actually saw and heard during instruction (showing what caught their attention and what did not); what distracted their attention away from the lesson (showing what distractions should be controlled); and how they felt during certain parts of the lesson (again, showing where their attention was and perhaps giving a clue as to why). For example, the teacher distributes (once a day, three times a week, once a week, or whenever appropriate) a slip of paper for students to fill out in no more than ten minutes, or in as little as two or three minutes, and return to the teacher, who reviews and files it.

Name:

Date: Unit/Topic:

What I learned most from this lesson/unit/exercise:

What I still don't know/understand/can't figure out:

The teacher would help me more if (s)he would:

LEVEL 2: The teacher evaluates own teaching occasionally and uses the results.

While the best teacher self-evaluation is continuous monitoring of student behavior, even occasional or periodic self-evaluation is beneficial. The techniques at this level are the same as those at Level 1, but a Level 2 evaluation schedule is rated higher in profile because of the greater possibility that student inattention will go unnoticed and untreated by the teacher.

Evaluation techniques at this level include:

Asking a teacher, administrator, instructor, supervisor, or trainer to observe your class and discuss with you your goals and methods.

Asking parents, "What do your kids say about this class when they come home? Is there anything they seem to particularly like or dislike? Do you see any signs of their learning?"

Using final exams or year-end standardized test scores to measure the effectiveness of your instruction.

LEVEL 3: (none.)

LEVEL 4: The teacher submits to evaluation when required and sometimes uses results.

Most school district teacher evaluation requirements today are inadequate both in quality and quantity. Teacher performance is usually not improved by such requirements, and students do not benefit either.

LEVEL 5: The teacher accepts only positive feedback from evaluation, rejects negative feedback.

Some teachers take credit for students' successes but deny responsibility for misbehavior (Bradley, 1978). This selective perception is only human: teachers, like everyone else, make their world what they want it to be in place of what it really is (Weiner, 1979; Shaver, 1975).

The teacher's tendency to accept positive feedback and reject negative feedback is understandable and human, but in most circumstances it is not professional. Teachers must resist their natural tendencies to call students "lazy," "dumb," "hostile," "unmotivated," "deprived," or any of the other attributes that excuse a failure to teach. Occasionally, however, when a teacher feels unusually depressed, it is quite reasonable to say to students or supervisors or administrators: "OK, I know there must be just lots wrong with what I'm doing today, but I don't want to hear that right now—just tell me what's right! I can only handle positive thoughts today; tell me the bad stuff some other time!"

LEVEL 6: The teacher ignores all evaluation of own teaching.

It is hard to imagine a situation that would justify such behavior, but there is one! The inventive teacher who tries out a new activity or system sometimes encounters immediate hostility from students; the proper response to premature evaluation is to ignore it, as in this example:

> **STUDENTS:** Aw, this is for the birds. This stinks! Let's go back to the old way we did it before!

TEACHER: Now hold on, let's give this thing a chance. We haven't seen what it can do yet, have we?

LEVEL 7: The teacher resists all evaluation of own teaching.

As in the case with Level 6, it is hard to imagine any justification for this teacher behavior, but there actually is one: when the teacher who is trying out a new idea knows that hostile parents or prejudiced administrators are waiting just outside the door ready to destroy the effort with premature and possibly unfair evaluation, the teacher may be justified in keeping the evaluators out of the classroom until the idea has a fair chance to prove itself.

EXERCISE: SKILLS OF MONITORING STUDENT ATTENTION

How do teachers decide which students are paying attention to the lesson and which are not? Before class begins, study and memorize the visual cues of student attention (chapter 1, Figure 1-2).

Then examine photographs A, B, C, and D on pages 72 and 73. It may be difficult to determine exactly what is happening in each scene, yet we teachers suffer the same problem in the classroom: we often cannot see clearly, so we make judgments not necessarily on good information, but rather on the best information available. The purpose of this exercise is to help you memorize and use the visual cues of student attention.

Using your best information, fill in the table below. For each picture, count the actual number of students in each attention state — attention, inattention, and unknown attention — according to the visual cues in Figure 2-2, chapter 2. Write those numbers in the table below.

TABLE 3-1: JUDGING STUDENT ATTENTION

	Number of Students in:		
	Attention	**Inattention**	**Unknown Attention**
Picture A			
Picture B			
Picture C			
Picture D			

1   To begin the exercise in class, join a group of four or five. Meet for ten minutes.

2   In your group, compare your judgments with the others, and try to get your group to reach consensus (not a majority vote) on each picture.

3   Returning to your class group, report any unresolved debates to the entire class. (The instructor will act as moderator.)

Conclusion   Some teachers confuse unknown attention with attention (they may think staring students are paying attention). Some teachers confuse unknown attention with inattention (they reprimand students who are occasionally talking about the lesson). The point of this exercise is to see that unless a student's cues are absolutely and clearly attention or inattention, you should always judge the student unknown, and act accordingly.

Assignment   Observe one student in your field placement or other class for ten minutes. (If possible, choose a student with whom you have had particular difficulty, or one whom you do not have good feelings about, or one who is making slow progress.) On a sheet of paper, record exactly what that student is doing every 30 seconds. Be objective. Code each episode with the appropriate label:

- Unk The student is judged to be in unknown attention.
- In   The student is judged to be in inattention.
- Att   The student is judged to be paying attention.

Then think about how your observations compare with your prior assumptions about that student. Do they support your assumptions totally or partially? Or do they not support them? If your assumptions differ from your observations, what action should you take? If your observations support your assumptions, what action should you take?

NOTES

1   Emmer, Evertson, and Anderson (1980), for example, describe effective teachers whose advance planning and preparation make their first days of class businesslike and efficient. They make clear their rules and procedures, particularly as they monitor and follow-through, and they spend little class time on housekeeping duties. In contrast, less effective teachers appear to create problems in the classroom through lack of planning, lack of clarity, lack of follow-through, and lack of consistency. These first-day experiences appear to characterize the way these classrooms perform thereafter.

   Moskowitz and Hayman (1976) demonstrate not only the power of establishing clear expectations early in the year, but also the desirability of establishing friendly, personable relations with students at the outset of the year rather than austere, harsh, unfriendly relations.

2   Brophy and Evertson (1976) found no positive correlation between teacher confidence and learning gains in young children. They assume, as we do in this Ab section, that teacher confidence "probably is vital for a teacher working with older students, particularly with students who have critical, judgmental attitudes toward the teacher" (p. 112), but they could find no evidence that teacher confidence is important in working effectively with young children.

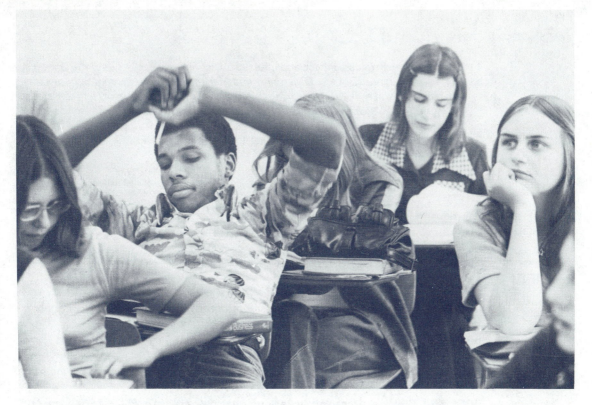

3 For further help in using these and other such techniques effectively, see the University of Texas training manuals, *Organizing and Managing the Elementary School Classroom* (Evertson et al., 1981) and *Organizing and Managing the Junior High Classroom* (Emmer et al., 1982) which you may obtain from the UT Research and Development Center at moderate cost. Write to:

Research and Development Center for Teacher Education
University of Texas
Education Annex 3.203
Austin, Texas 78712

REFERENCES

BOEHM, A., & WEINBERG, R. *The classroom observer: A guide for developing observational skills.* New York: Teachers College, Columbia University, 1977.

BRADLEY, G. Self-serving biases in the attribution process: A reexamination of the fact or fiction question. *Journal of Personality and Social Psychology,* 1978, *36,* 56–71.

BROOKOVER, W., et al. *School social systems and student achievement: Schools can make a difference.* New York: Bergin, 1979.

BROPHY, J. Successful teaching strategies for the inner-city child. *Phi Delta Kappan,* April 1980, *63,* 527–529.

BROPHY, J. Research on the self-fulfilling prophesy and teacher expectations. Paper presented at American Educational Research Association Annual Meeting, March 1982.

BROPHY, J., & EVERTSON, C. *Learning from teaching.* Boston: Allyn and Bacon, 1976.

BROPHY, J., & GOOD, T. *Teacher-student relationships.* New York: Holt, Rinehart and Winston, 1974.

COLLINS, M., & TAMARKIN, C. *Marva Collins' Way.* Los Angeles: J.P. Tarcher, 1982.

COOPER, H. Pygmalion grows up: A model for teacher expectation, communication, and performance. *Review of Educational Research,* 1979, *49,* 389–410.

DARLEY, J., & FAZIO R. Expectancy confirmation processes arising in the social interaction sequence. *American Psychologist,* 1980, *35,* 867–881.

EDMONDS, R. Effective schools for the urban poor. *Educational Leadership,* October 1979, *37,* 15–24.

EDMONDS, R. The characteristics of effective schools: Research and implementation (Testimony before the U.S. House of Representatives Subcommittee on Elementary, Secondary, and Vocational Education). East Lansing, Michigan State University, October 1981.

ELASHOFF, J., & SNOW, R. Pygmalion reconsidered. Worthington, Ohio: Charles A. Jones, 1971.

EMMER, E., EVERTSON, C., & ANDERSON, L. Effective classroom management at the beginning of the school year. *Elementary School Journal,* 1980, *80,* 219–231.

EVERTSON, C., et al. *Organizing and managing the elementary school classroom.* Austin, Tex.: The Research and Development Center for Teacher Education, the University of Texas at Austin, 1981.

FENNEMA, E., & SHERMAN, J. Sex related differences in math achievement and related factors: A further study. *Journal for Research in Mathematics Education,* May 1978, *9,* 189–203.

FLANDERS, N. Analyzing teacher behavior. Reading, Mass.: Addison-Wesley, 1970.

GOOD, T., & BROPHY, J. *Looking in classrooms* (2nd ed.). New York: Harper and Row, 1978.

GOOD, T., & BROPHY, J. *Educational psychology: A realistic approach.* New York: Holt, Rinehart and Winston, 1980.

JACOBS, J. (Ed.) *Perspectives on women and mathematics.* Columbus, Ohio: The Ohio State University College of Education, 1978.

MORINE-DERSHIMER, G. Instructional planning. In J. Cooper (Ed.), *Classroom teaching skills: A handbook.* Toronto: D. C. Heath, 1977.

MOSKOWITZ, G., & HAYMAN, J. Success strategies of inner-city teachers: A year-long study. *Journal of Educational Research,* 1976, *69,* 283–289.

PERSELL, C. *Education and inequality: A theoretical and empirical synthesis.* New York: Free Press, 1977.

RIST, R. Student social class and teacher expectations: The self-fulfilling prophesy in ghetto education. *Harvard Educational Review,* 1970, *40,* 411–451.

ROSENTHAL R., & JACOBSON, L. *Pygmalion in the classroom.* New York: Holt, Rinehart and Winston, 1968.

SHAVER, K. *An introduction to attribution processes.* Cambridge, Mass.: Winthrop, 1975.

SIMON, A., & BOYER, E. *Mirrors for behavior: An anthology of classroom observation instruments.* Philadelphia: Research for Better Schools, 1970.

TAYLOR, M. Race, sex, and the expression of self-fulfilling prophesies in a laboratory teaching situation. *Journal of Personality and Social Psychology,* 1979, *37,* 897–912.

WEINER, B. A theory of motivation for some classroom experiences. *Journal of Educational Psychology,* 1979, *71,* 3–25.

YINGER, R. A study of teacher planning. *Elementary School Journal,* 1980, *80,* 107–127.

CONTROLLING CONTENT AND EVALUATING LEARNING (METHOD B)

4

Many people say the root of effective classroom management and control is to select content carefully, with appropriate objectives, sensitive and timely pacing, and superb evaluation and feedback (Kounin, 1970; Popham and Baker, 1970; Doyle, 1979; Bloom, Madaus, and Hastings, 1981; Brophy, 1982a). This chapter examines skills and techniques of selecting, stating, and pacing content objectives, and of evaluating learning outcomes, monitoring student progress, and giving feedback to students.

METHOD Ba
Selecting Content Objectives: What content objectives does the teacher select for the students?

A "content objective" is what the student is supposed to learn from a lesson. Some objectives are low profile, others high, depending partly on content difficulty.

Today's educators have many methods to classify relative difficulty of content. Some of these methods classify readability: the Dale-Chall Scale, the Dolch Word List, and others. Others classify the concepts and organization of content (Bloom et al., 1956; Gagné and Briggs, 1979). The Ba section of the Taxonomy is based on a simple, arbitrary, operational model that classifies content difficulty according to the amount of time assumed necessary for the individual learner to master the content; for example:

- Mastered Content: Has been learned previously.
- Easy Content: Can be learned readily,[1] assuming the learner applies himself totally to the task.
- Moderately Easy Content: Requires 10–30 percent more time than easy content.
- Moderately Difficult Content: Requires 30–80 percent more time than easy content.
- Difficult Content: Requires 80–200 percent more time than easy content.
- Very Difficult Content: Requires more than 200 percent more time than easy content.

The first step for determining content difficulty is to pretest the planned content. Those students for whom the content will initially prove easiest are those who score highest on the pretest—they already know most about the material, and some may have already mastered it. Those students who score lowest on the pretest may initially find the content the most difficult, since they appear to know the least about the lesson content to start with and therefore have the most to learn. As you teach the lesson, however, different student learning rates will emerge as some students learn more readily than others.

Although content material is infrequently pretested in many American schools—for reasons easy to understand[2]—it is essential to truly effective instruction for many students (Kibler et al., 1981, pp. 121–127). How else is a teacher to know whether or not his lessons are appropriate to students?

LEVEL 1: Students can master next step in content with moderate effort.

The next step may be any task—a problem to solve, a speech to make, a fact to memorize, a physical skill to perform, an attitude to demonstrate—that helps learning occur. If the task is moderate, many students are more likely to stick with it and see it through than if it is difficult.

Most students like challenge (Kounin, 1970), and many can be induced to expend real effort to meet it (Good and Brophy, 1978). They are not distracted by the challenge to any significant degree, so the risk of distraction from nudging students ahead is rather low.

What techniques can teachers use to nudge students?[3] Try these:

- Assign content that requires the student to spend approximately 10 percent more high-attention time to master than easy content.
- Ask the student a follow-up inquiry question after he has answered a first one (see Method 0).
- Ask the student a thought test question in a professional manner (see Method 0).
- Ask the student a higher order question (see Method Tb).
- Encourage students through brief pep talks (see Method W).

LEVEL 2: Students can master next step in content with ease.

This is close to the premise of programmed instruction. The professional literature in this area is vast, and becoming dated.[4]

LEVEL 3: Students can master next step in content with some difficulty.

When the new content requires approximately 50 percent more high-attention time to master than does easy content in the same field, we assume that content selection is at Level 3. This amount of difficulty bothers some students and not others.

The most effective antidote to student distress, resistance, and distraction is content-oriented pep talking (see Method W) and provisions for extra help if needed (see Tutoring, Methods E3, Ia3).

LEVEL 4: Students can master next step in content with great difficulty.

At Level 4, the student runs the risk of becoming demoralized, an unsuitable frame of mind for high attention to the lesson (Jorgenson, 1977; Gambrell, Wilson, and Gantt, 1981).

This technique can be successful, however, if the teacher uses it for effect. Showing students in a pretest how much they will know by the end of the unit is often a good motivator. Assure students, however, that the pretest has nothing to do with their grade. Also remember the possibility that a student might freeze on a pretest, when he confronts unfamiliar materials; for example, an elementary student who is able to do single-column addition might add the single-column problems on his test, then stop when he reaches the double-column problems. But if the student looks over the entire test first, he might find himself freezing when he sees double-column addition and not even be able to do the single-column problems he knows.

LEVEL 5: Students have already recently mastered next step in content.

Our theory here is that there is greater probability of the student's being distracted by the lesson's going on too long than by the lesson's being difficult. When the lesson lasts too long, the able student, whether low or high achiever, can lose attention simply because of the sameness of the thinking. The risk of inattention and boredom is high.

Is teaching already-learned material ever justified in the classroom? Yes, particularly for introducing a new topic to fearful students. Some students need to be reminded they are able and successful. An easy initial task can be a strategic move on the teacher's part to get students into the swing of things in a new lesson. For example, the teacher might say, "Let's add three plus three. Everyone can do that, right? Now what does three *times* three mean?" Notice how quickly the familiar leads into the unfamiliar, the old into the new.

Another strategic reason for reteaching material, or teaching for "overlearning," is suggested by Brophy and other investigators who claim that overlearning is effective and appropriate for low achievers (Brophy, 1982b). Another reason, review, is a time-honored and legitimate teaching device to enhance retention of learned content (Gagné and Briggs, 1972, p. 132).

Yet we must think carefully about these strategies of teaching from the familiar, overlearning, and review. Each technique, when used properly, has the low profile effect of Bal or Ba2, not the distractive mid profile effect of Ba5. Thus, the teacher must use utmost skill in reteaching material, for the risk of student inattention increases as overfamiliarity increases.

LEVEL 6: Students cannot master next step in content in the near future.

Level 6 does not mean that students never rise to an extraordinary academic challenge; after all, fine teachers accomplish the impossible every day. But the risk of pitching the initial goal far beyond the student's grasp is high indeed. There is a significant difference between placing initial content far beyond a student's present grasp and placing the ultimate content far beyond him.[5]

LEVEL 7: Students have already mastered next step in content long ago.

This is the most distractive content condition; don't insult students with material they consider beneath them. On the other hand, elementary material from years before can occasionally be useful. When introducing a new topic or skill, an inventive teacher might begin with an elementary and familiar referent; for example:

"Now today we're going to talk about the tonic, the 3rd, and the 5th tones of the chord. Remember the tune, 'Row, Row, Row Your Boat?' Just for kicks, sing it through once right now. Ready? Good. You probably noticed that most of that song is sung to just one chord, right? The tonic of the chord is the note you sang on 'row,' the 3rd is the note of 'boat,' and the 5th is the note of 'stream.' So 'row...boat...stream.' Tonic, 3rd, 5th. Got it?"

METHOD Bb
Stating Content Objectives: How does the teacher state content objectives to students?

An objective is a statement of what the student is supposed to learn. Statements of content objectives may be low profile or high profile depending in part upon how specific or general they are.

LEVEL 1: The objectives are stated in specific learning terms.

"Everyone knows what's going on here; they know exactly what is expected of them," claims the teacher whose students are working toward specific objectives. The students know exactly what to do and under what conditions. Here is how this teacher introduces a new unit in social studies:

"When we get through with this chapter on the Progressives, you will be able to tell the names of fourteen prominent Progressives, what each person was proposing, who opposed each of these people and why, and what finally came of the proposal. You will also be able to tell at least one similarity between FDR's philosophy of government and the Progressive philosophy. And you will be able to tell how Ronald Reagan reacted to the Progressive philosophy, and give three reasons. You should be able to tell these things either out loud, as we discuss them in class, or on paper in an essay test. And you should be able to use this information as you watch TV news people trying to make sense of the Washington scene today."

The test of whether a content objective is stated specifically enough is whether it can be observed and/or measured by the teacher so as to determine when the objective has been reached.

LEVEL 2: (none.)

LEVEL 3: The objectives are stated in general learning terms.

Notice how much more general the following content objectives are than the examples in level 1; these objectives are impossible to observe or measure.

"I want you all to do this and do your best."

"I want you to learn to appreciate this."

"We're going to see how the Progressives changed American government and even American education. When we get through with this unit, you should have a better understanding of the Progressive Movement."

If you ask a student in this class what he is supposed to learn, the student will likely answer, "We're supposed to learn about Progressives." If you then respond, "But what exactly does 'learn about Progressives' mean? What, specifically, does your teacher want you to learn?" the student might shrug his shoulders and mutter, "I don't know, we just learn whatever she wants us to, I guess."

The problem with nonspecific content objectives is that the teacher cannot really tell when they have been achieved, nor can students. If the objective cannot be evaluated, at least a few students will consider it purposeless or "dumb."

LEVEL 4: The learning objectives are not announced to some students.

One reason some students are inattentive in the classroom is that they are not in school enough to know what is expected of them. The teacher must somehow compensate for the effects of absenteeism. Some methods are:

- Appointing other students to inform absent students of learning objectives and assignments.
- Holding special tutoring sessions with them at convenient times.
- Calling the parents and giving tutoring instructions over the phone, or meeting parents in conference.
- Organizing a standard set of worksheets or skill folders to use for informing absent students of learning objectives and providing them with instruction. (Audiotapes and visual aids can be included.)

Deliberately withholding learning objectives from a student may be justified when the teacher is working with a special student whose skills lag far behind those of the rest of the class. In these special cases, the teacher might work slowly from step to step (see Method Z2), telling the student no more than he absolutely needs to know in order to learn the next step, withholding learning objectives that might confuse or alarm him.

LEVEL 5: The objectives are stated in terms of a specific activity.

The specific activity is considered valuable for its own sake, not for its teaching potential; for example:

"I want you all to do this exercise; it's good for you—just do it."

"We're all reading this story because it is interesting."

"It's not important what you write; what is important is that you write! Do you understand what I mean?"

"We're doing this because it's fun to plant seeds. Kids love it!" Consider this dialogue between a teacher and a student who is fooling around:

TEACHER: I thought I told you to finish the chapter.
STUDENT: I did finish it.
TEACHER: Did you do the questions at the end?
STUDENT: Yeah.
TEACHER: Let me see…Look, half these answers are wrong!
STUDENT: You said do 'em, so I did 'em!

When objectives are stated in terms of a specific activity rather than specific behaviors to be learned, the teacher incurs significant risk that the student will consider the activity purposeless. Therefore, if there is an intrinsic purpose in the activity itself, the teacher needs to help students find it.[7]

LEVEL 6: The objectives are stated in terms of a general activity.

These are examples of general activity objectives:

- "We are reading this story because it's fun to read stories." (Compare with Level 5, "This story is fun to read.")
- "It's important for you to think mathematically—that's why we're doing these problems."
- "Government is the voice of the people—you owe it to yourself to learn about your government."

The risk of student distraction because of uninvolvement grows as objectives and purposes become more and more abstract and vague.

LEVEL 7: The objectives are never announced.

We rarely see this technique, probably because students would not stand for it. Teachers usually give some reason for an activity or procedure, although the reason may not always be clear. You do not have to announce objectives when students have their own reasons; in playing academic games or shooting basketballs or building wooden birdhouses, the teacher's reason may not be needed.

EXERCISE 1 STATING CONTENT OBJECTIVES (30–45 minutes)

Preparation for Class Exercise　Classify the following teacher statements by profile level, assuming that each teacher statement is a Method Bb technique. Example: <u>1</u> "I want you to cross your T exactly like this—see?"

_____ 1 "Why are we listening to the music? It illustrates the baroque style."

_____ 2 "The test is going to cover the Greeks. You should know the Age of Pericles pretty well for the test.... What about the Age of Pericles? Well, if I answered that question, I'd be giving away the test, right?"

_____ 3 "Now, a lot of this stuff you're not going to understand, but I want you to listen to it anyhow. That's all you need to do—just listen and don't fool around."

_____ 4 "When we come back from the apple cider mill, you can start work on your diagram of how a cider mill works. Be sure to take a note pad along!"

_____ 5 "On Wednesday, I'm going to ask you how you felt during this simulation game, I mean, what you were thinking about while all the negotiating was going on."

_____ 6 "You should be able to type without looking at the keys by now. Can you do it?"

_____ 7 "I'm glad you're curious to know how this is going to end up and what it means, but let's just take it one step at a time for now."

_____ 8 "You can read whatever you want for 10 minutes; after that I want you to take out your textbook and start..."

_____ 9 "Grammar is to help you understand your language better."

_____10 "Why are we doing this? You tell me!"

1 Join a small group of three to five persons. Meet for twenty minutes.
2 In your group, try to reach consensus on the proper classification of each teacher statement above. If, after reasonable debate, one or more in your group does not wholeheartedly agree with the others, mark the item with an asterisk and go on.
3 Reconvene the class and discuss the disputed items. (Your instructor will serve as moderator.)

Conclusion   This will have been a successful exercise for you if it has made you aware that many teacher statements make implicit references to learning objectives. These references are so subtle that they communicate the teacher's expectations for student performance without either teacher or students consciously realizing what is happening. The teacher's learning objectives need not be formally written down, but they should be sensible and clear. Avoid self-contradictory objectives such as: "Think about this carefully, but don't be the last one to finish!"

METHOD Bc
Pacing Content Objectives: How does the teacher pace learning for students?

Teachers usually think of pacing a lesson in terms of fast and slow: "Is there enough time to do this activity, or was it paced too fast?" or "Was this activity paced too slowly because there were too many interruptions that broke the momentum?" Fast and slow compared to what? When the student is ready for a next step in learning but the next step is not available, forcing him to wait, the pace is too slow. When the next step is begun but the student is not ready, the pace is too fast. When the student is ready, and the next step is available, the pace is appropriate or comfortable or just right.

In this section, we will consider pacing the skills students are supposed to master. Research and common sense suggest that when the pace of skill development is either too fast or too slow, classroom behavior problems grow, and student attention to lesson content diminishes (Kounin, 1970).

By *skills,* we mean what the student has learned or achieved in one step of content learning (see Ba). For example, in learning to drive a car with manual transmission, one must learn to release the emergency brake before disengaging the clutch; we will call releasing the brake a "skill"; releasing the clutch is the next "skill." Other types of skills might be the ability to conjugate a verb, identify a cowslip, recognize an example of "prudence," or be able to predict when a chord will resolve.

Students who are properly paced and stimulated are not always aware they are learning, but they often reveal telltale signs. They may show purposeful intensity as they walk directly from station to station, a kind of preoccupation that says "I mean business!" They may become very content-oriented in their talk, ready to discuss, debate, or argue content ideas at any moment, or they might become quietly reflective and seem to daydream as they talk. Their eyes might gleam a little more brightly than usual during class, showing unmistakable signs of high attention. They may be drawn to wherever there is something happening that relates to the content they are studying. In short, they are ready; the teacher simply feeds their enthusiasm. As soon as they master one skill, the teacher challenges them with the next. The pacing of content objectives determines the level of challenge. Some people believe the term "on-fire learner" applies only to gifted children, but any student can catch fire, no matter what his level of development.

LEVEL 1: When one skill is mastered, the next skill is immediately available.

How does the teacher know when students are ready for the next skill?

- Clear signs of mastery (e.g., high test scores, rapid performance of skills in class, ready and correct answers, etc.).
- A growing impatience with the class and even with the teacher.
- Increased "fooling around" and horseplay with other students.
- Expressed boredom at repeating the same skill over and over, even in different practice problems and new situations.
- Daydreaming and other signs of inattention even when the students seem able to answer questions, pass tests, etc.

How might the teacher respond to students' need for the next skill?

- Move right into the next phase of the lesson, ignoring the schedule.
- Preview the next lesson briefly and let individual students start it early.
- Drop hints of books and resources that pick up where their skills are now.

Should a teacher ever resist moving to the next skill when students feel they have mastered the last one? The answer is yes; when students are able to say it, but not do and apply it, the teacher must stick to his guns until the job is done right.

LEVEL 2: When one skill is mastered, students can prepare for the next skill immediately.

The teacher can maintain high student attention through a transition period (see Method Gb) if the transition requires students to prepare actively for the next learning experience. If the student has mastered the concept of "intransitive verb" before her classmates, for example, the teacher might give her the page numbers of the next skill, "transitive verb," and ask her to write designated problems in lists on the board. In this case, the student is not actually learning the next skill, but is preparing to learn it. The teacher's assignment is not busywork, which keeps the student's mind focused on a task or topic for no useful purpose; it is a preparation technique that builds anticipation for the next step of learning.

LEVEL 3: Having mastered a skill, one or two students must wait a short time for the next one.

When students become restless and impatient in content areas they do well in, they are growing. They are tired of waiting for the next interesting challenge. They are not just impatient for a new activity, but for a new skill. Busy teachers might complain at this point that theory and practice are quite different: "After all, there are 28 students in my room! How could I possibly individualize instruction for each one of them?"

The answer is that administrative problems never adequately justify poorly paced instruction. Effective teachers always seem to find ways to overcome administrative delays. (See Methods Be1, D1, E1, Ga, Gb, Ia, Ja, Jb, Jc, and Z1.)

The teacher may be justified in delaying a student from beginning the next skill if the student has mastered the last skill by rote, but does not yet apply it appropriately.

LEVEL 4: One or two students are pushed into learning the next skill before they have mastered the previous skill.

When a student is pushed on before he is ready, he may go docilely forward, as he is told, he may hesitate because of insecurity, or he may object. All three responses will distract him from the lesson content.

Is it ever justified to move a student to a new skill before he has sufficiently mastered the last one? If the previous skill is taking too long and is not prerequisite to those following, the teacher may be wise to move the student ahead. The transition is considerably easier if the teacher explains the situation to the student.

LEVEL 5: Having mastered a skill, one or two students must endure long delay until the next one.

Students become restless when they feel they are not learning anything. We should give them credit for that—they are, in effect, remarkably good self-diagnosticians even though we grow impatient with their symptoms!

Sometimes even a long delay is justifiable in activities such as dramatic plays, musical recitals, or some physical education games, where delays are an integral part of the activity and can be made worthwhile (perhaps as a time for reflection).

LEVEL 6: The entire class is pushed into learning the next skill before they have mastered the previous skill.

There can be considerable trouble in this situation, and you can usually rely on students to sound the alarm: "I can't do this!" "This stuff is dumb!" "I don't get it at all!"

Is a teacher ever justified in moving students ahead too fast, before they are ready? Yes, for the same reasons stated in Level 4. For example, students benefit from teachers' using long, unfamiliar words with precision and explanation[8]; and students with strong self-concepts appear to thrive on work that challenges them, or is even too hard, in contrast to students with lower self-concepts who seem to need far more repetition and reassurance (see Ba1 and Ba2).[9]

LEVEL 7: Having mastered a skill, the entire class must endure long delay until the next one.

The justification for long delay in the classroom is the same as that for Level 5.

METHOD Bd
Evaluation of Learning: How and how often does the teacher evaluate learning?

Evaluation of learning means the teacher observes a student's performance, measures it in some way, compares it with a standard, and judges the comparison as favorable or unfavorable. Evaluation of learning, student accountability, and student assessment all refer to essentially the same thing. There are many techniques for evaluation.

- Paper-and-pencil tests: choices (true/false, multiple choice), completions (short answer, close item), essay (short or long answer), compositions of style, and others.
- Recitation: question-answer, spelling drill, problem solving, inquiry skills, and others.
- Clinical Observation: role play behavior, simulation skills, gamed problem-solving techniques and strategies, and others.
- Field Observation: problem-solving techniques and strategies, goal achievement, and others.[10]

Evaluation may be continuous or sporadic.

Continuous: The evaluation process takes place continuously (the teacher steadily monitors and coaches the student), or so regularly that the effect is continuous (daily spelling quizzes and follow-up retests).

Sporadic: The evaluation process surges from time to time (e.g., end of chapter tests), or takes place at the end of the term or year.

Evaluation may be objective or subjective, depending upon the standard the teacher uses for comparison and judgment.

Objective: The standard is external, public, and easily agreed upon by all reasonable persons (e.g., "No paper shall have any run-on sentences").

Subjective: The standard is internal to the evaluator, private, and variable according to the evaluator's state of mind at the moment (e.g., "No paper shall be sloppily written").

Evaluation standards may be absolute (e.g., "Must lift leg to 120° angle"), or relative (e.g., "Must lift leg as high as average 12-year-old"). The evaluation standards may be announced before evaluation takes place, or afterward (e.g., "We want you to do the best job you can, and will let you know how you did").

The distractive effects of evaluation vary; objective evaluation is less distractive than subjective, continuous is less distractive than sporadic, and announcing standards before student performance is less distractive than announcing them afterward. Distraction is directly proportional to anxiety or distress, and whatever causes anxiety and distress in students will automatically distract them from lesson content.

LEVEL 1: Evaluation is objective and continuous; standards are revealed beforehand.*

Students in a well-taught ballet class know exactly how well they are doing at all times: the teacher demonstrates the standard, and the student watches himself in the mirror to see how closely he meets the standard.

Evaluating learning in mathematics is even more precise; the standards are objective and allow for continuous comparison and judgment. Evaluation in English literature is not as easy, since the skills and standards are not as readily demonstrable.

Another name for continuous evaluation is *monitoring,* the process of continually watching a student's progress and judging whether he is on the right track or wasting time. (See Method Be, Monitoring.)

LEVEL 2: Evaluation is objective and periodic; standards are revealed beforehand.

Most students adapt well to the common system of periodic evaluation — tests at the ends of chapters, weekly spelling quizzes, and so forth.

LEVEL 3: Evaluation is subjective, continuous, and arranged beforehand.

If the teacher's subjective evaluation is applied continuously and in full view of the entire class, most students can learn to live with it and function effectively in the system without undue distress. This is a logical approach if the teacher-student relationship is, by consent of all parties, that of Master-Disciple, a time-honored and reasonable relationship although not often condoned or trusted in the United States.

A problem with subjective evaluation is that some students fear the teacher might "get down on a student," and that worry is distractive.

LEVEL 4: Evaluation is subjective, sporadic, and arranged beforehand.

"All right, you folks have been working on this unit, and tomorrow I'm going to give you an essay test over this material, and on that test I want you to convince me that you know this material well. What is well? You'll just have to trust my judgment on that — I'll tell you if you know it well or not." An evaluation system like this does not disturb many students; a few are quite distressed by it, and will spend considerable energy, which they need for learning, worrying about and fearing the unknown. Some people call this lazy teaching. Whether lazy or not, it is risky.

Subjective evaluation is quite appropriate when students seek criticism and advice from a teacher whose judgment they trust; this profile level, when sought and desired by students, is similar to the Master-Disciple relationship mentioned in Level 3.

---

*"Beforehand" means the standards are announced before evaluation takes place.

LEVEL 5: Evaluation standards are revealed after the student's performance.

One often hears cries of outrage from students receiving graded test papers: "You didn't tell us we had to do that on the test!" The teacher feels she is right because she has worked hard on her evaluations; the students feel they are right because they didn't know what was coming. The war begins, and at the end, everyone feels defeated.

Level 5 evaluation is justified and routine in pretesting (see Bal). This technique can also be enormously effective as an instructional device: "You students have your grades, and you know how you did on the test, but what you don't know is how your performance matches up with [some other standard — the State average on the Mathematics Assessment tests, or my other class, fifth period, or my students in this class last year]."

LEVEL 6: Evaluation is premature or nonexistent.

Premature evaluation can be discouraging for students if the teacher is disapproving, or simply puzzling if the teacher, trying hard to be warm or supportive, approves of something that actually isn't there.

Premature evaluation can be justified when a student needs encouragement so strongly that what would be premature approval for most students is quite appropriate for him (see Method Yb, Professional Praise).

If evaluation of learning never occurs, interesting results follow. Some students stop working because they see no point in continuing. A few work even harder and evaluate themselves.

There are times when the teacher should observe but not judge a student's work. When the student is creating or first encountering what for him is a new idea or product, leave him alone; just observe and encourage him.

LEVEL 7: Evaluation results are inaccurate.

"What was she thinking of when she graded my paper!" cries one student. Replies another: "And she said I didn't put my proofs in my paper, and here they are, right here!"

The most disconcerting evaluation misses the mark entirely. Sometimes the root of the problem is unclear objectives, sometimes poor observation of results; in all cases, the teacher reports invalid assumptions rather than valid descriptions, so the evaluation is not objective but illusory.

Conceivably, inaccurate evaluation might be used as an exercise in critical thinking: "I have made evaluative comments on each of your papers. I want you now to go through your papers and tell me which of my comments are valid criticisms and which are invalid."

METHOD Be
Monitoring: How does the teacher monitor student learning?

A number of investigators declare that careful teacher monitoring of student progress is one of the important differences between effective and ineffective teaching (Kounin, 1970; Emmer, Evertson, and Anderson, 1980).

Monitoring is a complex combination of many techniques. In this section, we classify the most common techniques of monitoring in terms of their probable effectiveness in attracting student attention and inducing student learning.

LEVEL 1: The teacher continuously trains students in self-evaluation.

There are three advantages of training each student to monitor his own learning: first, he learns self-evaluation, an invaluable lifelong skill; second, he can evaluate immediately rather than waiting until the teacher comes around (see Bc1 and Ga1); third, his evaluation has greater chance of becoming part of his learning than when someone else evaluates and assigns a score to his work (see also O'Leary and Dubey, 1979).

Techniques of student self-monitoring include programmed learning, self-scoring quizzes and exercises, and posted performance goals for specific subject areas. Systems for helping students keep track of their own progress include student folders, posted records of test, quiz, homework, and lab project scores and grades, and progress charts using stars or colored circles — either private records or public.[11]

LEVEL 2: The teacher continuously observes and questions students to appraise their knowledge and progress in learning.

The common practice of patrolling the aisles and checking to see whether students are working is not monitoring, it is policing. It is not an acceptable substitute for observing what students are actually doing with lesson content (learning or mis-learning), then acting on those observations.

Instead of actually watching what students are writing or performing, the teacher may ask diagnostic questions to check their learning (see Method T).

LEVEL 3: The teacher uses frequent quizzes, tests, and/or drills, to appraise student learning.

When the teacher limits monitoring to this technique, the risk of mislearning begins to grow. Mislearning leads to later confusion and inattention. The risk of quiz-anxiety also grows, and becomes a real barrier for some students.

When quizzes and other such devices are used in conjunction with other continuous monitoring and supporting devices, the effect is low profile and powerful.

LEVEL 4: The teacher uses infrequent quizzes, tests, and/or drills to appraise student learning.

Fear of tests hampers some students' learning, and infrequent testing can give a distorted and incomplete view of each student's experience in the tested unit or course. Usually, the infrequent test is too late to help a student's learning; nevertheless, this technique is common practice today.

When used in conjunction with a regular monitoring system, however (see Be1 and Be2), infrequent tests can be useful.

LEVEL 5: The teacher monitors through standardized tests which are not specifically oriented to classroom lesson content.

Because standardized tests typically sample a broad array of student behaviors, a great deal of actual student learning may go unnoticed simply because the tests do not look for it.

Still, used in conjunction with Be1, standardized tests can be a useful way to watch student learning and compare students in one program with students in others. Standardized test scores sometimes show whether or not a particular class is being sufficiently challenged.

LEVEL 6: The teacher monitors through nonspecific third-party reports.

When a teacher asks an aide, "Well, how's Chris doing on his numbers?" and the aide replies, "I'm pleased — he's doing pretty well," the student is probably receiving sloppy monitoring and may, as a result, receive inappropriate instruction.

Consider this aide's more specific reply: "I'm pleased — he can recite his two's and ten's without a mistake now."

LEVEL 7: The teacher does not monitor but rather makes assumptions on the basis of non-content data or historical information.

"Oh, your boy is doing just fine! He enjoys his work so much, has a happy smile on his face all the time — he's just doing wonderfully!"

Brophy and Evertson (1976, p. 67) report studies showing that a teacher cannot simply assume that a student is learning; it is necessary for the student to *do* what is being taught. Therefore, the teacher must ask questions, or otherwise observe the student in action, to avoid being fooled by appearances.

EXERCISE: MONITORING STUDENT LEARNING BEHAVIOR

Refer to Exercise 1: Location, in chapter 11, Method N, and replicate all steps of the exercise except Step 4 (omit) and Step 5 (substitute "picture" for "doodle"). For the content of your lesson, Step 2, choose an abstract term (honesty, sincerity, integrity, loyalty, responsibility, cheating, duplicity, fickleness, disloyalty, irresponsibility) and announce to your students: "Today I want you to think about . . . ," then specify your topic. As you continue to talk about your opinion on the topic, at Step 3, each student will begin to draw a picture of what the topic means to him. Monitor all your students' drawings, and at Step 5, recall and describe each student's picture.

METHOD Bf
Feedback to Students. How does the teacher give students feedback on their learning?

Timing and specificity are two important factors in feedback to students; as to timing, students profit more from *immediate* feedback of evaluation results (Ammons, 1956, p. 285), and regarding specificity, students profit more from specific than from general feedback (Ammons, 1956, p. 287).

LEVEL 1: The teacher gives immediate, specific feedback to every student.

Immediate feedback helps prevent mislearning.[12] Effective teachers do this by monitoring continuously (see Method Be), by handing back quiz and test papers promptly, within 24 hours if possible, or even immediately after performance in some cases, and by using active listening skills (see Method O).

      Specific feedback requires more teacher effort than general feedback, as you can see from these examples.

      Specific: "Your first paragraph is very clear, Jo—here's your topic sentence, and here are your examples. Your second paragraph loses me; these three sentences seem to talk about three different things, and I don't know why."

      General: "Your paper is pretty good overall, Jo, but confusing in some places; you might want to proofread it again."

LEVEL 2: The teacher gives immediate, general feedback to every student.

General feedback does not show the student exactly what he needs to improve. Some students are mildly disconcerted by this, and signal their concern with statements such as "I'm not sure what you want me to do with this."[13]

LEVEL 3: The teacher gives delayed, specific feedback to every student.

Some students worry about tests, compositions, lab sheets, projects, and homework papers that are not returned to them promptly. While that worry itself may distract some students, the major distraction is the student's loss of interest. Delayed feedback means lost opportunity, and lost opportunity means lost learning.

      In special cases, delayed feedback is professionally justified. It is sometimes wise to let student composition work "cool off" before using it again for rewriting skills, for content analysis, for development of citations and research documentation, and other skill training that uses the students' own work as a vehicle.

LEVEL 4: The teacher gives delayed, general feedback to every student.

Imagine yourself as the student who sees a long term paper, on which you have worked hard, finally come back to you with "Nice job" written on the title page—and that's all. "Is that all there is to say about my hours of work?" you ask.

      The technique is justified when the teacher must leave immediately after a dramatic or other evaluated performance; it is right, proper, and necessary for the teacher, upon his return, to say: "I know this is now old business, but you kids were terrific!"

LEVEL 5: The teacher gives feedback to some students, not to others.

Some teachers reportedly give more feedback to high achievers than to low achievers (Brophy and Good, 1970). The loss to the low achievers would seem prejudicial and disconcerting. The technique is justified, however, when ignoring misbehavior, a low profile teaching technique (see Method Xb).

LEVEL 6: The teacher gives no feedback to any student.

This practice usually erodes class morale, and can destroy student attention and achievement. But, if the class has been engaging in inappropriate behavior, the teacher may treat it in various ways, including ignoring the offensive behavior (see Method Z2).

LEVEL 7:: The teacher gives incorrect feedback to at least a few students.

An example of incorrect feedback is the "character builder," a strategy whereby the teacher hands out low grades at the beginning of the semester to all students regardless of performance. Students waste a lot of energy worrying about the low grades and explaining them to their parents, who do not understand the logic of inaccurate feedback. In a few cases, however, incorrect feedback can be a superb technique for student learning (see the example for Bd7).

NOTES

1   "Readily" is specific to the learner; that is, what may be easy for one may be difficult for another. "Readily" implies no specified time limit; it is the time a student takes to complete any task about which the student can say, "I can do it pretty easily."

2   Among the reasons: much instruction today is activity-oriented rather than objective-oriented, and learning objectives are not specified. Moreover, content is predetermined for most subjects at most grade levels, and all students are assumed to need exposure to that content, so the notion of pretesting seems irrelevant in many classrooms (see Wilhelms, 1962).

3   Other techniques may be found in manuals on individualized instruction, such as Dunn and Dunn (1978).

4   Two places for teachers to start: Markle (1969, 2nd ed.) for writing programmed materials; and Jacobs, Maier, and Stolurow (1966) for evaluating existing materials.

5   See Gagné and Briggs (1979), pp. 289–298.

6   See Gronlund (1978), chapter 2.

7   See Yinger (1980).

8   See Good and Brophy (1978), p. 363.

9   See Brophy and Evertson (1976), p. 66.

10   See Gagné and Briggs (1979), chapters 9 and 12; Herman (1977), chapter 5; Schmuck, Chesler, and Lippit (1966), chapter 9; Bloom, Madaus, and Hastings (1981); Gronlund (1978).

11   See Rosenbaum and Drabman (1979) for a review of research and literature on training student self-control.

12   See chapter 1, "Schedule of Reinforcement."

13   See Popham and Baker (1970), pp. 37–38.

REFERENCES

AMMONS, R. Effects of knowledge on performance: A survey and tentative theoretical formulation. *Journal of General Psychology,* 1956, *54,* 279–299.

BLOOM, B., et al. *Taxonomy of educational objectives. Handbook I: Cognitive Domain.* New York: David McKay, 1956.

BLOOM, B., MADAUS, G., & HASTINGS, J. *Evaluation to improve learning.* New York: McGraw-Hill, 1981.

BROPHY, J. Classroom organization and management. East Lansing, Mich.: Institute for Research on Teaching, Michigan State University, 1982a.

BROPHY, J. Research on the self-fulfilling prophesy and teacher expectations. Paper presented at the American Educational Research Association Annual Meeting, March 1982b.

BROPHY, J., & EVERTSON, C. *Learning from teaching.* Boston: Allyn and Bacon, 1976.

BROPHY, J., & GOOD, T. Teacher's communication of differential expectations for children's classroom performance: Some behavioral data. *Journal of Educational Psychology,* 1970, *61,* 365–374.

DOYLE, W. Making managerial decisions in classrooms. In D. Duke (Ed.), *Classroom management,* 78th Yearbook of the National Society for the Study of Education, Part II. Chicago: University of Chicago Press, 1979.

DUNN, R., & DUNN, K. *Teaching students through their individual learning styles: A practical approach.* Reston, Va.: Reston, 1978.

EMMER, E., EVERTSON, C., & ANDERSON, L. Effective classroom management at the beginning of the school year. *Elementary School Journal,* 1980, *80,* 219–231.

GAGNÉ, R. *The conditions of learning* (3rd ed.). New York: Holt, Rinehart and Winston, 1977.

GAGNÉ, R., & BRIGGS, L. *Principles of instructional design* (2nd ed.). New York: Holt, Rinehart and Winston, 1979.

GAMBRELL, L., WILSON, R., & GANTT, W. Classroom observations of task-attending behaviors of good and poor readers. *Journal of Educational Research,* 1981, *74,* 400–405.

GOOD, T., & BROPHY, J. *Looking in classrooms* (2nd ed.). New York: Harper and Row, 1978.

GOOD, T., & BROPHY, J. *Educational psychology: A realistic approach* (2nd ed.). New York: Holt, Rinehart and Winston, 1980.

GRONLUND, N. *Stating objectives for classroom instruction.* New York: Macmillan, 1978.

HERMAN, T. *Creating learning environments: The behavioral approach to education.* Boston: Allyn and Bacon, 1977.

JACOBS, P., MAIER, M., & STOLUROW, L. *A guide to evaluating self-instructional programs.* New York: Holt, Rinehart and Winston, 1966.

JORGENSON, G. Relationship of classroom behavior to the accuracy of match between material difficulty and student ability. *Journal of Educational Psychology,* 1977, *69,* 24–32.

KIBLER, R., et al. *Objectives for instruction and evaluation* (2nd ed.). Boston: Allyn and Bacon, 1981.

KOUNIN, J. *Discipline and group management in classrooms.* New York: Holt, Rinehart and Winston, 1970.

MARKLE, S. *Good frames and bad: A grammar of frame writing* (2nd ed.). New York: John Wiley, 1969.

O'LEARY, S., & DUBEY, D. Applications of self-control procedures by children: A review. *Journal of Applied Behavior Analysis,* 1979, *12,* 449–465.

POPHAM, J., & BAKER, E. *Planning an instructional sequence.* Englewood Cliffs, N.J.: Prentice-Hall, 1970.

ROSENBAUM, M., & DRABMAN, R. Self-control training in the classroom: A review and critique. *Journal of Applied Behavior Analysis,* 1979, *12,* 449–465.

SCHMUCK, R., CHESLER, M., & LIPPIT, R. *Problem solving to improve classroom learning.* Chicago: Science Research Associates, 1966.

WILHELMS, F. The curriculum and individual differences. In *National Society for the Study of Education 61st Yearbook,* 1962, Part I. Chicago: University of Chicago Press, 1962.

YINGER, R. A study of teacher planning. *Elementary School Journal,* 1980, *80,* 107–127.

CONTROL OF STRATEGIES AND MEDIA (METHODS C, D)

5

This chapter examines some of the ways teachers plan for instruction. Although teaching strategies actually include decisions about media and materials, groups, facilities, time scheduling, and activities, we shall define "strategy" in a particular way here, then analyze the other decisions separately in this and the next two chapters.

METHOD C: INSTRUCTIONAL STRATEGIES

A teacher may choose to tell students the right answer or help them discover an answer for themselves. These choices are examples of instructional strategies.

METHOD Ca

Expository Strategy: How does the teacher tell and explain the lesson concept to students?

The expository strategy predominates in American teaching. When using this strategy, the teacher presents a concept, skill, problem, or generalization for students to learn, explains the concept in detail with examples, illustrations, or specific coaching, then expects the students to be able to learn exactly what they have been taught. Expository teaching may utilize lectures, demonstrations, recitations, or any other activity that permits the teacher to convey the idea to students, whether that idea is concept, facts, or skill.

LEVEL 1: The teacher states concepts clearly, then follows with relevant examples in proper sequence.

The term "advance organizer," coined by David Ausubel (1963), means any basic concept or structure that helps anchor or support the material to be taught. For example:

"Today we are going to talk about the Hawaiian Islands ... "

"As you look at this painting, notice the triangular composition formed by ... "

"When you start bending your knees, try to move so you keep your body vertical like a tall skyscraper."

(See also Joyce and Weil [1972, chapter 10] and Weil and Joyce [1978]).

LEVEL 2: The teacher demonstrates concepts or skills to be learned, then follows with relevant examples or practice in proper sequence.

When students see what they are to learn as well as hear it, their probability of learning increases. A risk in using visual demonstrations is that a student may focus on what he sees to the exclusion of what he hears.

LEVEL 3: The teacher begins the lesson with examples or details, then delays stating the concept, skill, topic, generalization, or organizer.

Although many students love a good mystery, and respond with pleasure and enthusiasm when the teacher says, "Why are we doing this? Where is this all leading? Well, I can't tell you right now, but hang on — we'll be there shortly," other students do not love a mystery, and need to know exactly where they are going and why. They would greet the same technique with confusion: "What's she talking about? Do you understand what's going on?"

LEVEL 4: The teacher supports concepts with relevant examples that are in illogical or incorrect sequence.

The problem of "skipping around" is that someone is bound to get lost. When history is not told in chronological order, when nouns get mixed up with adjectives, when the teacher has to say, "Oh, I'm sorry, this is all mixed up — let's go back to … ," we have sequence problems. The easiest solution is to stop and repeat examples in proper order; trying to hide the problem invites mislearning or worse.

On the other hand, as a special device in discovery strategies (see Method Cb), random presentation can be useful with able and self-confident students.

LEVEL 5: The teacher supports concepts with relevant examples that are inadequate to illustrate or explain the concepts.

The teacher's prime clue to distraction is the student's plaintive cry, "I don't get this!" The student who doesn't understand may not be focusing his attention on it. The best strategy is to give the student a fresh start with another example.

LEVEL 6: The teacher supports concepts with inappropriate or irrelevant examples.

This kind of lecture or presentation is guaranteed to create confusion; for example, "So what we're talking about today is capitalism. Now, the first thing you have to consider is that the U.S. is the only country that has a check-and-balance system in its constitution."

The only reason for inappropriate or irrelevant examples in the classroom is comic effect.

LEVEL 7: The teacher provides incorrect information either in the concept or in the examples.

Mislearning is more troublesome than nonlearning, because unlearning requires greater effort than learning for the first time. The teacher who does not know the subject area but attempts to teach it anyway creates havoc in students' minds.

You can present incorrect information in the classroom if the purpose is to invite objections and rejoinders from students. Some teachers say, "Just keeping you on your toes," or "Wanted to see if you were still awake." Other than these special cases, it is far better for the teacher to say candidly, "I don't know, but I'll find out."

METHOD Cb

Discovery Strategy: How does the teacher help students discover concepts for themselves?

The teacher has a concept in mind but prefers that students discover the concept for themselves rather than be spoon-fed the concept (Jacobsen et al., 1981). Or, the teacher wants students to develop their problem-solving skills rather than focus on the concept or solution they finally discover (Suchman, 1960).

The discovery strategy is usually described in these steps: (1) students encounter a problem or puzzle that intrigues them; (2) they formulate possible answers or solutions (hypotheses); (3) they gather information related to the hypotheses; and (4) they analyze the information and compare it with their hypotheses.

LEVEL 1: The teacher provides an intriguing problem or examples, then urges students to resolve or explain the matter.

A prerequisite of successful discovery teaching is an interesting problem or puzzle; for example: "In this section of *King Lear*, I want you to think about various reasons he might have behaved as he did. Write them down. Then, in your small groups, explore the text to see which explanation seems to fit the play best."

The second prerequisite to successful discovery teaching is to present good examples, examples that implicitly display the characteristics of the concept. The teacher might put the following words on the chalkboard: receive, receipt, perceive, retrieve, believe, relief; then say to the class: "What do you see there? ... Yes; what else do you see? .... Sure, and anything else? ... Is that true in all cases? ... Is there anything that is true in all cases? ... So what would you say about the spelling here? ... Could you make a rule that explains these spellings? ... Does your rule fit all the cases here? ... Yes, I agree. Your rule is easy to remember: '*I* before *E* except after *C*.' Right? Everyone say it with me. ... Now somebody tell me how to spell "deceive." ... Tell me how to spell "belief." ... Close your eyes, everyone, and everyone spell out loud the word "receive."

For further help in using this technique, see Jacobsen et al. (1981, pp. 156–162); also Joyce and Weil (1972, chapters 6–9, 12–15).

LEVEL 2: The teacher urges students to use efficient hypothesis-testing, then presents subsequent examples in strategic time and sequence.

A teacher of elementary school science lowers a heatproof glass pitcher over a candle until the flame begins to diminish, then raises the pitcher, then lowers it again, and asks, "Why might this be happening?"

Unskilled students begin by asking questions that yield little information:
"Does it get too hot in there for the flame to burn?" When the answer comes back "No," the student needs at least one more question to pursue the hypothesis that heat is the reason for the flame's dimming:
"Does the glass pitcher get too hot or something?"
"No."

"Does the candle get too hot?"

"No."

Skilled students may pursue the same hypothesis with far greater efficiency:

"Does it have something to do with heat?"

"No."

"Does it have something to do with air?"

"Yes."

In short, the teacher urges students to be efficient by training them to ask broad questions first and narrower questions later.

When the teacher finds that the first set of examples are insufficient, he may introduce subsequent examples, each of which takes students one more step toward seeing patterns. For example, imagine that the teacher in Cb1 felt the students needed another example; his questioning might have gone like this:

"What do you see there? ... Good, what else do you see? ... Sure, and anything else? Yes, and anything else? ... What if we were to add the word *conceive* to your list—how should we spell it? ... Why should we spell it that way?"

LEVEL 3: The teacher discourages nonstrategic questions and experiments.

The teacher can discourage nonstrategic questions in several ways:

"I could answer your question, Johnny, but you wouldn't learn much from the answer. Try asking a broader question."

"You have asked these two questions. Now what one question could you have asked that would have done the work of these two?"

LEVEL 4: The teacher gives hints to students.

There is a difference between helping students ask questions and giving them answers. When you give hints, the purpose of the students' inquiry often shifts from finding an explanation for the content question to finding other ways to make the teacher give more hints, a game that some students simply cannot resist.

LEVEL 5: The teacher provides inadequate examples or asks students to guess at the right answer.

Guessing games can either be fun or pointlessly boring. When skillful sequencing of questions is missing, some students are likely to get discouraged or disgusted; sometimes their attitudes affect others (see Good and Brophy, 1978, pp. 365–66). The purpose of discovery teaching is to train students to think in a rational and disciplined manner; you defeat the objective when you make students depend on guessing. Random guessing can be justified in discovery teaching when a student is unable to participate in any other way. The teacher might then permit the student to guess, since guessing is at least a place to begin.

LEVEL 6: The teacher tells students the correct answer at the outset, then structures the lesson to rediscover that same concept.

Some science teachers will object to classifying conventional science laboratory methods as high profile, but others will nod and say, "Yes, this has been the problem with traditional science teaching—telling them beforehand what they are looking for." When science laboratories feature mechanical recipes rather than exciting discovery, some students will consider labs pointless and science dull, and will avoid science. However, the technique may be justified when the teacher is using expository teaching (see Cal.)

LEVEL 7: The teacher assumes that students can solve problems or discover concepts without any structure or previous experience.

The math teacher says, "I gave each team a yardstick, a piece of paper, and a protractor and told them to go outside and figure out the height of the school chimney. I didn't tell them how—I just wanted to see if they could figure it out for themselves. What a mess."

A few highly curious, self-disciplined students love to be thrown into a problem with no guidelines or experience. But most students do not, and become confused and discouraged when they are inappropriately challenged.

METHOD D: MEDIA AND MATERIALS[1]

Teachers commonly refer to paper handouts and worksheets as "materials," to audiovisual equipment as "media." In this book, "media" refers to all physical means of carrying information to the senses, including the human voice.

METHOD D
Media and Materials: In what manner does the teacher use media in teaching?

LEVEL 1: The teacher establishes a medium so compelling that it becomes a total environment for the student.*

In *Education and Ecstasy* (1968), George Leonard tells of a student who steps into a special learning environment to find himself surrounded by sights and sounds that carry the lesson content to the student as powerfully as the carnival mystery house enthralls its young visitors.

In the everyday classroom, a skillful teacher can create the same kind of total-immersion experience at almost any moment, using almost any medium. Whenever one is engrossed in a book and feels himself part of the story; whenever one gets angry in a simulation game about urban crime because the city council representative refuses to vote for a street light program for the neighborhood; whenever one watches a mathematics puppet show and hopes the girl-puppet will successfully count to 20 to save the boy-puppet from the witch—all are total-immersion experiences that are possible in the classroom. They are wonderful for the spirit as well as the mind, because they let students escape the real world around them even as they learn.

---

*This technique assumes the teacher uses appropriate content at the proper skill level for students. Media alone cannot induce attention if other conditions are inappropriate.

No medium can compel complete student involvement; even television loses its attraction when it is badly used. Conversely, no medium is impossible either; a magician can fascinate us for a moment with only a handkerchief and a penny. Almost every medium requires some inspiration on the part of the teacher to make it fascinate students, and students become fascinated when teachers use media to build anticipation and suspense.

If you use a film, videotape, or sound-filmstrip that is awkward to interrupt, build anticipation in the students' minds beforehand; for example, in a math class: "You're going to see this equation build slowly, step by step, and I want you to watch for the very moment when all the pieces just fall together, bam! Like that!"

Anticipation building is necessary to prepare students for total involvement in live action as well as passive watching. It is essential for many instructional simulation games, which some teachers feel are the best total-immersion teaching tools available. For example: "In this game of Policy Negotiations, you each can use your influence tokens to vote for or against this policy, to lobby for a new issue, or to strengthen your position in office. Now what I am waiting to see is how each one of you will decide to use your influence. What decisions will you make? And why will you make them? O.K., let's start."

The most familiar live-action medium in many classrooms is the worksheet. While most worksheets are dull, occasionally one shows some inspiration as well as content. Its directions might read: "Learn how to spell some tricky words. Put the correct letter in each blank [multiple choice items]. Do you think you put the correct letter in each blank? (yes/no) Now put your six answer letters in the six blanks below. These letters will spell a hard spelling word. Check your dictionary carefully to be sure you have spelled that hard word correctly. Did you check? (yes/no) Now go back and make sure you spelled the tricky words correctly. Did you check them? (yes/no) Now write all seven words in the blanks below, just the way you will write them on the Hard and Tricky Word spelling test your teacher will give at the end of this hour."

A teacher can build anticipation during an activity: " ... So I'll just put this word up here on the chalkboard and—wow, just where do you think this is all going? Where do you think we're going to end up? Let's go on and see if you're right." These techniques do more than simply attract student attention; they hold attention and build concentration as well.

LEVEL 2: The teacher uses a variety of media in appropriate moderation to support the lesson.[2]

Whereas total-environment media techniques are intended to attract and sustain student attention over time, moderate use of media is intended to set the stage for learning and convey content information.

Set the Stage Stage-setting media should be absolutely content-oriented and free of distraction from lesson content. The teacher can decorate classroom walls and bulletin boards with charts, pictures, and other displays that immediately convey a content image. (An excellent source of specific suggestions is Leacock [1969], chapter 3, which discusses content-oriented wall displays.) You can also hang or display actual instructional paraphernalia throughout the year. Some teachers who use instructional games in their classes put the games in clear plastic bags or fasten game parts together with shower curtain hooks and hang them from the ceiling or from strings along the wall to make a colorful display. This frees shelf and other cabinet space for less showy materials.

You can also set the stage for individual lessons with sound or even sound-slide displays, appropriately content-oriented. For example, a music teacher plays a commercial recording of the band or choir's next assigned piece as the students enter the rehearsal hall. An English teacher plays a recorded recitation of a poem that students will study that class period. An elementary primary grade teacher plays quiet, soothing music to set the stage for nap time after lunch or for any other quiet time. Each device conveys the teacher's expectation for what the student is to pay attention to during the instructional time or other periods of the day. All of these are control techniques.

Sometimes stage-setting controls themselves become distracting; for example, a student who looks at a poster of Paris during French class may think more about the Eiffel Tower than about the conjugation of *avoir*.

Convey Content Information   The human voice is the most common teaching medium, and the most common instructional activity is lecture or "teacher talk." But most effective teachers try to vary verbal teaching with other kinds of teaching because many students appear to pay attention better when they can look at something as well as listen, whether television, books, slides, charts and maps, posters, demonstrations, overhead transparencies, models, or objects.

When you bring out a visual, use key words to call students' ears to attention along with their eyes; for example:
"Notice here that ..."
"Look! See how ..."
"In this little ... who can guess ..."
"Here is a picture of what we have just been talking about."
If your students' attention has started to lag, do not turn your back on the class while you draw on the board or search for a visual aid; when you lose eye contact, you may not be able to regain their attention by the time you're ready to face them again. Instead, face the class as you use the chalkboard, and ask questions or explain what you are doing. You can also send a student to fetch the visual aid you need for your demonstration.

LEVEL 3: The teacher uses media as novelty.

At Level 3, the media begin to attract attention to themselves rather than direct attention to content, and the lesson begins to look flashy.

Sometimes showiness helps get the attention of students who are not in the habit of paying attention in school, but the teacher who relies on razzle-dazzle teaching techniques and gimmicks finds that as the novelty wears off, the attention wears out.

LEVEL 4: The teacher uses media without integration with the lesson or explanation of purpose.[3]

Do you recognize this scene? We see teenagers spill into the room singly and in groups and settle in their assigned seats. The bell rings. The teacher finishes taking the role, walks over and turns out the lights, then asks a student to close the window shades. The teacher turns on the movie projector to run a film on the settling of the Old West during the nineteenth century. The film runs for 25 minutes. Most students have their eyes on the screen most of the time. Two girls exchange lipsticks and combs at one point, but after the teacher says "Hey," they look at the screen. One boy puts his head on his desk, face to the side, but the teacher moves over and taps him on the shoulder; the boy then puts his head in his hands with face toward the screen.

When the film is over, the teacher turns on the lights and turns off the projector. He asks the student to open the window shades. "All right, now on your reports," he says to the yawning and stretching class, "make sure you label your maps so you clearly show the different territories . . . ." This teacher has selected a relevant film, given it 25 minutes of class time, and then ignored it.

How should that film be presented? A simple, introductory statement of purpose would be barely satisfactory; a preliminary anticipation-builder (see D1) would be far better; best of all, perhaps, would be to teach that 25-minute film in segments. After previewing the film, the teacher could introduce it by saying, "There are four different topics in this film. I want you to watch for . . . ." Or, he could prepare students beforehand: "This is a long film, and we're going to stop it twice in the middle so I can ask you about what you've just seen." Then he could specifically build anticipation for the first segment: "The first question I want you to explore is what the film director wants you to believe about those early settlers."

There are some teaching occasions for which integration or explanation might not or should not be used. Special effects require no words of explanation. You might teach a lesson on math, then, without a word, turn on Tom Lehr's satirical song, "New Math." You might also begin a simulation game with no introduction at all, plunging directly into the activity, then stop the action after about 15 minutes and ask, "What's this all about? What does this mean? Anything? Or is it just a game?"

LEVEL 5: The teacher uses a few media constantly with no variation.

Some teachers complain that their students are addicted to television and will not sit still in school. A few of these teachers say they are unable to compete with television. The teacher who talks all day long, or uses worksheets all day long, day after day, is not competing with television; he is competing with human nature.

LEVEL 6: The teacher makes mistakes or incurs time delays in using media.

It is often better not to use an overhead projector at all rather than make the screen image crooked. Your students should not leave the lesson remembering your media mistakes instead of the content. Consider, however, the delightful exceptions: occasionally a teacher will be seen fumbling around looking for something, or falter in speaking for want of just the right word, or pin up a poster upside down. Are these mistakes? Perhaps, but they may also be carefully planned special effects for capturing attention and building suspense.

LEVEL 7: The teacher uses media that do not function or are irrelevant.[4]

Nothing is more distracting than a teaching medium that doesn't work—a ditto that students can't read, a wet chalkboard the teacher tries to use anyway, or a science demonstration that works in the first class but fails in the second.

What should you do when the medium doesn't work properly? Best to treat it for what it actually is, a distraction, and quickly move on (see Method X). Do not waste time explaining the failure, since that is even higher profile than the inoperative medium itself. An irrelevant medium is equally distractive. "I know it doesn't really fit," says the teacher, "but I came upon this yesterday and thought you'd enjoy it," and up goes a cute poster, or out comes a story or joke, and away goes the lesson. Do not assume the teacher should never entertain students during a lesson, but be aware that introducing irrelevancies automatically distracts student attention.

NOTES

1   See Schramm (1977), chapter 2, for a review of research on learning from media instruction. There is no one way or right way or right kind of media, but there is much evidence that people learn from media. Research on audiovisual materials (from 1950–1978) can be found in Kemp (1980), chapter 3.

2   Helpful resources can be found in the following: Gerlach and Ely (1980), especially pages 256–59; Heinick, Molenda, and Russell (1982), especially chapter 7 on multi-media for a single lesson. Johnston et al. (1978) demonstrate that learning centers should provide multimedia experiences. Dunn and Dunn (1978) also provide a wealth of ideas for all grade levels.

3   Refer also to Method Bb, Stating Content Objectives, and Method Bd, Evaluation Standards. Also see Kemp (1980), chapter 4, on relevancy.

4   See Gerlach and Ely (1980), chapter 10, on relevancy.

REFERENCES

AUSUBEL, D. *The psychology of meaningful verbal learning.* New York: Grune and Stratton, 1963.

DUNN, R., & DUNN, K. *Teaching students through their individual learning styles: A practical approach.* Reston, Va.: Reston, 1978.

GERLACH, V., & ELY, D. *Teaching and media: A systematic approach* (2nd ed.). Englewood Cliffs, N.J.: Prentice-Hall, 1980.

GOOD, T., & BROPHY, J. *Looking in classrooms* (2nd ed.). New York: Harper and Row, 1978.

HEINICH, R., MOLENDA, M., & RUSSELL, J. *Instructional media and the new technologies of instruction.* New York: John Wiley, 1982.

JACOBSEN, D., et al. *Methods for teaching.* Columbus, Ohio: Charles E. Merrill, 1981.

JOHNSTON, H., et al. *The learning center idea book.* Boston: Allyn and Bacon, 1978.

JOYCE, B., & WEIL, M. *Models of teaching.* Englewood Cliffs, N.J.: Prentice-Hall, 1972.

KEMP, J. *Planning and producing audiovisual materials* (4th ed.). New York: Harper and Row, 1980.

LEACOCK, E. *Teaching and learning in city schools: A comparative study.* New York: Basic Books, 1969.

LEONARD, G. *Education and ecstasy.* New York: Dell, 1968.

ROSENSHINE, B. Content, time and direct instruction. In P. Peterson & H. Walberg (Eds.), *Research on teaching: Concepts, findings, and implications.* Berkeley, Calif.: McCutchan, 1979.

SCHRAMM, W. *Big media, little media.* Beverly Hills, Calif.: Sage, 1977.

SUCHMAN, J. Inquiry training in the elementary school. *Science Teacher*, November 1960, *27*, 42–47.

WEIL, M., & JOYCE, B. *Information-processing model of teaching.* Englewood Cliffs, N.J.: Prentice-Hall, 1978.

CONTROL OF GROUPING AND SPACE
(METHODS E, F)

6

I n this chapter, we will examine the teacher planning skills of organizing groups and space in the classroom.

METHOD E: GROUPING STUDENTS

Some teachers are uneasy with the idea of grouping students for instruction in any way other than as one large class group. Other teachers are so enthusiastic about small groups that they use them all the time. Among the various purposes for grouping students, the most important is to permit different kinds of interaction to occur simultaneously.

METHOD E
Grouping Students: How does the teacher group students for instruction?

This section of Method E classifies the risks of grouping in terms of flexibility. Flexible grouping means the groups change when learning needs change. Inflexible grouping ignores such needs. Homogeneous grouping is of students who are alike, and heterogeneous grouping is of unlike students.

LEVEL 1: The teacher forms temporary groups according to the needs of the lesson and of students.

The reason for flexible grouping is to place students appropriately for a specific content objective, task, or activity. Students' needs change continuously, as do instructional purposes; therefore, the only sensible method of grouping within the classroom is temporary, to achieve the purpose of the moment for the people of the moment. Both homogeneous and heterogeneous groups are useful at different times and should be formed and disbanded whenever sensible. (For further help on techniques in this area, see Good and Brophy, 1978, chapter 9.)

LEVEL 2: The teacher forms permanent groups for specific learning tasks.

Some teachers organize their rooms into laboratory groups, spelling drill groups, homework checking groups, and other groups for specific learning tasks. The groups serve a useful administrative purpose without freezing students into inappropriate lesson content groups. If the teacher trains a group to perform its appointed tasks by a specified time, the group will usually work smoothly with little risk of distraction.

Notice the difference between a permanent homework checking group, which is primarily an administrative group, and a reading group, which is not primarily administrative (see Level 6).

LEVEL 3: The teacher groups students for peer tutoring.

Peer tutoring groups may be pairs or small groups. The advantages of peer tutoring clearly lie in three areas[1]: (1) students often do an effective job of tutoring, both because of their ability to act as peer role models and because of their awareness of student language and assumptions; (2) the teacher is freed to help other students; and (3) tutors can learn lesson material even better when they teach it to someone else.

Disadvantages and risks of distraction are that some able students are not able tutors; they lack teaching skills, patience, or understanding of their proper function. Also, some combinations of tutors and tutees will waste time chatting, fooling around, or arguing. Then, too, some students are embarrassed to be tutored, and will unconsciously resist their tutor's best efforts.[2]

LEVEL 4: The teacher uses the large class group exclusively.

The risk here is not of misbehavior but of missed opportunities. Any large group, even with the most imaginatively interactive teacher, reaches moments when a small group activity would be ideal for carrying the lesson; if the teacher is not sensitive to it, the moment is lost. If the teacher relies exclusively on any one type of organization, opportunities are lost.

LEVEL 5: The teacher uses the same permanent homogeneous small groups for all subject areas.

This is the practice of dividing the class into reading groups at the beginning of the year, arranged according to test scores, then using these groups for all subject areas throughout the year. The effect of this practice is to create a group that may be homogeneous in the one content area but heterogeneous for others, because few students are equally competent in all content areas — each has different areas of strength and weakness. In addition, placement in a particular group, regardless of the student's actual ability or interests, tends to label a student and thereby determines his subsequent grouping assignments (Rist, 1970). (Permanent grouping assignments may be satisfactory for administrative groups, as we noted in Method E2.)

LEVEL 6: The teacher uses a different permanent homogeneous small group for each subject area.

Administrative convenience causes many teachers to keep one reading group or one math group together throughout the semester or year. The risk of lost opportunities prevails as at Level 5. Although this practice is common, its potential disadvantages are currently under debate. For example, Good and Brophy (1978) argue that homogeneous ability grouping undermines the achievement and self-confidence of students who happen to be placed in low-ability groups, whether or not the placement is appropriate (p. 281). On the other hand, Kulik and Kulik (1982) find no evidence of deteriorated achievement or even of reduced morale in low-ability groups; in fact, they even find traces of higher morale in some students who are grouped with others of similar ability.

Nevertheless, one risk of permanent homogeneous grouping is the teacher's tendency to consider the students in such groups as similar and to treat them alike, even though they may be quite different; for example, teachers who teach low-ability groups sometimes expect their students to make little progress, and the effect on any one student can be unfortunate. Temporary homogeneous groups are often an effective teaching device, but never rely on them consistently.

LEVEL 7: The teacher uses groups for inappropriate or undefined purposes.

"I want you to read this story quietly to yourself, and to do that we'll divide into five small groups. You have half an hour to read this story in your groups. OK, begin." This teacher is so zealous about using small groups that he has formed groups for an inappropriate purpose. It would be more appropriate to use the small groups for discussion; for example, "I want you to read the first page of this story quietly to yourself, and to do this we'll divide into five small groups. When everyone in your group has finished, your group should decide whether Bill is being fair or not."

METHOD F: ORGANIZING PHYSICAL SPACE

How important is the physical classroom environment to student attention and learning? History suggests that it may be relatively unimportant. After all, Socrates did a notable job of teaching on street corners and in the public market, unsuitable places for instruction by modern standards, and another influential teacher, Jesus of Nazareth, taught wherever there happened to be people around.

Yet, a number of studies show that careful design of physical space can make considerable differences in students' classroom behavior.[3] We will consider various classroom arrangements that can enhance or detract from instruction.

METHOD Fa
Locating Low Achieving Students.

A low-achieving student usually has difficulty keeping his attention on the lesson. In an effort to make low-achieving students feel at home and comfortable in the classroom, you may be tempted to permit all students to sit where they want to sit. Resist that temptation, because low-achieving students will probably rush to the back and sides of the room, friends will sit together and talk incessantly, and you may find yourself unconsciously favoring small self-selected groups of high-achieving students. Instead of submitting to group pressure, take control.

LEVEL 1: Mix low-achieving students with high-achieving students when making seating arrangements (see Figure 6-1, A[e] and B[d, e]).

Good and Brophy find that low-achieving students participate in class activities more frequently when they sit next to high-achieving students (1977, p. 416).

LEVEL 2: Place low-achieving students close to the teacher rather than far away.

In earlier days, it was customary for teachers to seat the "slowest" student next to the teacher's desk so she could give the student more attention and keep the student's behavior under direct control. This is still a sensible technique.

LEVELS 3, 4, 5: (None.)

LEVEL 6: Place low-achieving students at the back or sides of the room, remote from the teacher's continual monitoring and direct supervision.

A remote location is not usually wise. "Low achievement students, who typically have shorter attention spans and perhaps less interest, may find it easier to tune the class out when they sit a long distance away from the teacher" (Good and Brophy, 1977, p. 420). The teacher must control personal feelings in such cases.

An exception might be when a low-achieving student is given a learning contract and trained to fulfill it—then he might conceivably be placed at a remote location for a period of time.

LEVEL 7: Group low-achieving and/or problem students together remote from the teacher's direct supervision.

A teacher might temporarily group low-achieving students together for a particular lesson that she will directly supervise. Under any other circumstance, this technique is sheer folly.

METHOD Fb
Seatwork

Because seatwork usually implies independent study, the most logical spacing of students tends to encourage independent work and discourage social interaction.

LEVEL 1: Separate student desks or study positions and avoid face-to-face eye contact between students (Figure 6-1 A[d]).

The traditional "auditorium" style of seating, with everyone facing the same direction, inhibits face-to-face student contacts in a natural way, automatically reducing both temptation and opportunity. The teacher is free to move anywhere in the room.

LEVEL 2: (None.)

LEVEL 3: Seat students around large tables (Figure 6-1 C).

When students are spaced around cafeteria or library tables, the separation is usually adequate to minimize socializing, particularly if the teacher monitors well and if students do not face one another. The same arrangement with smaller tables is also adequate.

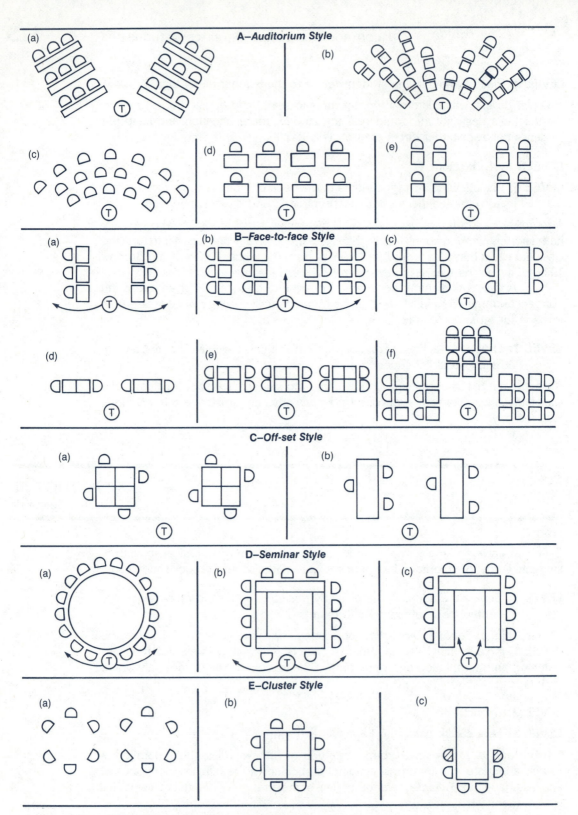

FIGURE 6.1 Classroom Arrangements

LEVEL 4: Arrange student desks in pairs, with both students facing the same direction (Figure 6-1 A[e] and B[f]).

This time-honored arrangement, typical of many nineteenth-century American schoolhouses, can be useful for mixing high-achieving and low-achieving students. For others, however, the risk of socializing begins to grow.

LEVEL 5: Cluster several small student desks with students facing one another (Figure 6-1 B[c] and B[e]).

Even under the teacher's watchful eye, this room arrangement offers almost irresistible opportunities to any student whose attention is wandering away from assigned seatwork. When the clustered students are working on cooperative projects, the arrangement can work very well.

LEVEL 6: Pair student desks facing one another (Figure 6-1 B[d]).

For any activity other than paired project work, this arrangement runs high risk of inattention to lesson content. For project work by teams of two, the arrangement in Figure 6-1 A(e) works better.

LEVEL 7: (None.)

METHOD Fc
Small Groups.

Unless your groups have been well trained, they will tend to sit exactly where they find chairs, even if the arrangements are strange. If you must rearrange chairs after small groups have formed and started work, do so, because if any group member cannot clearly see the face of every other group member, the entire group runs high risk of inattention and distraction.

LEVEL 1: Each group's chairs or seats on the floor are clustered, facing one another (Figure 6-1 E[a]).

LEVEL 2: Each group sits at small desks which are clustered, facing one another (Figure 6-1 E[b]).

Desks give students something to write on during discussion and give them a sense of importance. An occasional student will feel the urge to examine the contents of his desk, or see if he can reach the desk across from him with his foot, but the desk cluster is usually reliable.

LEVEL 3: Each group sits around the end of a large table (Figure 6-1 E[c] and C[a]).

There is a possibility that those on the fringe (see shaded positions) will tend not to participate. The arrangement in C(a) is adequate for small group discussion.

LEVEL 4: Each group sits in seats arranged auditorium-style or in rows facing one another (Figure 6-1 A and B[c]).

For lack of alternatives, some teachers must actually use an auditorium arrangement with fixed seating for small group meetings, which is not at all satisfactory. At least one student is likely to "tune out."

To make the best of this bad situation, you can have students in the front row kneel on their seats and face backward, or leave the seats and sit in clusters on the floor in the orchestra, on the stage, or in a wide rear aisle.

The arrangement in Figure 6-1 B(c) does not permit those in the end positions to see others' faces.

LEVEL 5: The group sits in a cluster with one member out of the circle (a modified version of the arrangement in Figure 6-1 E[a]).

"Oh, I just want to listen anyway," protests the odd-man-out, and the teacher smiles, nods, and firmly directs the group to rearrange itself in a circle. The student who is allowed to remain outside the circle will spend most of the time in unknown attention.

LEVEL 6: The group sits in two clusters or subgroups.

A split occurs in any group when someone turns his back toward another member of his group. When close friends are assigned to a group in which they are not interested, they will frequently pair off and form their own group, tangent to the other. The teacher's proper action here is to insist on a circle arrangement.

LEVEL 7: Two clusters sit adjacent to one another, with a member from one paired with a member from the other (a modified version of the cluster arrangement in Figure 6-1 E[a]).

Sam and Wally are buddies, but were assigned to two different groups. So they sit side-to-side in their own groups and talk with one another. Teacher action is necessary to save both groups from disaster. You may put more space between the groups, pretending that you don't want the talk in one group to disturb the thinking in the other group, or you may train students never to sit so as to place a group member at their backs, thus forcing them into an Fc1 configuration automatically.

METHOD Fd
Lecture/Presentation/Demonstration.

In a lecture or presentation, the teacher relies primarily on one-way communication from herself to the students. As every teacher knows who has attempted to lecture in front of students in a school cafeteria, there are some good physical arrangements for lectures and teacher-talk, and some bad.

LEVEL 1: Individual desks or long tables are arranged auditorium-style, with all students facing the teacher (Figure 6-1 A[a, b, d] and B[f]).

In the ideal configuration, the back row is well within range of the teacher's normal speaking voice and vision. Aisles down the center and sides and across the back and front of the room permit the teacher full mobility in a large class of thirty or more, while in smaller classes even more walking space between desks should be possible. The desks or tables are a symbol of work activity, and establish an excellent climate for high attention.

LEVEL 2: Individual chairs (without desks) or seats on the floor are arranged auditorium-style, with students facing the teacher (Figure 6-1 A[c]).

Like Level 1, this technique keeps all students within close eye and voice range of the teacher. Semicircles or V-configurations are best.

LEVEL 3: Seating positions are arranged in one large circle, square, or U-shape around the room, seminar-style (Figure 6-1 D[a, b, c]).

In large groups of ten or more, the seminar style increases the distance between teacher and students, and teacher movement becomes awkward; except in the U-shaped arrangement, the walking teacher speaks to the backs of students' heads, forcing the teacher into a small and confined teaching station within the group. Keeping those difficulties in mind, note also that this arrangement does eliminate most face-to-face contact among students, and therefore creates fewer distractions than the higher profile arrangements.

LEVEL 4: Seating positions are arranged in one or more pairs of rows, opposite and facing one another (Figure 6-1 B[a and b]).

A disconcerting factor in this arrangement is that students look directly into one anothers' faces at rather close range. Although the arrangement does not appear to foster misbehavior, students' minds tend to wander as they think about the people they're watching and about their own appearances. These distractions are noticeable in junior and senior high schools.

LEVEL 5: Seats are arranged around large tables, such as those in cafeterias and libraries (Figure 6-1 B[c] and C[b]).

Cafeterias are uncomfortable for lectures or presentations because the teacher must look at the backs of students' heads, and students face each other. Both drawbacks reduce student attention.

LEVEL 6: Individual student desks are clustered together in small groups of four (Figure 6-1 B[e] and C[a]).

A common configuration in elementary schools, this arrangement puts classroom control to a severe test during teacher talk. The teacher must look at the backs of students' heads, and students face one another in close proximity.

LEVEL 7: Individual student desks are paired, facing each other, or clustered (Figure 6-1 B[d] and E).

This arrangement is particularly poor during teacher talk, lecture, or presentation. It can be tolerated during brief instructional periods, but will not work as a long-term arrangement.

METHOD Fe
Recitation, All-Class Discussion.

"Recitation" means the teacher asks questions of students, and they respond with answers. Sometimes recitation activities expand into class discussions, with students talking to each other as well as giving answers to the teacher.

LEVEL 1: Seating positions are arranged in one large circle, square, or U-shape around the outside of the room, seminar-style (Figure 6-1 D).

This arrangement constrains teacher mobility, but gives the opportunity for face-to-face conversations across the table among students as the teacher permits.

LEVEL 2: Seating positions are arranged in one or more pairs of rows placed opposite and facing one another (Figure 6-1 B[a, b, c, f]).

Students have a good opportunity to speak across the aisle to each other, and teacher visibility remains quite good. Teacher mobility is considerably better here than in the Level 1 arrangements.

LEVEL 3: Seats, desks, or tables are arranged auditorium-style, with students facing the teacher (Figure 6-1 A).

The advantage of the auditorium style is that students can see and hear the teacher; the disadvantage is that students often can't hear one another.

LEVEL 4: Seats allow for odd-man-out seating in the room.

While teachers may be wise to isolate students during seatwork, especially those who cannot control their socializing, isolation may inhibit a student's concentration during recitation, if the student feels alone. It is better, if possible, to bring him into the group for recitation and discussion, and remove him again during transition to another activity.

LEVEL 5: Seats are arranged around large tables, such as those in cafeterias and libraries (Figure 6-1 B[c]).

Group inattention can mount rapidly with this arrangement, because the teacher must look at the backs of students' heads, and students who face one another at tables often strike up conversations during class discussions. You can alleviate some of the problem by having students turn around on their chairs or benches so you can see their faces during recitation.

LEVEL 6: Individual student desks are clustered together in small groups of four (Figure 6-1 B[e] and C[a]).

Students should turn their chairs around for recitation and class discussion.

LEVEL 7: Individual student desks are paired, facing one another, or clustered (Figure 6-1 B(d) and E).

This is a very difficult setting for recitation or class discussion.

METHOD Ff
Learning Centers/Laboratory.

Good learning centers and laboratory exercises sometimes hold student attention through visits from parents and strangers, through accidents and loud noises, or even through the bells that mark the beginning of recess or lunch. Nevertheless, factors of space and location can affect student attention in learning centers.

LEVEL 1: Provide a separate, self-contained and reasonably remote location for each learning center.

When the reading center is in one corner of the classroom, the math center in another, and the science center in still another, scheduling and logistics can be kept separate and simple.

LEVEL 2: Group two or more subject-matter centers together.

When both the reading center and the social studies center use the same tape recorders or the same dictionary, the possibility arises of conflicting demands and confusion. When the teacher wants to use centers but has limited resources, the risk is reasonable if the centers are well designed.

LEVELS 3, 4: (None.)

LEVEL 5: Place learning center(s) in an unmonitored location.

It is possible, but not probable, for a learning center to hold all students' attention with no supervision by the teacher.

You do not have to avoid using remote locations for learning centers if you pretrain students carefully and encourage strict self-monitoring (see Methods Be1, Ja1).

LEVEL 6: (None.)

LEVEL 7: Place learning centers in central classroom traffic areas.

Space limitations sometimes make it necessary to place a learning center next to the classroom sink or the pencil sharpener, where students often congregate. Considerable pretraining and monitoring is necessary to keep the obvious distractions from damaging instruction.

METHOD Fg
Resources and Materials.

Classrooms operate most efficiently when each student has his own resources and materials — text, pencils, and laboratory equipment — readily at hand. The risk of distraction grows as more people share resources and when resources are located farther from each student's learning station.

LEVEL 1: Provide each student with all necessary resources at his learning station.

LEVEL 2: Provide resources close to each student's learning station.

For example, class sets of dictionaries can be kept at nearby tables if student desks are too small to store a dictionary.

LEVEL 3: Provide resources to pairs of students.

Elementary students often share crayon boxes by pairs, and secondary students often share laboratory equipment. Be sure students are trained to share resources quietly and without squabbling.

LEVEL 4: Provide resources to small groups of students.

Small group projects sometimes require sharing materials, and the teacher should train students beforehand to cooperate and coordinate; for example: "Because you all must share the same paint jars, plan your work ahead. At any one time you should be able to use any one of three or four different colors, in case someone else is using your first choice. If you feel you have to argue about whose turn it is to use red to paint the five red balloons, then you are not planning well enough. Do you understand my reasoning?"

LEVEL 5: Provide several sets of resources, each in a different area of the room.

Where there are limited resources, you must do the same kind of training you do at Level 4.

LEVEL 6: Provide several sets of resources at one designated area.

For example, you may have three complete sets of paint jars, all located on the paint table, producing the problem you have at Level 5 with the additional problem of centralized placement. Students must thus move long distances to get paint, and inevitably incur distractions along the way.

LEVEL 7: Provide a single resource at one location in the room.

A classroom usually has only one pencil sharpener and similar equipment, and often only one of certain instructional artifacts such as wall maps and scientific models. The best ways to control their use are by: training students to use these resources during transition periods rather than during instruction; locating the resources away from instructional activities as much as possible (for example, locate pencil sharpeners at the back of the room, or away from the direction students face); and establishing procedures to control the use of central resources (for example, prohibit lining up at the pencil sharpener or the teacher's desk or anywhere else in the room). "Take a number" or "Row 1 always goes first this week" or similar policies can sometimes stop problems of taking turns before they begin.

NOTES

1   Justification for peer tutoring is established by Cohen, Kulik, and Kulik (1982).
2   Some of these disadvantages can be offset by training students. (See Method Ia3; see also an excellent guide to the use and training of peer tutors in Good and Brophy [1978], pp. 311–318).
3   See, for example, Nash (1981) and Evans and Lovell (1978).

REFERENCES

COHEN, P., KULIK, J., & KULIK, C. Educational outcomes of tutoring: A meta-analysis of findings. *American Educational Research Journal*, Summer 1982, *19*, 237–248.

EVANS, G., & LOVELL, B. Design modification in an open-plan school. *Journal of Educational Psychology*, 1979, *71*, 41–49.

GOOD, T., & BROPHY, J. *Educational psychology: A realistic approach* (2nd ed.). New York: Holt, Rinehart and Winston, 1977.

GOOD, T., & BROPHY, J. *Looking in classrooms* (2nd ed.). New York: Harper and Row, 1978.

KULIK, C., & KULIK, J. Effects of ability-grouping on secondary school students: A meta-analysis of evaluation findings. *American Educational Research Journal*, Fall 1982, *19*, 415–428.

NASH, B. The effects of classroom spacial organization on four- and five-year-old children's learning. *British Journal of Educational Psychology*, 1981, *51*, 144–155.

RIST, R. Student social class and teacher expectations: The self-fulfilling prophesy in ghetto education. *Harvard Educational Review*, 1970, *40*, 411–451.

CONTROL OF TIME AND ACTIVITY
(METHODS G, H)

7

I n this chapter we will examine the planning skills of pacing and varying learning activities.

METHOD Ga

Pacing Activities: How effectively does the teacher make a new activity, or the next segment of an activity, available to students at the moment they are ready for it?

LEVEL 1: When one activity or segment is completed, the next one is immediately available.

High attention from one activity sometimes carries over to the next activity if the transition between them is fast and smooth. Fine teachers like to build this momentum, especially when the next activity is a drill or a routine.

Kounin (1970) found that "momentum" (absence of slowdowns) and "smoothness" (absence of jerkiness, false starts, etc.) correlate significantly with task involvement (attention) during recitation in classrooms. Do not make a student sit around waiting; delay breeds inattention and mischief. The ideal way to pace activities is to build into the content and activities an answer to every question or problem that might arise, so that at the exact moment the student is ready to ask the question, the answer is automatically there. For example:

"What should I do with my worksheet when I have completed it?" (The instructions are at the bottom of the worksheet.)

"How should I organize this project?" (The outline is on the board.)

"What can we do after we finish the quiz?" (The question is answered by a little sign placed where the students turn in the quizzes.)

LEVEL 2: When one activity or segment is completed, the next one is ready to be prepared by the students.

A student's enthusiasm for an activity can sometimes be used to mobilize his help in preparing for the next activity; student assistance in transitions helps reduce the risk of inattention during subsequent instruction. For example, if you expect students to finish an activity at noon but instead they finish at 11:30, you can anticipate that possibility by planning something for them to do to prepare for the afternoon's lessons, such as write word lists on the chalkboard, collate exercise sheets, or sort through files.

LEVEL 3: Having completed an activity or segment, one or a few students must wait briefly for the next one.

Many students tolerate brief delays with no problem, but a few become agitated, impatient, or even anxious. There are two antidotes for such situations: one is to train students in principles of classroom life (see Method Ja1); the other is to prevent such situations through careful planning (see Ga1 and Ga2).

LEVEL 4: One or two students are forced to begin a new activity before completing the previous one.

In any group of students, someone is always slower than the others, and his frustration grows as pressure is put on him. Two options reduce the risk of student frustration and increase the possibility of his staying on-task: (1) let him continue, then have another student orient him to the new activity later; or (2) promise him time later on to finish what he is doing.

LEVEL 5: Having completed an activity or segment, one or a few students are forced into long delay until the next one.

Students with time on their hands, and nothing compelling to do, just naturally fool around. So: "You're done already, Ray? Well, marvelous. I don't have something else right now for you to do, I'm sorry to say. You'll just have to wait quietly till everyone else is finished."

LEVEL 6: The entire class is forced to begin a new activity or segment before completing the previous one.

The teacher is in a bind: he knows he is behind schedule and that the present activity is taking longer than expected; at the same time, students expect to finish what they start. What to do? Several options can help avoid the disappointments and inattention of Level 6. The teacher can:

- Discuss her dilemma openly with the class, asking them to think at least overnight and advise her the next day on what they think she should do.
- Begin the new material concurrently with the old activity, keeping time requirements well in hand so as to avoid overload, and training students in skills of keeping two projects going at the same time. Complete the activity on an accelerated but adequate schedule, then replan future activities.
- Complete the old activity on schedule and radically replan future activities for maximum efficiency.
- Assign the new activity, or part of it, as homework (preparatory readings, for example, or a data-gathering experiment).
- Assign the old activity, or part of it, as homework.

LEVEL 7: Having completed an activity or segment, the entire class is forced into long delay until the next one.

Long delays are sometimes unavoidable. If the field trip bus is supposed to return at 2:30, and at 2:53 the class is still waiting at the curb, what is a teacher to do? An effective teacher might hold class right there: "It looks like we'll be here a while longer, and I appreciate your patience. While you wait, you have some choices: you can close your eyes and start planning your paper right now, visualizing what major points you will make; or you can talk with one other person about the test coming up Thursday; or you can talk to your teammates about the panel reports next week."

But most classroom delays are not imposed on teachers; they are imposed by teachers on students. Lining up for the chalkboard or the pencil sharpener or the bathroom are delays. A more pernicious delay is waiting for everyone to quiet down before starting, which actually trains students for the next talking time when the teacher will again delay the lesson by waiting for everyone to be quiet. Most delays in school are unnecessary, and can be eliminated through effective low profile classroom controls.

EXERCISE 1 PACING ACTIVITIES (30–35 minutes)

Prepare a 4-minute lesson in this format: first minute, lecture; second minute, seatwork; third minute, pacing; fourth minute, lecture. During the third minute, you should plan to pace the students who will finish their seatwork early or late. Also, anticipate that some students may not be able to begin their seatwork exactly on time after your first lecture. Use only low profile pacing techniques—no waiting. Also make five "Pacing" Form G slips, each on an 8½" × 11" sheet of paper.

1   Join a group of four to six persons.
2   At your turn to be teacher, appoint a timekeeper in your group to mark 4 minutes.
3   Teach your lesson as directed above.

"PACING" FORM G

Name of "teacher" _____ Date: _____
Name of "student" _____
Activities: (list each in 1–3 words) Note: Put * next to any noncontent activity. Put start/end time (in seconds) for any wait.

During your lesson, each student will briefly list on Form G each activity he performs during your lesson. Any time a student waits for something to do, he writes "wait" on the slip and records the start and end of the wait time (in seconds); any time he is given a noncontent activity, he marks it with an asterisk.

4   After your lesson, collect your Form G slips. Immediately shift the teacher role to the next person.
5   Repeat steps 2 through 4 until all have been teacher.

Conclusion   If you are completely successful, all your Form G slips will begin and end with "Lecture notes" but will be different in between; furthermore, there will be no asterisks or "wait" entries. Hand in all Form G slips to your instructor. Repeat the exercise if desired.

EXERCISE 2 PACING ACTIVITIES (60 minutes) (Optional)

Repeat Exercise 1, but double the "class size."

METHOD Gb

Transitions: How quickly does the teacher make transitions within and between lesson activities?

Transitions are noninstructional times before or between lessons during which no learning takes place. The best transitions are fast, smooth, automatic, and routine. Effective teachers are frequently able to shift class activities in one to ten seconds. You can do so if you use these guidelines:

1   Be ready. Stack and sort materials for rapid distribution, write or chart explanations for easy presentation, and know exactly what to say when you begin the new activity or give instructions for it.
2   Be clear. Tell students exactly what will happen, what to do, what you expect, what the product is to be, and the significance or importance or reason for the new activity.
3   Be sensible. If you scold students for being noisy during transitions, you're wasting your breath and their patience.

LEVEL 1: Transitions are fast, automatic, and initiated by students when needed.

Think of a transition as procedures for beginning a lesson. There are essentially two styles for beginning a lesson. If you prepare to begin a lesson by reading instructions or giving directions or outlining upcoming activities or calling students to order or passing out papers or opening textbooks or announcing rules and procedures of the lesson, you are actually extending the transition, and are using a high profile technique. If you begin immediately with the content by posing questions or making statements or starting demonstrations or announcing goals, you are using a low profile technique. The low profile technique is fast, the high profile, slow.

Compare the two styles in these examples of a typing class in which several students are not ready to begin.

High Profile: "All right, class, we're ready to begin now. (Pause) Sue, Gail, and Martha, we're ready to begin now. (Pause) When we are first learning the keyboard, we unconsciously want to look at our fingers. It's perfectly natural for you to want to look at your fingers while you're typing—we all do, but...."

Low Profile: "When we are first learning the typewriter keyboard [Sue, Gail, and Martha are distracting across the room, and the teacher moves slowly toward them], we unconsciously want to look at our fingers." [The teacher raises her voice very slightly and points to individual students.] "Mike wants to do this, Amy does, Sue, Jim, Martha, Sarah—it's perfectly natural for you to want to look at your fingers while you're typing—we all do, but...."

The two introductions take the same amount of time (12 to 15 seconds) to reach the line "it's perfectly natural" if the high profile teacher's pauses are brief; however, if she has to wait for three seconds at each pause, the high profile method takes longer. In addition, it incurs three other obstructions to the lesson:

1   The teacher has subtly labeled Sue, Gail, and Amy "distractors." They may resent the label, and thus consciously or unconsciously resist the lesson, or they may welcome the special nonlesson attention, smile at their classmates, and plan for their next distraction.

2   The entire class is alert to the fact that someone is not ready to begin, and may begin their own distracting activities.

3   The high profile teacher has directed everyone's attention to the three girls, and now has a double task: to pull the attention of the distracted audience away from the three girls and onto the lesson.

The low profile method avoids all the risks of the conventional high profile style. The distracting students are most likely in full attention, and because Mike, Amy, Jim, and Sarah have also been named, they are less likely to drift into inattention during the rest of the introduction. (See also Method S.)

Students often need training to take the initiative in transitions. A girl who automatically closes her book and takes out her worksheet demonstrates the effects of that training; her teacher is exercising, through the student's actions, low profile control because the teacher expects, permits, or enforces this shift. (For techniques in training students, see Methods Ja1, Jb1, Jc1, and Jc2. For notions on speed, see Ga1 and Ga2.)

LEVEL 2: Transitions are fast, automatic, and initiated by students according to prescribed schedules and routines.

Effective classroom management usually features routines students can rely upon. At Level 1, these routines allow for considerable student discretion: "Whenever you complete an activity, move immediately to an unfinished task or assignment and do it. If you have no unfinished work, then monitor other students to see if someone else needs help, and offer help if asked. After monitoring, see your teacher for instructions."

Routines at Level 2 are defined and prescribed: "When a reading group student taps your shoulder, immediately put away your seatwork neatly, take out your reading book, and move quickly to the reading group."

LEVEL 3: Transitions are directly supervised by student monitors according to prescribed routines.

Even very young students are often able to supervise class activities, including transitions. Supervisory roles may be assigned at the time of the transition (a time waster), at the beginning of the day or the work period (a better procedure), or at the beginning of the month or semester (the best method for saving time).

Training students is important; the teacher cannot assume that supervisors will be efficient (see Method Jb2.)

LEVEL 4: Transitions occur on teacher cue, with teacher directions given at the time of the cue.

This is the most common technique, and one of the least efficient. In a well organized classroom management system, the teacher keeps quiet during fast, smooth transitions; in contrast, the teacher who must always give orders to students demonstrates lack of prior planning and organization and failure to train students.

Teacher direction of transitions is justified when time constraints make it impossible to train students for special transitions, and the teacher will save time by directing the operations.

LEVEL 5: Transitions are incomplete, resulting in false starts.

Occasionally, of course, teachers make mistakes, as we see in the following:

- "Oh, I forgot to tell you, class, to bring your books to your groups. Please get them now."
- "I am not happy with the way these chairs are arranged. Let's put them in circles instead—I just changed my mind."

LEVEL 6: Teacher announces transitions publicly to some students while other students are studying.

The teacher may make a loud announcement to reading group students while other students are busy at seatwork. Because such teacher habits are slow to fade, a conscientious teacher can build self-discipline in voice volume by placing a tape recorder in one corner of the room and leaving it on during an entire lesson. As you listen to your class afterwards, think about every statement you hear yourself make on the tape, and ask yourself:

Did everyone in the room need to hear that?
Did that statement distract any student's attention?

LEVEL 7: Transitions are lengthy or haphazard.

Transitions must be planned as carefully as instruction (see Ga1), and students must be trained to make transitions quickly and smoothly[1] (see Ja1). On rare occasions, long delays are inevitable; for example, the field trip bus cannot leave until all students are aboard. But in general, follow this transition rule: do not waste time waiting. Do not wait for stragglers when you begin a new activity. Expect students to be ready, and if they are not ready when you are, begin without them. If pokey students disturb the class as they continue to shift during your new lesson, treat their distractions as you would any others (see Method X techniques). Counsel chronically tardy students outside instruction.

When a student challenges you aloud ("I'm not ready yet!") you may say (1) "I see," and go on; (2) "Please do your best," and go on; (3) "I see; the class must go on now, but I will help you after class"; (4) "Joe, will you help Freddie find the proper place?" and go on; or (5) "I see," go on with the lesson, but move to Freddie and assist him without interrupting the lesson. Try to anticipate who the slowest student will be and move to that student automatically just before the transition, then help him make the shift quickly and smoothly.

EXERCISE 1
BEGINNING THE SEATWORK LESSON (5 minutes)

Prepare to teach a lesson that begins with seatwork. Your students will be talking among themselves noisily when you begin, and will not pay attention until you induce or force them to. Plan Level 1 techniques for beginning your lesson. To prepare for your own role as student, make four "Beginning" Form GG slips.

1 Join a group of three to five persons.

2 At your turn to be teacher, appoint a timekeeper in your group to mark 30 seconds.

3 Begin your lesson in any Level 1 manner; you have 30 seconds to get everyone's attention. When your timekeeper says "time," ask your class "Are you with it?" and they will chorus back to you "Yes!" Only then are you finished.

4 After you finish, each student will fill out Form GG. If the teacher did not secure a student's attention, the student will leave that line blank.

5 After your lesson, collect your Form GG slips and immediately shift the teacher role to the next person.

6 Repeat Steps 2 through 5 until all have been the teacher.

"BEGINNING" FORM GG

Name of "teacher" _____ Date: _____
Name of "student" _____
What did "teacher" do to focus your attention on the lesson content?_____
_____
What is the category of this technique on the Taxonomy?_____
  (e.g., Scolded me for talking, Yc6)

EXERCISE 2
BEGINNING THE LECTURE LESSON (5 minutes)

Repeat Exercise 1, substituting "lecture" for "seatwork."

EXERCISE 3
BEGINNING THE RECITATION LESSON (5 minutes)

Repeat Exercise 1, substituting "recitation" for "seatwork."

EXERCISE 4
BEGINNING THE CLASS DISCUSSION LESSON (5 minutes)

Repeat Exercise 1, substituting "class discussion" for "seatwork."

Conclusion   In a large group, report the techniques that seemed most effective to begin each type of lesson. Remember that an effective teacher needs a variety of techniques; a single pattern is usually effective only once or twice in any classroom. After the exercise, hand in all Form GG slips to your instructor.

METHOD H: VARYING STUDENT ACTIVITIES

Kounin (1970) provides empirical data to support our belief that variety in instruction is more effective than unrelieved sameness.

METHOD H

Varying Student Activities: How does the teacher provide variety in lesson activities?

There are not as many different types of student activities as we might imagine; the technique is to shift rapidly to a new activity if one does not hold student attention or is not producing learning.

- **LECTURES/REPORTS**   Teacher lectures/reports/reads/presents demonstration to entire class or to smaller group(s).
  Student lectures/reports/reads/presents demonstration to entire class or to smaller group(s).
  Panel of students lectures/reports/presents demonstration to entire class or to smaller group(s).
- **DEBATES**   Teacher debates with student(s).
  Student debates with student(s).
  Panel(s) of students discuss or debate within panel or with class.
- **DISCUSSIONS**   Teacher leads discussion among entire class.
  Student leads discussion among entire class.
  Small groups discuss (various size groups).
  Pairs of students discuss.
  Fishbowl groups discuss.

- **INDEPENDENT STUDY**   Students, individually or in groups, do assigned seat work in the classroom.
  Students, individually or in groups, do assigned research work in the classroom or library.
  Students, individually or in groups, do assigned laboratory work in the laboratory or classroom.
  Students, individually or in groups, do assigned physical activities in designated areas.
  Students, individually or in groups, do independent reading and study anywhere in the classroom.
  Students, individually or in groups, do assigned work in learning centers in the classroom.
- **EVALUATION/PRACTICE**   Teacher conducts recitation with students in class or small group(s).
  Teacher conducts practice with students in class or small group(s).
  Teacher gives written quiz or test to students in class or small group(s).
  Teacher gives oral quiz or test to students in class or small group(s).
  Students practice skills individually or in groups.
  Students perform individually or in groups for audience.
- **FIELD STUDY**   Class or smaller group explores field study outside the school.
  Class or smaller group explores field study within the school.
- **MEDIA**   Class or small group views TV, film, filmstrip, slides, VTR, etc.
  Class or small group hears audio recording, with or without visuals.
  Class or small group does art projects independently.
  Class or small group does art projects in group.
  Class or small group uses gaming or simulation device.
  Individual students work in media carrels or at other media stations.
  Students, individually or in groups, build displays, posters, models, grow plants, etc.

LEVEL 1: Student activity varies according to lesson content possibilities.

The effective teacher tries to get as much out of the lesson as possible, using imaginative, inventive, ingenious teacher planning: "I want them to recognize the different democratic forms of government, so how can I get the point across? Let's see, they can color all the countries in the world according to representational procedures. Maybe a game — 'Starpower' shows the need for controls. And the minority position in a democracy, what happens to it?" Effective planning of activities presumes that the learning objectives are continuously appropriate, properly stated, and sensitively paced (see Methods Ba, Bb, Bc).

LEVEL 2: Student activity is adjusted in response to student attention patterns and student needs.

When a lesson starts to drag, the teacher introduces variety in accordance with student needs, moods, and levels of tolerance. The shift in activity need not be conspicuous ; indeed, shifts can take place within the major ongoing lesson activity. For example, if you have been asking the questions, have the students ask you questions; if you have been writing problems on the board, have the students write on the board; or, if you have been interpreting the story, have them interpret the story. The point is that the students change activity, so they are doing something different from what they had been doing.

Humor can be a useful change of activity, but remember, while humor can be superb for focusing attention, it can also be extremely distracting. Make sure that what your students laugh about during instruction is the *exact content* you are trying to teach.

LEVEL 3: Students may vary their own activity within prescribed content limits.

"When you have finished looking up these words in the dictionary, you may then go to the tape recorder and take the spelling test." The criterion for change is always content-oriented; that is, the student always has a choice between two content-oriented activities, not between a content activity and a noncontent activity.

LEVEL 4: Student activity varies according to a preset pattern or schedule.

This is the way most traditional classrooms are organized, but it has inherent risks: every activity lasts too long for some students and not long enough for others. Consequently, traditional school schedules struggle against human nature. The most effective method of counteracting schedule rigidity is to watch students closely (see H2).

Preset patterns and scheduling are not necessarily wrong in teaching. The teacher is occasionally wise to ignore students' initial adverse reactions to an activity until they have become familiar with it, but when the teacher feels like a captain with a mutinous crew, other methods may be necessary to help orient students (see Methods W1, Pep Talk; V1, Directions; H2, Vary Activity Slightly; O, Active Listening; Td1, Diagnosis).

LEVEL 5: Students may vary their own activity within noncontent limits.

"When you get tired of looking up words in the dictionary, you can do free reading for a while until the tape recorder is free, then you can take your spelling test." In this example, the criterion for changing activities does not directly relate to content, so students have an opportunity to "opt out" of content learning for whimsical reasons. The accompanying risk of inattention is enormous.

LEVEL 6: The same student activity continues indefinitely.

Frequently, the teacher who complains most about poor student attention turns out to be one who primarily assigns all seatwork, day after day, or constantly lectures, day after day. The teacher can maintain a single activity without variation when he is pressed for time and class attention is uniformly high, but ordinarily, do not assume an activity will forever hold students spellbound; students even tire of games after a while.

LEVEL 7: Student activities vary without purpose or continuity, or stop altogether.

Occasionally a teacher changes activities without regard for the content or the students; when asked why, the teacher responds, in effect: "Well, it's good to change now and then, to keep things moving, to keep them on their toes." Without a rationale, however, change confuses students. Change for the sake of change normally makes no sense in the classroom.

Frenetic change is occasionally justified—a carefully planned kaleide-scopic effect can be intriguing and instructive. Occasionally, even cessation of all in-structional activity is justified. When Fundamental Principle No. 3, Sequence, has been carried to its ultimate, the teacher may be wise to stop everything and hold a class meeting in the manner proposed by Dreikurs, Glasser, Gordon, and others (see chapter 1).

EXERCISE 1
SHIFTING-ACTIVITIES DRILL (15–30 minutes)

Prepare a lesson and four copies of Form H for this exercise. The purpose of the exercise, a drill, is to encourage you to test and improve the skills you have been practicing in previous exercises. This is the time to strive for high efficiency and low profile, in a drill format.

1   Form a group of four or five persons. Arrange your chairs in a traditional classroom manner (facing front).
2   Assume the role of teacher and teach a 3-minute lesson with academic content. Appoint a student to also be your timekeeper.
3   During your 3-minute lesson, all students will be passive, sitting quietly and staring straight ahead until you activate them. They will respond appropriately to activation but will quickly revert to staring straight ahead as soon as they can.
4   The purpose of your lesson is twofold: first, teach them content; second, keep them jumping! Shift activity as many times as you possibly can in 3 minutes without distracting their attention from content in any way.
5   At the end of your lesson, give students 2 minutes to fill out Form H. They should hold these until the exercise is over.
6   Move quickly to the next teacher, then the next, until all have taught.

SHIFT ACTIVITY: FORM H

"Teacher": _____ "Student": _____ Date:_____

Directions: When the "Teacher" starts the lesson, write the activity in the first blank. Then note each succeeding activity in the blanks to follow. Note whether the "shift" was (L) low profile or (H) high (circle one).

L/H_____   L/H_____   L/H_____   L/H_____
L/H_____   L/H_____   L/H_____   L/H_____
L/H_____   L/H_____   L/H_____   L/H_____

Conclusion   Could you have done this exercise before you came to this training course? If you could not, and if you were able to change activities at least twice during the three minutes, you have learned well; keep working. If you already had the shift-activity skills before this session, you should have sharpened your skills and improved your flexibility through this intensive practice. You also should have been able to shift activity smoothly and with low profile at least six times. Remember, this exercise was just a drill. No one is asking you to shift at this rate in a normal class day. But everyone — your instructor, your students, and their parents — is asking you to be able to shift when shift is needed, and you should now be able to do it. After the exercise, hand in all Report Form H slips to your instructor.

NOTES

1   Brophy and Evertson (1976) report this observation from the two-year Texas Teacher Effectiveness Project:

> ...transitional periods in less well organized classrooms tended to be chaotic, with children wandering around, bumping into one another, confused, needing to ask the teacher what to do, etc. The teacher often was harried during these times, shouting out orders and attempting to do 10 or 15 things at the same time. (p. 58)

REFERENCES

BROPHY, J., & EVERTSON, C. *Learning from teaching: A developmental perspective.* Boston: Allyn and Bacon, 1976.

KOUNIN, J. *Discipline and group management in classrooms.* New York: Holt, Rinehart and Winston, 1970.

CONTROL OF STUDENT
PARTICIPATION (METHOD I)

8

To keep idle hands from mischief, some teachers are notorious for assigning busywork. Students despise busywork, but they like to be active.

METHOD Ia

Inducing Student Activity: How does the teacher induce students to participate actively in class?

LEVEL 1: The teacher selects and organizes instructional activities that induce student participation.

The probabilities of student participation vary according to the type of activity. Activities that require high student participation are worksheets, buzz groups, small group discussions, gaming simulation, group projects, group movement, group choral music or speaking, group problem solving, and competitive problem solving.

Activities that require only moderate or erratic student participation include panel discussions, chalkboard problems, all-class discussions, and notetaking. Low student participation activities include lectures, demonstrations, one-at-a-time drills, readings, recitations, and games such as spelling bees.

The teacher who wants to increase student participation should try to choose activities that automatically elicit high activity.

LEVEL 2: The teacher adapts activities to make them more active.

Ingenious teachers can make passive learning situations come alive for their students. How do they do it? They allow or demand that all students take some overt action at least once every minute. Countless techniques are available.

INTERACTIVE LECTURES

At all grade levels and in all kinds of schools and classrooms, the effective teacher avoids pure "teacher talk" lectures in favor of lectures that invite continuous audience participation. Participation does not function as an interruption when teachers use these techniques:

Question-Answer   The Question-Answer technique is as old as teaching; you ask a question and wait for a student to raise his hand: "The bee flies toward the flower, attracted by what, do you think? Tom? Sure, its bright colors, and what else? Jetta? Smell, yes, aroma, and now to what part of the blossom does the bee go? Jill? And why do you think that? Very logical, Jill. Actually, the bee heads for ... ." The technique is simple; as you talk or lecture to your students, check periodically to see whether they are understanding the message.

- Ask what they think comes next.
- Ask the implications, possible results, or possible conclusions of a certain fact or opinion.

■ Ask about what the teacher has just said.

The fine teacher does this very quickly, with little or no break in the pace of the talk or lecture.

Choral Response   The teacher gives a cue, and all students respond in chorus; for example:

> **TEACHER:**   The suspended solid formed by the reaction is called [hand signal—perhaps a downbeat motion]...?
> **STUDENTS:**   (chorus) Precipitate.
> **TEACHER:**   And when you put your test tube in the centrifuge...

Choral responses should not be used as a diagnostic tool, but rather as an attention focuser. For example, the teacher who wants to focus attention on a correct answer may first request the chorus, then echo with the correct answer:

> **TEACHER:**   And what is the name of this appendage of the lobster or crab? Everyone?
> **STUDENTS:**   (Chorus, mixed answers) Claw/Pincer/Chela/Pincher.
> **TEACHER:**   Chela. Chela is correct. And what is the name...?

Or the teacher can use choral responses to locate students who are ready to say something:

> **TEACHER:**   Think for a moment: why might Jody not want the fawn to come home with him that night? What is your answer? Everbody?
> **STUDENTS:**   (Extended cacophony of voices. Teacher looks for signs of response from heretofore nonparticipating students. Spotting one, he calls on her with a nod and hand signal.)
> **TEACHER:**   Cassandra?
> **STUDENT:**   Well, maybe because he was afraid his father might...

Students can be easily trained to respond in chorus; simply tell them what you want them to do and why. For example: "Sometimes when you know the answer and you want to say it but can't because it's somebody else's turn, that gets frustrating, doesn't it? [Look around, pause for "Yes" chorus, which will come almost automatically.] So I would like you to watch for this signal [demonstrate] because when I do or say that signal, that means you can answer right out without raising your hand, do you understand? [Signal for "Yes" chorus.] Again? [Signal for "Yes" chorus.] Sure. I like it already."

Verbal Cloze Item   This simple but powerful technique is the "choral response" without a signal. To use this technique, leave gaps or pauses in your lecture, and let your students fill them in spontaneously. Students can do this almost without training; for example: "When you pay for your hard candy and give the man a dime which is worth... [Ss: "Ten cents."] and he gives you a nickel back, worth... [Ss: "Five cents."], that makes your candy actually cost..."

Group Reflecting   This is a technique of embedding a message check right into the lecture. For example:

"Now, you may be saying to yourself..."

"I can hear you saying right now..."

"And you're thinking to yourself that..."

What are you, the lecturer, doing? Reflecting out loud your students' possible unspoken thoughts. Here is a math teacher using the technique: "When we bring down the next number, what do we do next? [No response from any student.] Well, you might be thinking, 'Gee, I don't know—this is different from what we've learned before,' right? But that's OK; watch what to do with that number..."

The power of group reflecting is fourfold (see Method O):

1   It shows the student that you know what he is thinking, or might be thinking.

2   It helps him clarify his thinking by making him check to see if your message check is correct.

3   It reassures and comforts the student when he is thinking, "I can't do this" or "I'm confused" or "I don't like this" or something otherwise disturbing. It tells the students such thoughts are normal, and nothing to worry about or be ashamed of; it helps relieve pressure and tension.

4   It gives the student an opportunity to be active; when you use group reflecting, you are actually inviting your students to respond overtly. Notice how audiences react when skillful public speakers use this technique.

Spot Seatwork   Seatwork, the most common instructional mode in American schools, is typically assigned for long periods of time, but spot seatwork can also activate students for three to five seconds during lectures or teacher-talk time. For example, in a French class:

TEACHER: The cedilla under the *c* in French [point to chalkboard] makes it sound like *s*. On your paper, write three c's with a cedilla under each. [Pause.] Now look at this word [point to chalkboard] and pronounce it properly. [Signal.]

STUDENTS: Garçon.

TEACHER: Garçon. And the *r* in French....

Or in a history class:

TEACHER: So William met Harold on a hilly battlefield at Hastings in 1066—draw a rolling set of hills like this on your note page [hand motion]—and their armies fought up and down the rolling Southern English countryside, and that was the end of brave Harold. Here's a photo of the battlefield; see the rolling hills at Hastings?

Or with an elementary writing group:

TEACHER: ...and it's important that you try to keep your writing line level rather than letting it slant. Hold your pencil up and level like this.

[Pause.] Now slant your pencil. [Pause.] Should your writing line slant like this? [Choral response: "No."] No; instead you should try to keep it... [Choral response: "Level."] level like this.

INTERACTIVE DEMONSTRATIONS

Use question-answer judiciously: "So we first cut up all the ingredients beforehand. What do you think we do next?... You're right, we could do that, but there's something else we should do first, and that is..."

Ask for a show of hands regarding simple opinions, and insist that all students, including passive listeners, raise their hands for one of the options ("Yes," "no," "maybe," or "I haven't raised my hand yet!").

ACTIVE RECITATIONS/DRILLS/READINGS/GAMES

The problem with most classroom recitations, drills, readings, and even learning games is that they are so boring! Students are forced to sit around watching other students learn! Effective teachers figure out ways to get every student active most of the time. For example:

Drills   Have the entire class drill briefly with you in chorus, then each student turns to a neighbor or to small groups of three or four to drill; then they return to large group where you spot-check those who are not yet comfortable with the drill, then divide class into "supervisory panels" of small groups who are responsible for drilling—judging, correcting, and supervising practice—their own members, one by one. Monitor your groups to ensure they are judging correctly.

Recitations   A powerful technique for activating students in recitation is asking them to respond to each other's answers or comments. For example:

> **TEACHER:**   Will the crystals form if we heat this solution? Think about that. Kim?
> **STUDENT 1:**   No, I don't think so.
> **TEACHER:**   Jeri, do you agree?
> **STUDENT 2:**   Yep.
> **TEACHER:**   Class, do you agree?
> **CLASS:**   (Choral) Yes.
> **TEACHER:**   Why do you think...?

Or:

> **TEACHER:**   Glena, Harry said a while ago that... You apparently think he misread the text.
> **STUDENT:**   Well....

Kounin (1970) found this technique used by more effective teachers; Good and Brophy (1978, p. 370) agree. I also found the technique used by some of the most dynamic teachers I observed in Japan (see Epilogue).

Readings   Have students read to their own small groups or read all together, in chorus, in the large class, as the teacher moves about the room, monitoring each student in turn, making notes for later individualized instruction during seatwork; or, have several students read aloud together in chorus, from two to ten at a time, as the teacher monitors and the rest of the class listens.

Learning Games   Redesign rules so there is something for everyone to do every minute of the game.

ACTIVE GROUP DISCUSSIONS

Pre-discussion Work   The major reason most class discussions fall flat is that students have not prepared for discussion. You can help your students prepare several ways, to help them get as much as possible from the discussion. For example: "In a few moments, I will ask you to discuss why Alice didn't want to go tell her friend about Billy. Right now, take a minute to write down six words that describe Alice's personality and character. [One minute pause] OK, now think to yourself: Do I have some good reasons for selecting each word? Take two minutes to look in the story for proof, some real evidence to back up your words. Write down page numbers next to each of your words."

Or: "When we form the panel, you will ask one of the panelists a question about his character from the story. Write now, in quick notes, a question you could ask." By the time the class discussion begins, these students are going to be hard to hold back. Pre-discussion work starts the brain working before discussion begins.

Start Debate   Some teachers are able to induce students to debate and learn from one another. While you need group discussion control skills (Method S) to maintain and focus debates, you can use these skills to start debates:

> **TEACHER:**   Jeff, how would you answer that question?
> **Jeff:**   Well, I think...
> **TEACHER:**   Anna, you don't look convinced.
> **Anna:**   Sure, because...?
> **TEACHER:**   Jeff, how would you reply to Anna's point? Go ahead, persuade her.
> **Jeff:**   See, what you're not getting is...

Or perhaps:

> **TEACHER:**   Melva, what do you say about that?
> **Melva:**   It couldn't have happened that way because...
> **TEACHER:**   Melva, did you hear Lonnie say a few minutes ago that...? How do you feel about that?

Start Buzz Groups   Buzz groups are informal temporary groups of two to six people that meet for a very short time—15 seconds to 5 minutes—to perform a specific task. Use a bell to signal the end of buzz groups. You can use them for content: "I've just been telling you about rational numbers. Now I want you to turn to your neighbor and decide between the two of you—or three of you if necessary — whether the number 39 is a rational number or not — and why. You have 30 seconds."

And buzz groups also have a place in problem solving: "We are a real problem for the 3rd graders now, do you see? When we are noisy in the hall, we disturb other classes. I want you to think hard about this problem. When I give you the signal, you will form buzz groups — with four persons in each group. In your buzz group, I want you to think of five things we can do to solve the hall problem. You will have two minutes to talk. OK, form your groups and begin."

You must monitor buzz groups constantly and carefully to make sure they are on-task.

LEVEL 3: The teacher organizes students for peer tutoring.

Call upon a helper to assist a student who does not understand a lesson and is not attending to it. Here are three guidelines.

1   Choose your helpers carefully — be selective — but use many different helpers on different occasions, not just one or two.
2   Give the helpers explicit instructions on what to do and for how long; do not be vague; for example, "Ellie, please help Jack understand the assignment for tomorrow in the red workbook. Don't disturb anyone else, and when you're done, go back to your seat. Thanks for your help."

   General instructions can be made standard policy for the classroom, so you don't have to repeat them in every case.
3   Follow up on your helpers — do not assume they did what they were supposed to do; for example, "Jack, did Ellie explain the assignment to you? Good. Tell me what you're supposed to do."

Any teacher who has used this technique will recognize the possible distractions. Some students emotionally rebel against being taught by their peers; arguments sometimes erupt over who is right, the tutor or tutee; and sometimes both tutor and tutee waste more time than they spend learning. Pretraining can help make peer tutoring productive (see Methods Ja1, E3).

LEVEL 4: The teacher assigns extra content-oriented work activities to keep students busy.

Whether or not students like the content area, they often perceive extra work as busywork. They may do the work, but their hearts and minds will not be in it. And when extra tasks are assigned to misbehaving students, the tasks seem to be punishment. Punishing a student with content is foolish.

The moral: if the student will not benefit from the extra work, don't assign it just to keep him busy — try something else.

LEVEL 5: The teacher assigns extra noncontent work activities to keep students busy.

After years of teaching, I am still not sure why this technique, while even more distractive than Level 4, is more popular with my students than assigning them extra content work. Could it be that the content I teach is so dull that anything, even clerical busywork, is a blessed relief from learning?

LEVEL 6: The teacher allows any activity students wish to pursue.

Student attention to lesson content during free reading or free study periods must be carefully prepared and administered (see Method J).

LEVEL 7: The teacher assigns noncontent activities during instructional class time.

Teachers sometimes use activities such as "movie day" or "Fun Friday" or "Free Game Day" as rewards: "The kids deserve a day off because they've been working so hard." Students who are really involved with content (see Method Bc1) can become impatient with "fun day" activities, and their parents may feel even more impatient. Effective teachers try to build the fun and excitement right into their lessons, instead of wasting instructional time.

EXERCISE 1
DRILL ON QUESTION-ANSWER SKILLS (10–15 minutes)

Prepare for this exercise ahead of time. When it is your turn to teach the full class, deliver a 15-second lecture (read from any portion of this text, perhaps, or choose another topic); at some time during your lecture, use question-answer to activate at least one student in your class. Your class will signal the end of your 15 seconds with brief applause. The next teacher will immediately begin until stopped by applause. Continue until all have practiced.

EXERCISE 2
DRILL ON CHORAL RESPONSE SKILLS (10–15 minutes)

Use Exercise 1 procedures to practice the choral response technique. All teachers should use the same downbeat signal for choral response (your instructor will demonstrate). Use the technique at least twice.

EXERCISE 3
DRILL ON VERBAL CLOZE SKILLS (10–15 minutes)

Use Exercise 1 procedures to demonstrate verbal cloze at least twice.

EXERCISE 4
DRILL ON GROUP REFLECTING SKILLS (10–15 minutes)

Use Exercise 1 procedures to demonstrate one group reflecting technique.

EXERCISE 5
DRILL ON SPOT SEATWORK SKILLS (10–15 minutes)

Use Exercise 1 procedures to demonstrate at least one spot seatwork technique.

EXERCISE 6
INTERACTIVE LECTURES (10–20 minutes)

Prepare for this exercise beforehand. In this exercise, you will teach a 3-minute minilesson to a lethargic class, using low profile interactive lecture techniques to activate your students. Prepare four copies of Interactive Lectures: Form I beforehand.

1 Form a small group of four or five persons and arrange chairs in a traditional classroom pattern.

2 Assume the role of teacher and teach a 3-minute lesson on a preplanned topic to your students. (Have one student act as your timekeeper as well.) Your students should have Form I ready.

3 During your 3-minute lecture, all students will be passive, sitting and staring at their desks except as you activate them. Use at least one example of each of the activating techniques listed on Form I. Your students will respond appropriately to each "activation," but will then quickly revert to passivity; therefore, you must continually make efforts to activate them, and you must use a variety of techniques.

4 As you lecture, your students will mark Form I, giving you a tally mark for each technique you use. For example, if you say, "Now you might be thinking," each student will score one checkmark for Group Reflect.

5 At the end of your 3-minute lecture, each student should hold your Form I until the Conclusion. Do not discuss your teaching performance now; give others their chance to teach by proceeding immediately to the next teacher and repeat steps 2 through 5 of this exercise.

INTERACTIVE LECTURES: FORM I

Name of "teacher": _____ Name of "student": _____ Date: _____
Write a Check Mark ✔ for each example of a technique used by the "teacher."
_____ Question-Answer   _____ Group Reflect
_____ Choral Response   _____ Spot-Seatwork
_____ Verbal Cloze
Return this form to instructor.

Conclusion After all have taught, each group member should give Form I to the proper persons. Discuss and make suggestions. Before leaving, hand in all Form I slips to your instructor.

EXERCISE 7
ACTIVATING GROUP DISCUSSIONS (15–20 minutes)

Prepare ahead for this exercise. Plan a 3-minute lesson which contains pre-discussion work, all-class discussion (debate), and buzz groups, in that order. Also prepare four copies of Activate Discussion: Form II.

1 Form a group of four or five persons, different from the group in Exercise 6. Arrange your chairs as in Exercise 6.

2 Assume the role of teacher and teach a 3-minute minilesson, perhaps in the same topic area you chose for Exercise 6. (Have one student act as time-keeper as well.) Your students should have the Activate Discussion: Form II ready for use.

3 During your 3-minute lesson, follow the format prescribed above. Finish your buzz groups before your time is up.

4 As your lesson goes on, your students will mark Form II.

5 At the end of your 3-minute lesson, students should hold all forms and move on immediately to the next teacher so that all get a chance to teach.

ACTIVATE DISCUSSION: FORM II

Name of "teacher": _____ Name of "student": _____ Date: _____
Pre-discussion: How effectively did it focus your attention? Much/Some/Little.
Debate: What did the teacher say to stimulate debate during all-class
discussion?_____
Buzz groups: Were they quickly formed? Yes/No.
　　　　　　　Did they finish on time? Yes/No.
　　　　　　　Were they relevant to lesson content? Yes/No.
Return this form to Instructor at end of class.

Conclusion Return Form II, discuss, and make suggestions; before leaving, hand in all forms to your instructor.

METHOD Ib
Inviting Passive Students: How does the teacher encourage passive students to participate actively in class?

A passive student says little or nothing in class, rarely if ever volunteers or initiates interaction with the teacher, and is often described by teachers in this manner:

"A quiet kid, you know, doesn't say much."

"Prefers to be left alone, doesn't mix much with the other kids."

"Pretty good, never causes me any trouble."

If left alone, the passive student shows visual cues of Unknown Attention (see Figure 2-2, chapter 2). Some teachers tend to leave this student alone:

"The kid is doing OK—that's just her nature, you know, just quiet."

"You never want to call on a kid like that—you might embarrass him."

The teacher should resist this tendency, and get the passive student to respond, because the professional teacher is responsible for keeping all students in attention, not in unknown attention. There are many low profile techniques for bringing a passive listener into attention during the lesson, techniques to which almost no student can object because few will be aware the techniques are being used.

LEVEL 1: The teacher uses name-dropping (Method U), general eye contact (Method L), and open body position to establish a receptive climate for passive students.

Here is a teacher using a passive student's name (Becky): "Now Sue, I don't think Becky would agree to that—nor would Sam or Freda. If you said that to Becky, wouldn't you make her mad? Or Sam? Or Freda? Or would you?" In the process of being recognized and included in the lesson at no risk to her, Becky is also being shown subtly how she can appropriately chime in and respond when she is ready—and indeed the teacher is giving Becky strong signals that her opinion will be welcome when it comes. Few passive students can continually resist the lure of invitations like these.

The teacher also creates a receptive climate using general eye contact with all students during the lesson (see Method L). Be sure the student knows you have been talking to him as well as to other students near him.

"Open body position" means your face and the front of your body face the student. Smile or nod to the student occasionally when someone else is talking—in response to and in the context of what the second student is actually saying.

Monitor each passive student carefully but unobtrusively for any nonverbal sign of interest or response to any aspect of the lesson: a shake of the head, a spoken "yes" or "no," or a puzzled look are important overt responses that you can acknowledge informally, with a nod or by quietly murmuring the student's name as you exchange glances. None of these techniques is forcing; they are simply friendly, open, encouraging, and reassuring.

LEVEL 2: The teacher uses direct address (Method U) to several students concerning content without pausing for response.

You can personalize an all-group activity, such as choral responses, by immediately following the activity with quick questions to individual students, in turn, down a row, or across aisles—asking three or more students by name, "Sylvia, do you agree with the answer 'quadrilateral'? Alan? Becky? Pete?" Make it fast, do not wait for answers, and move quickly on. The passive student, as one person in a row or aisle, is forced to respond privately, and can do so with virtually no public notice.

LEVEL 3: The teacher gives the student a special content-oriented task during the lesson.

For example, you can ask a student to write a problem on the board; read a brief passage aloud; help adjust or hold a display; or explain a picture or graph or chart. Excellent teachers seem to have an endless supply of activities for students, and are able to assign them smoothly with no obvious break in the lesson and without causing a reaction from their students, whether elation or chagrin. (Pass the privileges around.)

When the teacher uses this technique too often with one or a few students, the effect is no longer low profile because other students will complain that they are never chosen.

LEVEL 4: (None.)

LEVEL 5: The teacher uses direct address (Method U) and waits for a response.

This is the most common technique for rousing passive students, despite the fact that it often embarrasses them and diverts others' attentions from the lesson to the student's embarrassment. A direct question is appropriate for almost any student in attention but should rarely be used with students in inattention or unknown attention.

It should now be clear that the traditional practice of throwing out questions randomly to students — perhaps to keep them on their toes — is decidedly risky, even though it is stoutly defended by many teachers.

LEVEL 6: The teacher publicly signals a passive student's nonparticipation.

"We haven't heard from Becky yet today" or "My, you're quiet today, Becky — are you feeling all right?" Teachers often use this high profile technique to set an example for the rest of the class; in such cases, the technique usually diverts other students' attention away from the lesson topic to the passive student, then to their own uneasiness about whether the teacher will call on them next.

The technique can sometimes be an effective vehicle for goodwill, however; the teacher might use it to recognize and reward a normally active student, as if to say, "Hey, you're important here, and I haven't forgotten you even though I have not called on you earlier."

LEVEL 7: The teacher publicly rebukes the passive student for nonparticipation.

This technique is unpleasant to hear, and rarely justified: "Now, it's time you woke up, Benny, and started taking part in this class. We do not teach auditors here."

EXERCISE 1
INVITE PASSIVE STUDENTS (15–20 minutes)

Use the same procedures as Section Ia, Exercise 6, except that you will substitute Interactive Lectures: Form II. Use only Level 1 and Level 2 techniques in this exercise. The teacher should strive to have every student check every blank on Form II.

Although remaining passive throughout the exercise, each student should at one point show a sign of interest for the teacher to acknowledge with a nod, smile, wink, or other response.

INTERACTIVE LECTURES: FORM II

Name of "Teacher": _____ Name of "Student": _____ Date: _____

Write a check mark (✔) for each example of a technique used by the "teacher" with *you* during this exercise, e.g., ✔✔✔ Name Drop

_____ Name Drop   _____ Eye Contact
_____ Direct Address   _____ Open Body Position
_____ Notices your nonverbal sign of interest

Return this form to Instructor at end of class.

REFERENCES

GOOD, T., & BROPHY, J. *Looking in classrooms.* New York: Harper and Row, 1978.

KOUNIN, J. *Discipline and group management in classrooms.* New York: Holt, Rinehart and Winston, 1970.

CONTROL THROUGH MANAGEMENT STRATEGIES (METHOD J)

9

Educators today debate whether classroom control should be primarily external or whether students should be expected to exercise self-control; whether the teacher should plan the course of study alone or whether students should be involved in some way; whether the teacher should directly supervise every learning activity or whether students should be expected to monitor their own learning.

METHOD Ja
Student Self-Control: How does the teacher train students for self-control in the classroom?

Although teachers differ as to their definitions of student self-control, two views predominate. One is that students must take the initiative for self-control; the other is that the teacher establishes the ground rules. Those who subscribe to the first viewpoint feel that student self-control means the student takes complete responsibility for his own learning, follows through on that responsibility, and, in effect, teaches himself. Terms such as "self-reliant," "self-starting," and "self-motivated" label this type of student behavior.

Other teachers feel that student self-control means the student works cooperatively and effectively within the classroom system established by the teacher. Terms like "responsible," "trustworthy," "reliable," "dependable," or even "honorable" label the student who can be counted on to follow the teacher's directions explicitly.

Either definition of self-control is acceptable if the teacher trains students appropriately. Training can take place before content instruction begins (we will use the term "pretraining") or during instruction. Pretraining is the lowest profile form of training.

LEVEL 1: The teacher pretrains students to behave appropriately during instruction according to certain general principles.[1]

The goal of pretraining is to enable students to behave appropriately without prompting or cues. Two approaches to pretraining are joint planning and management training. When he uses joint planning (described in Method Jc1), the teacher makes students part of the lesson planning team. When he uses management training, the teacher might set forth basic principles, then help students understand and apply them to various types of problem situations. For example, basic principles might be stated like this:

- Do not do anything that might distract another student's attention from lesson content.
- Do not do anything that distracts your own attention from lesson content.
- Do not do anything that interferes with your teacher's instruction.

Having announced these principles, the teacher might say: "Let's assume for a moment that your pencil breaks during seatwork. What all could you do to solve your problem and still observe the general principles? Anyone?" or "If your pencil broke during a test, what all could you do and still observe the general principles? Anyone?"

Because the purpose of pretraining is to help students behave appropriately without teacher prompting, students should practice the skills in simulated settings and situations so they know exactly how the skills *feel*.

LEVEL 2: The teacher assumes a set of rules, guidelines, and procedures, and applies them consistently without special announcements.

Amazingly, some teachers never post lists of rules, rarely talk about rules, and never threaten students with rules or with consequences, yet from the first day of school, they convey a sense of purpose, direction, and order to their students, who behave accordingly. How do they do it? Most often, the answer lies in consistent and highly skilled use of low profile techniques, any of which a teacher can develop with concentration and effort.

Compare the following two "First Day of School" speeches:

Teacher A: "All right, if I can have your attention now, please, I'd like to welcome you to Algebra I. Now there are a few things you will need to remember in this class. First you must bring your notebook to class every day, got that? *Every* day!"

Teacher B: "Hello everybody, welcome to Algebra I. This class will begin with some of the same math you have learned before. Look at this equation, $X - 4 = 7$. Doesn't that equation look familiar? Write it down in your notebook, which we will use in this class every day...."

Popular opinion notwithstanding, most students need no more than Teacher B's announcement to understand what the teacher expects. How does Teacher B get her kids to bring their notebooks? She simply expects them to, and they probably will (see Method A). When Teacher A says, "Oh no they won't! I know kids!" he is using the same laws of expectation to decrease the probability that his students will bring their notebooks.

But Teacher B is not naive; she knows students fail to hear messages sometimes, and she knows they sometimes fail to understand what they hear—she expects that. So she uses a follow-up technique to repeat and reinforce her original message.

Teacher B: "Isn't that a fancy way to do it? Now copy this example in your Algebra notebook. No notebook? Here are slips of paper you can use now and paste into your Algebra notebook tonight when you buy it. As you write, remind yourself of the difference between $3(4 + 1) + 5$ and $3(4 + 1 + 5)$...."

Notice that Teacher B never leaves her lesson to lecture on housekeeping; every administrative detail supports the subject matter. The teacher who begins teaching immediately, taking care of administrative details through careful planning and organization, conveys a strong message of expectation to students ("I do not waste time; our time together is too valuable to waste"), and her students get the message. (See Method V1, Directions.)

LEVEL 3: The teacher pretrains students in routines and standard classroom behaviors.

The teacher anticipates certain occasions when students should behave in special ways, then expects the exact student behavior at the proper time, such as:

- How to behave in small groups.
- How to get ready to begin a lesson.
- How to begin a new activity.
- How to tutor other students.
- How to be tutored by other students.
- How to keep notebook in order.
- How to keep desk, locker, file, shelf in order.
- How to ask questions during recitation or lecture.
- How to ask questions during seatwork or independent study.
- How to care for laboratory equipment.
- How to check spelling in the dictionary.
- How to do homework at home.
- How to get help from other students (nontutorial situations).
- How to move in and out of reading groups.
- How to line up for recess, bathroom, lunch, gym, dismissal, etc.

Writers on classroom management frequently recommend routines and assigned tasks, for good reason: some important classroom tasks do not require much thought, so we make them automatic. Most students feel comfortable with routines, because they offer predictability, security, and a reassuring sense of order. Assigned tasks also help students feel part of the classroom enterprise, whether or not they like their tasks.

There are at least two risks in pretraining techniques. One is the potential for interruption. Any system seems to invite its own destruction, and there will be inevitable squabbling over who is supposed to do what according to the assignment sheet. Another risk in cued routines is that teachers sometimes forget to give the cues. To be able to depend on students' doing the proper thing without being reminded, the teacher should train students at Level 1.[2]

LEVEL 4: The teacher posts rules in the classroom.

So ingrained is the practice of posting classroom rules that many school districts require it, even though researchers are unable to find evidence that posted rules help establish or maintain classroom control. Merely displaying rules, and even elaborate styles of presenting, reviewing, and calling attention to those written rules, seems to have little observable effect on student behavior (Madsen, Becker, and Thomas, 1968).

The technique may be warranted for students who simply cannot remember a rule, but the teacher should first consider whether the students perhaps have too many rules to remember, and whether all of them are necessary, and whether the students actually understand the forgotten rule.

LEVEL 5: The teacher reminds target students privately, during the lesson, of proper behavior.

When reminding privately, state the rule, don't give a reprimand: "This is a place and time for studying English, remember?" In contrast, a reprimand labels the misbehavior: "Quit fooling around and start studying."

Since a reminder of the rules almost always *sounds* like a reprimand, it is potentially distracting to the target student.

LEVEL 6: The teacher reminds students publicly, during the lesson, of proper behavior.

Teachers in American classrooms frequently say such things as:
"What's the rule for sharpening pencils?"
"Remember, all eyes on the page as we read."
"Everybody should be taking notes on this—it's going to be on the test."
You can avoid Level 6 simply by putting content words into your statement of the rule, thus making it a low profile Level 1:
"We don't sharpen pencils while we are so deeply into slang expressions like 'the fuzz'—what are some other slang terms?"
"Remember, all eyes on the page to see what Jody will do next."
"As you take notes on this, be sure to include the date 1718—yes, write 1718 in your notes right now—because that was when...."

LEVEL 7: The teacher interrupts the lesson to train students in proper behavior. (See also Method Xa7.)

Students think of this technique as "sermons" or "lectures," particularly when the person reciting the rules is a parent or a teacher. So distracting are these sermons that, in the midst of them, an occasional student can be heard to mutter, "Aw, let's get on with it"—by "it," he means the lesson.

Most teachers who deliver sermons on rules operate from the logic that students should know what the rules are, and if they forget them, it is much more efficient to recite the rules once for everyone than to repeat them privately to individuals. The logic seems reasonable, so it is strange to find that researchers question it. Madsen, Becker, and Thomas (1968) found that rewarding desired behavior with praise together with ignoring undesired behavior produced significant behavior change, but announcing rules, even frequently, affected student behavior rather little. Therefore, we might wonder if most teacher lectures on classroom rules not only divert student attention away from lesson content but are also a waste of time.

On the other hand, interruption for training is appropriate when the teacher uses it as a preplanning strategy, preceding each small segment of the lesson with training in the specific skills the lesson demands. These alternating lessons are the mark of superb teaching.

EXERCISE 1
CLASSROOM MANAGEMENT PRINCIPLES (10–15 minutes)

In this exercise you will experiment in first establishing principles, then training students to observe them, as suggested in Ja1. Prepare this exercise in advance, including three copies of Form J.

1 Join a group of three persons (four, if necessary).
2 At your turn as teacher, announce one general principle you wish your students to follow hereafter. Then train your students according to General Principles: Form J for 3 minutes. (Appoint a timekeeper among your students.) As you teach, your students will fill out Form J. They should hold them until the discussion period after the exercise.
3 At the end of 3 minutes, do not discuss your performance, but let the next person be teacher.
4 Repeat Steps 2 through 4 until all have practiced. Then exchange forms.

GENERAL PRINCIPLES: FORM J

Name of "Teacher":_____ Name of "Student":_____ Date:_____
Check each task each time it is done by "Teacher":
_____ 1. Invite questions/comments from students on principle.
_____ 2. Propose/invite sample situations for applying the principle.
_____ 3. Provide actual student *practice* for all students in a simulated situation.
_____ 4. Critique the practice with feedback to students.
Return this form to Instructor at end of class.

Conclusion Exchange forms, discuss ways of improving your skills, and return Form J to your instructor.

EXERCISE 2
CLASSROOM MANAGEMENT PRINCIPLES (10–15 minutes)

In this exercise, practice negotiating basic principles with your students (you might use the skills described in Chapter 22, Section BB) as you use the general format of Exercise 1. You will need to extend your lesson to at least 5 minutes for this exercise.

METHOD Jb
Supervision: How does the teacher provide for supervision in the classroom?

We will consider only the quantity, not the quality of supervision. For example, if a teacher provides an aide to supervise students continuously, the Jb control is

Level 1, regardless of whether the aide is effective or not. Other elements of classroom control become relevant after the amount of supervision has been determined.

LEVEL 1: The teacher directly supervises all learning activities at all times.

Some teachers avoid dividing their classes into smaller working groups because direct teacher supervision is easiest when there is only one group to supervise. Yet a teacher who has withitness and overlapping skills (see Kounin, chapter 1) can adequately supervise three, four, or even five groups simultaneously in the classroom.

LEVEL 2: The teacher pretrains students to use an adequate self-monitoring system.

When the teacher pretrains students in the skills of a lesson, she automatically establishes expectations for appropriate behavior during the lesson. A self-monitoring system shows whether or not the expectations have been fulfilled. Notice, for example, how most of the exercises in this book have monitoring forms or evaluation procedures that serve a supervisory as well as a training function.

Without either direct teacher supervision or an effective self-monitoring system, any student activity incurs high risk of off-task conversation and horseplay, regardless of age level.

LEVELS 3 and 4: (None.)

LEVEL 5: The teacher provides random, occasional, direct supervision of learning activities.

In the absence of pretraining, occasional teacher supervision visits to a learning activity group are not enough to ensure that all students in the group will maintain attention, even when the visits are random.

When the group is working on a clearly defined project for which they have been training, the risk of distraction is considerably reduced, and continuous teacher supervision may not be required.

LEVEL 6: The teacher provides regular but occasional direct supervision of learning activities.

The library research groups common to English and social studies classes often fail because students are not skillfully trained to do their work. In the hope that everything will somehow turn out all right, the teacher roams the area, putting out brushfires of inattention here and there.

The technique is justified when the activity requires only limited teacher supervision: cheerleading teams are an example, as are some science laboratories, debate teams, physical education classes, or arts classes.

LEVEL 7: The teacher makes no provision for supervision of learning activities.

Homework is poorly done in U.S. schools because it is not carefully pretrained, and is not supervised (evaluated) after it is completed. The same risks befall unprepared, unsupervised groups.

EXERCISE 1
PLANNING SEQUENCED CONTROLS (20–30 minutes)

This exercise is useful at the end of a training course or program since it applies Fundamental Principle No. 3, Sequence, to the entire Taxonomy of methods and techniques.

Before class, write down responses to the following two problems:

1   Ned is persistently reading a comic book during seatwork. Describe a sequence of at least six steps before you take the comic book away from him.
2   Suzie and Bud are talking constantly during class. Describe a sequence of at least six steps before you reprimand them or move their seats.

Also prepare six Sequence: Form JJ sheets.

1   Form a group of three persons (four, if necessary). Put seats in a traditional classroom arrangement, facing front.
2   At your turn as teacher, teach a 1-minute lesson in which the first situation occurs. (Do not use your written notes here.) Student Ned will be covertly persistent. As you teach, your other students will act as both students and observers, filling out a Sequence: Form JJ sheet (save forms till Conclusion).
3   When you finish teaching, the observers should hold your Form JJ until the Conclusion. Immediately switch roles.
4   Repeat steps 2 through 4 until all have taught.

SEQUENCE: FORM JJ

Name of "Teacher": _____ Name of "Observer": _____ Date: _____
Situation 1 / 2   (Circle one.)
Briefly note each control technique used by "Teacher" and apply the proper label from Taxonomy: e.g., Scold (Yc6).
1. _____ (   ) 4. _____ (   ) 7. _____ (   )
2. _____ (   ) 5. _____ (   ) 8. _____ (   )
3. _____ (   ) 6. _____ (   ) 9. _____ (   )
Return this form to the instructor after class.

Conclusion   Your small group should examine each form and, using the Taxonomy, apply the proper label to each technique. Then decide how closely the pattern follows the Fundamental Principle No. 3, Sequence, particularly the provision for using low profile techniques simultaneously. Some teachers feel that direct supervision (re: Jb1) means only that the teacher is present and ready to act; the Sequence principle shows how such action may be taken.

PLANNING SEQUENCED CONTROLS (15–20 minutes)

Repeat Exercise 1, this time using situation 2.

PRETRAINING STUDENTS IN SELF-MONITORING

Plan beforehand a 5-minute lesson in which students will monitor their own work (re: Jb2). Also prepare three copies of Form JJJ (below).

1 Form a group of three (four, if necessary). Place chairs in traditional arrangement.

2 At your turn as teacher, teach a 5-minute lesson in the following format: pretraining in self-monitoring your lesson activities; and lesson activities with students monitoring their own work. As you teach, your students will fill out Self-Monitoring: Form JJJ. Time your own lesson.

3 After your lesson, take 3–5 minutes to confer with your group on your performance, including suggestions for improvement.

4 Repeat Steps 2 and 3 for the other members of the group to act as teacher.

Conclusion   Did you feel confident that if you were to leave the room during the lesson activities, your students would probably have completed the activities successfully? That level of competence should be your goal; your actual practice should be to monitor *all* instruction.

SELF-MONITORING: FORM JJJ

Name of "Teacher": _____ Name of "Student": _____ Date: _____
Check a blank whenever the "teacher" does the task:
PRETRAINING:
_____ Announces content.
_____ Announces goal/purpose.
_____ Explains/demonstrates desired skills/behaviors (content).
_____ Explains/demonstrates how to observe desired behaviors.
_____ Explains/demonstrates how to record desired behaviors.
_____ Explains/demonstrates what to do in case of questions.
_____ Explains/demonstrates what to do in case of undesired behaviors.
_____ Conducts practice drill.
LESSON ACTIVITY:
_____ Begins the lesson/conducts the lesson.
_____ Monitors student self-monitoring.

JOINT PLANNING

METHOD Jc
Participatory Management: To what degree are students involved in the decision making for classroom instruction?

In large measure, the classifications in this section are speculative; we have little solid research data to tell us the relative impact of management strategies on student attention. However, the logic of the classifications is consistent with the limited research available.

LEVEL 1: Students participate in planning and management of limited aspects of instruction.

Here are two examples: (1) an elementary teacher sits down in a meeting with his students and asks, "What should we do with our bulletin boards that would be good for our learning about astronomy? And to whom should we assign the tasks, and how can we monitor the job?" And (2), a high school English teacher meets with individual students and cooperatively draws up a two-week learning contract with each student; students help plan and/or manage a part of the instructional program within limits established by the teacher. Both teachers are engaged in "limited participatory management."

LEVEL 2: Students advise the teacher on instructional policies and procedures.

Smart teachers ask for their students' advice all the time, letting the students know they are being asked for their wisdom, not for decisions. For example, "I planned to have small group discussions today, but frankly I'm worried that you might just fool around the way you did yesterday, and I don't want that. I hate to waste your time. What do you suggest?"

The possible distraction here is that one or two students may feel they are entitled to make the decisions; their discomfort with an advisory role, while unwarranted, is nevertheless real.

LEVEL 3: Students participate in planning and management of all aspects of instruction.

How can teachers help students take responsibility for their own learning during instruction? A joint planning/management approach assumes that each student develops a vested interest in the program for which he has some responsibility.

Joint planning can assume infinite shapes. The teacher might involve students in selecting content ("What do you think the major problems are that we face in the world today and tomorrow, problems we ought to study?"); setting goals ("What do you feel you should have learned after this unit on energy is complete?"); deciding on teaching strategies and activities ("How might we go about learning about the physics of our energy problem?"); and evaluating ("How am I going to know exactly what you have learned from this unit, without having to guess?").

Joint management of instruction may be handled through learning contracts, student supervisory committees, student review and evaluation committees, group project organizations, etc.

Success relies on the teacher's abilities and time. Teachers who lack talent in these techniques can produce considerable confusion, and communicating about management matters can be time consuming. Nevertheless, the learning that comes from these programs can be memorable and noteworthy (see Schmuck and Schmuck, 1975; also Johnson and Bany, 1970, pp. 236–328).

LEVEL 4: The teacher changes prior agreements for clearly stated reasons.

Sad to say, even the best, most sensible, most necessary reasons are likely to offend someone, and will absorb at least some of that person's time and energy, perhaps even diverting his attention from his studies. That is the risk of unilateral decisions in a cooperative system.

LEVEL 5: Some students participate in planning and management, some do not.

Favoritism is unfair; whether the teacher excludes some students from joint planning or whether they exclude themselves and blame the teacher, ill feeling will result.

Occasionally, selective joint planning is appropriate when the teacher is working with several different groups, each with its own needs and goals. The teacher must then use different methods, including those of supervision and management, with the various groups.

LEVEL 6: The teacher ignores prior agreements and/or student advice for no apparent reason.

Ignoring a student is a high profile technique; the risks of rage and resentment are great. Is ignoring students ever justified in the classroom? Yes; see Methods Z2 and Xb1.

LEVEL 7: The teacher changes or violates prior agreements for no apparent reason.

To break a promise, even an unwritten promise, is to destroy the trust that teachers and students must share for one another.

Although breaking agreements and promises is undesirable, the teacher may do so when student welfare is clearly jeopardized, whether students understand or not. For example: "I know we planned to climb trees, and I know you're disappointed, but I suddenly realized that we didn't have enough adults to help supervise. I'm sorry. I just didn't want anyone to get hurt."

EXERCISE 1: PARTICIPATORY PLANNING (10–15 minutes)

Use Section Ja, Exercise 2 for building skills in participatory planning.

NOTES

1 Brophy and Putnam (1979) suggest that general principles are probably superior to specific rules in structuring effective classroom management.

2 For further help in using this technique effectively, see Evertson et al. (1981); Good and Brophy (1978), pp. 70–78; Schmuck and Schmuck (1975), chapter 5, and pp. 40–42.

REFERENCES

BROPHY, J., & PUTNAM, J. Classroom management in the elementary grades. *Classroom management*. The Seventy-Eighth Yearbook of the National Society for the Study of Education, Part II. Chicago: University of Chicago Press, 1979.

EVERTSON, C., et al. Organizing and managing the elementary school classroom. Austin, Tex.: Research and Development Center for Teacher Education, University of Texas at Austin, 1981.

GOOD, T., & BROPHY, J. *Looking in classrooms* (2nd ed.). New York: Harper and Row, 1978.

JOHNSON, L., & BANY, M. *Classroom management: Theory and skill training.* New York: Macmillan, 1970.

KOUNIN, J. *Discipline and group management in classrooms.* New York: Holt, Rinehart and Winston, 1970.

MADSEN, C., BECKER, W., & THOMAS, D. Rules, praise, and ignoring: Elements of classroom control. *Journal of Applied Behavior Analysis,* 1968, *1,* 139–150.

ROSSWORK, S. Goal-setting: The effects on an academic task with varying magnitudes of incentive. *Journal of Educational Psychology,* 1977, *69,* 710–715.

SCHMUCK, R., & SCHMUCK, P. *Group processes in the classroom.* Dubuque, Iowa: William C. Brown, 1975.

CONTROL THROUGH VOICE AND EYES (METHODS K, L)

10

T wo major instruments of teacher control are voice and eyes.

METHOD Ka
Voice Volume: How does the teacher use voice volume to control student attention during the lesson?

Changing voice volume is a technique few teachers use, probably because most do not think about how varying volume can control attention. Are most teachers able to vary their voice volume? Of course; and silence — that is, no voice volume — is one of the teacher's most powerful tools.

LEVEL 1: The teacher changes voice volume strategically for content effects.

The teacher can use a variety of voice volume techniques to capture and maintain student attention. Raising the voice on key words and phrases is the most familiar and common technique: "And so, when you think of *corn* production, you've got to think of *rebuilding your soil* — corn is very *hard* on soil."

But lowering the voice on key words and phrases often is even more effective — a "stage whisper" conveys words dramatically. Remember, however, that the softer your voice becomes, the slower and more distinctly you should speak. Some teachers use a technique of pronouncing the first part of a word loudly, the second part softly, for effect. Building a sentence or phrase gradually from soft to loud, or vice versa, is another way to build emphasis. You can also try making an exclamation just before an important point: "And what do you think is attached to that carbon? *What!* Right, a hydrogen, and so now we can see that...."

LEVEL 2: The teacher uses silent pauses for content effects.

Silence is one of the teacher's most powerful tools. It attracts attention to ideas, and invites thinking. For example, pause after making an important lesson point — and again, just before repeating it softly or in a whisper. Or, pause noticeably after asking an open question of the class, without calling on anyone or giving anyone reason to disturb the silence: "Now just think for a moment, without raising your hand or saying anything out loud, just think for a moment about...."

LEVEL 3: The teacher uses content-word voice-overs to mask small distractions.

Using this technique, the teacher tries to drown out the noise students are making. If students are not making much noise, the technique works well; when students are quite noisy, another technique is necessary.

LEVEL 4: The teacher uses exaggerated volume changes.

Exaggerated volume, either too loud or too obviously soft, can sound "phony." Whatever voice changes the teacher makes should be logically consistent with lesson content.

Exaggerated volume changes can be a humorous device, but remember to focus on lesson content if the humor is shared during instruction.

LEVEL 5: The teacher uses loud volume throughout the entire lesson.

In an effort to make students hear and pay attention, some teachers consistently use a single loud voice volume. In fact, supervising teachers frequently comment that student teachers do not have loud enough teacher voices, so the tradition of the loud teacher voice is perpetuated to new generations of teachers. To some students, a loud teacher voice is stressful and irritating. Many truly effective teachers have soft voices; their students must work to hear what is being said. If a student has a hearing or attention problem, simply move that student closer to the teacher.

LEVEL 6: The teacher uses brief silence to wait for order or to respond to student comments or questions.

This is a favorite technique in American classrooms, based on the assumption that if you don't have every student's attention before you begin, you will have to repeat everything. The problem is that even brief delays are distracting to students who are ready to listen.

When a student says something and the teacher does not respond, or perhaps even looks away, the distraction to that student is likely to be acute. If, however, a student makes a comment in extraordinarily bad taste (an insult or profanity), the teacher may be wise to greet the comment with silence, then continue the lesson.

LEVEL 7: The teacher uses prolonged silence or shouts to restore order.

Prolonged silence while waiting for order is a common and frequently recommended device. Unfortunately, it wastes an extraordinary amount of time, irritates some students enormously, and gives others the opportunity to delay the lesson and fool around.

A new teacher often shouts for order, instead of using other, better techniques to open a lesson (see Method Gb1, "Beginning the Lesson").

You can, of course, use prolonged silences or shouting to directly support lesson content; for example: [Silence] . . . ."Now that you have looked at the outside of this box, I want you to think to yourself, without speaking out loud, about how that box is connected on the inside. When you have an answer, raise your hand." [Prolonged silence] Or, you might shout, "And then Alexander envisioned what might be. 'Ho!' he proclaimed, 'I will conquer the world!'" Then whisper, "And he almost did!"

EXERCISE 1 VOICE VOLUME (5 minutes)

Prepare a 1-minute speech to give to a small group of students. (If necessary, read an appropriate passage from this text.) Also, prepare three copies of Form K.

1   Form a group of three or four persons, and sit in a circle.
2   Each teacher makes her 1-minute speech in turn, while students have their heads down, looking at a copy of Form K and filling it out. One student also serves as timekeeper.
3   Students hold their Form K slips until discussion (Step 5).
4   Repeat Steps 2 and 3 until all teachers have spoken.
5   Exchange Form K slips and discuss.

VOICE: FORM K

Name of "Teacher": _____   Name of "Student": _____   Date: _____
Every 5 seconds, place a mark on the line to represent the "teacher's" voice volume at that moment. "Average" represents the "teacher's" normal or "average" volume. Number the marks below the line from 1 to 13.

Very soft   Average   Very Loud

Each time you make a mark and number it, record in the space below how *appropriate* you felt the volume to be to the meaning of the content: If the volume *carried* the meaning, record ++; if volume helped the meaning, record +; if the volume interferred with your getting the meaning, mark −. If you are not sure one way or the other, mark ?.

1. _____   2. _____   3. _____   4. _____   5. _____   6. _____   7. _____
8. _____   9. _____   10. _____   11. _____   12. _____   13. _____

Conclusion   In judging the expressiveness of a voice, we need to consider both volume and pitch, but here we try to separate them for training purposes. You probably have good control over voice volume if your range spans approximately one-half the length of the line, and you have only ++ and + marks recorded for meaning.

METHOD Kb

Voice Pitch: How does the teacher use voice pitch to control student attention during the lesson?

The monotonic teacher is likely to bore students. In contrast, the teacher who varies voice pitch, going higher, then lower, has the same effect as varying chord patterns in music—the effect of newness or surprise.

Radio personalities rely heavily on voice pitch to capture and sustain audience attention as well as to convey their message. Teachers can use the same technique to good effect.

LEVEL 1: The teacher varies voice pitch strategically for content effects.

Rosenshine reports an early study which claimed that voice pitch variation correlates with pupil achievement (1970, p. 509). Even without a formal study, we assume that skillful voice inflection influences student attention. These are ways to achieve skillful inflection:

- When a student's attention is wandering, try raising the pitch (not volume) of your voice very high, in a manner appropriate to your message, or dropping the pitch very low, even comically so. Smile when you do so, and watch for high attention responses you are almost sure to get.
- When a group of students displays inattention or unknown attention, try varying pitch very high or very low, again with a smile, and combine this technique with changing your voice volume and perhaps with changing your position in the room.

LEVEL 2: (None.)

LEVEL 3: The teacher briefly uses a monotone for content effect.

This technique is sometimes called "the dry voice." Teachers use it to mimic a talking computer or an evil witch. It can also be effective for reciting familiar information before a point of interest. For example, you might say in a rapid monotone, "So Columbus sailed out to find the passage to India, and after three long weeks out of sight of land" then, in a slower, more animated tone, "what happened? What did Columbus actually find?" Here, the monotone is a traditional signal that something exciting is about to be said; it is a favorite device of storytellers. The technique may prove disconcerting to one or two students, but most will recognize and understand the device and not be distracted by it.

LEVEL 4: The teacher exaggerates voice pitch changes for content effect.

The sing-song style of some elementary teachers can be disconcerting to some students, but exaggerated inflection can also be a humorous or attention-getting device.

LEVEL 5: The teacher uses a monotone throughout the entire lesson.

If students seem more inclined to sleep than to take notes during a lecture, the teacher's voice, rather than the content, may be at fault.

LEVEL 6: The teacher uses shrill, whining tones in speaking to students.

Students tune out this monotone voice pitch. It is difficult to imagine a constructive use of this technique, except for special content effects.

LEVEL 7: The teacher has a voice disability.

When the teacher suffers from laryngitis or some other malady, the effect can be distracting; a pronounced lisp can be even more so. And students can be sent into gales of laughter when the teacher's voice squeaks. You can either grin and bear it, or use teaching activities that do not depend on your voice.

An inventive solution is to teach the class as usual, but write your instructions, lectures, or questions on the chalkboard or newsprint charts. The quiet in your classroom will amaze you—for a time—and students will find learning primarily through their eyes a novel change of pace.

EXERCISE 1 VOICE PITCH (5 minutes)

Use the procedures of Exercise 1: Voice Volume. Change Form K to Form KK by relabeling the line this way:

VOICE FORM KK

Very Low   Average   Very High

METHOD L

Eyes: How does the teacher use eyes to control student attention during the lesson?

At low profile levels of control, the teacher's eyes do not distract the student from the lesson; at high profile levels, the student stops thinking about the lesson and thinks instead that the teacher is looking at him.

LEVEL 1: The teacher looks at all students almost continuously during the lesson.

The novice teacher is easy to identify: he focuses all his attention on the student he happens to be talking to; the rest of the room is far away from his eyes and his mind. The professional teacher's "eagle eyes," in contrast, are always on the move, from student to student, from one area of the room to another. Even while talking earnestly with one student, her eyes dart periodically to see what is happening elsewhere.

During seatwork or independent study, it is most natural and comfortable for you to keep your attention focused on the student you are working with. *Resist nature!* Look at other students periodically as you talk and listen. During a lecture or presentation, look at your students at least once every ten seconds. During brief transitions, while passing out materials or moving equipment, and even when you show a movie, watch the students. (You should normally preview movies.) During class discussions or recitations, watch the listening students more than the speaking students.

In general, reserve no more than one-third to one-half of your eye contact for the student who is speaking to you or to whom you are speaking; keep the rest of your eye contact for the other students. Watch the people who are listening to the speaker. It is they who do or do not understand what the speaker says, or who do or do not want to respond to him. Watch for cues of attention, inattention, or unknown attention.

Memory is an important skill for eye contact; the teacher must not only notice visual cues of attention, but must remember them, so she can ignore some student behaviors as they occur but take corrective action following instruction. The teacher who tries to correct all students behaviors all the time ("Sit up straight, Jim," "Take your finger out of your mouth, Glenella") ends up doing a lot of correcting and not much teaching.

LEVEL 2: The teacher looks at all students continuously during the lesson, at target students slightly longer than others.

Look at a target student not only when the student is not attending to the lesson, but when he *is* attending, to reward and hold his attention. We are more likely to pay attention to someone who is paying attention to us than to someone who is ignoring us.

LEVEL 3: The teacher looks at all students continuously during the lesson, at target students more frequently than others.

Look at the student often while you talk to the class or look about the room, but do not fix your gaze on him at any one time. If he is aware that you look at him frequently, he may become nervous and distracted.

LEVEL 4: The teacher looks at target students constantly during the lesson, occasionally checks other students.

While you talk to the class or look about the room, you let your gaze linger on the student, clearly talking to him or focusing on him during seatwork. To overcome the risk of distracting your target student, try to be conversational, and invite the target student nonverbally to interact with you about lesson content. Even with such friendly efforts, however, this technique risks making target students ill at ease and even sullen, because they may feel singled out.

LEVEL 5: The teacher looks at target students constantly during lesson and signals with eyes.

This is the old-fashioned and familiar eye signal that says, in the blink or squint of an eye, "OK, I've got your number, and that's enough of that!" Other students are likely to notice your eye signal, but may not be inclined to look to see where you are directing it.

LEVEL 6: The teacher gives target students a brief glare.

The first problem with this technique is the almost sure distraction to other students, since some are certain to look where the teacher is glaring; the second problem is the certain distraction to the target student.

LEVEL 7: The teacher gives target students a long glare or frown.

This popular technique makes teachers feel better, by providing them with a kind of emotional release, but it is one of the great distractive time wasters in teaching.

EXERCISE 1 EYES (15–20 minutes)

Before this exercise, prepare five copies of Form L, and prepare step 2 below.

1 Form small groups of four to six, sitting in a circle. Write names of other members of your group on Form L.
2 Assume the role of teacher and begin to read (anything) or speak (any topic) for 30 seconds (timed by another member of your small group).
3 During your 30-second lecture, each student (group member) will listen to you and also, as inconspicuously as possible to avoid your detection, will do any one of the following behaviors at least twice:

                                  1   2   3   4

A Look at ceiling / door / clock / neighbor.

                                            1   2   3   4

B Pick up something from floor / sleeve / sock or shoe / under chair.

                                1   2   3   4

C Draw on paper a doodle / notes on teacher talk / tic-tac-toe / his own name. (Note: The student must not cover the paper when the teacher looks at it.)

4 At the end of 30 seconds, the timekeeper will say "Stop." On Form L, write the code (e.g., A3, C1) for each student's behavior in the blanks marked

---

FORM L   TEACHER, WHAT DID YOU SEE?

Directions: Write the name of each other person in your group (each "student").

Names of "students"	OBSERVED	ACTUAL	MATCH
Example: _____	_____	_____	_____
_____	_____	_____	_____
_____	_____	_____	_____
_____	_____	_____	_____
_____	_____	_____	_____

PERCENTAGE TABLE: Number of "Match" ✓ /Number of "students"

In Group of 3 "Students"	In Group of 4 "Students"	In Group of 5 "Students"
0/3 = 0%	0/4 = 0%	0/5 = 0%
1/3 = 33%	1/4 = 25%	1/5 = 20%
2/3 = 66%	2/4 = 50%	2/5 = 40%
3/3 = 100%	3/4 = 75%	3/5 = 60%
	4/4 = 100%	4/5 = 80%
		5/5 = 100%

Effectiveness of Classroom Observation: _____ %

"Observed," announcing them to your group as you do so. Then ask each person for his actual behavior and write those codes in the proper column.

5 Calculate your score for effectiveness of classroom observation:
   a. Put a check mark in the Match column for each Observed code that exactly matches the Actual code (see Example).
   b. Count the total Match check marks and use the percentage table to calculate your effectiveness score.

Conclusion   Your instructor may wish to tally the effectiveness scores for the entire group. Ask for suggestions if your score is lower than you would like.

You can see that remembering is an important skill in this exercise. The teacher must not only notice visual cues of attention but must remember them. Your students can sense how well you remember, and they judge your competence, in part, on how well you notice and remember. Kounin calls this skill "withitness" (see chapter 1).

You might have wondered why, in this exercise, we stress inconspicuous off-task student behaviors. The purpose is to simulate the same façade of attention that students develop and use in the classroom. Teachers must see through this façade and identify unknown attention, or, in the case of Tic-Tac-Toe, inattention. The teacher must not assume the façade means attention.

It is harder to score 100 percent with a group of five students than a group of three; if you want to test and develop your skills, repeat the exercise with groups of five or more—all the way up to 25 or 30, normal class sizes in most schools.

You should learn from this exercise that the effective teacher almost never focuses full eye attention on one student, one table, or one small group of students; instead she keeps one eye on the student and both eyes on the rest of the class. (Every student knows the effective teacher seems to have eyes in the back of her head!)

REFERENCES

ROSENSHINE, B. Enthusiastic teaching: A research review. *School Review*, August 1970, *78*, 499–514.

CONTROL THROUGH GESTURES AND LOCATION (METHODS M,N)

11

Besides voice and eyes, the other major instruments of teacher control are gestures and physical location in the classroom.

METHOD M: GESTURES

To say that teacher gestures can help or hinder student attention is to belabor the obvious. Yet, teachers easily forget the power of their gestures, so we will examine again this important control method (see Smith, 1979).

METHOD Ma
Pointing: To what does the teacher point during the lesson?

LEVEL 1: The teacher points to or nods head toward a lesson object or prop.

The effective teacher makes sure that students see the lesson as well as hear it. Pointing to lesson content invites students to do what they are inclined to do naturally—to look to see what is going on.

LEVEL 2: The teacher uses gestures to emphasize topical points.

Rosenshine reports two studies in which teacher gestures were observed and pupil learning of lecture content was measured; in both studies, students remembered teacher statements significantly more often when statements were accompanied by gestures (1970, p. 510).

Orators have always used nonverbal language. The carefully-timed closed fist or pointing finger or slapped hand or nodded head are all familiar devices. The teacher must refrain, however, from overdoing it (see Ma7, Irrelevant Gestures).

LEVEL 3: (None.)

LEVEL 4: The teacher privately removes a student's distractive object.

On the theory that what is out of sight is also out of mind, the teacher hopes the student will pay attention after the cap pistol or comb or comic book is safely tucked away in a desk drawer. Unfortunately, the student's mind often follows the object, so the technique of removal can sometimes be as distracting as the offending object (see Xb4). This is not to say that the object should not be removed; only that you should try other techniques first (see Xb2).

LEVEL 5: (None.)

LEVEL 6: The teacher publicly removes a student's distractive object.

The teacher need not hold the offending object in the air; as long as everyone knows the object is being removed is enough to create a diversion from lesson content.

LEVEL 7: The teacher points at distracting objects or makes irrelevant or inappropriate gestures.

Do you make a habit of pointing at students who misbehave during your lesson? Or do you make ideosyncratic gestures or motions that express your own personality or give you personal comfort but distract your students?

METHOD Mb
Touching: In what manner does the teacher touch students during the lesson?

Because touching is such a personal matter, Americans are generally very careful of offending other people through touch. Teachers are particularly sensitive to the sexual connotations of touch for students above the middle-elementary level. Thus, this control method requires careful distinctions among different age groups.

LEVEL 1: The teacher physically guides the elementary student in accordance with lesson content.

Guiding a student's hand in handwriting, an arm in throwing or swimming, the head in scanning, and other such situations, are all appropriate for, or even require, touching.

LEVEL 2: The teacher physically comforts or rewards elementary students in conjunction with content.

Some teachers use touch effectively. A shoulder-hug reassures a distressed student, a squeeze of delight shows pride in a student's accomplishment. These are characteristic of teachers who call themselves "touchers" and "huggers." These techniques work well for students who are conditioned to parental touching and hugging, and are not distractive when they accompany content words.

LEVEL 3: The teacher physically guides the secondary student in accordance with content.

At the secondary level, physical education teachers, especially coaches, must often physically control student movements during instruction, as must typing teachers, vocational arts and fine arts teachers, and others. Instructional use of physical touch means limiting body touch or proximity to that required for instruction. Effective use involves public and businesslike procedures, unaccompanied by jokes or entertaining remarks about the physical proximity of teacher and student. Remarks are in bad taste, and distract the attention of students in an already vulnerable situation.

LEVEL 4: (None.)

LEVEL 5: The teacher touches the arm or shoulder of target students not in attention.

The teacher usually places a hand firmly—and momentarily—on the student's shoulder or arm in passing. The effect on the student is extremely distracting, but few other students will be distracted if you are skillful.

LEVEL 6: The teacher physically comforts or rewards a secondary student.

Teacher hugs are not customary means of reinforcing learning in secondary class-rooms, and can therefore be immensely distracting. Unfortunately, handshakes and other physical forms of reward are also not customary, nor are hugs as an expression of comfort, although when a student is so dramatically distressed that the entire class is affected, an arm around the shoulder or a hug is both human and appropriate.

When done publicly and appropriately, handshakes, pats on the back, and an arm around shoulders create a climate of acceptance. During a lesson, these behaviors take students' minds off lesson content.

LEVEL 7: The teacher physically restrains or punishes the student during instruction.

When you have tried all other conceivable forms of student control to no avail, then physical restraint and punishment may be warranted.

Some educators argue that physical restraint and punishment save time over other measures; the problem with this argument is that when you or I grab, pinch, or push students who are not paying attention to the lesson, we run the risk of poisoning the time following the punishment, while the student works through his anger, resentment, embarrassment, and hatred, unable to focus attention on the lesson. So great is the risk of distraction with these techniques that we often call them "losing our cool" (see Z7 also).

EXERCISE 1 DEMONSTRATION—Gestures (5–10 minutes)

1 Your instructor will read or speak for one minute, using any prop desired, such as a wall chart or chalkboard, and making any gesture or body move-ment desired. (The best demonstration will include both low and high profile examples.)

2 During the instructor's presentation, you will write notes in the spaces below on six gestures, motions, body movements or contortions that catch your eye.

_____ ( )	_____ ( )	_____ ( )
_____ ( )	_____ ( )	_____ ( )
_____ ( )	_____ ( )	_____ ( )

3 After the presentation, report your observations to the instructor, who will write and tally them on the board (reports from five or six students will suffice).

4 Examine each gesture and decide among members of the group whether the gesture distracts attention from the content or topic (D), focuses attention on the content or topic (F), or has no significant effect either way (N). Put the proper label (D,F, or N) in the parentheses.

Conclusion It is amazing to discover how many gestures that would seem to draw people's attention to what we say actually distract their attention or have a neutral effect.

In the next exercise, you can discover this about your own habits, both conscious and unconscious.

EXERCISE 2 GESTURES (15–20 minutes)

Before the exercise, prepare a 1-minute lecture you can teach without holding notes in your hands. Also copy five slips of paper, each with nine blanks and parentheses of the same format as in Exercise I.

1 Form a small group of four or five members. Seat all members in a traditional audience style, facing one direction.

2 Assume the role of teacher. Ask your students to take out a slip and write your name on it. Then, for one full minute, read or speak on some topic you might teach to students. (A group member should keep track of time for you.) If your presentation is a demonstration, use whatever props you need, such as a wall chart or chalkboard.

3 During your presentation, your students will take notes on six gestures or other body motions that attract their notice or stay in their memories.

4 After your minute is over, your students should mark each observation in the parentheses:
D - Distracted my attention from topic/lesson/content
F - Focused my attention on topic/lesson/content
N - Neutral; did not affect my attention

After marking their slips, your students will give them to you. Calculate your low profile gestures score this way:

   a. Count all the observations and write them here:_____
   b. Count all the D's and write them here: _____
   c. Count all the F's and write them here: _____
   d. Count all the N's and write them here: _____
   Low profile gestures control score $= c/a =$ _____
   High profile gestures control score $= b/a =$ _____
   Neutral gestures control score $= d/a =$ _____

Your goal in this exercise should be to achieve a higher low profile score than your neutral score, and to achieve a high profile score close to zero.

Conclusion One purpose of this exercise is to help you think about what your students see as well as hear during your lesson. After all, most students' eyes are working as busily as their ears, and the question is, how are you controlling what they look at? Is your lesson visual as well as auditory?

In addition, some students notice more what you do than what you say because their dominant sense is sight rather than hearing. Talk doesn't convey as much to them as do pictures, diagrams, charts, written words, symbols, objects, or visual action. Too much meaningless talk bores them, and when they get bored, they fidget, fool around, and get into trouble. So the effective teacher makes sure her lesson can be seen as well as heard.

Another purpose of the exercise is to help you become more aware of what mannerisms distract student attention from lesson content. (Notice the similarity of this exercise to the first impressions exercise in chapter 3.)

Now think about all those observations marked N. How can they be truly neutral if they were noticed and recorded? Since they were probably distractive, if only for a split second, you might be wise to treat them as high profile.

ASSIGNMENT   Take one or more of the following opportunities to look at yourself in the classroom.

1   Request that you be filmed on videotape for at least 15 minutes. Many school districts and most universities have VTR equipment and sometimes staff to run it. If you have never seen yourself on TV, you are in for a big surprise.
2   Ask a colleague, friend, supervisor, instructor, or principal to map your movements in the classroom, observe your gestures as in Exercises 1 or 2, and tell you what they see.
3   Consciously practice in your classroom, with actual students, the same skills you practiced in Exercise 2. See what a difference it makes not only in what you know about your students' work but also in how they behave.

METHOD N: CHANGING LOCATION

We are concerned here with the dynamics of teacher and student location rather than with particular seating or group patterns (see Method F).

METHOD Na
Teacher Location: How does the teacher change location in the classroom?

The traditional position for the teacher is at the front of the room, with an occasional brief foray up the center of the room and perhaps around the outskirts (Adams and Biddle, 1970, p. 49). Associated with this traditional teacher location is what Adams and Biddle call "The Action Zone" (Figure 11.1), an area of the classroom that seems to be literally and figuratively the center of activity, usually directly in front of the teacher and in the center of his vision, where almost all pupil participation occurs. Very little pupil participation occurs outside the Action Zone.

Most students who sit in the outer areas tend to remain inactive as long as the teacher stays at the front of the room. Adams and Biddle explain this student inactivity in terms of physics rather than personality: it is physically difficult to carry

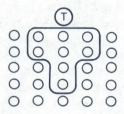

FIGURE 11.1   The Action Zone

on an ordinary conversation with someone who is thirty feet away. The question then is, what can the teacher do about the Action Zone?

LEVEL 1: The teacher periodically changes location in the classroom during instruction.

As a routine maneuver during lecture, class discussion, seatwork, and all other modes of teaching, effective teachers change position in the room, taking notes and materials along as needed and as practical. They avoid holding to the traditional teacher position except for lectures and presentations that demand central location. Instead, they use the entire room (see Figure 11.2). Notice how the action zone shifts as the teacher moves. The difference in students' behavior is immediately apparent; students in the corners begin to sit up, look more alert, and participate more frequently.

If you cannot move freely about the room as you lecture, transfer your speaking position from the front of the room to prepared positions at the sides of the room or even, on occasion, at the back of the room, to eliminate perpetual "dead spots" in the classroom.

When a student is speaking during recitation, move away from that student while still facing him, so he is forced to speak more loudly to reach you, thereby

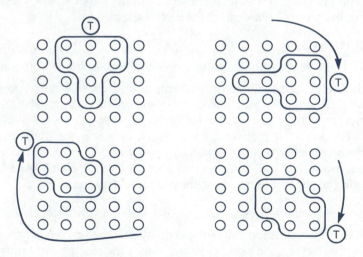

FIGURE 11.2   Variable Action Zones (as teacher changes positions)

reaching the rest of the class as well. This is a simple way to get students to speak to one another and to listen more attentively to one another in recitation or open discussion. Another technique is to move toward a speaking student who is far away from you until you have clearly established this movement, then stop or move slightly away again. Do *not* stand next to a student who is reciting; other students will begin to ignore this private conversation between you and the student.

While students are doing seatwork, you may be tempted to sit behind your desk with an eye on the rest of the room. Resist the temptation. Your responsibility is to monitor student work (see Method Be). When students work in small groups, teachers often wonder, "While I sit in the corner working with a reading group, how can I control the rest of my class with low profile techniques?" The answer is that you cannot just sit in the corner. Effective teachers seat themselves in reading groups so they can see the entire room, and give themselves easy passage through the room. During student reading or problem solving in the small group, the teacher periodically rises and moves out into the room, quickly checks work, and returns. (Smart teachers seat their most likely inattentive students near the reading group.) The control is impressive, because the reading group carries on without disruption, and the teacher's movements are those of routine teacher monitoring.

LEVEL 2: The teacher moves into the area of target students as the lesson continues.

When you notice inattention or unknown attention, move into that part of the room as you continue the lesson. Do not distract the attention either of the target students or of the rest of the class. Frequently, unknown attention corrects itself automatically as you move, especially if you are an effective monitor.

LEVEL 3: The teacher passes by target students as the lesson continues.

When you notice inattention or misbehavior, move directly to the target students, pass by, and perhaps teach from near that position. Keep the lesson going without a break. You are likely to distract the attention of the target students in conscious inattention, but you will not distract the rest of the class.

LEVEL 4: (None.)

LEVEL 5: The teacher stands next to target students as the lesson continues.

The teacher stops next to the target students and teaches from that position for a short time. Another option is to place a firm hand on the student's shoulder or arm, usually momentarily, as you stand there. Other nearby students are likely to notice. This is a very distractive technique for consciously inattentive students.

As an excellent technique with a hyperactive or distractible student during transitions, move near the student when you anticipate a shift in activity, and be ready to aid the student at the moment you announce the shift.

LEVEL 6: The teacher remains continuously stationary throughout instruction.

When making a presentation that requires many overhead projector transparencies or showing slides without a remote control switch, the teacher must remain in one location next to the machine.

But a fixed, unchanging teaching station is usually not necessary, and is never ideal because of the action zone effect discussed earlier (Na1).

LEVEL 7: The teacher moves continually and constantly during instruction.

Conceivably, a teacher may have a strategic reason for pacing frenetically around the room, but without a strategic reason, constant frenetic motion is highly distractive and should be avoided.

METHOD Nb
Student Location: How does the teacher position/reposition students during instruction?

Every new teacher debates whether to assign seats or allow students to sit where they wish. Evidence shows that self-selection can produce problems, including reduced attention (Good and Brophy, 1980, p. 416). In this section we will discuss the dynamics of student location, in contrast to static seating patterns (see Method F).

LEVEL 1: The teacher designates student positions before the lesson begins.

The teacher can be quite flexible in seating students according to the demands of each lesson and the needs of each student. Effective teachers exercise their prerogatives at will; they do not wait until problems arise before making appropriate moves. (See "Beginning the Lesson," Method Gb1.)

LEVEL 2: Students shift positions in and out of buzz groups or their equivalent.

When students are trained to use buzz groups and the teacher executes them well, they are not distractive. Almost no furniture need be moved, and transitions are almost instantaneous (see Method E).

LEVEL 3: Students are allowed to choose their own seating positions before or during the lesson.

LEVEL 4: Students move furniture to form small groups with others in adjacent positions.

LEVEL 5: (None.)

LEVEL 6: The teacher quietly moves a target student's location during instruction.

Move the student with a whispered comment: "Gerald, I think you'll concentrate better on your work if you move to that empty seat in the corner. Please move now without disturbing anyone else." You can use this technique during any class activity. Other students will notice and be distracted, of course, but the technique may be necessary if the student has not responded to earlier lower profile teacher actions in sequence.

LEVEL 7: The teacher stops the lesson to move the target student's location or rearrange room.

For example, "I'd like you people over there to come back to your seats and sit down, now."

      This high profile technique is rarely necessary because, in normal circumstances, most problems can be resolved at low profile levels. The technique can be useful, however, as a public demonstration of "withitness" (see Kounin, chapter 1). You may occasionally want to plan a shift of student seating patterns into your lesson. For example, when breaking students into working or discussion groups, you might announce: "Walk at least 12 feet to find a partner."

EXERCISE 1 TEACHER LOCATION (15–20 minutes)

1   Form small groups of four to six members. Write the names of other members of your group on Form N. Arrange chairs or desks in a line, facing the same direction, for your students in this exercise. Separate the chairs by at least 3 feet. Each student has a piece of blank paper and a pen or pencil before him.

2   Assume the role of teacher and begin to read or speak on any topic for one full minute (timed by another member of your small group of students).

3   During your 1-minute lecture, each student will listen until you pause beside him and simply look at the sheet of blank paper before him, at which signal he will begin to take notes. Activate all your students as soon as you can.

4   Also during your 1-minute lecture, each student will doodle in the margin of his paper when you are not looking. Students may not cover their papers in any way. Observe all the doodles and remember the doodle each student drew.

TEACHER, WHAT DID YOU SEE? FORM N

Directions: Write the name of each other person in your group (your "students").

Names of "students"	Doodle (1–3 words)	"YES"	"NO"
Example: _Sue G._	_Arrows, circles_	_____	_____
_____	_____	_____	_____
_____	_____	_____	_____
_____	_____	_____	_____
_____	_____	_____	_____
_____	_____	_____	_____

Percentage table: Number of "yes" ✔ /Number of students

                                    (See Form L, Exercise 1 for Method L.)

Effectiveness of classroom observation = _____ %

5 At the end of one minute, your timekeeper will say "Stop," and each student will turn his paper over and wait. On your Form N, use one to three words to describe the doodle each student was drawing on his sheet, announcing it aloud as you write. Then call each student's name in turn; he will say "Yes" or "No" as to whether you correctly remembered his doodle. Put a check mark in the proper place.

6 Then calculate your effectiveness of classroom observation score as before.

Conclusion Your instructor will tally the effectiveness scores. Ask for suggestions if your score is lower than you would like.

This exercise stresses again that you must observe what students are actually doing rather than simply stand at the front of the room making assumptions. Teachers cannot see unless they move. And notice again the multitopic thinking required of the teacher who is really "with it": the teacher must think both about content and process, about subject matter and student behavior. Teaching is not a profession for lazy people.

Is it harder to do this exercise with six students than four? With ten students rather than six? Of course; practice with larger groups as your instructor directs.

REFERENCES

ADAMS, R., & BIDDLE, B. *Realities of teaching: Explorations with videotape.* New York: Holt, Rinehart and Winston, 1970.

GOOD, T., & BROPHY, J. *Educational psychology: A realistic approach* (2nd ed.). New York: Holt, Rinehart and Winston, 1980.

ROSENSHINE, B. Enthusiastic teaching: A research review. *School Review*, August 1970, *78*, 499–514.

SMITH, H. Nonverbal communication in teaching. *Review of Educational Research*, Fall 1979, *49*, 631–672.

CONTROL THROUGH ACTIVE LISTENING (METHOD O)

12

Many people think good listening means shutting your mouth while someone talks to you. Other people think good listening means nodding your head vigorously and occasionally saying, "Yes...Yes...I see...hmmm...imagine that!" while someone else talks to you. But a few people have active listening[1] skills that keep the listener, rather than the speaker, in control of the conversation.

METHOD O

Active Listening: How does the teacher respond to student statements with questions during instruction?

All questions can be classified as one or more of three types:

1 Inquiring: These questions ask for new information. They comprise between 90 and 100 percent of the questions most people ask. (Example: "What do you think we should do?")

2 Message checking: These questions "send back" the message, from listener to sender, to see if the listener received the message properly. Professional interviewers or reporters, and others skilled in conversational arts, frequently use these questions. (Example: "So you're saying that we should...?")

3 Thought testing: These questions test the implications of the message just given in order to make the sender think. These questions are used by those skilled in negotiation or debate. (Example: "If, as you say, we should draft women, should we draft mothers with young children?")

Many statements masquerade as questions. For example, the so-called *rhetorical question* is not a question at all, but rather a statement of opinion: "Don't you think it would be a good idea if you handed in your homework on time for a change?" There is also the "fighting rhetorical question": "How would you like a trip to the principal's office?"

Then there is *acknowledgment,* a response that tells the speaker the listener is aware a message has been sent but not necessarily whether the message has been heard or understood:

"Oh, really?"

"Hm, you don't say?"

"Well, what do you know about that!"

EXERCISE 1 IDENTIFYING ACTIVE LISTENING TECHNIQUES

In the following Demonstration Script, exactly half the lines are questions, even though they may look like declarative statements.

ACTIVE LISTENING: DEMONSTRATION SCRIPT

(A)   I sense that you're feeling confused about active listening.

(B)   Naw, I can understand it OK.

(A) Anything bothering you about the text, the way it's written?
(B) Naw, the text is OK.
(A) Text is OK, and you understand the concepts OK—you ought to be feeling good about this stuff!
(B) Well, it's OK, I guess.
(A) You guess?
(B) (Laugh) Yeah.
(A) You're not sure?
(B) Well, I'm not sure I can do this active listening stuff, you know? I mean, active listening is fine for professional interviewers, you know, but I'm no interviewer—I'm a teacher!
(A) Oh, so you're saying that teachers can't do active listening.
(B) Well, no, but I've never been very good at this teaching skills stuff.
(A) I thought teaching skills were the reason you were taking this training course—or is there another reason?
(B) Well, as a matter of fact, yes; it is the reason, but there are so many other people in this course that already know this active listening stuff, you know?
(A) And you figure they will make you look bad.
(B) Well, not bad exactly, but not good either.
(A) Why does that bother you?
(B) Because they can already do active listening almost as well as the instructor can, and I can't.
(A) How many of them are as good as that?
(B) Maybe...six or eight.
(A) So if there are eight students as good as the instructor, does that mean that you actually have nine instructors in that course?
(B) (Laugh) Yeah, you could say that, I suppose.
(A) And you have only paid for *one* instructor?
(B) (Laugh) Yeah.

Now, think about the script. Who was in control of that conversation, A or B? And who was giving all the opinions, A or B?

The Demonstration Script shows how a listener who merely asks questions, without using rhetorical or fighting questions, can control a conversation, even while another person gives all the opinions.

As a teacher, you can use questions to control any class discussion in which your students do most of the talking. To learn the techniques, go back over the Demonstration Script and classify each of A's questions as follows:

I = Inquiring about new information (not previously suggested)
M = Message-checking what the speaker has already said (verbally or nonverbally)
T = Thought-testing the logic and implications of what the speaker has already said.

_____ 1. I sense that you're not...
_____ 2. Anything bothering you about...?
_____ 3. Text is OK, and you can...You ought to be feeling...
_____ 4. You guess?

_____ 5. You're not sure?

_____ 6. Oh, so you're saying that teachers can't...

_____ 7. I thought teaching skills were the reason that...?

_____ 8. And you figure they will...

_____ 9. Why does that bother you?

_____ 10. How many of them are as good as that?

_____ 11. So if there are eight students...?

_____ 12. And you've only paid for one...?

Compare your answers with these explanations:

1 "I sense..." = message check (The listener (A) earlier "read" some non-verbal signals from the speaker (B) and is checking to see if the signals are real. Notice how "fuzzy" the signals are.)

2 "Anything bothering..." = inquire (A is asking for new information not previously given by B, but which the speaker can be expected to know.)

3 "Class is..." = thought-test (A is pressing the logic of the information given thus far by B, showing B what conclusion A draws.)

4 "You guess?..." = message-check (A is actually checking to see if he heard the word "guess" correctly; in effect, however, A is asking, "What do you mean by that?")

5 "You're not..." = message-check (A is again asking, in effect, "What do you mean by that?")

6 "Oh, so..." = thought-test (A is testing the limits and logic of what B has said.)

7 "I thought..." = inquire (A is asking straightforward questions to get new information that B has not given before.)

8 "And you..." = message-check/thought-test (In one sense, A is checking B's feelings, which have not yet been fully revealed. In another sense, A is expressing one logical conclusion that any listener might draw from what B has just said. This question serves two functions at the same time.)

9 "Why does..." = inquire (A is asking a straightforward question to get new information B has not given before.)

10 "How many..." = inquire (Same as 9.)

11 "So if..." = thought-test (A is pressing the logic of B's point to determine whether a student who is "as good as the instructor" actually is an instructor himself.)

12 "And you..." = inquire/thought-test (In one sense, A is asking a straightforward question to get new information; in another sense, he is stretching the logic of students-as-instructors to imply that the slow student in a fast class enjoys the benefits of learning from unpaid teachers.)

Conclusion   Notice the power we get from a question, such as no. 8, that serves more than one function. In the next sections of this chapter, we will examine and practice each type of question. You will probably miss the variety and balance of questions in the Demonstration Script; in fact, the drills may seem monotonous when they repeat a single type of question over and over. Do not become impatient: no musician plays scales over and over in a public concert, and you will not play these drills in your classroom, but both musical scales and question skill drills are important learning tools.

INQUIRING QUESTIONS

You can use exactly the same techniques professional question-askers use in journalism to improve your effectiveness with inquiring questions. Reporters use the formula: *who-what-where-why-when-how*. When these prove insufficient, pull out the old classic teacher techniques that work for any occasion: "Tell me about that..." or "Tell me some more about that ..." or "I don't understand your point about..." or "What happened?" or "What happened then?"

As you use a series of inquiring questions, try to develop two subtle skills. First, pursue a line of inquiry: concentrate your questions on one theme or topic and investigate it, probe it, discover and reveal it through your questions. Let each answer lead to your next question. You can do this even on topics you know nothing about.

Second, develop your skill of imagery. Build a mental picture of what your student is telling you; put each piece in its place as he gives you information. Are all parts of the picture absolutely clear? You may be tempted to leave the fuzzy parts of the picture alone because they are, after all, mysterious, but resist your natural impulse to ignore the fuzzy parts; instead direct your questions toward the areas you do not fully understand—in other words, fill out your mental picture.

EXERCISE 2 (15–20 minutes)

In this exercise, you are to ask as many inquiry questions as you can in 4 minutes. Here is how the game will work:

1   At the signal, find two other people with whom you have not worked recently, and form a group of three.

2   At your instructor's signal, one person becomes teacher, one becomes student, and one becomes observer.

3   Teacher asks the student, "What have you been thinking about?" Student answers in one sentence only. Teacher continues asking inquiring questions until bell rings. Student continues giving one-sentence replies. Observer records a check mark on a slip of paper every time teacher asks an inquiry question. The point of the game is for the teacher to ask as many inquiry questions as she can in 4 minutes.

4   Your instructor will signal the end of 4 minutes, at which time you should rotate roles so the original observer becomes the teacher, the teacher becomes the student, and student becomes observer; work for 4 minutes, then rotate roles for the final time. If the group does not divide well into threes, form one or two pairs. Student will then double as observer and record check marks on a slip of paper.

Suggestions for teacher and observer: If your student takes a long time to answer a question, look at the observer, who will remind the student, "Answer in one sentence only."

Suggestions for student and observer: If the teacher asks a message-check question, answer it, but observer records a check mark *only* when teacher asks for new information. (Even if the student answers "I don't know," tally the question if it's inquiry.) If the teacher asks the student a thought-test question, do what you'd normally do — take a lot of time to answer it! But observer should not make a check mark.

Strategic suggestions for the teacher: Use the formula who-what-where-why-when-how. When these are insufficient, use the classic "Tell me about that."

Conclusion   Tally scores. How many observers tallied a total score for a teacher of 1–10 check marks? 11–20? 21–30? 31–40? 41–50? 51–60? Over 60? What techniques were particularly useful to the high scorers? (Open discussion.) The purpose of this exercise is to develop your confidence in asking questions of matters you know nothing about. If you use these techniques well, you will never again experience that sinking feeling that you have nothing to say — in an interview, at the dinner table, at Parent-Teacher Night, and certainly in the classroom. You will never run out of questions to ask.

This was a rapid-fire drill, and is not easy for most people the first time they try it. But its speed gives you a lot of practice in a very short time, and makes you concentrate under pressure, the real working condition of the teaching profession.

EXERCISE 3 (10–15 minutes)

In this exercise, concentrate on developing two professional skills of asking questions; first, the line of inquiry, and second, the skill of imagery.

1   Repeat Steps 1, 2, 3, and 4 of Exercise 2, this time working with different people and with only two-minute time intervals.
2   During your turn as teacher, incorporate the techniques of line of inquiry and imagery in your questioning.

Conclusion   You have heard skilled teachers and other professionals say things like, "One part of what you are saying isn't clear to me; help me with that." By this time you should understand what they were doing in such cases, and you should appreciate the skill of competent inquiry.

Assignment   Report a conversation in which you use inquiry questions, especially a conversation in which you knew nothing about the subject, topic, or incident. Include at least one example of each trusty standby, "Tell me something about...," "Tell me more about...," and "I don't understand..."

Report this dialogue in a line-by-line series of quotations. You can use any appropriate type of question, but label each inquiry question with an I.

MESSAGE-CHECKING QUESTIONS

We commonly believe that when someone says "I agree," or "I know exactly what you mean," he is *proving* he understands us. We want to believe he understands us. These acknowledgements, however, are not proof at all. They are only sophisticated forms of grunting. If you tell somebody something he doesn't agree with, he grunts, "Uh" or "Uh huh." Or if he's very diplomatic, he says "You don't say." If he's a college professor, he pauses, puts a finger on his chin, looks you straight in the eye, and says, "That's very interesting." But these responses are only grunts to acknowledge that you have spoken; they do not prove that you have been heard and understood.

Message-checking is by far the most efficient way to *convince* your student you understand what he is saying. There are three kinds of Message-checking.

Parroting   Repeating one or more of the student's words exactly as he says them, in the same order. For example:

> **STUDENT:**   I left it at home on the kitchen counter.
> **TEACHER:**   At home. Hmm.

Parroting is not undeniable proof of listening, but it is better than a grunt.

EXERCISE 1 (2–5 minutes)

The instructor will read aloud some prose materials from this chapter*; at each slight pause in the reading, each student in turn will quickly parrot one to four words before the instructor moves on. When it is your turn, break in quickly to parrot.

Conclusion   Parroting is certainly not proof the speaker has been understood. Consider this sample dialogue:

> **A:**   Dad, are you busy?
> **B:**   Naw, I'm just reading the paper. What do you want?
> **A:**   Dad, there's a big deal tomorrow night, and I want to go to it. Dad, are you listening to me?
> **B:**   Yeah, sure, go ahead.
> **A:**   And I want to go — it's at the Paladium...
> **B:**   Paladium...
> **A:**   and I need to use the car...
> **B:**   the car...
> **A:**   and I need it at five o'clock to midnight...
> **B:**   five...
> **A:**   Can I have it, Dad?
> **B:**   Have what?
> **A:**   The *car*!
> **B:**   When?

---

*Instructor's choice. Pause every 5 seconds, and keep this drill moving *quickly*.

Paraphrasing Repeating the same idea but in different words (as few as possible). For example:

> **STUDENT:** I don't get this stuff at all.
> **TEACHER:** It's too hard?
> **STUDENT:** Well, it's just confusing.
> **TEACHER:** So if we take it step by step...
> **STUDENT:** Yeah.

or

> **A:** Once you develop the skill, you can paraphrase anything...
> **B:** You mean *nothing* is impossible to paraphrase?
> **A:** Right, anything a student says to you can be paraphrased, and the effect will be that you know you've been heard.
> **B:** He'll be convinced.
> **A:** Right.

Some people confuse parroting with paraphrasing. If you have this trouble, try using these cue words:

"In other words, you feel that/think that...?"

"I hear you arguing for..."

"So you're saying that..."

"If I understand you correctly, you want..."

Then, after you are proficient in paraphrasing, omit the cue words. Your use of message-checking is much more low profile if you use brief paraphrases without cue words. (Exception: When a student is getting emotional, you may need to use cue words to convince him you understand his viewpoint.)

EXERCISE 2 (5–10 minutes)

The instructor will read aloud as in Exercise 1. This time, at the pause when it is your turn, try to paraphrase the last idea you heard read. Remember, once you develop the skill, you can paraphrase anything, even awkward silences:

> **A:** Can't think of anything to say right now?
> **B:** Right.

Reflecting Sending back a message that someone did not actually say, but which you sense was there. You may receive a nonverbal message, especially an emotion or attitude, and send it back to see if you received it correctly. For example:

> **STUDENT:** This is stupid stuff. What a waste of my time. Why do I have to do such stupid stuff?
> **TEACHER:** You really feel frustrated, don't you?

or:

> **TEACHER:** Sam, you look like something is bugging you. Want to talk about it?

You may receive a complex message; simplify it by reducing it to a few words, then send those back to see if that's what is meant. You cut through all the words to get to the essential meaning. In effect, you title the thoughts. For example:

> **STUDENT:** They wouldn't let me... and then they... and I couldn't... and there was so much....
> **TEACHER:** It wasn't fair, was it?
> **STUDENT:** No.

or:

> **STUDENT:** Mrs. Burns, I did *this* right, and you said *this* was OK.
> **TEACHER:** Yes?
> **STUDENT:** And you said this was right, and I got *this* right, too, and...
> **TEACHER:** Bobbi, are you trying to tell me that you want a higher grade?
> **STUDENT:** Right!

EXERCISE 3 (10–20 minutes)

The instructor will speak to each person in turn; sometimes the message will be one of these nonverbal signs: shrug, deep sigh, stretch and yawn, look up at ceiling, cover face with hand, wink or slow blink, or frown. Sometimes the message will be a rapid reading of a short paragraph selected at random.

When the message comes to you, try to reflect it back. In the case of a nonverbal message, translate it into words to see if you understood it. In the case of a rapid, complex message, summarize it in only a few words — in effect, writing a title for the message — then check. Remember, if your student says "No, that isn't what I said" or "That isn't what I meant," reply with something like, "Oh, tell me again what you really mean." For example:

> **A:** (A shrug.)
> **B:** Tired?
> **A:** No.
> **B:** What's up?
> **A:** I've got so much going on, I'll *never* get caught up.
> **B:** Oh, discouraged.
> **A:** Yeah.

Conclusion Notice how often message-check questions sound like statements. In fact, a skilled message-checker uses more periods than question marks.

Again, recall three important skills in message-checking: (1) If a student becomes impatient and snarls, "No, no, no, that isn't what I said!" or "Of course that isn't what I meant!" be patient with his bad manners and say something like "Oh, I see. Well, tell me again what you *really* mean. I want to know." (2) A careful "mistake" on your part can be highly revealing of what is going on inside a student's mind, and may indeed help him to realize just what he was saying, thinking, or feeling. For example: "This is dumb stuff!" "You can't do *any* of it?" "No, I can do the first part OK, but the second part..." (3) Keep it short.

EXERCISE 4 (15–20 minutes)

You should do this exercise at least twice for it to be effective. It is not only powerful but fun, not only fun but challenging.

1 On signal, find a partner and, between the two of you, quickly choose a topic about which you genuinely disagree. (Use the Topic List below.) Designate one person A, the other, B.

2 A asks: "Tell me your opinion."

3 B gives his opinion on the topic in no more than one sentence. (In later trials, expand this to two or three sentences.)

4 A then paraphrases or reflects B's opinion, to B's satisfaction (that is, B must nod or say "yes" or in some way agree that A understands B's opinion). Then A gives his opinion. (If A does not get B's agreement, A must keep trying until successful. If necessary, A can ask B to repeat what he said.)

5 A gives his opinion, in response to B, in no more than one sentence (later, more) and B paraphrases or reflects as in 4. A and B then repeat steps 3 and 4 continuously until time is up.

6 The instructor signals time after 5 minutes.

Remember that as you debate the topic with your partner, you cannot state your own opinion until you have convinced your partner you understand his. (Parroting is not allowed in this exercise.) For example:

A: Tell me *your* opinion.
B: I think grades stink.
A: They're not useful.
B: Right.
A: I disagree because...
B: So you *like* grades.
A: No, I just think they're necessary.
B: Students *need* them.
A: Yes.
B: Well, what you're not considering is...

The instructor should demonstrate this procedure with at least one student for a minute or more so the entire class can see the procedure work, and monitor every pair during the exercise and assist as needed.

If a pair cannot find a topic they disagree on within 30 seconds, one party should take an advocacy position and simply make the best argument he can for one side of an issue—that is, defend the position of those who do believe that argument.

Topic List

■ Women are biologically more emotional than men.
■ Children should be spanked when they *severely* misbehave.

- Smoking should not be permitted in public places.
- The government should replace all property taxes with income taxes.
- To succeed, politicians must be dishonest.
- Schools should not teach morality.
- A teacher should never say "I give up on you—I can't work with you any more."
- College athletics are more harmful than helpful because they exploit just about everybody.
- Plumbers, electricians, and carpenters are grossly overpaid.
- Most doctors are grossly overpaid.
- The U.S. needs socialized medicine.
- Newspapers should not have to reveal sources of information about serious crimes such as murder and treason.
- Reverse discrimination, that is, favoring minority groups over whites, is a good thing.
- When a student cannot do what the teacher wants, it's the teacher's fault.
- Students should respect their teachers or parents just because they are teachers or parents.
- (Or give your own opinion on something and see if your partner disagrees.)

Conclusion   If you are still unskilled in paraphrasing and reflecting, you will run out of things to say before the end of 5 minutes. (If this happens, immediately separate from your partner and listen to another pair; learn from them.) If you are already skillful in this technique, five minutes will not seem long enough—you will feel frustrated at being cut off.

Parroting was not allowed in this exercise because it is not sufficient proof that you understand the message. It is nevertheless valuable as a way to stay in a conversation.

These message-check skills are basic to many other low profile teaching skills (see Methods P, Q, R, S, T, Y), so develop your skills to the point that you can apply them automatically and easily, at any time.

Assignment   Skillful message-checking is a powerful tool to reduce tensions when students' emotions begin to rise. Imagine that a student has a gripe against you or the class or the school. He may be angry with you for something you said or did, or something you made him do. Your natural impulse is to let your own anger flare; instead, try using message-checking to "pour oil on troubled waters."[2] Divert tensions with message-checking. Be aware that message-checking is not a solution to a problem; it can *soothe* the problem, however, and help people get control of themselves so they can begin to think.

THOUGHT-TEST QUESTIONS

Thought-testing, perhaps the most intellectually challenging set of skills in this book, makes your students really think about what they are saying while you avoid disagreeing with them or making them feel defensive. It shows your student that you are a thinking person who is trying to understand all the implications of what the student is saying.

Imagine that a student says, "I think women should have to register for the draft." Five questioning techniques will force him to think more deeply about what he has said:

Test the logic   With this question, you try to extend his statement's logic to the extreme; for example, test the definition to see all the cases it covers.

"Women should be forced to kill?"

"You'd favor drafting women for front line combat?"

"Pregnant women should also be drafted?"

Test by analogy*   With this question, you try to apply his principle to an entirely different situation, testing to see if it applies in the same way.

"And men should be drafted for domestic duty?"

"You'd endorse the Russians' drafting their women, too?"

Test consequences/Test applications   Explore what happens when the principle is applied in the real world.

"So when war comes, will we send our mothers overseas?"

"If we were to draft women, would women share barracks with men, or would we set up separate camps for women?"

Probe origin/source/reasons   Explore where the student got the information or opinion and why it's important to him.

"You've held this view a long time? Do your parents hold this view?"

"Do you feel this policy is vital to the security of the U.S.?"

Hypothetical counterargument   Explore how the student would respond to counterarguments, making sure you never suggest them as your own arguments.

"I hear people say that women can't withstand the physical demands of combat. How do you answer that argument?"

"If somebody were to call your argument sexist, what would you say?"

Always follow a thought-test question with at least one message-check question; your follow-up question is added insurance that your thought-test question will succeed. For example,

> **STUDENT:**   To be fair, see, we should require women to register for the draft, too, see?
> **TEACHER:**   You feel that women should be forced to kill people?
> **STUDENT:**   Well, no, see, they could do other things besides fight.
> **TEACHER:**   Supporting roles, rather than combat.
> **STUDENT:**   Yeah.
> **TEACHER:**   I see. Janine, do you agree with Sam?

---

*In the analogy, the situations are different but their elements correspond one-to-one; the same principle is applied to both situations. In the first example, "men" corresponds to "women," "domestic duty" corresponds to "war duty," and the common principle is "draft."

As with inquiry and message-check questions, certain cue words often (but not always) signal a thought-test question:

"If that's true, then is it also true that...?"

"Then, is what you're *really* saying..."

"What would happen if..."

"What do you say to someone who says your idea..."

"Why do you say that...?"

EXERCISE 1 (20–30 minutes)

In class, the instructor states an opinion in one sentence (the earlier list of topics may be used); for example: "There is no such thing as a good *natural* teacher."

Members of the group will then ask thought-test questions that illustrate logic testing (5 minutes); then questions that illustrate testing by analogy (5 minutes — these are harder); then questions that test consequences, probe origin, then offer hypothetical counterarguments. Do not spend time trying to correct incorrect examples; instead, listen hard to all the correct examples and try to understand why each one is correct. These are not easy skills, and take time to acquire; don't worry about their initial difficulty, but work to master them gradually.

Conclusion Notice that the hypothetical counterargument is easiest of all. All you do is add a few cue words to the front of a statement of disagreement, and you have a thought-test question. These few cue words depersonalize the disagreement.

When you become skilled at thought-testing, experiment with leaving out cue words and occasionally omitting the automatic message-check follow-up. Until you attain that goal, do not leave out any elements.

EXERCISE 2 (20 minutes)

The goal of a thought-test question is thinking. Two observable signs of thinking are a silent pause and a voiced pause ("Well...," "Ah...," "Hmm...."). The purpose of this exercise is to help you make students pause while they think.

Modify each statement below so that it states your own opinion. Then add to the list another strong opinion you hold about schools, teachers, students, or teaching. (Do all this before class.)

- Teachers should be paid according to their students' scores on standardized tests.
- Schools should be run by professionals, not by parents.
- The classroom is a place for quiet.
- A teacher's experience is his/her badge of office, to be respected by all.
- (Statement of your own)

1   In class, form groups of three (or four where necessary) and assign names A, B, and C (and D) to each group member.

2   At the instructor's signal, B will ask A: "What is your opinion?" A will then respond.

3   B will then ask any kind of question he wishes, hear the response, and continue until he sees an opportunity to ask a thought-test question (using any of the five techniques you have already learned). C will act as monitor and watch for the tell-tale sign of a thought-test question — a pause followed by "well" or "uh" or "hm," or a similar sign from A. C will then announce "thinking!" and the group will proceed to Step 4 below.

    If B asks what *he* thinks is a good thought-test but fails to get the pause, he must continue until he can get the proper sign from A. After C announces "thinking!" the group will proceed to Step 4 below.

    If B has not gotten a *pause* from A in one minute (C will act as timer), then C will say "Switch roles," and the group will proceed to Step 4 below.

4   C will then replace B, and B will replace A in Steps 2 and 3 above. After "thinking!" or one minute, whichever comes sooner, proceed to Step 5 below.

5   A will replace B, and C will replace A in Steps 2 and 3 above.

After the group has completed a round, repeat Steps 2 and 3 again, this time using different opinions.

    After completing a second round, begin a third. Give yourself as much practice as you can, both listening to others' active listening and also practicing your own. This exercise should last no longer than 20 minutes. For example:

> **B:** What is your opinion?
> **A:** I think parents should determine how the school is run.
> **B:** We shouldn't have any professional administrators? (Thought-Test)
> **A:** Sure we should have them, but they should follow the wishes of the parents.
> **B:** *Every* parent's wishes. (Thought-Test)
> **A:** Right.
> **B:** And if two parents disagree, they should close the school. (Thought-Test)
> **A:** Well, *no*, of course not, but...
> **C:** Thinking!

Conclusion   The real secret of success in this exercise is not whether you actually produce "thinking!" or not — after all, the cards are stacked against you, since your partner knows exactly what you are doing — but whether you feel yourself asking the kinds of questions most likely to produce a "thinking" response. When you *do* produce "thinking!" enjoy your feeling of success — and congratulations!

    You may have noticed that some logic testing questions (thought-testing) sound a lot like reflecting questions (message-checking), and that when thought-testing questions are asked with real low profile skill, they sound like inquiring questions. If you noticed these similarities, you are learning well: testing logic and reflecting do overlap, and you can count twice any question that serves both functions. It is also true that a well-placed thought-test question is so low profile that it sounds like a simple, straightforward inquiring question, until you start to think about it; that is why it works so well.

Assignment   Carry on a conversation — tape recorded, if possible — with one of your students, your supervising teacher, your instructor, or someone else, duplicating the type of questioning you did in Exercise 2. Use cue words to help you, and follow every thought-test question with a message-check. Report a line-by-line sample of your conversation and label the different kinds of active listening:

> I   = Inquiry
> M-C = Message-Check
> T-T = Thought-Test

Also, if you can, label the different kinds of thought-test questions:

> L: Test Logic
> A: Test Analogy
> C: Test Consequences/Application
> O: Probe Origin
> H: Hypothetical Counterargument

Remember that a thought-test question is not just any question that makes someone think (see Figure 12.1). Inquiry makes someone think of information you're asking for, and message-check makes him think about whether what you said is the same as what he said. But thought-test makes a person think *again* about what he has already stated, whether it is his own assumption, opinion, attitude, perception, or his own thinking.

For example, let's say he has been thinking and talking this way: "A, then B, then C, and then..." When you ask your thought-test question, his mind automatically retraces the same pattern, and he is about to speak, when he realizes that "C" may no longer fit the pattern — and he pauses. That is the effect of the true thought-test question.

PROFILES OF ACTIVE LISTENING CONTROLS

LEVEL 1: The teacher uses limited and appropriate acknowledgement, parroting, paraphrase, and inquiry regarding content.

LEVEL 2: The teacher uses appropriate reflecting or thought-testing regarding content.

LEVEL 3: The teacher uses long paraphrase during instruction.

The teacher increases the risk of distraction by asking long paraphrase questions; she may confuse students with her rendition of what they said. To avoid this possibility, the teacher should keep paraphrases short—only a few words.

LEVEL 4: The teacher uses continual message-check with target students.

"Excess" can be defined as "too much of a good thing," and new teachers are frequently guilty of excess when they repeat everything students say. As Good and Brophy point out (1974, p. 368), teachers who repeat everything students say actually send two messages: (1) "I can say it better than you can," and (2) "Don't bother to listen to other students because the teacher will repeat what they say."

Continual message-checking can be useful, however, for helping students vent emotions, that is, to "pour oil on troubled waters."

LEVEL 5: The teacher uses continual message-check with cue words.

New teachers often depend heavily on the cue words that signal the technique. Some students detect the signals and find them artificial and offensive. Ordinarily, the teacher's best use of message-check is low profile—limited and appropriate use, without cue words, in short statements. When a student is emotionally upset, however, heavy use of cue words may be necessary to convince the student he is being heard.

LEVEL 6: The teacher uses active listening to maintain noncontent talk about lesson procedures or mechanics during instruction.

During instruction, *any* nonlesson topic must be considered high profile. Unless they are the content of the lesson, instructional mechanics and activities are simply a vehicle for learning; therefore, any classroom discussion about them is off-task and noninstructional (see Method V).

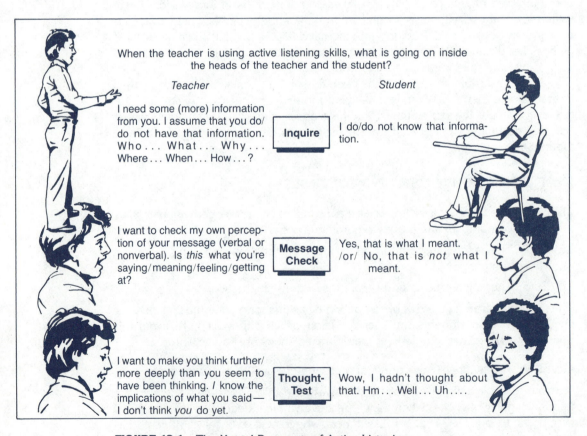

When the teacher is using active listening skills, what is going on inside the heads of the teacher and the student?

Teacher

I need some (more) information from you. I assume that you do/ do not have that information. Who... What... Why... Where... When... How...?

Inquire

I want to check my own perception of your message (verbal or nonverbal). Is *this* what you're saying/meaning/feeling/getting at?

Message-Check

I want to make you think further/ more deeply than you seem to have been thinking. *I* know the implications of what you said— I don't think *you* do yet.

Thought-Test

Student

I do/do not know that information.

Yes, that is what I meant. /or/ No, that is *not* what I meant.

Wow, I hadn't thought about that. Hm... Well... Uh....

FIGURE 12.1   The Mental Processes of Active Listening

The key to successful classroom management is to make all conversation during instruction support content learning. For example:

TEACHER X: You say you couldn't hear, boys?

TEACHER Y: You say you couldn't hear the pronunciation of *garçon*, boys?

Does this devotion to lesson content seem fanatical to you? In conventional terms, perhaps; in professional terms, we would use the word "committed."

LEVEL 7: The teacher uses active listening to maintain off-lesson topics during instruction.

Any noncontent talk during instruction is, by definition, off-task; when the teacher uses it, we call it high profile.

BALANCE IN QUESTIONING: THE "INTERVIEW CONVERSATION"

Combining all the active listening skills gives a teacher immense power, for each type of question elicits a different emotional response. Inquiry elicits interest, a tolerance for continuing the topic; message-check elicits a sense of well-being, warmth, of feeling listened to and understood; and thought-test elicits a sense of excitement, surprise, or even drama. All the question types are necessary in the classroom.

The next two exercises will help you become aware of how you can balance active listening techniques.

EXERCISE 1 (15–20 minutes)

Remember the almost equal numbers of I, M, and T questions in the Demonstration Script at the beginning of this chapter? Your instructor will demonstrate "balancing questions" in an interview or conversation. The point of this experiment is not to achieve perfect balance (a difficult skill to master), but rather to help you think about how a teacher can train himself in questioning skills.

Any group member may volunteer to be interviewed by the instructor on any topic either party wishes. When the instructor (whom we will call the teacher) asks a question, the group member (whom we will call the student) must limit each answer to one sentence or 15 seconds, to allow time for many questions. The total interview will be 3 minutes long; it should be tape recorded if possible.

During the interview, the other group members will act as monitors, and use the Monitor Form, following its instructions exactly. After the interview, compare your Monitor Form with others; your instructor may replay the tape, with pauses, to check your classifications.

Conclusion A few professional radio and television interviewers know how to ask questions in an interesting, congenial, even exciting way. They often demonstrate the balanced and stimulating use of active listening questions that should be part of every teacher's repertoire.

THE INTERVIEW CONVERSATION: ACTIVE LISTENING EXERCISE

MONITOR FORM

On a separate paper, write down first 1–6 words of *each teacher question* (do *not* write student responses), then classify each question using these symbols: M = message checking; I = inquiring; T = thought-testing. Example:

> *I = tell me (what you want to talk about)*
> *M = you mean*

Suggestions to Teachers: (a) Balance your M, I, T questions. (b) Avoid using obvious cues. (c) Keep control—break in every 15 seconds with a message check to keep control, then either let your "student" continue or ask another question.

EXERCISE 2 (20–30 minutes)

If you had a chance to be interviewed by a professional interviewer or a skilled teacher, on any topic you chose, what would it be? What hobby, activity, event (personal, local, state, national, international, cosmic, religious, professional, historical) interests you the most? Write it here: _____

1   Form groups of three or four.
2   In this exercise, you will be interviewed by another group member for exactly 5 minutes on your topic. The third person will act as monitor and fill out a Monitor Form during the interview, then give it to the teacher after the interview. When you are the student, relax and enjoy yourself; let the teacher do all the work!
3   Switch roles.
4   When it is your turn to be teacher, try to:
    (a) Begin smoothly (e.g., "What would you like to talk about?" or "What's interesting to you these days," etc.)
    (b) Work for balance in your I, M, and T questions
    (c) Remember to follow every T question with an M question, whether you get a response or not.
    (d) Do not use rhetorical questions; they weaken the effect of your T question.
    (e) Work hard; concentrate; make your conversation interesting for both your student and the monitor.
5   When it is your turn to monitor, be alert for questions that serve more than one function—for example, M/T or I/M or even M/I/T. They are *good* questions!
6   After all the interviews, confer with the other group members and ask for their suggestions on how to improve your skills.

Conclusion   Most people do not stop to analyze what makes a good question— they just know they like it. While there is considerable art in effective teacher conversations with students, there is not much mystery, for you have just practiced some techniques that almost guarantee effectiveness. Your task now is to practice for mastery and facility.

EXERCISE 3 (5–15 minutes)

Repeat Exercise 2 in different groups. Shorten each interview to one minute or even to thirty seconds. See how balanced you can be in that brief time.

The purpose of this exercise is to test and develop your quickness and facility; because life in the classroom moves so rapidly, control skills that require long periods of class time are rarely useful.

Conclusion This exercise required you to think fast on your feet. Welcome to teaching! If you can perform these exercises well under pressure, you can be confident of your ability to perform well in regular classrooms of students. But you must continue to practice.

Assignment Practice balancing your questions until you can do it in 15 seconds or fewer. Report a conversation with students (or others designated by your instructor) in which you demonstrate good balance in a brief time. For example:

> **TEACHER:** Are you all finished? (I)
> **STUDENT:** Yeah.
> **TEACHER:** Done for the day? (T)
> **STUDENT:** (Laugh) Naw.
> **TEACHER:** You're still on the job? (M)
> **STUDENT:** Yeah.
> **TEACHER:** Good. Let me know when you're ready to start the next unit, OK?
> **STUDENT:** OK.

Write your report in line-by-line dialogue, like the example, and label each type of question.

NOTES

1   Thomas Gordon (1974) applies the term "active listening" to techniques that I call "message checking." My notion of active listening includes not only "message checking," but "inquiring" and "thought testing" as well, techniques that Gordon sometimes terms "roadblocks." Despite our differences, we agree that the message checking/active listening technique is a fundamental teaching skill.

2   Gordon (1974) uses this term and technique in the same way.

REFERENCES

GOOD, T., & BROPHY, J. *Looking in classrooms* (2nd ed.). New York: Harper and Row, 1978.

GORDON, T. *T.E.T. Teacher effectiveness training.* New York: David McKay, 1974.

CONTROL OF SPEAKER AND TOPIC
(Methods P, Q, R)

13

Usually, the speaker controls a conversation. Knowing this, some teachers fear that class discussions will get out of hand, and may avoid open-discussion activities altogether. Yet skilled teachers, like professional interviewers, know how the listener can control a conversation. Listener control is essential in classrooms where students dominate and take over, interrupt other students, stray off the topic and talk about irrelevant things, or just sit, saying nothing at all.

METHOD P
Conversation Control: How does the teacher as listener control the conversation?

What we shall call "conversational control" is a basic skill in low profile techniques.

STEP 1: Break in

Usually at the end of a sentence or at a *pause* in the student's talking, you break in with Step 2. If *no* pauses occur, you may break in by talking *over* the student (call his name first to get his attention if necessary).

STEP 2: Paraphrase

You break in using a message check (see Method O) of what your student is saying.

STEP 3: Wait for assent

You wait until your student nods or says "yes" or otherwise says that your message check was correct.

For example:

> S: ...and then we went back and...but Herbie couldn't climb the rope because...so we...
> T: (breaks in) You had quite an adventure, John—John, you *really* had a lot of fun, didn't you?
> S: Boy, I'll say!

> S: If the glass was *pushed* down into the water, then you've got the guy's arm pressure making the water rise, and the arm pressure you got to, you know, measure, 'cause...
> T: (breaks in) So, there's more to it than just the volume.
> S: Yeah.

> S: Mrs. Grodin, can we do down to the library, 'cause we gotta get some books on the...
> T: (breaks in) You're working on your term project?
> S: Right....

The obvious purpose here is to help the teacher control the conversation even while a student is speaking. New teachers sometimes object vigorously to this technique. They protest that it's rude to interrupt someone, to which I reply, it is rude to interrupt, but "breaking in" is different from "interrupting." When we interrupt someone, we disregard what he is saying or doing and try to replace it *immediately* with our own concerns. But when we break in with a message-check, we are recognizing and restating what the person is saying or doing. The properly used message-check respects the person, which is exactly the opposite of interrupting him.

Assent (at Step 3) says, in effect, "Yes, that was indeed my message." While you may think your student is saying "yes" to *you*, he is actually saying it to *himself*. He is talking aloud to himself so you can hear him; he is saying, "Did this teacher actually hear me and understand what I said? Did the teacher really get my message? Have I been understood?" When the answer is "yes," the student may say it aloud, nod, grin, or make some other outward sign of assent, but the real communication is inside the student's head. That internal dialogue is critical; do not rush this step. Give your student time to convince himself he has been heard correctly. After he convinces himself, you can control the conversation as you wish.

LEVEL 1: The teacher uses brief paraphrase to control the conversation.

In most cases, paraphrase is the best vehicle for conversation control. Parroting (Level 2) may sound perfunctory, and reflecting (Level 3) may interrupt the student's train of thought. Paraphrasing avoids these problems, but to be low profile, it must be short:

> **S:** I think the British should have just left the Colonies alone—
> **T:** Just given them up.
> **S:** Yeah, because the Colonists didn't want them over here.
> **T:** *None* of the Colonists.
> **S:** Well, a lot of them didn't anyway, and besides we were so far away.
> **T:** Remote.
> **S:** Yeah.

LEVEL 2: The teacher uses acknowledgement or parroting to control the conversation.

Acknowledgement is any verbal or nonverbal expression that says, "I realize you are speaking to me." (See Method O.) So a grunt, "I see," "Hm," or a nod are all forms of acknowledgement. They add nothing to the conversation except to encourage the speaker that he is perhaps being listened to and is cleared to continue.

Parroting is slightly more powerful than acknowledging, since it shows the speaker that at least certain words have been heard; it does not prove those words have been understood.

> **S:** I think the British should have just left the Colonies alone—
> **T:** Uh, hun.
> **S:** Because the Colonists didn't want them over here—
> **T:** Yes.

S: And we were so far away.
T: Far away.
S: Yeah.

LEVEL 3: The teacher uses reflecting or extended paraphrasing to control the conversation.

Reflecting is a powerful form of message checking (see Method O), but must be used with care in conversation control because it can break the student's speaking momentum and train of thought. The extended paraphrase runs the same risk:

S: I think the British should have just left the Colonies alone.
T: They were intruders.
S: Well, yeah, actually, because the Colonists didn't want them over here.
T: So the wishes of the Colonists should have been respected by the British.
S: Sure, because we were so far away.
T: The long distance between America and England is an important factor in determining how the Colonies should have been governed?
S: Well, yeah, I guess so.

LEVEL 4: The teacher uses continual message-check to control the conversation.

Rapid-fire message-checks distract, annoy, and sometimes unnerve the speaker. Most other students, oddly enough, appear not to notice the control, perhaps because it suggests great earnestness on the part of the teacher.

LEVEL 5: The teacher overrides the speaker with the teacher's own comment.

Some students are unaffected by this technique—they keep right on talking. Others are distracted and annoyed by it. Other students may be amused, bewildered, and occasionally mildly disgusted. With the talk-over technique, the teacher seizes control of the conversation without recognition of the student.

LEVEL 6: The teacher interrupts the speaker with support for the speaker's view.

"I know *exactly* what you mean. I was thinking the same thing myself. It is *true*, isn't it, that ...?" It is professional for a teacher to break in; it is rude to interrupt. Nevertheless, interruption is the most common technique for controlling interrupting! For example, "Now just a second, Jean, let Phil finish what he was saying."

LEVEL 7: The teacher interrupts the speaker with a contradiction.

"Wait just a minute before you go on. I disagree strongly with what I think you are saying..." The attention shifts from the speaker's idea to the interrupter. During a classroom debate, however, the teacher might purposely use this high profile technique in the role of "devil's advocate," a legitimate teacher device.

EXERCISE 1   DEMONSTRATION DRILL (5 minutes)

Each member of the group in turn reads something aloud as the instructor demonstrates conversation control within 5 seconds of the start of each reading. When it is your turn to read, notice the effect on you of conversation control. The message you send comes back to you for verification; you are not subjected to an abrupt disregard or denial of what you were saying.

If one of your group objects that the conversation control technique feels high profile and distracting to him, your instructor (or you) can talk to the person and, in the middle of the conversation, use conversation control in a low profile manner; if the conversation control is successful, the person will not be aware that the technique he found objectionable actually went undetected outside the context of a drill. In any case, do not stop the class to debate; understanding often comes only with mastery, so move on.

Use this drill to rehearse conversation control in your own mind even while your instructor demonstrates it; just before your instructor breaks in each time, do so yourself, whispering your paraphrase quietly to yourself.

Conclusion   During the drill, did group members feel the instructor was arguing with them? Insulting them? Embarrassing them? Correct conversation control is almost invisible! Remember that paraphrase is the best method of conversation control. Parroting may sound perfunctory, and reflecting may interrupt the student's train of thought. Use paraphrase, and keep it brief.

EXERCISE 2   DRILL (10 minutes)

Repeat the procedures in Exercise 1, except that your instructor will read aloud, and each group member in turn will use conversation control within 10 seconds, permitting the instructor to continue reading. Break in within 10 seconds. Again, whisper quietly your own conversation control during other people's turns.

EXERCISE 3   DRILL (about 20 minutes)

Pair off and begin the following procedure:

1   One person reads from this chapter, or talks on a topic he wishes. (This person also keeps track of time.)
2   The other person breaks in every 15 seconds, using conversation control and encouraging the speaker, in low profile, nonverbal ways, to continue speaking after each control. Work on developing your conversation control skill to the point that you can break in any time, even in the middle of a sentence, without forcing your partner to lose track of what he is saying. In other words, help him to keep going.

3   Continue steps 1 and 2 for 5 minutes (allowing you to practice 19 conversation controls), then switch roles and repeat.

4   Your instructor will signal the end of 10 minutes.

Conclusion   What problems did you encounter? What suggestions can you give other group members? What techniques worked especially well for you and your partner that you can offer to others?

The purpose of this exercise is to help you develop a rhythm in conversation control, so it begins to feel easy and automatic. In the next exercise, omit the rhythm and rely on technique. Remember, these are drills, not simulations of real classroom behavior. You are using Level 4 techniques to help you master a Level 1 skill.

EXERCISE 4 (about 20 minutes)

In this exercise, the other group members depend on your skill just as your students do.

Form small groups of four, five, or six persons. Each person speaks to the group in turn (reading something, perhaps) for a 2–3 minute period. (The speaker keeps track of the time.)

At your turn, direct your talk to one member of the group until he successfully uses conversation control, preferably within 10 seconds; use eye contact or body position to show you are speaking to him. After his conversation control, address another member, then another, randomly selecting your targets but ensuring that all group members have approximately the same number of chances at conversation control by the time your turn is over. After 2 or 3 minutes, another group member will speak.

Conclusion   By this time, conversation control should be almost automatic. You should have few of the worries you had at the beginning of this chapter, for you now know how to use conversation control techniques in a truly low profile manner, and you also feel confident in your ability to use it any time you wish.

Assignment   Using a standard dialogue format, report at least two different conversations in which you demonstrate conversation control with your students, your supervising teacher, and/or any other persons your instructor designates. Label each example of conversation control with CC in the margin. Provide at least four examples.

METHOD Q

Control of Speaker Role: How does the teacher shift the speaker in a conversation?

Every teacher has students who dominate the class, interrupt, always volunteer first to speak, repeat themselves, cut in, and who talk on and on and on. The problem for the teacher is letting others have a turn.

In middle class American culture, we are conditioned to let someone finish speaking before we speak, so we are occasionally helpless victims of compulsive talkers. Some teachers let students talk on and on, subverting lessons, taking control of classes, and destroying the academic attention of other students. Other teachers become so frustrated that they interrupt students ("I'm sorry to stop you here, Jeannie, but we have to move on") or insult the students ("Thank you, Tom, I think that's enough; let's let someone else talk for a while"). The shift-speaker technique, though not easy for everyone, is a sensible low profile alternative. The teacher shifts speakers by using a conversation control in conjunction with inviting another student to speak. The following examples describe students who are difficult to control effectively with conventional techniques; the shift-speaker technique, however, makes it easy.

Run-on

S: ...And they couldn't have done anything else, see, because there was all that stuff in the cave, and...
T: Their options were really limited, right?
S: Right.
T: Cindy, did you read it the same way?

Repeat

S: I dunno, maybe you could sort of, well, you know, if you really wanted to, I suppose...
T: It's hard to figure out right away, isn't it, George?
S: Yeah.
T: Steve, you found it hard, too?

First to Speak

T: Which is it, the dermis or the epidermis?
S: Oh, I know, Miss Rowley, I know, I know.
T: Angie.
S: The dermis.
T: The dermis?
S: (Nods head vigorously.)
T: Sharon, would you say dermis, and if so, *why*?

Imagine the problem of students who continually interrupt one another. If you use this technique properly, no one will know you are taking action against a rude interrupter.

Interrupt

S: ...and so, I tried to tell her that it wasn't my fault because...
S$_2$: (interrupts,) Yeah, that happened to me, too. She always does that to me too...
T: (breaks in) You have the same problem, S$_2$?
S$_2$: Boy, I'll say.
T: And S$_1$, she wouldn't listen to you?
S$_1$: (Nods.)
T: What happened then, S$_1$?

Notice that the teacher is careful not to use the word "but" (as in "but S_1, as you were saying...") or any other word that signals a contradiction or recalled statement. A high profile technique would announce to the class that S_2 has interrupted S_1 and that the teacher is trying to get back to S_1; this directs attention toward the interruption and away from lesson content.

Low profile shift-speaker is one of the most powerful classroom control techniques. The secret to its success is continual practice, and as you practice, remember the psychology behind the technique. Every talker wants to be heard and recognized, and the compulsive talker needs recognition more than most. If you try to fight this need or suppress it, later problems arise: resentment, retaliation, or simply intensified efforts to be heard. These conscious or unconscious student reactions become more probable as you suppress talkative students. Better to work with human nature than fight it: give those students the recognition they need, then quickly move on. If you are concerned about good manners, make that the topic of another lesson; don't let it interrupt the lesson for today.

MORE TIPS ON USING SHIFT-SPEAKER

1   As a rule, break into student talk at the end of a sentence. But you can also break into the middle of a sentence in very difficult cases: look directly at the student and lean toward him with obvious full attention, paraphrase quickly (two or three words) and wait for his assent. Then quickly but quietly invite someone else to speak.

2   Frequently, students will use assent to continue what they were saying; they are delighted to have such a skillful listener. In that event, simply repeat, or recycle, the shift-speaker technique. You will probably not have to recycle more than two or three times, even with the most persistent student, because when you recycle a third time, you replace paraphrase with reflecting:

> T: So, Tom, you think we could use the straw pieces.
> S: Yeah, and then we could put them in the basket...
> T: [Leaning forward] Put them in the basket to make it soft, right?
> S: Sure, and then...
> T: [Leaning forward even more and nodding head] Tom, you really want that basket comfortable for those baby chicks, don't you?
> S: Yeah.
> T: I can tell! Sarah, what would *you* suggest?

3   Never shift speaker and change topic simultaneously; always invite your new speaker to respond to the same topic you were discussing with the previous speaker. If you change them simultaneously, your previous speaker will notice—and feel ignored.

LEVEL 1: The teacher uses conversation control (paraphrase), then invites a new speaker on the same topic.

LEVEL 2: The teacher uses conversation control (reflecting), then invites a new speaker on the same topic.

The reflecting technique (see Method O) forces a slight pause while the student considers the accuracy of the teacher's message-check. In that pause, the teacher prepares, by turning his head or his whole body to another student, to invite the next student to speak as soon as the first student gives assent to the message-check.

LEVEL 3: The teacher uses conversation control (parroting), then invites a new speaker on the same topic.

Parroting does not satisfy the speaker as do paraphrasing and reflecting, so it increases the risk the speaker will continue to speak after assent.

LEVEL 4: The teacher acknowledges the speaker, or waits for a pause, then invites a new speaker on the same topic.

Acknowledging gives the speaker no assurance he has been understood, which he is likely to realize. The period of silence gives no evidence the teacher has understood or even heard the student.

LEVEL 5: The teacher interrupts or overrides the speaker, or shifts speaker and topic simultaneously.

Teacher interruptions may be justified in the guise of a pseudo-message-check; when a student is giving wrong information, it may be necessary for the teacher to act quickly:

> **S:** ...so when the Congress impeaches the President, the Supreme Court then has to decide if he's guilty or not—
> **T:** You mean, when the *House* impeaches the President and the *Senate* decides his guilt?
> **S:** Oh, yeah. So they...

This type of conversation control, however, can be highly distractive.

Another form of teacher interruption is to override the speaker by talking louder, as loud, or sometimes even more softly. The override technique is justified when the teacher is beginning a lesson (see Method G) and many students are talking all at once; here the teacher combines override with other low profile devices (pointing to the chalkboard or a lesson object, moving about the room) while talking about lesson content. The override is also justified when a student does not respond to lower profile forms of conversation control.

Still another form of teacher interruption is to shift speaker and topic simultaneously. Either of these techniques is low profile by itself, but together they tend to distract the target student. Simultaneous shifting of topic and speaker is justified during freewheeling discussion in which all students are actively participating, but the technique must still be used cautiously.

LEVEL 6: The teacher signals an interruption, then invites the original speaker to resume.

A familiar example might sound like this (B interrupts A, teacher interrupts B): "B, I believe that A was not finished yet. A, what were you saying?" Whether or not the teacher interrupts tactfully and diplomatically, the distractive risk remains the same.

This technique may conceivably be justified if the teacher has been training a student to control his interrupting behavior and has agreed beforehand to cue the student when he inadvertently interrupts someone because he isn't paying attention.

LEVEL 7: The teacher reprimands the speaker, then invites another speaker.

Conventional high profile techniques for shifting speakers are uncomfortably familiar:

"Be quiet, Donald; I want to hear what Alice has to say."
"Thank you, Richard, that's enough. Lonnie?"

EXERCISE 1 DRILL (10–15 minutes)

1   In the regular class group, quickly choose a topic of common interest or concern. One person, who acts as the first student, begins to state an opinion; before 15 seconds have elapsed, the next person, as teacher, uses the shift-speaker technique to pass the speaker role to another student; continue leap-frogging around the group in this manner until the first student is in the position of teacher (the instructor will take a turn as student if necessary, to make this happen), and continue until all in the class group have practiced shift-speaker once.

   A natural tendency in this drill is to state the invitation as, "And Sue, what do you think?" Avoid this obvious formula if you can. Remember, also, this is a drill to help develop a teacher skill; it is not intended to be an actual discussion, so the instructor should discourage a "teacher" who delays the drill with a plea for politeness.

2   Repeat the drill as in 1, this time breaking in with shift-speaker before five seconds of each student's opinion. This is not simply a repeat drill, however; now you will begin to build mastery and rhythm and confidence, and you will be amazed at the improvement in everyone's performance, even those who had difficulty the first time around.

EXERCISE 2 (15 minutes) "THE THUMB EXERCISE"

In this exercise, your fellow group members will depend on your skills to bring them into the group discussion. Without you, they are as helpless as the quiet students who do not participate in class discussions without help from the teacher.

1   Form groups of four to six. Each group will confer in a 10-minute meeting on a topic chosen before the meeting by the entire group. (See list of topics in chapter 14, Exercise 6.)

2   At the signal, one member of each group will begin to speak on the topic.

Anyone else who wants to speak must raise a thumb; he cannot speak until another group member, as teacher, uses a shift-speaker technique and invites him to speak. He will continue speaking until still another member raises a thumb, and so on. (A speaker may not act as teacher at the same time.) If a group member does not raise a thumb to speak, he may be called on anyway by another group member on the basis of visual cues (see Method Ib).

The measure of your group's effectiveness is the number of times each person in your group is invited to speak: if all members are invited an equal number of times, your group is a complete success. If some members are invited and others not, the group should practice the exercise again.

EXERCISE 3 (5–10 minutes)

In this exercise, you will try to control an interrupter without alerting anyone to the interruption.

1 Form groups of three or four. Designate A, B, C (and D).
2 A says or reads something, B quickly interrupts with "I know just what you mean!" and says or reads something similar. C uses shift-speaker back to A, and A then nods and says, "You did it" to signal that the shift has been successful.
3 Switch roles so that B now reads, C interrupts, and A uses shift-speaker techniques.
4 Switch roles again. Continue switching roles until each person has had at least three chances to use the shift-speaker technique.

EXERCISE 4 (5–10 minutes)

In this exercise, practice using repeated shift-speaker techniques, ending with a reflecting technique to control particularly difficult students. Use the same procedure as Exercise 2, but this time each speaker will continue talking after assent, forcing the teacher to repeat conversation control at least once, finally getting a pause with reflecting, and then inviting. Avoid the trite formula, "And Susan, how do you feel about that?"

Conclusion   You have been practicing some of the most powerful low profile classroom control techniques available. The secret of success is continued practice. Make the following assignment work well for you.

Assignment   Using a standard line-by-line format, report at least three occasions in which you use a conversation control and invitation to speak with your students or with other persons designated by your instructor. Use labels CC and INV for appropriate lines.

METHOD R

Control of Topic: How does the teacher change the topic in a conversation?

Students often ramble, leaving the topic to say things completely irrelevant to the lesson. Occasionally the irrelevancy is a game, leading the teacher on a merry chase after nonlesson topics that waste time and demonstrate student ingenuity in delightful ways. But typical irrelevancy is unintentional.

What should we do with students who issue irrelevancies, non sequiturs, and distracting, silly remarks? Ignore them? Scold them and tell them to stop daydreaming and pay attention?

Conventional teacher topic control techniques are often unpleasant and high profile: "All right, Jason, I think we're getting off the track here. Let's try to stick with the topic, shall we?" or "Michelle, are you listening? Where have you been? Now you start paying attention, young lady."

With low profile techniques, however, teachers can control the topic in such a way that students' minds quickly focus on lesson content without embarrassment to the students. To change topics, the teacher uses conversation control along with an inquiry (to the same speaker). This technique utilizes the conversation control technique (see Method P) and adds an inquiry question (see Method O), thus affording an excellent low profile device for shifting a student's mind from one topic to another. For example, if a student says something completely irrelevant to the topic:

> **T:** And did the Romans do any important things?
> **S$_1$:** Sure, they built good roads...
> **S$_2$:** And conquered lots of countries.
> **S$_3$:** Mr. Finch, where's my spelling test?
> **T:** It's lost?
> **S$_3$:** Yeah.
> **T:** We'll find it, Cindy; Cindy, think for a moment: What else did the Romans do besides build roads and conquer nations?

Or when a student says something almost relevant to the topic, but not quite:

> **T:** And what makes the leaves green? Anybody? James?
> **S$_1$:** They got green stuff in 'em that makes 'em like that.
> **S$_2$:** Yeah, yeah, clarapill!
> **S$_3$:** I wish they'd stay green all year.
> **T:** And stay on the trees?
> **S$_3$:** Yeah.
> **T:** (To S$_3$) What do you think makes the grass green?

Or a student gives a completely incorrect answer:

> **T:** How many times will 4 go into 16? Jim?
> **S:** Three.

> **T:** You mean that 4 will go into 12 three times?
> **S:** Yeah.
> **T:** Good. If 4 will go into 12 three times, Jim, how many times will it go into 16?

The teacher can also use this technique when students are talking about their topic instead of the lesson:

> **S:** Mrs. Hunt, can we go outside today and have our class out there? It's so crummy in here.
> **T:** The sun looks good out there, eh?
> **S$_s$:** Right on/Yeah man/Yippie.
> **T:** You believe fully, with all your hearts, that we could really concentrate on reviewing for the test outside?
> **S$_s$:** Sure/No sweat/Right on.
> **T:** Well let's see for a moment just how good your powers of concentration actually are today. For example, somebody tell me about mores and folkways...

Again, the goal for the change-topic technique is to keep student attention riveted on the lesson, preventing students from thinking about hurt feelings or other distractive emotions. Remember the psychology behind this skill—every student needs to be heard. To satisfy this need, we prove through message-check that we have heard them. After they have been heard, students are often surprisingly receptive to thinking about a new topic. The inquiry question forces them to think, at least for a moment, about the new topic. Low profile controls work with human nature, not against it.

When changing topics, do not substitute a statement for the inquiry question. Students can ignore a statement more easily than a question. When a student rapidly continues the same topic after giving assent, use a sequence. Keep breaking in with paraphrases or reflecting until the pause comes (it will, eventually—don't be discouraged) and then shift topics. Repeat this technique as often as necessary. For example:

> **T:** And so we have four circles and five—
> **S:** I won a doll at the fair last night, Miss Reid.
> **T:** You won, Cindy?
> **S:** Yeah, and my gramma made the doll for me, and—
> **T:** That was very special for you, wasn't it?
> **S:** Yeah, and—
> **T:** You were very proud, weren't you, Cindy?
> **S:** Yeah.
> **T:** Cindy, how many squares do you see here?

Work to refine and smooth your technique, making it appear natural, effortless, and above all, low profile. For example, after you get assent, you might acknowledge with "OK" or "Um-hm" or some other neutral sound that is characteristic of your normal speech. Then immediately ask your inquiry question with no break or pause, giving the impression of eagerness to ask your question. Also, accompany your inquiry question with strong eye contact and a slight forward tilt or motion of your head or body.

As you gain confidence and skill, notice that the new topic, the subject of your inquiry question, may either be very close to the student's topic or very far — it makes no difference. When you are skillful, your students do not notice.

LEVEL 1: The teacher uses conversation control (paraphrase), then changes topic.

LEVEL 2: The teacher uses conversation control (reflecting), then changes topic.

The risk of distraction is slightly higher at Level 2 than at Level 1 because reflecting questions require more thought; thinking about the question may lead the student on to other thoughts before he formulates an answer.

LEVEL 3: The teacher uses conversation control (parroting), then changes topic.

Parroting is not as satisfying to the speaker as paraphrase and reflecting (see Methods O and P), but it can bring an assent:

> **S:** ... and this is such boring stuff to study.
> **T:** Boring.
> **S:** Right.
> **T:** How does one go about...?

LEVEL 4: The teacher acknowledges the speaker, or waits for a pause, then changes topic.

This technique is perhaps most common among people with reputations for being diplomatic or artful at avoiding certain topics.

> **S:** ... and this is such boring stuff to study.
> **T:** I see. Hm. Tell me, how does one go about...?

The power lies in the congenial manner of raising the new topic; the weakness is that the technique is transparent.

LEVEL 5: The teacher interrupts or overrides the speaker with a new topic, or changes topic and speaker simultaneously.

LEVEL 6: The teacher signals that the prior topic is not favored, then changes topic.

For example:
> "I see. Well, that's not the topic. The topic is..."
> "That is also an important consideration. May we deal with that one after we finish this topic?"
> "I'm sorry, I realize we have shifted the topic on you..."

Here the teacher gives the student a clear signal that the student's prior statement was off-target; even when the teacher takes the responsibility off the student's shoulders, the effect is high profile.

LEVEL 7: The teacher denigrates the speaker's topic, then changes topic.

For example: "I do not find that amusing. What I want you to discuss now is…" or, "There is no place for that here. The topic is…."

   This technique is, however, preferable to a reprimand, because it depersonalizes the situation and emphasizes the topic rather than the student.

EXERCISE 1 DRILL (10–15 minutes)

Before class, establish three topics you very much want to talk about today. Write them here:

(A) _____

(B) _____

(C) _____

In your regular class group, your instructor begins talking or reading aloud about any topic. Each group member in turn, before 10 seconds have elapsed, breaks in as teacher and uses the change-topic technique. In response to each correct technique, the instructor says, "That's a good question" and continues talking or reading, either on the original or the new topic until the next teacher breaks in.

Conclusion   Avoid formulas such as, "How do you feel about…" Remember that your purpose is to avoid signal words that make your technique noticeable, obtrusive, and high profile.

EXERCISE 2 DRILL (10–15 minutes)

1 Pair with another person. (If your group has an odd number, form pairs and one group of three.)

2 Assuming the role of student, begin to talk about your topic. Your partner will act as teacher and listen to your first sentence or two.

3 The teacher will try to change to his own topic. If he uses the technique correctly, say "That's a good question" and continue talking about your topic. If he does not change correctly, ignore his interruption and keep talking. Stop and help him if he's confused, or call your instructor.

4 Repeat Step 3 until the teacher has practiced five shifts, then reverse roles. (In the group of three, one person will monitor each session.) For example:

   S: I like dogs a lot, and…
   T: Dogs are favorites of yours?
   S: Yes.
   T: Have you ever tried to teach a learning disabled kid?
   S: That's a good question. I like to teach my dog tricks. Why just the other day I…
   T: You're a dog-teacher, eh?
   S: Right.

> T: How many L. D. kids do you think are in the schools today?
> S: That's a good question. One of my dogs is hard of hearing, and...

Conclusion   This drill can be fun, and a superb skill-builder if you work hard to do it correctly. The purpose is to try to concentrate on two topics at once.

EXERCISE 3 DRILL (30–40 minutes)

In this exercise we add a few more distractions to help you develop your concentration. Remember, if you can change topic quickly and effectively in this exercise, you can do it effectively almost anywhere.

1 Form a group of four persons (if necessary, three or five).
2 Assuming the role of student, begin to talk about your topic. The others will assume the role of teacher and listen to your first sentence or two.
3 The first teacher on your left will try to change topic. You should answer his question as briefly as you can, then immediately drift back to your own topic, at which time the next teacher will change topic, then the next, then the next.
4 After each teacher has a turn, turn to the person on your left and ask: "What did you want to talk about?" Your small group then repeats Steps 2 and 3.

Conclusion   By this time you should have observed many smooth techniques for changing topics, and should have practiced at least nine yourself.

Assignment   Using a standard dialogue format, write a report of at least three occasions in which you use these techniques of changing topic with your students, supervising teacher, or others designated by your instructor.

CONTROL OF GROUP DISCUSSION
(METHOD S)

14

roup discussion is most successful in small groups of three to fifteen, but a skillful teacher can manage groups of fifty or even a hundred.

METHOD S
Controlling Group Discussion: How does the teacher control student discussions during instruction?

The purpose of any group discussion is to help students think out loud and learn from each other. Five low profile group leadership skills help teachers lead discussions, and students can learn them as well (see Table 14–1). These are some examples of low profile teacher remarks to encourage discussion:

MC — "So you enjoyed this story, Dan?"

TT — "How could it be that he both wants to marry her and doesn't want to marry her?"

Dir — "Does anybody have an idea?"

Inv — "Alex, what were you going to say?"

R/S/Dir — "Dan said a while ago that the dragon was not the problem. Are we all agreed on that?"

TABLE 14–1   Group Discussion Control Skills

Skill	Teacher Action	Effect
Skill 1 — Message Check (MC)	Paraphrases, reflects feelings and general ideas; on occasion, parrots	Students feel they are truly being heard and understood
Skill 2 — Thought Test (TT)	Asks for implications and possible consequences; tests analogies and probes for reasons	Students think and rethink
Skill 3 — Direct (Dir)	Starts things off, sees that decisions are made or discussion continues Asks open-ended questions (to entire group) Asks inquiring questions of speaker Raises new topics Asks if group is ready to make a decision	Gives students directions for thinking
Skill 4 — Inviting (Inv)	Opens way for *individual* group members to join group discussion or activity	Students feel welcome
Skill 5 — Recall/ Summarize (R/S)	Recalls what individual students have said earlier; summarizes what group as a whole is saying	Helps students organize their thinking and understand importance of what they say

Notice that each skill in Table 14–1 helps students formulate and express their own positions; none of the group leadership skills pertains to the teacher's expressing his position (opinion, facts, information, experiences, feelings, testimony, agreement or disagreement, interpretations, etc.) to the students, except to mobilize student discussion. There is a difference between group leader functions and group member functions. We use the label "other" when the teacher functions as a *member* of a class discussion by responding to a question, expressing the teacher's own opinion, agreeing or disagreeing (verbally or nonverbally), or otherwise making statements as would any other group member.

The teacher's goal in controlling group discussion should be to balance control skills and orchestrate them according to the group's goals, needs, and behavior. To do this, the skilled teacher often makes one statement serve more than one function. Here are more examples of teacher talk during a lesson:

Dir—"What should we talk about? What is not clear to you in this assignment?"

Inv—"Yeah?" (Nod to person who hasn't spoken.)

MC/TT/R—"You said before, Mary, that angle X and angle Y are not equal. Were you *actually* saying that these triangles are not congruent?"

Inv—"Does that seem right to you, Judy?"

MC—"I'm not making myself clear, am I?"

MC/R—"Are you saying, Bill, what Lou was saying?"

MC/Inv—"Are you confused?" (Look at passive listener.)

S—"There's no question in our minds about that any more, right?"

MC/Inv—"William, you look like you don't agree."

Dir—"Who has a suggestion?"

Dir—"Have we covered everything? Are we ready to go on?"

To lead a good discussion, say as little as you can while facilitating the group members' ideas. Use these low profile techniques: message-check skills (Methods O, P1, Q1, and R1); thought-test skills (Method O); and directing skills.

DIRECTING SKILLS

1 Open-ended questions
   "Well, we're talking about.... Is this a good thing or a bad thing?"
   "Does anyone have an opinion?"
   "How can we start talking about this?"

2 Raising new topics
   "Has anyone thought about...?"
   "Now that we're done with that point, how do you feel about...?"

3 Keeping the group on target
   "When we were talking about...a while ago...."
   "What about [original topic]? Does anyone have an idea about...?"

4 Raising decisions
   "Are we all agreed, then, that...?"
   "Is there anything else on...?"
   "Are we ready to decide?"

INVITING SKILLS (also see Method Ib)

The skill required in inviting someone to speak is contrary to natural instincts; you must watch the *listeners* in your class discussion group, not just the speaker. Look for small signs of reaction or emotion or interest, then use low profile techniques to invite new speakers into the discussion. The quiet members of your group often have a long history of sitting on the sidelines watching their classmates, but quiet students can be reached and awakened by a teacher with good discussion control skills. When you detect a small sign, try one of the following:

Turn easily to the student and say, "How do you feel about that"/"Do you agree?"/"Does that sound right to you?" etc.

Nod your head to the student now and then; make friendly eye contact now and then.

"*You* know about that; what would *you* say?"

"And was your experience the same?"/"Did you read it the same way?"/"Is that what you thought when you saw it?"

If your invitation visibly jars the student, you have probably misread the student's sign of readiness, failed to make sufficient nonverbal contact beforehand, or failed to be low profile in your invitation.

In short, your inviting skills are successfully low profile when your student speaks without hesitancy or awkwardness, even if he has not spoken before.

RECALLING/SUMMARIZING SKILLS

RECALL WHAT SOMEONE HAS SAID

"Joe said something earlier that I think we should...."

"As Sue said a while ago, we are facing a problem of...."

The main difference between message-checking and recalling is that message-checking is directed to the student who has *just* spoken, while recalling is directed toward someone who has spoken earlier.

SUMMARIZE WHAT THE GROUP SAYS

"It seems to me that we are all saying that...."

"Are we agreed, then, that...?"

"We seem to be divided on this issue, right? That is, we...."

"Aren't we trying to do *two* things at once here? And it just isn't working...."

Summarizing helps pull a discussion together, giving it an overview and perspective. "This is what we have been talking about," says the teacher, and the students think, "Oh, yeah, now I see." Students are particularly fortunate when their teacher is able to acknowledge differences of opinion and put those differences in useful perspective without taking sides. The technical skill here is simply a message-check of what the entire group has been saying.

HOW TO BEGIN GROUP DISCUSSION

Several low profile techniques for preparing and starting students in group discussion are content talk, preparatory seatwork, debate-primer, and buzz groups.

CONTENT TALK

The teacher is usually wise to begin group discussion with content talk rather than talk about lesson mechanics or methods. Compare these two beginnings; the first uses a mixture of high and low profile talk, the second uses only low profile:

> **TEACHER X:**   We are now going to have group discussions on pollenation reproductive systems.
> **STUDENTS:**   Do we have to discuss this? What's there to discuss? This is stupid!

> **TEACHER Y:**   I've been talking about "budding" as a reproductive system in some plants. Now would you say that a pollenation reproductive system is more advanced or less advanced than budding? Is it more adaptive or less adaptive? Anyone?

PREPARATORY SEATWORK

Many class discussions fail because students do not prepare themselves for discussion. The teacher can help students in ways such as these:

> **TEACHER:**   In a few moments, I will ask you to discuss why Alice didn't want to go tell her friend about Billy. Right now, I want you to spend one minute writing down six words that describe Alice's personality and character.

or

> **TEACHER:**   When we form the panel, you will ask one of the panelists a question about his character from the story. Write down a question you could ask.

By the time discussion begins, these students are going to be hard to hold back. Preparatory work starts the brain working on the discussion topic *before* discussion begins.

DEBATE PRIMER

Some teachers are able to induce students to debate with and learn from one another without acrimony or confusion. While group discussion control skills are necessary for maintaining these debates and keeping them focused on lesson content, other skills can be used to start the debates. For example:

> **TEACHER:**   Jeff, how about the question of loyalty of the Colonists?
> **JEFF:**   Well I think that, technically, the Colonists were disloyal. The Tory's were the loyal ones.

> TEACHER: Anna, you don't look convinced.
>
> ANNA: Sure, because what were they being loyal to? A king who wanted to exploit them? What kind of loyalty is that?
>
> TEACHER: Jeff, how would you reply to Anna's point? Go ahead, persuade her.
>
> JEFF: See, what you're not getting is . . . .

BUZZ GROUPS

Buzz groups are informal, temporary groups of two to six people each, which form suddenly and meet for a very short time — 15 seconds to 5 minutes — to perform a specific task. Signal the end of buzz groups with a bell.

> TEACHER: I've just been telling you about rational numbers. Now I want you to turn to your neighbor and decide between the two of you — or three if necessary — whether or not the number 39 is a rational number, and why. You have 30 seconds. Ready? Go.

or

> TEACHER: And if we do take this field trip, it ought to have a focus, I think, a central theme or question. But what question? I'd like your best ideas. When I give you the signal, you will form buzz groups — with four persons in each group — when I give the signal. In your buzz group, I want you to think of five possible questions or themes. You will have two minutes to talk. OK, begin.

It is important when teaching with buzz groups to monitor them constantly and carefully to make sure they are on-task; do not assume. And stop on time.

LEVEL 1: The teacher induces total group participation and total group effort.

LEVEL 2: The teacher assigns formal responsibilities to different students in the group and trains students for those responsibilities.

Students are reassured when they know exactly what is expected of them. For example, the teacher may announce debatable topics ahead of time and assign students to prepare to defend one side or the other. Or various students might be trained in particular group discussion skills (Table 14-1) and monitor and record their small group participation in actual small group discussions (see exercises at the end of this chapter).

LEVEL 3: The teacher leads all group interaction.

This traditional teacher role in group leadership succeeds most of the time. Teachers enforce it with talk like this:

> "Please do not talk until I call on you."
>
> "If you want to talk, raise your hand first."
>
> When students get very excited, this technique can be frustrating. The waits seem endless to eager students who feel they have something important to say. (When everyone wants to speak, buzz groups are ideal.)

LEVEL 4: The teacher permits one or more group members to be passive or absent.

The teacher may not be aware that he is ignoring a student, but those who do not participate in group discussions will not learn, and their insights and suggestions will be lost to the others. When a student is just learning discussion skills, however, the teacher might give him some time to observe before expecting him to become fully active in the group.

LEVEL 5: The teacher excludes one or more group members.

It is difficult to consider one a group leader who cannot keep his group together. When a teacher dismisses or excludes group members, the group no longer exists; a new group automatically forms, testing anew the leader's ability to lead.

When a student is momentarily uncontrollable or so beset with personal concerns that he cannot function in the group, the teacher should allow him to be absent from the group, but this should be a last resort in handling behavior problems.

LEVEL 6: The teacher uses the group discussion as a platform for the teacher's own ideas.

Imagine, for example, that a teacher forms a small group and says: "In this group you should feel free to give your opinion about the short story, because this is a time for independent thinking about *your* interpretation of the story." If the teacher then lectures the group on her interpretation of the story, she is misusing the group.

This technique is justified for trying out an idea on a small group before taking it to the entire class. In this case, the small group acts as a sounding board.

LEVEL 7: The teacher allows group discussion without leadership.

A group in which neither the teacher nor any student exhibits leadership skills is worthless. Group members will soon tire of squabbling and wasting time. There is no reason for a leadership vacuum in a classroom group.

EXERCISE 1 WARM-UP DRILL (1 minute)

Referring to Table 14-1, your instructor will say aloud little bits at random from the table, and your group should chorus, from memory, the corresponding skill titles. For example:

"Open-ended questions." "Direct."
"Talks about what individual students have said earlier." "Recall."
Do these quickly. When you monitor a group discussion later in the class, you will have to know these labels well to evaluate your partner's control skills.

EXERCISE 2 DRILL (10 minutes)

In this drill, your instructor will read aloud, at random, from the following sample statements. After the first few words of each statement, group members will name aloud the skill—or "other"—of which that statement is an example. Then the instructor will repeat the *correct* classification and move right on. Save discussion until the end; use the drill to learn through successive examples:

> Then this looks OK to you? (MC)
>
> How could it be that he both wants to marry her and doesn't want to marry her? (TT)
>
> Does anybody have an idea? (Dir)
>
> Alex, what were you going to say? (Inv)
>
> Dan said, a while ago, that the dragon was not the problem. (R)
>
> Don't you think the correct answer is b? (O)
>
> Oh, so what you *say* is that Amy did it, but what you *mean* is that.... (MC)
>
> Then if *he* should not be forced to return, does that mean that *she* shouldn't either? (TT)
>
> We started off talking about the collection. What else was needed there? (Dir)
>
> Does that seem right to you, Judy? (Inv)
>
> We all agree, right? (S)
>
> That's crazy. (O)
>
> So you want to make one, too, right? (MC)
>
> So what would happen if she left right away? (TT)
>
> Have we covered everything we need to cover? Are we ready to go on? (Dir)
>
> I'd like to hear your idea, June. (Inv)
>
> It seems to me that we're arguing for dismissal. (S)
>
> Are you saying that they go together? (MC)
>
> Why not? Why shouldn't they? (TT)
>
> Who has a suggestion? (Dir)
>
> Donna, I can't tell if you agree or not. How do you feel about it? (Inv)
>
> So what we've been saying is that we *can* work it out, right? (S)
>
> Sure, and then you could go in and ask. (O)
>
> I'm not making myself clear, am I? (MC)
>
> Are you implying, Joe, that Raskolnikov should *not* have gone back to his room? (TT)
>
> What shall we talk about? (Dir)
>
> Yeah? (Nod to person who hasn't spoken.) (Inv)
>
> There's no question in our minds about that any more, right? (S)
>
> I agree, right. (O)
>
> Let's get back to Pam's point. (Dir/R)
>
> Then are we ready to decide now? (S/Dir)
>
> If everybody agrees $a + b = c$, let's look at number 3. (S/Dir)
>
> I think the real question here is the word "practical." Would anybody else agree? (O/Dir)
>
> Are you saying, Bill, what Lou was saying? (MC/R)
>
> That doesn't make sense to me. (O or TT or Dir)
>
> Are you confused? (Look at passive listener.) (MC/Inv)
>
> William, you look like you don't agree. (MC/Inv)

You said before, Mary, that angle *X* and angle *Y* are not equal. Were you
actually saying that these triangles are not congruent? (MC/TT/R)
So we agree on . . . . But now . . . is impossible. Was that your point, Bob? (15
words, and both recall and summarize are here. A very powerful control.)
(MC/TT/Inv/S/R)

EXERCISE 3 DRILL (10 minutes)

This drill, the same as Exercise 2, will *add* the task of monitoring a teacher and
recoding/classifying her discussion control skills on paper. For recording and classifying, make a skeletal monitor's form. Your instructor will read — rather slowly —
12 statements at random and without pause; follow directions 1 and 2 on the
Monitor's Form.

Conclusion   First, review the statements and check your classifications. Second,
check the facility of your monitoring. You should have written only one to six words
to refresh your memory later of what was said. (This is fast, hard work, but it will
be important to your teacher-partner in later exercises.)

GROUP DISCUSSION CONTROL SKILLS — MONITOR'S FORM

Directions to Monitor:
1 Fill in the date, your teacher-partner's name, your own name, and code letters of the assigned skills announced by the instructor.
2 During the discussion, record the first one to six words of *every* statement made by your teacher-partner (or note relevant gestures, facial expressions, etc.). Also record a Code Letter for each statement/gesture.
3 After the meeting, fill in the actual observed skill(s) blank.

Date: _____

Name of teacher: _____

Name of monitor: _____

Assigned skill(s): _____

Actual observed skill(s): _____

Code	Skills	Code	Skills
MC	Message-check	Inv	Inviting
TT	Thought-test	S/R	Summarizing/Recalling
Dir	Directing	O	(Other: opinion giver, etc.)

Record of Participation:
e.g., _Inv_ Do you agree, Jim?

___

___

EXERCISE 4 DRILL ON INVITING SKILLS (10–30 minutes)

The class or group should form a circle. Your instructor will initiate an open discussion on a topic of the instructor's choice and will invite you to share your views, relying on your visual cues of readiness. You will then be the speaker for 1 minute or less. The rest of the group will do two things as you speak:

1 Listen to what you say and keep occasional eye contact with you as you speak.
2 Watch the rest of the group, looking for small signs or visual cues of readiness to speak. (After you have been speaker, put a check mark here: _____)

When you have finished speaking, someone else will act as the inviter and invite still another group member to be the new speaker. This process continues until every group member has been both a speaker and an inviter. (After you have been an inviter, put a check mark here: _____)

The exercise is over when all group members have performed both roles. Follow these rules for the exercise:

1 No one may speak unless invited.
2 The speaker may not invite.
3 Only low profile skills are allowed; the question, "Who hasn't spoken yet?" is absolutely prohibited.
4 No listener in the group may look at the speaker for more than five seconds at a time; when you are a listener, you may either shift your eyes away from the speaker every five seconds and then return, or you may let your eyes wander around the group and check in with the speaker occasionally to let him know you are listening to him. (Your instructor should monitor all listeners for "five-second-violations" just as the basketball referee watches the foul lane for three-second violations.)

Conclusion　This exercise requires you to do three unnatural, inconvenient, and frustrating things:

1 You may not look at the speaker with your full attention. Instead, you must keep your eyes on the rest of the class as the speaker talks.
2 Other people cannot speak until you invite them. That is a lot of responsibility.
3 To make this exercise work, you must think about the topic under discussion, keep track of who has and has not spoken, and watch for visual cues of readiness—all at the same time!

Welcome to the world of professional teaching. The competent professional teacher does all these things, every day, and does them well. If you had trouble with this exercise, do it again. Or do the drill on eyes below. Your inviting skills could change the school life of a shy, withdrawn student whose previous teachers either did not have this skill or did not care how the student behaved.

EXERCISE 5 DRILL on EYES (2 minutes)

If you had difficulty with the 5-second limit in the inviting drill, try this: as your class group sits in a circle, the instructor reads or talks for two minutes. Hold up one or more fingers on one hand continuously as you take notes. As you listen to the instructor, look at others in the group who are holding up various numbers of fingers, and jot down on your note paper the name of each person and the number of fingers he is holding up, at the same time you take notes on what is being said. You are trying, in this mini-exercise, to break old habits. They are hard to break, so expect some discomfort, but also realize that you can and will break those habits.

EXERCISE 6 FISHBOWL (20 minutes)

The fishbowl technique in this exercise is excellent, though rarely used, for class-room discussions in upper elementary and secondary classrooms. (Students must be carefully trained to use it.)

1   Form groups of six, eight, or ten. (If an odd number, put an extra person in the largest group.)
2   Divide each group into an inside circle and an outside circle. The inside circle will hold a discussion. (They are the teachers, those in the outer circle, monitors.)
3   When you are monitor, be sure to sit exactly opposite your partner so you can see her face and hear what she says, and outside the discussion circle. Do not participate in the discussion in any way, no matter how interested you are in the topic. Follow the directions on the Monitor's Form and make your own form for the discussion.

Fishbowl

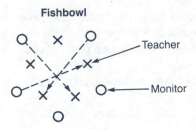

4   When you are teacher, you will hold a discussion with a group for 5 minutes on any topic listed below, designated by the instructor, or preferred by your group. Choosing the topic is part of the discussion, not a preliminary. During this discussion, strive as teacher to use, in low profile, each of the five skills (all are the Actual Assigned Skills on the Monitor's Form) in addition to any O's you feel like using. All members of the discussion group have the responsibilities of

teacher: every teacher is expected to use at least one example of each control skill in addition to other statements she may make.

5 If your group has an extra member, pair two monitors with one teacher for the first meeting.

6 The instructor will announce the start and end of the first 5-minute discussion period.

7 At the end of the first discussion, change places with your partner and start at new 5-minute discussion period, following Steps 3 through 6 above. (Note: at Step 5 above, the new monitor will have to maintain two separate Monitor Forms for the two teachers assigned to her.)

TOPICS

- Should teachers be held accountable for the performance (success *and* failure) of their students?
- Is it the teacher's fault or the principal's fault when a teacher is continually ineffective?
- Is cheating always wrong?
- Should schools teach sex?
- Is teaching *really* a profession?
- Is a silent, quiet student harder to teach than a noisy one?
- Should a tutor aide or student teacher tell a supervising teacher exactly how she feels when the aide disagrees with the supervising teacher's opinion or methods or goals?
- Is cheating always bad?
- What should a teacher do when a student tells him to "Go to hell!"
- The best student does what she is told and does not talk back.
- When a parent knows more about the child than does the teacher, the teacher should follow the parent's advice.
- Schools should not teach morality.
- Students should respect other students' ideas, even crazy ones.
- The job of the professional teacher is to manipulate people.
- A teacher should never say, "I can't work with you; I'm sending you to counselor/principal/...."
- When students misbehave in class, it's usually because the teacher has not prepared the lesson properly.
- Schools should teach students to think independently, not to parrot their teachers or to conform.
- (Other)

Conclusion   The first fishbowl discussion is often frustrating for the group. First, if you are conscientious, you are trying to think about using all five skills while thinking at the same time about the topic and about what other people are saying. It seems impossible. Second, you are trying to use your skills, but so is everyone else, and the conversation sounds weird with everybody competing for message-checking, summarizing, and inviting. There just does not seem to be enough time for everyone to have a chance to use their skills in a relaxed and appropriate way.

Third, many first-time groups cannot even find a topic in five minutes. Finally, it seems odd to form a group and then make every member the leader. In normal groups, we choose one leader and let her do all the work.

All your frustrations are real, and all result from one factor: lack of skill. If you are ever permitted to sit in a group of truly skilled discussion leaders, you will be amazed at how delightful the experience can be. These people really know how to listen, to encourage each other to speak, and to challenge each other's thinking. They help each other stay on target, and get their job done efficiently. No one says "Hey, I'm the discussion leader here!" Instead, everyone accepts her fair share of responsibility for helping the discussion run smoothly, and every member of the group is heard.

It will not be long before you will sit in such a group; by the end of this chapter, you and most of your fellow group members will be competent enough in discussion control skills to conduct an excellent group discussion. More important, you will then have the skills to control discussion in almost any classroom. While the student is free to think only about the topic, the teacher must think about both the topic and the group process.

EXERCISE 7 MEETING (20–minutes)

After one or more of the drills described earlier, repeat Exercise 6 and consider the difference. This time, increase each meeting time to 7 minutes, and do not debate long on which topic to choose. If one person is interested in a topic, speak to that topic until the person is satisfied, then change topics.

EXERCISE 8 MEETING (20–30 minutes)

This exercise repeats all the procedures of Exercise 6 except that the meeting time increases to 8 minutes. Your goal in this exercise is to use every discussion control skill at least once, and to vary your patterns of activity by following every "O" with a Control Skill. For example, your pattern of group discussion control might originally have looked like this:

O O MC O O O O Dir O R

In this exercise, try to produce a pattern closer to this one (remembering that "O" is not a teacher control skill, but a statement or response):

O Inv O Dir S MC O TT MC O

In leading a class discussion, the natural impulse to state one's own views should be rigorously controlled. Sometimes we should state our opinions; at other times, we should use low profile techniques to make students think for themselves. (Note: "No, I don't want to tell you *my* opinion; I want to know how *you* think" is mid to high profile.) The professional teacher has the self-control to choose and implement either option as appropriate.

Assignment   Using a standard dialogue format, report a discussion you have with at least two other people, preferably a discussion with students on subject matter. In this discussion, demonstrate your use of all five discussion control skills. Label each skill by its code letters along the right-hand margin so the instructor can read it easily.

CONTROL THROUGH INSTRUCTIONAL QUESTIONS (METHOD T)

15

METHOD Ta

Standard Procedures: What is the teacher's usual style of asking instructional questions?

Some teachers think that calling on a student requires nothing more than the student's name and a question. This is not so; the teacher can ask questions in high profile or low profile ways. For example, notice how important the timing of each student's name can be in the teacher's style of asking questions.

LEVEL 1: The teacher asks a question, waits, calls on volunteers, then waits for answer.

The question comes first, before any names are mentioned (see Good and Brophy, 1978, p. 366). This technique induces all students to think, rather than just the student whose name is called. Also, calling on volunteers means no student is likely to "freeze" when his name is called. If the teacher's habit is to call *only* on volunteers, other students may be inclined not to think, knowing they will not be called upon. A combination of Level 1 and Level 2 techniques is desirable in most cases.

LEVEL 2: The teacher asks a question, waits, calls on nonvolunteer, then waits for an answer.

The teacher *expects* an answer, even if it is "I don't know." The student is not a passive student for whom special techniques are necessary (see Method Ib).

LEVEL 3: The teacher asks a question, waits for an answer, then immediately repeats the question to another student.

This is the technique some writers refer to as *redirection* (Jacobsen et al. pp. 177–179). While this technique may disconcert a student who is not ready with an answer, it works quite well for speeding up a dragging discussion or recitation.

LEVEL 4: The teacher calls on students before stating the question.

"Holly, what is the capital of California?" With this technique, there is the possibility that only the student whose name is called will bother to think about the question, and that hearing his name will unnerve and disorient the student because he does not know what is coming (Good and Brophy, 1978, p. 366).

As a variation in classroom recitation, this technique can be fun and exciting for students because it feels "dangerous" to them, the very reason it is a popular procedure on television quiz shows.

LEVEL 5: The teacher asks question, pauses briefly, then shifts quickly to another student before the first student answers.

"He didn't even give me time to answer!" complains the student, who is understandably embarrassed and resentful, but for a rapid drill, the technique can be exciting and profitable for students.

LEVEL 6: The teacher directs uncued questions to inattentive or unknown attention students.

Asking a question of the inattentive student, providing no cues or context, and using the question to wake him up or set an example for the rest of the class, is popular teacher practice, but usually distractive.

LEVEL 7: The teacher interrupts student answers with his own.

This technique would be rude except in this kind of circumstance:

> **TEACHER:** ... and the moment arm should be how long, Theresa?
> **STUDENT:** Lessee, I think maybe about—
> **TEACHER:** — 14 inches. Theresa, I asked you an unfair question, I realize, because I hadn't told you beforehand that...

METHOD Tb

Types of Questions: What types of questions does the teacher ask during instruction?

No one type of question is intrinsically better than another type, but different instructional purposes require different types of questions. Classroom control requires that any specific type of question be appropriate to the lesson.

Cognitive questions ask for intellectual responses, while affective questions draw on attitudes and emotions. Convergent questions have only one right answer. They cause students to draw ideas together, recall facts, summarize, and conclude. For example:

"What makes the generator turn?"

"How does the water actually turn the blades?"

"Does the turning blade make electricity all by itself?"

"What is the relationship between the electrical current and the magnetic field?"

Divergent questions do not have a single correct answer; rather, they allow students to arrive at one of several acceptable or appropriate answers. For example:

"When you think of electricity, what comes to your mind?"

"How has electricity changed the way wars are fought?"

"How are electric motors different from electric generators?"

"How can you tell if a wire is large enough to carry a given current?"

Low level questions ask for facts, simple definitions, terms, names, dates, or events—any information that can be memorized and recalled.

"Who is the current President of the U.S.?"

"How many oxygens are there in heavy water?"

High level questions require intellectual processing:

"Who has been the most effective President of the U.S.?"

"How could you manufacture hydrogen peroxide most cheaply?

Closed questions call for statements of fact, description, definition, or naming. Open questions require statements of opinion, evaluation, explanation, or inference.

LEVEL 1: The teacher asks lower level, closed, convergent questions on lesson content.

A growing body of evidence shows that lower level closed questions correlate more closely with student achievement than higher level open questions (Wright and Nuthall, 1970, p. 487; Brophy and Evertson, 1976, p. 129).

LEVEL 2: The teacher asks higher level questions on lesson content, in series, when appropriate.

A full discussion of higher level question techniques may be found in Bloom et al., 1956.

LEVEL 3: The teacher asks open, cognitive questions, inviting students' own experiences that relate to lesson content.

When students think about open questions, their minds reach out. How far are they likely to reach? We cannot predict each student's response to an open question, but we know that open questions incur greater risk of off-task thinking, hence the teacher must be vigilant and skillful in controlling conversations and group discussions in which open questions are asked. Bull sessions and aimless talk are the result of ineffective teacher controls.

LEVEL 4: The teacher asks affective questions related to lesson content.

The teacher should not avoid asking these kinds of questions simply because they are mid-profile; to the contrary, empathetic questions can be powerful tools to involve students in their learning: "Imagine now: Your family has lived on this land for as long as anyone can remember. Now these strange-colored foreigners arrive and start building houses on your land. And they laugh at you and your family—they call you stupid. So what should you do?"

In this case, the student's feelings may or may not be relevant to the topic, or the student may get mired in his feelings (including daydreams) and be unable to think.

LEVEL 5: The teacher asks vague, overlong, embedded questions.

Good and Brophy (1978, pp. 360–370) report the work of Grossier, Rosenshine, and others who show that effective teacher questions are clearly content-centered rather than vague ("What tense is used here?" rather than "What do you see here?"); brief rather than lengthy (because the longer a question, the more difficult to understand); ask one question at a time (otherwise students do not know which question to answer and waste time trying to decide); and avoid continuous repetition of questions (students otherwise get the implicit message that they need not listen the first time). An embedded question repeats and rephrases the same question several times in succession, an irritating custom; for example: "What is the most reasonable answer? What makes the most sense to you? Which seems right? What do you think?"

LEVEL 6: The teacher asks questions with no purpose, direction, or relevance to lesson content.

When the teacher is off-task and requires students to be off-task as well, the results are obvious. On occasion, the candor or humor of such spontaneous moments can enhance a lesson, but the teacher must control the risks of distraction during such moments.

LEVEL 7: The teacher asks an inappropriate type of question for the lesson purpose.

A teacher may ask a higher level question of interpretation before students are familiar with basic facts.

EXERCISE 1
DIFFERENT TYPES OF QUESTIONS (5–10 minutes)

In your large group, consider each of the following questions and classify it in two ways:

1 Decide whether it is lower or higher level, closed or open, convergent or divergent, affective or cognitive, content-oriented or noncontent oriented.
2 Decide, on the basis of (1), the profile level of the question. Check your decision against the Taxonomy.

> "Who was the U.S. President during the Civil War?"
> "Give me an example of reciprocity."
> "Why?"
> "What's wrong with his analysis?"
> "Was it the same in the first problem we studied?"
> "What is the largest planet?"
> "Where else could she have gone?"
> "What page are you on?"
> "What could Washington have meant by no entangling alliances?"
> "And how do you feel about it? Do you approve?"
> "When will you have it ready?"
> "Name one of the dinosaurs."
> "What is a French word for 'sickness'?"
> "Can you hear me?"
> "Why isn't it done?"

Conclusion Many of these questions are purposely ambiguous. Given one interpretation, you can classify a question one way, or another way according to a different interpretation. If you can give different interpretations to a question as well as classify each interpretation appropriately, you are definitely engaged in higher level thinking!

METHOD Tc

Wrong Answers: How does the teacher treat students' incorrect or inadequate answers?

Some teachers get angry when students give wrong answers to instructional questions. Some feel hurt, betrayed, cheated, indignant, curious, or determined. Regardless of the teacher's feelings about wrong answers, the teacher must solve the problem of student fear of appearing foolish, because fear is distracting.

LEVEL 1: The teacher automatically identifies the source of the wrong answer, then asks again.

Wise teachers make their students look and feel wise, as in this example:

> **TEACHER:** Who was the last U.S. President to be impeached? Angie?
> **STUDENT:** Uh, Kennedy?
> **TEACHER:** If you were thinking of assassination, you were right— Kennedy *was* the last President to be assassinated. Impeachment is different. Do you know what it means?
> **STUDENT:** No.
> **TEACHER:** OK. Phil?

LEVEL 2: The teacher uses probing questions to help students rethink incorrect answers.

A student can become glib when the teacher accepts anything he says, but when teachers expect him to re-examine partially correct answers, add to incomplete answers, or explain correct answers, he becomes thoughtful. Compare these two examples:

> **TEACHER:** Which of the ingredients is adding that mellow flavor? Sam?
> **STUDENT:** The garlic?
> **TEACHER:** The garlic. Well, that's an interesting answer. Does anyone else have an idea? [The teacher here abandons thinking in his search for the correct answer.]
>
> **TEACHER:** Which ingredient adds the mellow flavor? Sam?
> **STUDENT:** The garlic?
> **TEACHER:** Why do you think the garlic? [The teacher is using a probing technique.]

(For an excellent discussion of and suggestions for probing questions, see Jacobsen et al. [1981, p. 182 ff].)

LEVEL 3: The teacher uses prompting devices to help students respond successfully to questions.

Prompting is a technique of providing hints, clues, or clear avenues to a correct answer without stating the answer itself. For example:

TEACHER: And what is the major 3rd above E flat? Rickie?
STUDENT: Uh. A flat?
TEACHER: If the major 3rd is two full steps above the tonic, what is it...?
STUDENT: Oh yeah, G.
TEACHER: Correct.

Using this skill with elementary age students, the teacher provides each student with conspicuous cues or clear context: "Bert, Columbus didn't start out with just one ship on his first voyage, did he? Nor did he sail with just two, but in fact he had how many? Three, that's right. Now what did Columbus...?" The secret is to make the question so clear and so easy that it sounds routine; the question is quickly asked, quickly answered, and the teacher moves along to the next thought, without giving the student time to think about how easy the question was. (Jacobsen et al. [1981, pp. 180–182] discuss and suggest prompting techniques.)

LEVEL 4: The teacher asks why the student has answered that way, identifies the source of error, then asks again.

The following example illustrates this technique:

TEACHER: Who was the last U.S. President to be impeached? Angie?
STUDENT: Uh, Kennedy?
TEACHER: Why do you say that?
STUDENT: Well, he got shot and...
TEACHER: Right, Kennedy was the last President to be murdered or *assassinated*. Now my question is, who was the last to be *impeached* ...?

In contrast to Level 1, the teacher here asks the student why he answered as he did. The student may think, "Uh oh, she doesn't like my answer." At Level 1, the teacher simply assumes why, then quickly moves to other lesson content.

LEVEL 5: The teacher corrects a wrong answer.

This sensible, common technique is justified in most cases of incorrect answers, but may still embarrass the shy student who has just ventured to volunteer an answer. It can also unnerve the insecure student who did not volunteer, but was called on anyway; offend the student who is sure of his answer, right or wrong; or anger the student who thinks the teacher is being arbitrary.

For secure, inquisitive, and highly involved students, the technique works well—it is quick and highly focused. But for other students, or even for secure students in a bad moment, it can be distractive.

LEVEL 6: The teacher ignores a wrong answer.

The risk in ignoring any student answer is obvious, except when special rules are operating, and ignoring answers is temporarily standard procedure for all students.

The risk of embarrassment and resentment is greatly reduced (although not eliminated) if the teacher announces, "OK, let's see if you can guess what happens next. I'll let you keep guessing until you get it right, so keep on guessing even if your first guess isn't correct."

LEVEL 7: The teacher accepts a wrong answer as if it were correct.

Teachers sometimes use this technique to protect students' feelings, perhaps by not correcting the erring student. Unfortunately, the result of these good intentions is more mischievous than helpful, and more disruptive than humane. As a "devil's advocate" technique to arouse student protest and debate, this technique may be justified, but even then, the teacher must be careful to avoid confusing students who are slow to recognize the game and why it is being played.

EXERCISE 1
DRILL ON WRONG ANSWERS, LEVEL 1 (10–30 minutes)

This is an important drill that the instructor should monitor. It is also fun, so enjoy it.

1   As the teacher, ask any content question you wish of the student across the group from you.
2   Your student will give an incorrect or inappropriate answer.
3   You will then respond at Level 1, and your student will answer correctly.
4   The person to your right becomes teacher and goes through steps 1 through 4, using a different student across the group. Continue around the entire group.

At Step 3, your instructor or other group members may coach as appropriate. As each person takes a turn at Step 4, the others should rehearse quietly to themselves.

EXERCISE 2
DRILL ON WRONG ANSWERS, LEVEL 2 (10–30 minutes)

The Exercise 1 procedure may be used, or the instructor may establish small groups to drill on probing techniques, Tc2.

EXERCISE 3
DRILL ON WRONG ANSWERS, LEVEL 3 (10–30 minutes)

Like Exercise 2 except for drill on prompting techniques Tc3.

METHOD Td
Diagnosis: How does the teacher diagnose students' learning needs and problems?

Some say that once we identify the real problem, we are halfway to the solution. *Diagnosis* is the process of identifying real problems.

LEVEL 1: The teacher asks questions about the student's prerequisite knowledge, then moves forward step by step until the problem is identified.

For example:

> **TEACHER:** What's your problem?
> **STUDENT:** I can't do this stuff.
> **TEACHER:** You sound discouraged about the whole thing.
> **STUDENT:** I am. I can't do these problems.
> **TEACHER:** OK, now tell me the answer to this question. Can you do this one?
> **STUDENT:** Yeah. It's...
> **TEACHER:** Yes. Now tell me this one...

This approach supports the student; he suddenly leaves the failure of the present and experiences again his successes of the past, enabling the teacher to find out exactly where the difficulty lies.

LEVEL 2: The teacher asks the student to demonstrate what he was doing at the moment he encountered the problem.

This technique is so simple and obvious that one wonders why it is not used more often:

> **STUDENT:** I can't do this dumb stuff!
> **TEACHER:** OK, show me exactly what you were doing just before you got bogged down.

LEVEL 3: (None.)

LEVEL 4: The teacher asks the student why he is having trouble.

Once in a while, this technique yields helpful results; for example:

> **STUDENT:** I can't do this dumb stuff!
> **TEACHER:** Why is this a problem for you?
> **STUDENT:** Because I wasn't here the day you explained logarithms.

Just as often, perhaps, the technique can delay diagnosis:

> **STUDENT:** I can't do this dumb stuff!
> **TEACHER:** Why is this a problem for you?

> **STUDENT:** I just can't do it, that's all.
> **TEACHER:** Well, then...

LEVEL 5: The teacher asks questions that have already been answered.

Well-meaning teachers often ask questions to convey warmth and friendliness that serve merely to make students impatient.

> **STUDENT:** I don't know the answer.
> **TEACHER:** What? Don't you know the answer?

LEVEL 6: The teacher stops diagnosis before completion.

A few teachers have the unfortunate habit of walking away from legitimate student learning problems.

> **STUDENT:** I can't do this dumb stuff.
> **TEACHER:** What's the trouble?
> **STUDENT:** I just can't do it, that's all.
> **TEACHER:** Well, you better figure it out. It's going to be on the test tomorrow.

The only justification for stopping diagnosis prematurely is when the student is clearly playing games (see chapter 20, S-9, "Helpless.")

LEVEL 7: The teacher asks the same diagnostic question over and over.

An untrained and frustrated teacher sometimes repeats the same question over and over in an inept effort to diagnose a learning problem:

> **TEACHER:** What don't you understand?
> **STUDENT:** Any of it.
> **TEACHER:** Well, *what* don't you understand?

Teachers should use inept questions only for the sake of humor:

> **TEACHER:** All right, the topic today is the Pythagorean Theorem. Tim, what do you know about the Pythagorean Theorem?
> **STUDENT:** Nothing.
> **TEACHER:** Nothing, eh? Would you like to tell us about that?
> **STUDENTS:**   (Laughter.)

EXERCISE 1 DIAGNOSIS (5 minutes)

Recall a recent situation in which you were having trouble learning or understanding something. If possible, select a topic that would be possible for someone else in the group to ask questions about.

1 Pair with another member of your group. Begin by saying, "There I was, and I just couldn't....." The other person, as teacher, will practice the techniques of Td1 for 1 minute.
2 Critique, offer suggestions, then switch roles.

EXERCISE 2 DIAGNOSIS (5 minutes)

Switch partners and repeat Exercise 1, substituting techniques of Td2.

EXERCISE 3 DIAGNOSIS (5 minutes)

Switch partners and repeat Exercises 1 and 2 as needed. (The instructor should monitor these sessions closely and offer suggestions freely.)

REFERENCES

BLOOM, B., et al. Taxonomy of educational objectives: The classification of educational goals. Handbook I: Cognitive domain. New York: David McKay, 1956.

BROPHY, J., & EVERTSON, C. *Learning from teaching: A developmental perspective.* Boston: Allyn and Bacon, 1976.

GOOD, T., & BROPHY, J. *Looking in classrooms* (2nd ed.). New York: Harper and Row, 1978.

JACOBSEN, D., et al. *Methods for teaching.* Columbus, Ohio: Charles E. Merrill, 1981.

WRIGHT, C., & NUTHALL, G. The relationships between teacher behaviors and pupil achievement in three experimental elementary science lessons. *American Educational Research Journal,* 1970, 7, 477–492.

CONTROL WITH NAMES, DIRECTIONS, AND PEP TALKS (METHODS U, V, W)

16

In conventional classroom control, lesson content words are spoken at special, appointed times: "Now we are going to talk about the Battle of the Alamo." In low profile classroom control, content words are attached to everything—to student names, to instructions on lesson mechanics, and to teacher pep talks.

METHOD U
Student Names: In what way does the teacher say student names out loud during instruction?

The teacher can use names in classroom control either in direct address or in name dropping. In direct address, the teacher addresses the student directly, which makes the student feel a need to acknowledge or respond in some way. For example, "The situation was out of hand, wouldn't you agree, Dave? And so they began to..." or "The situation was definitely out of hand, and so, just as if you had suggested it to them, Dave, they began to..." In name dropping, the teacher talks about the student, in the student's presence and within the content of the topic, so the student overhears his name. The student feels no need to acknowledge or respond to the sound of his name. For example, "The situation was definitely out of hand, Dave might agree, and so, just as if Doug or Deb had suggested it, they began to..."

Direct address, a common practice, allows the teacher the option of waiting for a response from the student ("Would you agree, Dave?") or not waiting ("Just as if you had suggested it to them, Dave, they...").

Name dropping, a relatively infrequent teaching practice, is a pretense or excuse to use a student's name inside your story or topic. Feel free to smile when you drop names, and watch for the attention students show. For example, in a teacher lecture: "Then Mr. Lincoln was really angry because his generals weren't doing anything, just as Mary or Lou would be angry if they were in Mr. Lincoln's shoes, so Mr. Lincoln decided to..."

During a recitation: "So you're saying, Randy, that dividing both sides by five will clear the left side of the equation; I assume that Chris and Matt would agree, so let's go to the next step."

Or, when a student asks a question and the teacher must respond: "Well, let's see, Joe; let's say that Ralph wanted to buy a coat at Sue's store, and Sue speaks only Spanish, so Ralph would have to..."

A student is almost always attracted by the sound of his name, so if we can put our students' names right into the content we are teaching, we increase our chances of getting their minds into the content and holding them there. Review again the example of Teacher Y in chapter 2, who uses name dropping skillfully.

This technique has great power to rouse and encourage quiet students to participate in the class. Often, when a quiet student's name is used in this technique, he will watch the class proceedings quietly for awhile, then suddenly burst out with a question, comment, or answer. My informal estimate is that between 60 and 80 percent of passive students respond effectively to this technique.

LEVEL 1: The teacher uses name dropping of all students periodically in the content of the lesson.

LEVEL 2: The teacher includes a target student's name, with others, in the content of the lesson.

Two devices are frequently effective for students in unknown attention or inattention. When students are talking among themselves out of turn, embed their names in the context of the lesson, preceding and following with the names of attentive students. (Use primarily name dropping.) Or, you may gain a target student's attention by using the names of persons near the student rather than the target student's name; for example, if Julie is leaning over talking to Lee, while Lee keeps her eyes on her desk, the teacher's first impulse may be to call on Julie. But using this technique, the teacher would use Lee's name in the context of the lesson. Lee attends, and so does Julie.

LEVEL 3: The teacher uses a target student's name alone in the content of the lesson.

You can use either direct address or name dropping. In this situation, unlike Levels 1 and 2, the student's name is mentioned alone, thus increasing the risk that the target student may be disconcerted by hearing his name.

What determines the risk of distraction? Primarily, it is the student's present attention level. If a student is already attentive, you may use his name alone, either in direct address or name dropping. If your target is inattentive or in unknown attention, then embed his name in the topic and with the names of attentive students.

LEVEL 4: (None.)

LEVEL 5: The teacher uses noncontent name dropping or direct address without pause to call a target student's attention to the lesson.

With this technique, you briefly depart from content to restore order in a familiar way: "I like the way Elsa is sitting up straight in her chair" or "If you'll look up here, Dave, you can see...."

You run the risk of beginning the "Who, me?" game (see chapter 20, S-1), if Dave looks around at his friends, smiles or frowns, fiddles with his pencil or interrupts the teacher with "Who, me?" If you use the technique frequently, the student may be heard to complain "You're picking on me."

On the other hand, if the teacher is striving to change a student's wandering attention habits, with prior notice to the student, the technique might be effective.

LEVEL 6: The teacher uses noncontent name dropping or direct address with a pause to call a target student's attention to the lesson.

At this level, the teacher uses noncontent words, which automatically distract attention, then adds names and a pause to complete the distraction:

"So Jeff can now do his work without bothering Ginny."

"So can you see what I mean, Harvey?"

LEVEL 7: The teacher uses a target student's name in a reprimand.

The examples below sound familiar because this is perhaps the most frequently used technique in American teaching:

"Tommy, turn around."

"Sid, sit up."

"Carl, cooperate."

"Gary, go back where you belong."

Where names are commonly used in reprimands, students jump when they hear their names. Some teachers try to mix name dropping (Levels 1 and 2) with reprimands (Level 7), but the result is usually self-defeating: "So we can see that the real battle in this region — Tommy, turn around — was between the French and the English. Now if Tommy had been hunting and fishing in that area (Tommy looks at his neighbors, grins, and mouths, 'Who, me?')..."

EXERCISE 1 DRILL ON DIRECT ADDRESS (5–10 minutes)

Seating the class group in a circle, your instructor will read aloud or speak for 30 seconds on any topic of choice. During this talk, the instructor will use Level 2 direct address with the names of the three persons directly on his left. After 30 seconds, the next person to the left will do the same, continuing in turn until all have spoken. You may use any of these forms of direct address along with others:

"...would you agree, X, that ...?"

"...just as if you, X, had..."

"...and you, X, might..."

"...if you, X, or you, Y, want to, you can..."

"...as you can see, X , this..."

"...it might occur to you, X, that..."

"...it might seem to you, X, that..."

"...so if you were to..., X, you might find that..."

"...and can you see, X, how this...?"

"...so do you understand how..., X, and how...?"

These forms are all embedded in the content, using the same content words that students are supposed to learn. They differ from noncontent direct address, which only talks *about* the content:

"So can you see what I mean, X?"

"Do you understand, X?"

"Would you agree with this point, X?"

EXERCISE 2 DRILL ON NAME DROPPING (5–10 minutes)

Repeat the procedures of Exercise 1, but substitute low profile name dropping.

EXERCISE 3 DRILL ON DIRECT ADDRESS AND NAME DROPPING (5 minutes)

1 Pair off with another person. Begin reading or speaking, and use as much low profile direct address and name dropping as possible in one minute, using the

names of other group members as if those people were present. If your partner senses that your technique is not low profile, he should stop you, offering suggestions, if possible. (If he can't offer suggestions, call your instructor.) This drill builds facility, forcing you to use as many different styles and devices as you can in one minute.

2 After one minute, switch roles and let your partner practice low profile uses of names.

EXERCISE 4 SLEEPY STUDENTS (10–15 minutes)

1 Form groups of five or six.
2 Each person in turn will be teacher of a class of sleepyheads for one minute by the clock; another group member should act as timekeeper. Read or speak to your class with low profile name usage. Having been sprawled "asleep" in his chair, each student will wake up and pay attention when he hears his name used in low profile direct address or name dropping. Each name must be properly embedded in the names of attentive students ("attentive" here means either not in the group or already "awake"); if the technique is not properly low profile, the student will not wake up! If you use a student's name in reprimand, he should immediately begin to snore!
3 In this exercise, you may not mention more than one sleepy student's name at a time in either direct address or name dropping.
4 If group members are not well acquainted, you may use name tags.

Conclusion This exercise is fun and poses the same realistic challenge classroom teachers face during instruction. Repeat the exercise if you feel you are not yet proficient.

Assignment Report an excerpt from a lesson you teach or a conversation you have, illustrating at least one example of direct address and one of name dropping (both low profile). Label the first DA and the second ND.

METHOD V
Directions: What is the teacher's style for giving directions during instruction?

The most common type of teacher direction does not focus the student's mind on lesson content, but on lesson mechanics:

"Now look at the map."

"Turn in your book to page 57."

"I want you to listen carefully to what Robert is saying; all right, Robert, you may continue."

These instructions seem perfectly reasonable until we consider what goes on in the listening students' minds.

The *map* is "a thing at the front of the room that's got a bunch of stuff written all over it."

Page 57 is "another page of this book that has more printing all over it."

Robert triggers thoughts of "So Robert is talking, so what else is new."

In contrast, notice how easily the following approaches turn high profile instructions into low profile:

"Now look at the map where Pakistan borders India on the North and also..." [The student's mind focuses on Pakistan and India, not on "the map."]

"Turn in your book to page 57 and find the definition of *noun* ...." [The student's mind focuses on *noun*.]

"I want you to listen carefully to what Robert is saying about why Chicken Little was afraid..." [The student's mind focuses on Chicken Little's fear.]

This style makes the difference between a student's daydreaming or thinking about lesson content.

Should the teacher always use content-oriented low profile directions during instruction? If possible, yes, because during instruction, the teacher should strive for 100 percent high attention from all students, with no distractions.

LEVEL 1: The teacher directs students to attend to specific lesson content.

Directions may be verbal or nonverbal.

LEVEL 2: The teacher tells students how they should attend to or think about specific lesson content.

For example, the teacher might lean forward and cup her ear, a signal to the class that listening is important, or she might say "Listen to what Dorella is saying about..." or "As the music plays, think about the conversation between the woodwinds and the strings."

LEVEL 3: The teacher gives directions to target students publicly regarding specific lesson content.

For example, the teacher may say to Gippy: "Gippy, make your eyes trace the outline of each state in this area so you can see which boundaries are natural, like rivers, and which are political."

LEVEL 4: The teacher gives noncontent directions to target students privately. (Same as Yc4).

The teacher leans over Heather's desk and says quietly, "Cool it, Heather." Heather gets the message.

Or the teacher gives other noncontent instructions to a student regarding the mechanics of the activity: "I want you to put your crayons back in the box when you finish, Tercell, got that?" or "We do not run to the door, Mildred; we walk to the door." Because these directions are not content-oriented, they are not low profile.

LEVEL 5: (none.)

LEVEL 6: The teacher gives noncontent directions to target students publicly.

Common examples of this technique are "Shh" directed toward a particular student, or the nonverbal index finger to the lips, also directed at particular students. These are *desist orders.*

LEVEL 7: The teacher gives noncontent directions to entire class.

Directions may be necessary on rare occasions, but desist orders such as the prolonged "shhhh" to the entire class, "It's getting too noisy in here," and "I want to see more work and less play" are highly distractive—and common in schools.

EXERCISE 1 LOW PROFILE DIRECTIONS (15–20 minutes)

1 Before the exercise, prepare a 2-minute lesson to teach, preferably materials you will soon actually use in a classroom.

2 Form a small group of three or four. The others in your group will be your students when you are the teacher. Teach your prepared lesson for two minutes; ask one to watch the time for you.

3 Your students will assume whatever age group you designate, and will limit their off-task behavior to those listed below. Each student will select a single behavior to do three times while you teach your lesson: slouch down in seat; put hands over ears; look at ceiling; look at another "student" (but not talk); look at floor; put head down on table; look at pocket mirror; play with hair or fingers or clothing; or whisper to neighbor.

4 The teacher's control task is to resist the urge to use high profile reprimands, and instead give low profile direction to each student. When you are properly low profile, the student will then look attentive for at least 10 seconds. If you are not low profile, the student will ignore you.

5 Shift roles so someone else can teach the lesson.

Assignment   Write a brief report of your use of low profile directions with someone you are instructing. If you cannot provide out-of-class examples, report your work in the class exercise. Record exactly what you said in your controls.

METHOD W

Pep Talks: What style of pep talk does the teacher give students during instruction?

Teachers occasionally interrupt lessons to deliver sermons on "Why we should not talk when the teacher is talking" or "Why we should be as considerate of others as we would want them to be considerate of us" or "You people have got to learn that..." These are worthy sermons, but should they interrupt lessons? Effective teachers have other techniques to control student attention during instruction; after instruction, they sermonize without sacrificing content learning.

Shouldn't the teacher strike while the iron is hot? Sometimes what we see as an ideal moment is actually our own impulse to vent emotions. Nevertheless, students of all ages need pep talks from time to time, and those talks can be either high profile or low profile.

LEVEL 1: Pep talk to class on teacher's high expectations for content learning.

This pep talk is oriented strictly to the content of the lesson, not to the mechanics of learning. For example, "Now I want you to learn these states and where the capitals are and how to spell them. You can remember that Boise is the capital of Idaho; and the capital of Delaware is Dover, and the capital of New York is — what? Not New York City, where you might expect it, but somewhere else — right, Albany, up here. You all can remember Albany."

Notice how the focus remains on lesson content at Level 1. The control technique is low key, low profile, almost invisible. Here is another example for boosting tired students: "Don't give up on this division problem — it's just a variation on the division problems you have already been doing. You looked for the highest multiple in those, right? You can look for the highest multiple here, too. OK? Try it again, look for the highest multiple."

LEVEL 2: Pep talk to target students privately on teacher's high expectations for content learning.

Imagine a teacher giving the above pep talks quietly to one or two students during seatwork. When the teacher speaks directly to a student, the teacher is more visible, but the control is still low profile.

LEVEL 3: Pep talk to target students publicly on teacher's high expectations for content learning.

LEVEL 4: Pep talk to target students privately on teacher's expectations for noncontent behavior.

The emphasis shifts from lesson content to other matters: "Johnny, I want you to work harder on your homework. I know that if you put in 10 minutes, even 5 minutes, each day, and just run through these things quickly in your mind, you can do it."

LEVEL 5: (None.)

LEVEL 6: Pep talk to target students publicly on teacher's expectations for noncontent behavior.

"Jeff, now you *can* do better if you just try, I *know* you can!" With the rest of the class as audience, the teacher encourages a student who has made mistakes, become dispirited, or refused to work. The noncontent topic makes this technique high profile.

LEVEL 7: Pep talk to class on teacher's expectations for noncontent behavior.

There are no content words in this exhortation, so content will not be in the listeners' minds: "You all should sit up and not slouch. You *can* remember!"

EXERCISE 1 LOW PROFILE PEP TALK (20–30 minutes)

1 Before the exercise, recall the most difficult teaching moment you have experienced, a moment that called for stopping the lesson for a sermon. Jot down some notes for a full 30-second low profile pep talk which, if the situation were to arise again, you could deliver to the students involved.

2 Form a small group of three to five persons. Assume the role of teacher in your group and tell the group the situation. Have one or more members briefly role-play the students who made your most difficult teaching moment so memorable, to set the stage for you, then deliver your low profile pep talk. Ask a group member to time you.

3 As you speak, group members will tally your pep talk on scratch paper with a check mark each time you mention a noncontent behavior that is linked to a specific content (see Column C), and with a check mark each time you mention a noncontent student behavior, teaching method or device, rule or principle, or an exhortation that is not linked to specific content (see Column N).

4 After you finish, ask your group members to report their tallies; after all are recorded, ask for suggestions as to how you could increase your score.

		Content-linked checks (C)	Noncontent checks (N)
Tallies:	Person 1:	_____	_____
	Person 2:	_____	_____
	Person 3:	_____	_____
	Person 4:	_____	_____
	Total:	(C)	Total: (N)

Effectiveness score: Total $(C/C) + (N) =$ _____ / _____
$=$ _____ %

Conclusion If you scored 100 percent, you were unusually effective in embedding your pep talk in content. If you scored 80 percent, you were very good; 50 percent is satisfactory. Below 50 percent, you should ask for lots of suggestions. Regardless of your score, you need lots of practice. This skill does not come easily.

Assignment Write a report in which you quote your use of at least one example of low profile pep talk with a student (or other persons designated by your instructor).

CONTROL OF DISTRACTIONS
(METHOD X)

17

Distractions in the classroom are inevitable. Every teacher knows that sooner or later, something will go wrong during the lesson, and student attention will be distracted from content. Teachers anticipate distractions in different ways.

METHOD Xa
Anticipating Distractions: When does the teacher anticipate distractions that might occur during instruction?

In this section, we examine different anticipation techniques to use both before and during the lesson. The lowest profile techniques are *proactive;* they are used before the lesson (see the discussion of proactive and reactive teacher controls in chapter 1).

LEVEL 1: The teacher anticipates and solves problems automatically in the lesson content, media, and activities.

If we accept the theory that almost all classroom management problems can be resolved through proper lesson design, most of us will suffer forever from guilt. Every lesson design has flaws, and no group of students always behaves exactly the way the lesson design assumed. Teachers are not and will never be omniscient, theory notwithstanding, but while we can admit our fallibility, let us not make excuses. We can and should anticipate most of the problems we will meet in the classroom. In fact, effective teachers rehearse. Like actors and actresses, they go through their lines during breakfast, on the way to work, during preparation periods, even in the shower; they think about what they will do in the classroom, and about the possible effects of their media and activities. While they rehearse, they see the faces of their students. They hear Jodie say, "This is dumb" and Lorena say, "I'm done—now what do I do?" and Tim whine, "I don't get it." They think beforehand about what they can do or say to avoid having students say those things. The controls a teacher uses before the lesson begins are the lowest profile controls possible, and often the most effective.

LEVEL 2: The teacher anticipates and answers problems briefly during orientation and directions.

"Students, on the ditto sheets I'm passing out, please notice a misspelled word in Item K." Beware of piling all your solutions into long orientation instructions; students often stop listening after the first 15 seconds.

LEVEL 3: The teacher observes and meets problems as they arise during instruction.

If you cannot foresee a problem, the next best response is to detect it early. For example, be alert to appearances of puzzlement or inattention; move in to ask questions and redirect attention. When lecturing, notice whether or not students are taking notes, and take action as you continue lecturing. Watch for upraised hands and move quickly to students who need help.

LEVEL 4: The teacher stops a student's work to correct a procedure.

If a student is not following instructions, the teacher will stop him, give directions again, and start him off once more.

      If the teacher knows that Stevie may not be working correctly because he is often slow to understand instructions, she may move to his area immediately after orientation to check his work and give him special help.

LEVEL 5: (None.)

LEVEL 6: The teacher stops the lesson to answer students' questions about proce-
         dures, evaluation, or other matters.

You should rarely need to use this technique, but sometimes a lesson falls apart; these are the signs:

- Different students in different parts of the room are asking the same *basic* question.
- A high percentage of on-task students are not getting correct or reasonable answers.
- A significantly high number of students are inattentive.

The wise teacher will stop the lesson, answer students' questions, then restart the lesson.

LEVEL 7: The teacher stops the lesson to reorganize.

The conditions for using this technique are the same as for Level 6 (see the "class meetings" notions of Dreikurs, Gordon, and Glasser in chapter 1.)

EXERCISE 1 ANTICIPATING DISTRACTIONS THROUGH REHEARSAL (20–30 minutes)

The first teaching of a lesson is, in effect, a rehearsal for the second and third teachings. In this exercise, try to simulate the first lesson, discovering what elements distract students' attention from content. Your goal is to focus student attention completely on lesson content by asking questions that make them think; by moving their eyes and filling their ears and occupying their hands with activities you want them to think about. Anticipate any and all distractions, and counteract them beforehand.

1   Before class, plan a 5-minute lesson for students, designating an age and grade level and subject area. Plan to teach so that your students have little opportunity to notice you, your teaching methods or lesson mechanics, their own mistakes, or any other noncontent distraction. In short, anticipate. Write in the spaces of Form X the three most important things you want your class to notice and remember from your lesson; all three must be objective and content-related (concepts, facts, skills, etc.).

2   In class, meet with a group of three or four persons. At your turn as teacher, teach your lesson for 5 minutes, striving to focus student attention on your

CONTROL DISTRACTIONS: FORM X	Student	Student	Student	
WANTED : _____				
WANTED : _____				
WANTED : _____				
————————————————————————				LINE
DIFFERENT : _____				
DIFFERENT : _____				
DIFFERENT : _____				
DIFFERENT : _____				
DIFFERENT : _____				
DIFFERENT : _____				
DIFFERENT : _____				
DIFFERENT : _____				
DIFFERENT : _____				

(a) Total checks above line: _____
(b) Total checks on sheet: _____
Score for effectiveness of control = a/b = _____ / _____
Percentage of effectiveness = _____%

three identified lesson elements. At the end of 5 minutes, each student writes your name on a slip, then turns it over and writes the three major elements, each in six words or fewer, that he noticed most during your teaching, whatever those happened to be. Spoken words should be written with quotation marks. (Allow one minute for this writing task.) All students should keep their slips.

3   Move quickly to the next teacher and lesson, then the next, until all have taught. Note: The instructor should directly control and announce times in this exercise, 5 min., teach; 1 min., write; 5 min., teach, etc.

4   After the presentations, collect the slips with your name and complete your Form X like the sample. In this sample, the teacher wanted students to remem-

SAMPLE FORM X		Student	Student	Student	
WANTED :	*location of Niger River Valley*	X		X	
WANTED :	*"Timbuktu was very prosperous"*	X	X		
WANTED :	*"Timbuktu was an important trade center"*				
————————————————————————					LINE
DIFFERENT :	*hair over face*	X		X	
DIFFERENT :	*"you guys are creeps"*		X		
DIFFERENT :	*rolled your eyes*		X	X	

ber the Niger River Valley and hear two important remarks. One student mentioned the Niger River, so the teacher checked "Niger" in the first column. The same student heard "Timbuktu was wealthy," hence another check in the first column. The student also noticed something different—hair falling over the teacher's face—and so the teacher entered "hair over face" *below* the line and put a check mark for it. The next student heard "Timbuktu was very rich" (check above the line) but noticed two different things which the teacher had not intended. The third student also noticed the hair plus the river and eyes.

5   Count your checks above the line, then all the checks above and below, and calculate a percentage according to the table below. How effective are you now in controlling your students' attention? Ten percent effective? Sixty percent?

TABLE 17–1   Percentage of Effectiveness

For Group of 3	For Group of 4
1/6 = 17%	1/9 = 11%
2/6 = 33%	2/9 = 22%
3/6 = 50%	3/9 = 50%
4/6 = 67%	4/9 = 44%
5/6 = 83%	5/9 = 56%
6/6 = 100%	6/9 = 67%
	7/9 = 78%
	8/9 = 89%
	9/9 = 100%

Conclusion   How many in the class scored 50 percent or above? What techniques seemed particularly useful or successful for you? (Open discussion.) If you scored a low percentage, do not feel discouraged, and if you scored high, do not feel smug! The purpose of this exercise is to help you think more clearly about why or why not students succeed in learning from your teaching. It is an experiment, not a test, but if you are not satisfied with the results, you should do it again. Try for a score of 75 percent or better.

ASSIGNMENT   Write a critique of your success in the exercise. What do you do that successfully catches and holds student attention? What do you fail to do? How can you improve your skills of controlling student attention?

METHOD Xb

Acting on Distractions: What action does the teacher take to control classroom distractions during instruction?

Just as some remedies are worse than the disease, so are some teacher control techniques more distracting than the distractions the teacher wants to control.

LEVEL 1: The teacher ignores the minor distraction or diverts student attention from it.

It is remarkable how many classroom distractions go away when teachers ignore them or teach over them. Students who create the distractions do so unconsciously —they tap on the desk or pull out a mirror and look at it simply because a stray idea passes through their minds. If your lesson is well conceived, well organized, and well administered, the student's distracting thought will depart as suddenly as it came, and he will be swept back on task by the momentum and climate of the lesson.

Ignore the Distraction   Ignoring does not mean the teacher fails to notice the distraction, nor that she pretends she didn't notice it. Rather, to ignore a distraction professionally means to notice it, remember it, but not act on it immediately. If you simply look at the student who is creating a distraction, he will often immediately cease the action. If the distraction does not disappear, remember it and take action sooner or later.

In ignoring distractions, beware of making a game of it with a distracting student. If you ignore his distraction and he persists, he may be *trying* to get you to react and give him attention. In such a case you may feel an urge to use high profile techniques, but resist the urge; instead, divert the student's attention to your lesson content.

Divert Student Attention   Magicians know how to direct attention toward what they want their audience to notice and away from what they want to conceal. Effective teachers use some of the same techniques.

There are countless low profile techniques for diverting student attention away from distractions and focusing on lesson content; in fact, the following techniques are all low profile.

- Name drop the distracting student's name along with others (Method U)
- Directly address the distracting student along with others (Method U)
- Give content-oriented directions or instructions to the entire class, automatically including the distracting student (Method V)
- Use content-oriented gestures while looking at the distracting student (along with others) and moving in his general direction (Methods L, M, and N)
- Elicit choral response from all students (Method Ia)
- Initiate spot seatwork (Methods Ia, H)
- Shift the activity (Method H)
- Ask open questions of the entire class, looking at the distracting students as well as at others while you wait for answers (Methods Ib and T)

LEVEL 2: The teacher incorporates the distraction into lesson content.

You must be reasonably clever and quick to use this technique, as in this example: "So what we're after is a kind of material in that rod, right? [Class nods; one student, Bob, starts tapping his pencil.] Now is the rod made of just one substance? Or might it be made of two substances, like Bob's pencil? And if the rod has two substances, would those two substances be arranged as they are in Bob's pencil, or arranged in another way? Any ideas?"

With this technique, the teacher immediately turns the distraction to her advantage. Many good public speakers know how to do this. Consider the politician whose speech is interrupted by an electrical storm that dims the lights; the politician wisecracks, "And I'll turn some lights on in Washington, too, if you'll vote for me in November." Effective teachers recognize opportunities the same way.

When a book accidentally drops to the floor during a math lesson, an infinite number of remarks can link the event with the lesson, depending upon the students' ages:

Grade 1:   "See? One plus one is two: one book dropped on one floor makes us all jump two feet!"

Grade 4:   "Wow. Now that's what one whole book sounds like! If you cut that one book into four equal parts, and dropped each part separately, how would you compare the sound of each part with the sound of the whole book? One-half the sound? One-third the sound?"

Grade 7: " . . .so that when you bring down the 9 to divide again, you can . . .[book drops on the floor] . . .well, bring down that 9, Eddie, that's good, but don't bring it down quite so hard! [Smiles, general laughter] So now we're bringing that 9 down softly [smile], and what do we do next in this division problem, Jane?"

Grade 11: "Well now! [Slow take as students laugh.] That's a noisy demonstration, I'll admit, but now tell me mathematically about the path that book followed through the air as it fell to the floor. How do we graph that curve?"

This technique is fun. Let yourself go momentarily and allow your imagination a spontaneous field day!

The technique is even useful for administrative interruptions, as we see here: a loudspeaker announcement interrupts the lesson on parts of speech to alert students to the bake sale that will be held the following week. "Everybody should bring their money," says the announcer, and afterward, the teacher says, "Think about that bake sale announcement, and tell me about the grammar of the line, 'Everybody should bring their money.'"

You can train your imagination to incorporate distractions into your lesson content, as we will see in Exercise 3.

LEVEL 3: The teacher uses content-word voice-over to mask small distractions. (See Ka3.)

LEVEL 4: The teacher quietly removes a distracting object as the lesson goes on.

This technique seriously distracts the target student who "loses" his bubble gum, her comb, his cap pistol, her magazine to the teacher.

LEVEL 5: The teacher gives the distracting student a private desist order during instruction.

Privately may mean in the classroom during seatwork when students are somewhat isolated from each other. This technique is not a reprimand or scolding; it is a simple desist order; that is, a request to stop, using various methods (L, M, N, and others), either verbally ("That's enough," "Please don't," or "No") or nonverbally (a shake of the head with direct eye contact; a hand on shoulder, arm or offending object; a shake of the index finger).

LEVEL 6: The teacher gives the distracting student a public desist order during instruction.

LEVEL 7: The teacher removes distracting student from the group.

If the class must be disrupted by a high profile method, it is often most efficient to remove the student from the group quickly, and as quietly as possible.

EXERCISE 1 Ignore Minor Distractions (10–15 minutes)

If a distraction does not disappear of its own accord, the teacher must remember it and take action later. We are bombarded with millions of images and sounds

---

TEACHER, WHAT DID YOU SEE?   Form XX

Teacher's Name: _____

Directions: Write the name of each person (student) in your group.

Names of "students"	Observed	Actual	Match
Example: _Sue Q._	A_3	A_3	✓
_____	_____	_____	_____
_____	_____	_____	_____
_____	_____	_____	_____
_____	_____	_____	_____

Percentage Table: Number of Match // Number of students

In group of 3 students	In group of 4 students	In group of 5 students
0/3 = 0%	0/4 = 0%	0/5 = 0%
1/3 = 33%	1/4 = 25%	1/5 = 20%
2/3 = 66%	2/4 = 50%	2/5 = 40%
3/3 = 100%	3/4 = 75%	3/5 = 60%
	4/4 = 100%	4/5 = 80%
		5/5 = 100%

Effectiveness of classroom observation and recall = _____ %
Give this form to instructor at end of class.

every minute; which do we actually remember? We want our choices to result from skill, not chance.

1. Repeat chapter 10, Method L (Eyes), Exercise 1, substituting the following directions for Step 3; during your 30–second lecture, each student will listen to you, the teacher, and then, as inconspicuously as possible, create any one of the following distractions:

1   2   3   4

A—Tap pencil on table/teeth/fingernails/another object.

1   2   3   4

B—Drop something on the floor: Books/pencil or pen/piece of paper/other object.

1   2   3   4

C—Make a verbal noise: hum quietly/clear throat/cough quietly/grunt quietly.

1 2 3 4

D—Whisper to neighbor who is located: in front/behind/to left/to right.

When the teacher simply looks at the student who is creating the distraction, he should immediately cease the distracting action. If you make facial expressions of reaction to any distraction in this exercise, he should continue the distraction until you break eye contact, then regain it with a glance.

2. After your 30-second lecture, follow the chapter 10, Exercise 1 procedures at Steps 4 and 5. Complete the "Teacher, What Did You See?" Form XX.

Conclusion Hand your Report Form XX to your instructor. The instructor may wish to tally the effectiveness scores for the entire group. Ask for suggestions if your score is lower than you would like.

EXERCISE 2 Divert Students' Attention Away from Distraction (15–20 minutes)

1. Repeat the procedures of Exercise 1, but with a different group.
2. When you are teacher, extend your instruction time to one minute. When your students create distractions (as in Exercise 1), you will control their distractions by using all eight low profile techniques listed on Report Form XXX. Each time you use one of these techniques, the students, properly controlled, will cease distracting for 10 seconds then repeat the distraction until controlled, cease for 10 seconds, then repeat. Also as you teach, your students should make notes on their copies of Report Form XXX.
3. After your one-minute lesson, your students will complete copies of Report Form XXX; collect all copies and give them to your instructor after your discussion.

REPORT FORM XXX: CONTROLLING DISTRACTIONS

Name of Teacher: _____   Name of Student: _____

Directions to student: Tell how many times (in the "No." blank) each control was used by your teacher during the one-minute instruction time. Then fill in the blanks.

No.

_____ 1. Name drop. Names used: _____ _____

_____ 2. Direct address. Names used: _____ _____

_____ _____ _____ _____

(High profile uses of names do not count; note only content-oriented uses.)

_____ 3. Content-oriented directions. What were you asked to do? _____
_____

_____ 4. Content-oriented gestures. Specify: _____
_____

_____ 5. Choral responses. What did you say? _____
_____

_____ 6. Spot-Seatwork. What did you do? _____
_____

_____ 7. Shift Activity. What was the first? a. _____
         Second? b. _____

_____ 8. Open Questions. Specify   (a) _____
         (b) _____   (c) _____
         (d) _____   (e) _____

Give this form to instructor at end of class.

Conclusion   There are no recipes in teaching, no set patterns of control that always work. This exercise is a drill, just as playing piano scales is a drill. Do not assume that the drill itself is a recipe for problem solving in the real world; instead, think to yourself: "When I want to use skill X — or when skill X is needed — am I able to use it just as I was able to use it in the drill?"

To evaluate your proficiency in this drill: you have a good mastery of basic skills for low profile control of distractions if you had no problem using all of them at least twice in this exercise, especially if you combined them in ways such as these: "Now I'd like everybody, including Bill, Sarah, and Joe, to write a synonym for "go fast" on your paper. How else could you say, "go fast"?" (Name drop, content directions, spot seatwork, shift activity)

You have excellent mastery if you used all the skills at least four times during the drill. If you had fewer than two examples of any technique, you are not concentrating. You may be distracted by other matters (your self-consciousness, perhaps); you may have not learned the skills well enough to do them automatically; or, instead of concentrating on your teaching, you may be trying to remember "what the book said to do." Keep working — you will be able to use low profile controls eventually.

EXERCISE 3 Incorporating Distractions into Lesson Content (30–45 minutes)

This technique is fun to use. The distractions many teachers feel are disturbing threats actually present opportunities for the low profile teacher to enjoy the job! (Recall the examples of Xb2.)

1 Before entering class, imagine yourself teaching a lesson in which any one of the following distractions occurs: student taps pencil on table or teeth, drops something loudly on floor, belches loudly, starts to whistle or hum or grunt, yawns noticeably, two or more students whisper obviously to one another, student laughs out loud, not in response to lesson, lets fly a paper airplane or paper wad, loudly pops bubble gum, pokes another student who loudly says "Quit it!" or "Stop that!" Given your lesson content, think of a low profile technique to use for each distraction; plan for every distraction mentioned.

2 In class, form groups of eight to twelve people. When it is your turn to be teacher, leave the group while your students decide among themselves which three distractions might occur during your lesson, in what sequence, and which student will do each one. The students should decide quickly, then summon you back.

3 Enter your classroom and begin teaching your lesson. After 10 or 15 seconds (no more than 20 seconds), a single distraction will occur somewhere in your classroom; your task is to incorporate that distraction into your lesson content using only Level 2 techniques. If you are not 100 percent low profile, the distraction will simply cease and you should go on with your lesson until a second and different distraction occurs within 10 or 15 seconds. Again, try to incorporate that distraction into your lesson content using only low profile; the distraction will cease, and you will continue until a third distraction occurs at which time you again try to use a low profile incorporation technique.

4 As they watch your attempt at low profile incorporation, your students will decide whether or not you were successful; each person will have to decide for himself if your actions actually focused his attention back on the lesson without distraction. If his attention was focused through a low profile technique, he will turn and *nod* his head to all the other students; if all students nod to each other, they will applaud. If one student shakes his head, that means the teacher did not focus his mind on lesson content; no applause is given, and the teacher continues until the next distraction occurs.

5 At applause, the lesson is over, and another teacher leaves the group. Repeat steps 2 through 4 for each member of the group; after all members play teacher once, go around again using different distractions.

6 Continue steps 1 through 5 until each member of the group has had three turns, or until 15 minutes is up, whichever is sooner (instructor should time).

When your students are nodding and shaking their heads at one another, you must continue your lesson smoothly without a pause. If students notice you are waiting for applause, they should not applaud, because your pause is high profile.

Do not discuss or critique any performance until the exercise is over, otherwise someone will be deprived of actual practice. A teacher who is puzzled by the students' lack of applause should write down her question and ask it later.

No student should lie about her experience. If she knows a teacher's technique was actually high profile but she applauds anyway so as not to hurt his feelings, she is unfairly preventing him from learning, an inexcusable crime for any teacher if done knowingly and willfully.

Conclusion Some discussion can take place in the small groups, some in the reconvened class. Now you can ask your students, "Why didn't you guys applaud when I ... ?"

This exercise can be great fun. Enjoy it! When your colleagues are clever, applaud them with gusto. There are not many boisterous moments in teacher education that are valuable to our learning as well, so remember them warmly!

Assignment If you can demonstrate these skills in the drills and exercises, you can do them anywhere. Report at least one example each of diverting student attention and incorporating a distraction in a real classroom where students do not know what you are doing. Discipline yourself to use the techniques.

CONTROL THROUGH CRITICISM
(METHOD Y)

18

The conventional American style of giving criticism is typically dishonest, and this dishonesty carries into our schools. A teacher may tell a student that a paper is unacceptable because it is full of spelling mistakes, when in fact the teacher values several aspects of the paper, implying that he cares *only* about spelling. Or an exasperated teacher may complain, "You always have the late paper, don't you, Roger?" when in fact Roger did turn in a classroom assignment promptly three weeks ago. Because conventional criticism frequently tells half-truths, and because half-truths are not only dishonest but also unpleasant and hurtful, teachers react to criticism as does anyone else—they either avoid giving criticism entirely, even when it is needed and appropriate, or else they try to dress up their criticism with so-called tact and diplomacy, techniques that only add to the dishonesty of conventional criticism. Criticism is a muddle for many people, but it should not be so for teachers because they are *hired* to criticize—that is their primary job. The question is not whether teachers should criticize, it is whether they do it well or poorly.

Criticism is any set of verbal or nonverbal behaviors designed to change someone's behavior. Common criticism has three parts:

- Part 1: What I *value* in you or your behavior.
- Part 2: What I *disvalue* in you or your behavior.
- Part 3: What I suggest or request that you maintain or change.[1]

The first part, valuing, is often called "praise" or "positive criticism," and the second part, disvaluing, is often called "negative criticism."

Professional criticism disciplines common criticism in two ways: first, each part of the criticism must be absolutely specific and clear, not general, abstract, or ambiguous; and second, the valuing and disvaluing parts must be two aspects of exactly the same thing—they must be tightly linked. Compare these two examples of criticism:

"Joe, you're really a nice guy, and I like you a lot, but you have been expecting other people to do your cleanup work for you, and I wish you'd do your own work like you're supposed to."

"Joe, I realize you've been busy on your art project, which you feel is really important, but you haven't been doing your cleanup work, so other people have to do it. I wish you'd help with the cleanup."

Which is professional criticism? Both examples say both "good" and "bad" things, and both make a request, but the first example sweetens the bad with feelings irrelevant to the problem at hand. The second example "values" as well as "disvalues" exactly the same thing, the way Joe uses his time. The link is tight, and the criticized behavior is specific and clear.

When both the valued and disvalued portions of professional criticism are clearly expressed and linked, the criticism is balanced.

The Success of Professional Criticism

Professional criticism is complete and honest. The criticism gives a student the complete picture of what the teacher is thinking, not just one part which might mislead or confuse the student. For example, if you say "Johnny, your work is really sloppy! I can't believe it!" Johnny will think you're down on him. If you really can't believe it, say so: "Johnny, last week your work was neat and attractive. This week it's sloppy. I can't believe the change!"

Professional criticism is clear and therefore more likely to be understood. The model requires a clear value statement and a clear disvalue or request statement. If the teacher says, "Well, I tried to be diplomatic about it, you know? I gave him the general idea; I hope he takes the hint," she risks not being understood.

Professional criticism anticipates the student's emotional response, addresses that response, and strives to keep the student in a thinking mood. Imagine these hypothetical reactions to conventional criticisms:

Steve: "OK, so I'm late on the math problems, but if you'd only recognize that I was kept late by my music teacher, and I didn't have a chance to start math with the rest of the kids."

Joan: "I know I shouldn't have gone to the pencil sharpener right then, but if you'd only recognize that I get too stiff sometimes — I need to stretch."

Ned: "Sure I didn't answer your question with the right date, but if you'd only recognize that I did have the right century."

Notice the common theme in these reactions: "if only you'd recognize" — a highly predictable response to conventional criticism. Professional, balanced criticism anticipates and defuses latent bad feelings by stating them out loud as part of the criticism:

To Steve: "I know you were delayed starting your math problems — that's why you're behind now, right? Hurry and try to finish with the others."

To Joan: "We've been a long time on this, Joan, I realize, but it's not time yet for your pencil."

To Ned: "OK, Ned, you're in the ball park, but not on base yet. Try again."

VALUING

Imagine that a student suddenly stands on a chair and knocks down the small projects hanging on the bulletin board. Could you find any part of that student's behavior to value? The fact is that a skillful teacher can handle any situation professionally. In the case of the student who was carelessly grabbing for her project on the bulletin board, use the three steps in "valuing": like, accept, and understand.

1 If you can find something to *like* in the student's disvalued behavior, say so. ("Sarah, I am glad you're so eager to start fixing your project, but ... ")

2 If you cannot honestly find something likable in the student's behavior, you might be able to *accept* that the behavior exists. ("Sarah, I know you want to get your project first — everybody does, but ... ")

3 If you honestly find nothing to like or accept in the student's behavior, you can at least *understand* the circumstances that led to the behavior. ("Sarah, I can understand that you might have worried that you'd never get your project, but .... ")

The purpose of the professional criticism model is not diplomacy, tact, or kindness; rather, the purpose is honesty and effectiveness.

METHOD Ya
Balanced Criticism: How effectively does the teacher use balanced criticism during instruction?

LEVEL 1: The teacher directs specific, content-oriented, balanced criticism to the entire class.

This criticism is professional in every respect: "Class, you have been working well up to now on fractions; now I see your minds are *off* fractions. I want you to think about how to multiply $1/8 \times 1/4$"

LEVEL 2: The teacher directs specific, content-oriented, balanced criticism to target students.

This too is professional criticism, with only a slight chance that the target students will be disconcerted by the criticism: "You there in the second row, get your head straight up when you come up; you're touching your toes fine, just come up higher on your recovery. That's right. Now you over there .... " (A shorter version: "You there ... good toes, feeble stretch!")

The following example follows the model and invites the student to analyze his problem: "This week's workbook assignment was due Monday, Paul, and I still don't have yours. When you hand them in, they look very good, but you've been late on the last two. I want your work to be both good and on time. Now, is there something I can do to help you? What's the problem?" (Notice the teacher's lead into choice counseling, discussed in chapter 22.)

LEVEL 3: (None.)

LEVEL 4: The teacher directs unclear or unlinked content-oriented criticism to target students privately.

"Sue, you raised your hand just fine — thank you for that. However, you haven't got the right answer yet to 7 times 6."

The problem in this criticism is the link; the balance is weakened, allowing a greater chance that the target student's emotion will rise. The value statement is irrelevant to the disvalue statement, so the student is likely to take offense at the transparent attempt to offer praise with the criticism.

LEVEL 5: (None.)

LEVEL 6: The teacher directs unlinked, content-oriented, overgeneralized criticism to students.

The problem with this technique is that the teacher risks sounding sarcastic. There is no clear link between the value and disvalue statements, and at least one of the statements is usually overgeneralized. Consequently, the value statement sounds artificial: "You'll go far in the art world, Donald, but you've got too much blue in this painting." Or: "She's a nice girl, you know, but her pronouns don't fit." There is little reason for a teacher to use this technique except perhaps for purposes of humor, and even then you must be careful to avoid insult.

LEVEL 7: The teacher directs noncontent criticism to students during instruction.

"Class, there is entirely too much noise in this room, and I want it quiet, just the way you did it yesterday, which was good. I want it that way again today."

Any criticism, no matter how artful, becomes high profile when it focuses attention on matters other than content.

EXERCISE 1 Balanced Criticism Drill (15–20 minutes)

Your instructor gives a 15-second talk to the class, including any or all of the following: mispronounced words, tugging at clothes, scratching, lack of eye contact, monotone voice, or other.

On a scrap of paper, write a Level 1 balanced criticism to hand in. Do not sign your name.

Your instructor will read each slip aloud, then ask the group to chorus "correct" or "not correct." If "not correct," group members should correct the criticism immediately. (Repeat the drill as needed.)

EXERCISE 2 Balanced Criticism (15–20 minutes)

Prepare for this exercise by writing down three student behaviors that irritate you continually or currently. (If you are not teaching, use situations at home, at work, or among your friends.) For each behavior, write a professional Level 1 balanced criticism.

In a group of about eight to twelve, act as the teacher. Deliver your criticism out loud to the person on your left, by *name*, as if that person were the actual offender. If your criticism is completely clear and linked, the group will chorus "correct." If anyone does not understand the criticism clearly, he should say "problem." Every group member must chorus each time.

Repeat the cycle until all group members have been teacher three times.

EXERCISE 3 Balanced Criticism (15–20 minutes)

Use the Section Ab Exercise 3 procedures, modifying as follows: the teacher may watch the student's paper and talk to the student, but the student may not talk or see the teacher's paper. When you are teacher, make every statement or direction a balanced criticism plus a request. For example, to begin the exercise, you may say, "I'm glad you've got your paper out and ready, but there's nothing written on it yet. Draw a … " If you make any statement your student thinks is not a correct Ya1 criticism, he will put his pen or pencil down and refuse to work until he hears a correct criticism. After five minutes, trade roles.

Conclusion   While it may at first seem a gimmick, this exercise is actually a good simulation of actual classroom events: the teacher instructs, the student follows, and when the teacher upsets the student ever so slightly, the student's motivation decreases and learning lags.

METHOD Yb
Praise: How effectively does the teacher use praise during instruction?

Praise is the valuing portion of the conventional criticism model. Mid and high profile praise are familiar in schools:

"That's a nice job, Amy." (Mid profile)

"Very good, Sam." (Mid profile)

"I like the way Ernie is sitting up straight." (High profile)

Most praise yields significant benefits; students feel good about themselves, their work, the class, and about school. But low profile praise captures the same good feelings and uses them to focus the student's mind on content. For example:

"That's a nice job on the introductory paragraph, Amy; I get a good idea from it of what your paper will tell me." (Low profile)

"Very good, Sam—you got your 6-times tables just right, that time, especially 6 times 7 equals 42. Good!" (Low profile)

"I like the way Ernie is sitting up straight to see what Goldilocks does next!" (Low profile)

Does it seem that we are splitting hairs? Is the notion of low profile praise too theoretical to be important in teaching? If you think so, try to remember how betrayed you felt the last time you praised a student, only to have him misbehave immediately afterwards. Why do you think he misbehaved? Quite possibly your praise focused his mind on himself and his own feelings of pleasure and self-satisfaction; it was then easy for him to drift off into thinking about something else.

Low profile praise has two other advantages for teachers and students. First, it is specific; the student knows exactly what he is being praised for, and can use that information. Compare these examples: "I really like your paper, Greg; it's a good one." What can Greg do with such global praise? It is equivalent to telling someone he has a nice personality, pleasant to hear, of course, but of no practical use.

"I really like the way you set up your paper, Greg, with good, clear examples for each argument." This praise gives pleasure, *plus* good implicit advice: "The next time you write a paper like this, Greg, make sure you have good examples the way you did here."

The second advantage of low profile praise is its honesty. When you say, "I really like your paper, Greg; it's a good one," you suggest that the entire work is of fine quality. To give this praise knowing full well that misspellings, faulty grammar, and illegible handwriting make the paper difficult to read, despite its excellent organization, misleads the student.

In short, the principle of low profile praise is to praise only in terms of lesson content, and only that which merits praise.[2]

LEVEL 1: The teacher gives specific, content-oriented praise to the class.

No one can feel singled out when the entire class is praised, and few minds are likely to wander if the praise is associated with content words: "You listened well to my advice on clamping your drawings—all the corners on these projects are true."

LEVEL 2: The teacher gives specific, content-oriented praise to target students privately.

The teacher's individual attention may conceivably concern some students, especially when they're praised in public, but the likelihood is slim: "Jerry, you pronounced the word *expliqué* very well."

LEVEL 3: The teacher gives general, content-oriented praise to target students privately.

"Nice job on organizing that chart, Amos," or "Shirley, you've really improved in your chemistry homework."

LEVEL 4: The teacher gives target students noncontent praise privately.

General praise now and then (Level 3) does not distract significantly, but when it comes continuously, it begins to appear meaningless; even the student may sneer.

> **TEACHER:** Nice job, fellas, nice job, nice job. (Teacher exits.)
> **STUDENT:** Jeez, what's *that* all about?

LEVEL 5: (None.)

LEVEL 6: The teacher gives continuous public praise to students.

Too much of anything becomes absurd. Perhaps the best example is "good," a word that new teachers seem to think they must say over and over. In fact, the word is rarely necessary, and often distractive:

> **TEACHER:** Everybody say this word.
> **STUDENTS:** *Garçon.*
> **TEACHER:** *Garçon.* Good.

In this case, the experience of saying *garçon* and hearing the teacher's echo reinforcement is itself sufficient and rewarding; "good" is superfluous, and used over and over, becomes cheap and meaningless. New teachers should discipline themselves not to say "good," and instead develop other forms of praise.

LEVEL 7: The teacher gives noncontent praise to the class or to target students publicly.

The notion that noncontent praise can be distractive may strike some as heresy, but it is true.

"That's a handsome cover you've got on that book, Kim."

"I like the way Gwenella moves her chair quietly, without scraping, when she comes to reading group."

"You guys got that experiment set up in good time."

Each compliment, if expressed during instruction, calls all the students away from content toward whatever the teacher is praising.

EXERCISE 1 PRAISE (10–15 minutes)

1   Join a group of five to eight persons.

2   At your turn as teacher, teach a 1-minute lesson (timed for you by a group member) on one of the following: how to do a certain dance step; how to pronounce certain foreign language words correctly; how to do certain exercise motions; how to do certain math operations; how to do a certain athletic game maneuver (e.g., "a pick" in basketball); how to divide a word into syllables; or how to do something of your choice.

3   During your lesson, praise every student at least once with a low profile technique. Each time you do so correctly, the student will say, "That's it"; if your praise is not low profile, the student will say nothing. If you use "good" at Level 7, all students will murmur "booo." (It takes strong action to break strong habits!)

4   Pass the teacher role around the group until all members have a turn.

METHOD Yc

Requests and Reprimands: How effectively does the teacher make "start" and "stop" statements during instruction?

LEVEL 1: The teacher makes a specific content-oriented request.

This is a request rather than a direct disvalue statement; often the disvalue is implied:

"Here, try it *this* way: make that top curve over the line."

"Remember to bring down the very next number."

You can also state the disvalued behavior directly to clarify the request or suggestion:

"Use a piece of Kleenex instead of your finger to shade or smooth that chalk—it's cleaner."

"Bring down the next number, not the second one over—the next one is 5, right?"

LEVEL 2: (None.)

LEVEL 3: The teacher makes a specific, content-oriented disvalue statement to target students privately.

This statement says, "No, you're wrong." (At Level 1, the teacher avoids saying "no" directly, but rather poses a request, such as "Now, Tom, think of it this way for a moment.") The teacher keeps the risk of distraction within limits at Level 3 by confining the disvalue to content only:

"Mike, you do not pour the water in on top of the powder."

"No, if you multiply them before you find the least common denominator, you'll end up with ..."

"Remember what we said before: if it fills that position, it is *not* adverbial."

LEVEL 4: The teacher makes a noncontent disvalue (or desist) statement to target students privately.

Of all control techniques, the verbal reprimand (desist order) most characterizes the institution of formal schooling to the general public. For example, if Gus is tipping back in his chair at a precarious angle, the teacher passes him and quietly says "Don't," and continues the lesson without a break. There is no way to give a noncontent reprimand without distracting the student's attention from the lesson.

LEVEL 5: (None.)

LEVEL 6: The teacher makes a noncontent disvalue statement or request to students publicly.

Again, this is the classic reprimand, or desist order. The reprimand may be verbal or nonverbal.

- Pointing or wagging finger at a student to indicate "stop that" or "sit down"
- Writing student names on the chalkboard as a warning
- Frowning at a student

Despite its power to distract attention from learning, some teachers insist that the all-class reprimand is necessary; they say "That's the only language these kids understand, that's all they hear at home" or "You've got to let them know who's boss, or they'll walk all over you." Yet each time the technique is used without the sequence prescribed by fundamental principle no. 3, we are left to wonder whether a low profile technique might have worked better, without the distraction.

LEVEL 7: The teacher turns out lights, orders heads down, makes a loud noise for order, or makes some other dramatic public reprimand.

My teacher education students are usually impressed with the elementary school technique of turning out the lights until everyone is quiet, because it works. The children quiet down, and even hush one another. The teacher can comment in a quiet voice about how noisy the class has been, and the class can get back to work. Unfortunately, this technique is highly distractive. The lights-out device is a time-waster, albeit a popular one.

Making students put their heads down on desks is another crutch, but an inventive teacher can use it at Level 1. Imagine a 5th-grade class: "All right, everyone, put your head down on the desk and close your eyes. It seems we all have different ideas in this discussion, and that's why so many of us wanted to talk at once. Now I want you to think about your own idea. First, what you think should be done; second, who would benefit from your plan [pause]. Third, who would be hurt by or would be opposed to your plan [pause]. And fourth, how and by what means your plan might be improved so more people would benefit and fewer would suffer or object [pause]. When you're ready, lift your head, take out paper, write down the four parts — I'll write them on the board — and after you're done, we'll continue our discussion."

Making a loud noise for order sometimes makes sense in physical education classes, or perhaps in music classes, and occasionally during loud learning activities such as game-simulations, but most of the time, slapping rulers and ringing bells are artless teaching techniques.

The dramatic reprimand is overdone; most teacher lectures about manners and cooperation are a waste of time unless they are backed by concrete training of students (see Method Ja1).

EXERCISE 1
DRILL on CONTENT-ORIENTED REQUESTS (10-15 minutes)

Prepare for this exercise by writing your response to each situation in the list below. In your class or group, take turns reading aloud your responses to each situation. When a response is properly content-oriented, forcing the students to think about content, your group will chorus "correct." If a response is not clearly content oriented, members of the group should chorus "problem." Discuss the problems.
Repeat this procedure for each problem.

1 Students won't settle down for a general discussion of their pending science projects on leaf types and structures.

2 While talking with two students at your desk about the compositions you have just returned with comments, two kids in the corner are throwing paper wads at each other.

3 In home economics, you are standing next to a chart explaining the different cuts of meat. A kid in back sighs "Geez" loud enough to be heard by all.

4 During a math lesson on decimals, you discover the students have removed all the chalk and erasers from the board.

5 While one student is reading his civics report aloud, on the topic of unicameral and bicameral legislative forms, Benny reaches his foot across the aisle toward Fred.

Conclusion   Our goal is to respond as low profile as possible, hence these requests must be quick. We are assuming that these situations do not call for balanced criticism because the total climate of the classroom is balanced, with value and disvalue, requests and praise.

NOTES

1   This model is derived from the "Resent-Demand-Appreciate" model in Simon, Howe, and Kirschenbaum (1972).

2   Brophy (1981) concludes that praise has been oversold to teachers; it is actually a weak reinforcer for many students, particularly above the primary grades, and can even be counterproductive.

REFERENCES

BROPHY, J. Teacher praise: A functional analysis. *Review of Educational Research,* 1981, *51,* 5–32.

SIMON, S., HOWE, L., & KIRSCHENBAUM, H. *Values clarification: A handbook of practical strategies for teachers and students.* New York: Hart, 1972.

CONTROL THROUGH REWARDS AND PUNISHMENTS (METHOD Z)

19

METHOD Z

Rewards and Punishments: How does the teacher administer rewards and punishments during instruction?

A teacher may say she doesn't approve of behavior modification techniques because she disapproves of manipulating people, but ironically, the same teacher
undoubtedly uses behavior modification techniques continuously. She cannot possibly do otherwise, for everything a teacher says, does, and even thinks has a
conditioning effect on student behavior—sometimes an immediate and observable effect, sometimes an imperceptible effect. The teacher who does not believe
in behavior modification might as well not believe in the law of gravity. The significant question is not whether teachers believe in behavior modification but whether
or not they condition students effectively.

Teachers should know that much of the work in behavior modification has
been done with difficult students, those with emotional problems, severe learning
disabilities, discipline problems, poor motivation or short attention spans, and
immature coping habits or antisocial attitudes. Behavior modification techniques
have been successful with difficult students, and teachers can learn to apply the
techniques successfully as well.

Some teachers claim that nothing can be done to control children today,
and that teachers are not responsible for the chaotic classroom conditions that
society creates. These claims would be justified if teachers had only commands
and reprimands available for classroom control, but in light of all we know about
shaping and controlling human behavior, the claims are hollow. (See Hall, Lund,
and Jackson, 1968; Thomas, Becker, and Armstrong, 1968; Madsen, Becker, and
Thomas, 1968; Madsen and Madsen, 1974; Walker and Buckley, 1972; Alberto and
Troutman, 1982.)

LEVEL 1: The teacher ensures that content objectives, lesson materials, and learning activities provide intrinsic, positive reinforcement.

This means that learning is in itself interesting. The student needs no external
rewards or encouragement; he simply likes what he is doing, and does it.

John Condry and Barbara Koslowski (1977) surveyed research concerning the advantage of intrinsic over external rewards in learning, and report that
when children are offered external rewards for performing various learning tasks,
they tend to choose easier tasks, to use task information less efficiently, and to be
more answer-oriented and less logical in problem solving than do children who are
asked to perform the same tasks without external rewards. In addition, external
rewards produce products of lower quality, higher error rate, and lower creativity.
Finally, external rewards *lessen* the probability that students will return to an activity
they previously considered interesting. This research simply confirms the obvious
notion that if a learning activity is interesting, a student is more likely to do it without
prompting or prodding.

What can the teacher do to build intrinsically interesting lessons? The
answer fills volumes on human motivation, but we can mention six elements that
effective teachers build into their materials and activities to catch, hold, and build

student interest. These are novelty, surprise, completion, suspense, competition, and identification.

1 Novelty is the different combinations of ideas or images that intrigue the student: an alligator playing the tuba; someone trying to eat the square root of two for breakfast; an engineer building a bridge across a stream with boards that are too short. Any novel idea can be expressed in the spoken word, in print, in picture, or in action.

2 Surprise is the same as novelty, but exaggerated.

3 Completion is a built-in motivator, an activity or task that begs to be finished. Why do some people stay up all night to finish a novel or watch a TV movie or complete a jigsaw puzzle? Why do students stay in from recess to continue a debate or finish a workbook exercise that permits one to fill in the picture after doing the exercise?

4 Suspense is the need for completion heightened by emotion — fear, hope, etc. What is going to happen next?

5 Competition provides a sense of excitement and the prospect of accomplishment. The allure of instructional game-simulation is that there is something to win by participating in the activity. Sometimes the player wins from another player (a zero-sum game), and sometimes from a "dummy player," the author of the game or the designer of the puzzle.[1] The concept of a dummy player is particularly important, for when the student is matching wits with a designer or author, he must learn what is being taught in order to win; for example, the young reader who tries to figure out the clues that lead "Encyclopedia Brown" to the culprit is playing a game of wits with the author.

6 Identification is the fascination with heroes and heroines who are struggling with the same problems that confront us, and who are doing what we will shortly be doing too.

LEVEL 2: The teacher rewards on-task behavior and ignores off-task behavior (contingent reinforcement) or rewards approximate behavior (shaping).

CONTINGENT REINFORCEMENT

The basic behavior modification technique, *contingent reinforcement,* consists of two parts: (1) giving praise or attention when the student does what is desired of him; and (2) ignoring student behaviors that are not desirable.

Contingent reinforcement[2] can be given in various forms and degrees at various levels of control. At Level 2, the teacher pays close attention to consistency, making sure to note and treat appropriately every instance of on-task behavior early, with regular rewards, and later treating them with decreasing and intermittent rewards as the on-task behavior grows stronger, more self-sufficient, and self-rewarding. The teacher who uses this technique ignores undesirable behaviors that are not severe enough to disturb other students.

These are examples of contingent reinforcement[3]:

Situation 1: The student gives a wrong answer.

Technique 1: Say nothing at first. If the student continues talking and finally gives a correct answer, praise.

Technique 2: Ignore the wrong answer and prompt the student with cues or clues to the correct answer — give him more information to deal with, perhaps in this form: "If *X* and *Y* were true, now what would you say?" Then reward the correct answer.

Situation 2: From time to time, the student does not pay attention.

Technique 1: Ignore the inattentive moments, wait until the student is paying attention, then praise him in terms of content, not in terms of social behavior: "I'm glad you remembered that the remainder is not dropped but is shown here — good for you" or "Good for you — you know exactly where that river goes: To the East. That's right."

Technique 2: Ignore the inattentive behavior, but use the student's name or other Level 1 or 2 technique, then ask a question about content the student can answer easily. Then reward the answer: " . . . as Johnny, Suzie, and Therese already are aware; would you agree, Suzie, that a comma should not be placed here? That's right." Or "George Washington worried about treaties and their potential restraint of this country's foreign policy. If, for example, Becky were President and I were to urge you, Becky, to promise France that if they ever got into any trouble with England, we would come to help France, well, you'd be just a bit wary of that kind of treaty, wouldn't you? Sure, and that's precisely what Washington was worried about when he wrote the advice you find on page . . . . "

Contingent reinforcement works more effectively for a whole classroom than traditional orders and reprimands. Here is the report of one researcher who was assisting teachers of first graders. Students were getting out of their seats and wandering around the room; observers noted, on the average, 2.9 children standing up out of their seats during seatwork at every 10-second mark. The teachers took four actions; notice the results of each (Madsen and Madsen, 1974, p. 116):

Action 1 — Teachers told specific children to sit down; the children sat. Teachers then told children who stood up without good reason to sit down.

Result 1 — Amount of standing up increased; individual children obeyed, but more stood up (average 4.14 standing up).

Action 2 — Teachers reduced their orders to sit down.

Result 2 — Standing up decreased to average 3.14.

Action 3 — Teachers then repeated Action 1.

Result 3 — Standing up increased to average 3.94.

Action 4 — Teachers praised other individual students for "good sitting."

Result 4 — Standing up decreased to average 1.89.

Here is another practical example: an elementary student, Rose, continually left her seat to have the teacher check her papers and answer questions. The teacher began to ignore Rose when she approached the teacher's desk, but attended to her immediately if she raised her hand while seated. Rose soon stopped her out-of-seat behavior and began to spend more time on her studies (Hall, Lund, and Jackson, 1968, p. 5).

SHAPING

Contingent reinforcement works well if a student demonstrates the desired behavior within a reasonable time, but if the student shows no sign of the desired behavior, the teacher may begin the process of *shaping*.

Shaping is the technique of continually rewarding those behaviors that are closest to the goal. Consider Rose again; Rose refused to study in class during seatwork; after using reprimands and punishments to no avail, Rose's teacher decided to try a new technique:

> On the day her teacher was first to reinforce Rose's study behavior, Rose did not study at all, and the teacher was thus unable to provide reinforcement. Therefore, beginning with the second reinforcement session, the teacher attended to behavior that approximated study (e.g., getting out pencil or paper, or opening her book to the correct page). Once these behaviors were reinforced, study behavior quickly followed.... (Hall, Lund, and Jackson, 1968, p. 4)

Here are more examples of shaping:

Situation: Student is writing on the wrong page in his workbook during seatwork.

Technique: Praise what you can. "Mike, you've got the right book here, good. Now what I want you to do, as you go through the words on the other page [turn pages] is notice how the *-ure* and *-ation* words all derive from Latin. Understand?"

Situation: The student is not paying attention and gives a wrong answer.

Technique: Praise what you can. "No, but you got the first part right, the part about . . ." or "No, but you are in the right ballpark in terms of . . ." or "No, but I can see how you might have thought that . . ."

Notice that at Level 2, all rewards refer only to lesson content, never to procedures, methods, study habits, or good or bad behavior outside of lesson content. At Level 4 and higher, the teacher rewards noncontent behaviors, with increasing probabilities of distraction from the lesson.

LEVEL 3: The teacher waits for on-task behavior, then rewards it with a token.

A token system is any technique for rewarding students with tokens (coins, other objects, check marks, stars, credits, merit points) which the student can then use as a medium of exchange for other commodities or privileges (extra recess time, first choice of games, candy). The student earns tokens and then is entitled to spend them. The token system is a controversial technique of behavior modification; critics condemn it for being manipulative or materialistic, or because they think it makes students habitually depend upon immediate external rewards.

My impression is that teachers have used token reward systems for centuries; grades are a form of token, as is the granting of privileges for good work.

LEVEL 4: The teacher withholds rewards from target students but rewards others, or rewards noncontent behavior.

These techniques are common in elementary classrooms; for example, when a student is not paying attention, the teacher often praises other students who are paying attention, but says nothing to the student who is not. "I am pleased that Jim, Jane, and Jerry are paying attention so well," or "Almost everyone is paying attention now, and that's good." The risk of distraction lies both in the noncontent talk and in the possible embarrassment of the targets of control.

This technique is justified in proper sequence (see fundamental principle no. 3), particularly when a goal is set for the student along with the denial: "Wendy, you did not qualify for points this time, so here is what I want you to do for next time—so you can get your points."

LEVEL 5: The teacher uses nonphysical punishments.

This favorite technique for controlling classrooms is also one of the most distractive, and appears in the form of negative comments, extra assignments, and withholding privileges.

NEGATIVE COMMENTS

While some people think behavior modification advocates punishment, most behavior modification research actually discredits punishment. Thomas, Becker, and Armstrong (1968, 129, p. 44) studied the effects of teacher disapproval (negative comments) on children's disruptive behavior. Beginning with a baseline or average of several teachers' normal behaviors, the investigators asked teachers to change behaviors several times so they could observe student reactions. First, teachers shifted to a 10-day period of withholding approval and using only disapproval to control students; the result was that 81 percent of the students increased disruptive behavior. Second, the teachers returned to their normal baseline controls, which included approval; 75 percent of the students improved their behavior within two weeks. Third, the teachers shifted back to disapproval, with the result that 78 percent of the students became more disruptive. Finally, with the teachers reverting to approval controls, 71 percent of the students decreased disruptive behavior.

None of these research findings will surprise experienced teachers, who recognize that their own worst days are also their students' worst days. The more they scold and discipline, teachers report, the noisier their students become.

EXTRA ASSIGNMENTS

It is difficult to imagine how students can be expected to develop motivation for their studies if studies are meted out as punishment.

WITHHOLDING PRIVILEGES

We have all been recipients of withheld privileges, and we all know the risks. When the student's resentment is stronger than his remorse, the technique of withholding privileges is bound to fail.

LEVEL 6: The teacher isolates target students.

A student can be isolated in various ways: excluded from a small group in which he has been working, moved to a remote part of the room or away from his friends, or excluded from the room.

Some teachers regularly send students who misbehave out of the room. Effective teachers almost never do so, for the obvious reason that you cannot teach an absent student. The professional teacher looks for help from other professionals. Because the exclusion technique is so totally distractive, it should be used only after a long series of lower profile controls have been tried without success.

The distractive power of isolation inside the classroom must not be underestimated, either. The risk is that the student will tune out the lesson and let himself be distracted by someone or something else later on, as if to say, "I'm stuck over here anyway, so what have I got to lose?"

As one of the final steps in a long professional sequence, time out is a persuasive technique. It can be beneficial to the student if he becomes aware of the reasonable purpose for the teacher's action, and is an excellent technique for resolving emotional flare-ups.

LEVEL 7: The teacher administers physical punishment other than isolation.

Physical punishment is only justified as a last resort. Even then, its use should be decided not by an individual teacher or administrator but by a committee of professionals who design a strategy for directing student's attention. Even when administering punishment, however, the educator should be aware that investigators and experienced practitioners of behavior modification generally eschew physical punishment. Excellent teachers almost never use it; they do not need to.

EXERCISE 1 INTRINSIC REWARDS (30–60 minutes)

Bring to your class group a one- to six-page example of learning material you believe has intrinsic reinforcement built into its presentation. (Do not assume the content itself is rewarding.) Attach to the back of your material a sheet of paper in the following format:

Your Name _____ Subject Area* _____ Grade Level* _____
1. Reviewer's Name _____ Rating (circle one) 1 2 3 4 5
Reasons:**

2. Reviewer's Name _____ Rating (circle one) 1 2 3 4 5
Reasons:**

Etc., through 5 reviewers.
Rating: 1 = Low reinforcement value; 5 = High reinforcement value

*These refer to the classroom where you propose to use the materials.
**Refer to Novelty, Surprise, Completion, Suspense, Competition, and/or Identification.

Circulate your materials to others in the group. Each reviewer should examine and judge the material before looking at your form. Each statement of reasons should refer to one or more of the categories in Section Z1: Novelty, Surprise, Completion, Suspense, Competition, and Identification.

Conclusion The purpose of this activity is to compare your judgments of intrinsic reinforcement (Method Z1) with others' judgments, to learn from the comparison, and to enhance your awareness of lesson appeal.

NOTES

1   Goodman (1973, p. 928) explains this concept well.
2   I am using the term as defined in Gage and Berliner, 1979, p. 286.
3   See "Behavior Modification" in chapter 1.

REFERENCES

ALBERTO, P., & TROUTMAN, A. *Applied behavior analysis for teachers.* Columbus, Ohio: Charles E. Merrill, 1982.

CONDRY, J., & KOSLOWSKI, B. Can education be made "intrinsically interesting" to children? Educational Resources Information Center, 1977, ED 153 706.

GAGE, N., & BERLINER, D. *Educational psychology.* Chicago: Rand McNally, 1979.

GOODMAN, F. Gaming and Simulation. In R. Travers (Ed.), *Second handbook of research on teaching* (American Educational Research Association). Chicago: Rand McNally, 1973.

HALL, R., LUND, D., & JACKSON, D. Effects of teacher attention on study behavior. *Journal of Applied Behavior Analysis,* 1968, *1*, 1–12.

KOUNIN, J. *Discipline and group management in classrooms.* New York: Holt, Rinehart and Winston, 1970.

MADSEN, C., BECKER, W., & THOMAS, D. Rules, praise, and ignoring: Elements of classroom control. *Journal of Applied Behavior Analysis,* 1968, *1*, 139–150.

MADSEN, C., & MADSEN, C. *Teaching/discipline.* Boston: Allyn and Bacon, 1974.

THOMAS, D., BECKER, W., & ARMSTRONG, M. Production and elimination of disruptive classroom behavior by systematically varying teacher's behavior. *Journal of Applied Behavior Analysis,* 1968, *1*, 35–45.

WALKER, H., & BUCKLEY, N. Programming generalization and maintenance of treatment effects across time and across settings. *Journal of Applied Behavior Analysis,* 1972, *5*, 209–224.

THREATS TO CONTROL:
GAMES STUDENTS PLAY

20

Teachers and students often behave predictably; their relationships become patterned after a time, and each can predict the other's moves and actions (Shipman, 1968, p. 136). Some predictable patterns of teacher-student interaction are helpful to learning. For example:

> STUDENT: Mrs. Jones, would you help me?
> TEACHER: Sure, Sue, what's the problem?

I will call these functional teacher-student interaction patterns "routines." Other patterns of teacher-student interaction are dysfunctional, that is, not helpful to learning. For example:

> TEACHER: Jill, what are you doing over there?
> STUDENT: Who, me?
> TEACHER: Yes, you.
> STUDENT: Me?
> TEACHER: That's what I said!
> STUDENT: What did I do?

I will call these dysfunctional interaction patterns "games." A game is any set of patterned teacher/student classroom behaviors whose motives are generally hidden and which distract from, delay, or prevent learning. (This use of the term *game* is not to be confused with legitimate instructional games. Dysfunctional games are the kinds of patterned behaviors Eric Berne originally called *games* in his popular book, *Games People Play* (1964).

Routines are part of the fabric of American classrooms. Unfortunately, games are also: experienced teachers often play games without knowing they are doing so; new teachers are often baffled, frustrated, even enraged by the games students successfully play with them. Experienced and new teachers alike need help to deal effectively with games in the classroom, and they *must* deal with them, because games waste time that could otherwise be spent on learning.

ORIGINS OF STUDENT CLASSROOM GAMES

Why do students play transactional games? One reason is the natural and inevitable conflict between the teacher's self-fulfillment and the student's growth.[1] The teacher is fulfilled by providing a sheltering, supportive environment to which the student responds positively and, to some degree, dependently: the student pays attention to the teacher and follows the teacher's instructions. However, as the student grows in this supportive environment, he wants to become more and more independent of that environment. He wants to ask probing, even critical questions, to know the rationale of every activity and policy, to raise alternative suggestions at every turn, and to pursue his own interests rather than the teacher's planned program of instruction. So the teacher's needs conflict with students' needs; I believe students sense this conflict and play with it. Other specific reasons for student game-playing include the need for attention, for social position, to relieve boredom, to test the system, to combat restrictions, to express frustration, and the need to survive.

MOTIVATIONS FOR PLAYING GAMES

NEED FOR ATTENTION

The most ready audience for a student's game is her classmates. Sometimes the student gets others in the audience to join her in the game, an added stroke of attention and recognition.

NEED FOR SOCIAL POSITION

Most students need to be a visible, active *somebody;* for the student with a particularly strong need for status, "oblivion may be worse than infamy."[2] Therefore, anything the teacher does to diminish the student in the eyes of peers threatens the student's most basic social need. It is ironic, then, that the first impulse most teachers feel is to quash students' games with a put-down. Of course, they do it for their own protection, but such action is like engaging in an arms race for peace.

NEED TO RELIEVE BOREDOM

Sheer boredom is the root of much student game playing. Eric Fromm reminds us that humans cannot tolerate an environment devoid of stimulae, nor an existence devoid of activity. Yet much of the traditional classroom routine is devoid of stimulation for students, and much is passive. The glaze that comes over most students' eyes can cover boredom for just so long before they must do something, so the games start.

NEED TO TEST THE SYSTEM

"The system" consists of the rules, the student, and the teacher. Students naturally test the limits of the rules that constrain them, for three logical reasons:

1 To find out what the rules really mean, and whether the announced rules are really rules or simply a verbal smokescreen.
2 To discover their own limits in terms of the extent to which they will risk danger in the game of testing. For some students, testing is a source of great joy, and we must recognize that fact and work with it.
3 To discover what kind of person the teacher is. Does the teacher really know the rules? Is he strong and reliable or weak? Can he handle the student's testing in a caring way, or does he retreat into authoritarianism or strike out? To the student, the real question is whether or not he can trust the teacher. The teacher who does not know the rules, does not understand the proper role of teacher, and who retreats passively or attacks viciously when teased, fails the test—leaving students disgusted. Students want their teachers to succeed. What most students ultimately want from the teacher is to learn; if students don't learn, the teacher fails.

NEED TO COMBAT RESTRICTIONS

The traditional American school is authoritarian, bureaucratic, and generally insensitive to individuals. The tensions of this environment cannot be denied or underestimated. Although the logical end of continual restriction and restraint is violence, schools rarely experience violence, even in the inner city; students usually express their hostility in other ways. When the teacher permits no latitude in the classroom, no room to think independently, students rebel by turning to dysfunctional games.

In a typical school, students believe teachers and administrators hold all the cards. In fact, students have immense power to influence and to disrupt the school—but if they *perceive* themselves as powerless, they may work hard to subvert the efforts of their superiors. A student's response to the teacher may have little to do with the teacher as a person; the student may simply be reacting to the traditional system the teacher represents.

NEED TO EXPRESS FRUSTRATION AT FAILURE

Students use both fair and foul devices in competition for rewards. Gordon's study of American high schools reveals just how far apart teacher and student perceptions of rewards can be. Most students interviewed wanted up to twenty percent better grades—deserved or not, we do not know—than they were assigned for their work. (Gordon, 1957, p. 42).

NEED TO SURVIVE

It is possible that the motives for student game playing represent a search for some means to maintain the student's integrity, dignity, identity, and sanity—in short, survival in school.[3] The strategies the student develops may be quite unconscious. If you ask, "Why do you do this even when I ask you not to?" the student may be truly at a loss to tell. Some of the underlying reasons are common to all students. For example, the predominant form of classroom control today is high profile, and students must often struggle to keep their minds on content. The predominant classroom activity in many classrooms is ditto worksheets which require continually quiet, passive behavior in students.

GENERAL PRINCIPLES FOR CONTROLLING STUDENT GAMES

I am always impressed when a teacher can respond to an apparently threatening student challenge with a smile and a casual comment, "Oh, I know that old game." This response takes away the emotion of the challenge. Second, it signals a halt to the challenge; simply knowing the game is often enough to end it. Finally, the teacher suggests that both parties must behave reasonably; unreasonableness, like games, has already been discredited and discarded.

Remember in reading and studying the interaction patterns in this chapter that most of them should not be considered games unless they both distract from the lesson and *recur.* The teacher who challenges a student while he is engaged in classroom routine can generate considerable confusion and bad feeling; overreaction may appear as foolish to students as the teacher who is unaware that students are playing games. So recognize games and counter them when you see them, but don't be paranoid. Wait until games become quite obvious. This advice should be reassuring for new teachers—take your time, relax, don't hurry your judgment. *When* you stop a game is not nearly so important as *whether* you stop it. And to stop it, you will apply the same fundamental principles that control inattention or unknown attention.

Who, Me?   S–1

KEY WORDS:

"Who, me? (What did I do?)"
"Were you talking to me?"

Functional Routine   Sometimes teachers do not speak clearly or loudly enough for students to hear. "Who, me?"/"Yes, I meant you" is a simple and useful message check.

Dysfunctional Game   The teacher begins with an innocent inquiry or request, such as, "Bill, did you happen to see what happened to my scissors?" or "Bill, could I talk with you for a moment?" Or the teacher wants Bill to stop goofing around and simply says, "Bill."

The student begins the game with "Who, me?" and an optional tag ending of "What did I do?" or "Why me?" The teacher continues the game by responding, "Yes, you!" or "Because I asked you!" or "I don't see anyone else here whose name is Bill" or some reply that counters the "Who, me?" inquiry with a challenge. If a teacher's reply is challenging or petulant, she unwittingly falls into the student's game.

Each episode is usually brief, but can accumulate considerable classroom time when it becomes a customary student response to teacher inquiries or requests.

How to Stop the Game   The student may be trying to create an image with his peers as a mysterious person who has something to hide, or he may seek the image of class clown or class hero who can bug the teacher and get away with it.

The trick is not to stop one episode, but rather to stop the student *custom* of playing "Who, me?" Remediation follows a step at a time. Make up your own remedies; these examples are arranged in ascending order of control levels:

- The teacher calmly says "yes," and continues the current activity without further notice of the student's game playing. (Level 2)
- The teacher responds with a smiling sidelong glance or a wink, and goes along with business as usual. (Level 4)
- "Are you playing your 'Who, me' game again, Bill?" (Level 6)
- The teacher says privately, "You are playing the 'Who, me' game a lot lately, Bill. Why are you doing it?" (The teacher might begin Dreikurs' four goal questions, as discussed in chapter 1.)

I Have an Excuse[4]   S–2

KEY WORDS

"Somebody stole my pencil."
"I'm sick."

"I left it in my locker."

"He did it to me first!"

For this discussion we must distinguish between reasons and excuses. Reasons are causal events; excuses are pseudoreasons. Students don't play games with reasons, but with excuses. While reasons are a natural part of education, excuses are nonproductive and expendable.

Functional Routine   Reasons are an integral part of teaching and learning. The functional routine consists of a student's expression of fact, sometimes accompanied by genuine frustration, and a teacher's accommodating and artful response to the student. For example:

> STUDENT: Somebody stole my pencil.
> TEACHER: That's too bad. Perhaps Mary can help you for the moment [or] That's too bad. We'll get one for you in a moment. Lucky you don't need a pencil right now to think in your head about . . . . [Back to the lesson.]

> STUDENT: I left it in my locker.
> TEACHER: I see. Well go ahead now, and then see me after class to discuss what you missed while you were out [or] I see. Look on with Jim for now, and I will discuss it with you later. [Back to the lesson.]

> STUDENT: He did it to me first!
> TEACHER: Well obviously you both have a problem; let's have the three of us think together about that problem at break time. Right now think about this: What would you do — anybody — if . . .? [Back to the lesson.]

The teacher must be accommodating, for when a teacher who is supposed to be helpful gives an unfeeling response to a student who has had a momentary lapse of memory or control, the student is justified in being miffed and resentful. Yet the teacher must also be professionally artful so as not to provide too easy a rescue for a young person who is supposed to be learning to take care of herself, and not to allow the lesson to be further disrupted. So the responses in the examples strive to accommodate or recognize the immediate problem while signaling that future action will be taken as well. In private conference with chronic excusers, losers, and leavers, the teacher may eventually want to do some choice counseling, to help the student think through problems, see all options and consequences, and make choices based on real consequences and personal values. (See chapter 22.) In short, the teacher patiently trains the student to break a habit and solve problems.

Dysfunctional Game   There are countless versions of the "I Have an Excuse" in which an excuse substitutes for a legitimate reason. The student offers an excuse, and the teacher treats it as a reason, thus entering into the game.

> STUDENT: I lost my pencil.
> TEACHER: Why haven't you got one?

STUDENT: I left it in my locker.
TEACHER: Well, bring it to class next time.
STUDENT: Yes, but I don't have the combination.
TEACHER: Who has it?
STUDENT: Pat.
TEACHER: Why don't you get it from Pat?
STUDENT: She's home sick.
TEACHER: Well, call her up.
STUDENT: She hasn't got a phone.

And so on. The game for the student is to get the teacher to accept each excuse as a bona fide reason. The game recurs daily, and can drive a new teacher to distraction. The student wins when the teacher continues being helpful or folds her arms, stamps her foot, or otherwise shows irritation, because the student has successfully foisted some responsibility off on the teacher. Now the teacher must solve the student's phony problem.

HOW TO STOP THE GAME

1 The game ends most easily when the teacher ignores it — perhaps talking over the student's words as if they had not been spoken — and directs student attention to lesson content.

2 The teacher says, "Well, that's quite a problem," and continues the activity. (Level 3 if spoken privately, Level 5 if publicly)

3 The teacher says, "I'll be interested to see how you solve that problem, Fay" or "I'll talk with you about that problem later, Fay," and continues the lesson as before. (Level 4 if spoken privately, Level 6 if publicly)

Irrelevant[5]   S—3

KEY WORDS

"It sure is hot in here."
"Wonder what's for lunch today."
"Hey, did you hear about . . .?"
Irrelevant comments are natural in any conversation, yet they never cease to surprise us in schools.

Functional Routine Some student comments that seem irrelevant are actually a reasonable leap beyond a current topic to the next logical consideration. Furthermore, some student comments are faulty interpretations of a current topic, and even though faulty, are nevertheless high attention behaviors. If the teacher really listens, she can detect the student's thinking process immediately and respond appropriately:

"That's good, Bill, that's where we're going. We're just not there yet. Where we are now is. . . ." (Level 1)

"I think I see why you say that—it's like what we're talking about in that it. . . . Am I right?" (Level 1)

When the student comment seems irrelevant but the teacher has a faint suspicion or hope that it might relate, she can use these Level 2 techniques:

"I don't understand how that relates to the topic of. . . . (Can you explain it?) (Can you help me?)"

"I just don't understand what you're saying, and I want to. Try again."

Sometimes a student comment is so far off the topic that the teacher cannot relate it without intellectual gymnastics. In this case, try a technique for shifting topics at Level 1 (see also Method R):

TEACHER: So now we know this shape is called a triangle.
Angie: My dog is going to have puppies!
TEACHER: You're happy about that, right, Angie?
Angie: Yeah, and. . . .
TEACHER: Angie, if this shape is called triangle, what is. . .?

Some student comments have nothing to do with the current topic, but show instead how the student feels at the moment. Again, use a shifting topic technique at Level 1, or move to Level 3:

TEACHER: When you think about why the South wanted to secede, the first thing you think about is what? Anybody? Darryl, did you have your hand up?
Darryl: Yeah, when's this period over?
TEACHER: We've been at this a long time, eh?
Darryl: Well, yeah.
TEACHER: Darryl, what's the first thing that comes to your mind when somebody asks, Why did the South fight the North?

When it is clear the student is having trouble concentrating, the teacher's task is twofold: first, recognize the student's feeling; second, refocus the student's attention on the lesson. Level 5 controls work well here:

"Does anybody else feel that way? Let's fix it. . . . OK, good. Now think with me a moment about [lesson topic]. . . ."

"You're having trouble thinking about this, aren't you Bill? Tell me, Bill, if you were [pose a hypothetical problem from the lesson]. . . what choice would you make?"

So, the principles of dealing with functional irrelevancies are first, to protect the student; do not embarrass him or call attention to his blunder, thereby running the risk of further distracting his attention from the lesson. Second, to protect the lesson by returning to the topic without delay, thus protecting the rest of the class from the distraction of the single student.

A bright and inventive teacher can occasionally turn an irrelevant distraction into a teaching point of the lesson itself. Consider the following example in a high school English class on *Macbeth*:

> **STUDENT:**   What's for lunch today?
> **TEACHER:**   You're hungry, aren't you? Well, it won't be long now, but you just can't wait, can you? Neither could Macbeth. What was he hungry for? (Power)

or

> **STUDENT:**   The top of this desk is dirty.
> **TEACHER:**   I see, Jan. Bothers you, does it? [To the class:] How is Jan's preoccupation with the dirt on her desk like Lady Macbeth? Can anyone think of an analogy? ("Out, out damned spot. . . .")

Teachers like this acquire reputations that spur students to test their ingenuity..

Dysfunctional Game   Students work diligently to get the teacher off the subject at hand. The teacher strives to get back to the topic but is led off again, and the game goes on. The students con the teacher, who tries to accommodate what she thinks are legitimate interests. Students want control, and the teacher doesn't want to offend or alienate anyone.

HOW TO STOP THE GAME

First, treat the student comment as if it were a reasonable and functional routine. If all efforts fail, you are clearly locked into a game. Try your next step at Level 6, voicing what everyone in the room already knows:

"Are you talking about the topic of . . . or are you talking about something else? I realize you want to change the topic, but I'd like to talk about this now, please."

"Your attention seems to be wandering, Bill; we are talking now about . . . ."

At Level 7, the class is completely distracted from the lesson:

"You are interrupting the lesson, Bill, and I'd like you to stop."

"I'd like to see you after class, Bill."

"I don't dig the game you're playing, Bill. Please stop."

The final step is to remove the student who continues to willfully disrupt the class.

Let Me Help You   S—4

KEY WORDS

"Can I help you?"
"Let me do that (for you)."
"Now *I'm* the teacher!"

Functional Routine   Younger children in traditional classrooms are thrilled to have the privilege of helping the teacher, but the thrill fades over the years. An offer of help and its acceptance or graceful rejection is a highly functional transaction, signifying honest communication and shared responsibilities for the classroom, its members, and its activities.

Dysfunctional Game   A student's offer of help is sometimes insincere. His motive may be disruption—to parade, to play for laughs, to masquerade as the teacher's assistant or "teacher." The game is fun when the teacher is out of the room, and even more fun when the teacher is present because of the element of risk. The intrigue comes from the ambiguity of motive, the teacher's guessing game: "Is he really trying to help me, or to bug me?"

When the teacher needs help, there is no reason to question motives; any motive will do as long as someone helps, assuming the student's clowning can be reasonably controlled.

HOW TO STOP THE GAME

When the student is passing out papers, or doing whatever she was told to do, but at the same time clowning, the teacher can use any low profile control technique. Or at Level 5, the teacher can move near the student and say in a low voice, "Pass the papers quickly and quietly now, Sarah, then go back to your seat."

When the distractions outweigh the benefits of a student's help, the teacher can go through a sequence of actions:

"Thank you. I appreciate your help, and when I need more, I'll call you." [Level 3 when stated privately or publicly]

"I see you didn't understand what I said. I'll call you when I need help; please sit down now." [Level 4 when stated privately, Level 6 publicly]

"I don't want to play that game. See me after class." [Level 5 when stated privately, Level 7 publicly]

(Willard Waller's *The Sociology of Teaching* [1932, p. 154] vividly describes "The Assistant Teacher Game" for any reader who thinks these games were invented only recently.)

S–5   You're Neat

KEY WORDS

"I like you."
"You're a neat teacher."
"I learn a lot in this class."
"That's good; now I understand."

Functional Routine   A student rarely gives a genuine compliment to a teacher in public. Usually it happens privately, and often furtively, as a glance, smile, a "Well, thanks." Whether furtive or open, teachers meet a compliment adequately with "Thank you" or "You're very thoughtful to say that." Compliments from students are treasures. It is also fun for students to tease their teachers with compliments, particularly exaggerated ones. The game is pleasant and harmless.

Dysfunctional Game   The term *brownnose* taints any sincere compliment a student might give a teacher, casting suspicion on both the compliment and the student. Teachers are permitted to compliment students, but students are not permitted to reciprocate; the risk of ridicule from other students is too great. This attitude adds excitement to the game. Sometimes students play it openly for the benefit of an amused audience, and sometimes they play it simultaneously with "Irrelevant."

> **STUDENT:**   You're the greatest teacher in this school, Mr. Jones, did you know that? (Giggles from the audience.)
> **TEACHER:**   Thank you, thank you, Gus. Thank you very much.

A student often pays an insincere compliment in a semiprivate or private conference.

The subtlety of this game makes it much like a cat-and-mouse transaction, with the teacher thinking, "Does he mean it or doesn't he?" and the student thinking, "Is he digging it or isn't he?"

HOW TO STOP THE GAME

A single "Thank you" does it nicely. Shifting topic completes the transaction and begins a new one. When compliments are clearly forced, a smiling retort ("Oh, you always say that") should get the message across to the eager student without embarrassing her. The teacher can get mileage out of the game by stopping it with a joke:

> **STUDENT:**   You're the greatest teacher in this school, Mr. Jones, did you know that?
> **TEACHER:**   Now that you mention it, Frank, I think you're absolutely right!

Shocking Behavior   **S—6**

KEY WORDS

> Expletives, belches, etc.
> "This class stinks!"
> "I hate you!"

Functional Routine   Accidents happen; some students are unstable and lose control easily, and usually placid students lose their tempers once in a while. If there is any good to be gained from these incidents, it is that the individual student releases tension, and the teacher, by handling the incidents professionally, builds trust and respect. Students are impressed when a teacher passes a crisis test. The best teachers react to crises with equanimity by anticipating problems, being prepared for them rather than surprised by them. For example:

STUDENT: Goddamn you, Mike, gimme back my damn pencil!
TEACHER: (In quiet tone of voice with hint of a smile) Sounds like he means it, Mike. . . . Have you two each got a pencil now? . . . Let's talk about (topic) now, and I'll discuss the pencil matter with you later.

STUDENT: (Loud belch during seatwork, loud laughter from many other students.)
TEACHER: Well, Rose, I hope that takes some of the pressure off you so you can concentrate now on your multiplication tables. (Smile, shift topic to a lesson-oriented directive, then continue to walk through the class, whispering compliments to students who are working—business as usual.)

STUDENT: This stuff is boring shit!
TEACHER: Well, Zed, I know some parts of the class are not very interesting for you or anybody else; I doubt that I would have chosen those exact words to report my feelings about the matter, but let me explain once again, so everybody knows, just exactly why we're doing this.

Notice in the last example how the skilled teacher, always looking for a dramatic moment to motivate students, has an ideal opportunity to explain the purpose of the lesson and the importance of the students' learning the material.

Dysfunctional Game Foul or aggressive language, and lewd smiles and body gestures are techniques students use to shock, intimidate, and overpower the teacher. The problem with "Shocking Behavior" in the classroom is that teachers are not prepared for it. "The usual college teacher preparation programs rarely discuss students' use of foul language" (Foster, 1974, p. 310).

Herbert Foster's *Ribbin', Jivin', and Playin' the Dozens* (1974) reviews games calculated to unnerve and shock, imported from black inner-city street cultures into the school. These brief descriptions are labeled with their page numbers from Foster's book for your convenience.

Man-maning—look and act like wild man, scare Whitey but don't touch him (p. 58)
Ribbin'—denigrating or making fun of someone (p. 183)
Shuckin' and jivin'—deceptive subservient behavior (p. 193)
Jivin'—deceiving in jest, often through double entendre (p. 196)
Woofin'—vicious verbal attack (to accept a challenge to fight is to accept a "wolf ticket"); loud mouthing, offensive threatening (p. 197)
Signifying—baiting two others to fight by means of reporting to one what the other said about him (p. 203)
The Dozens—foully insulting someone's mother (p. 210)
Putting 'em on—leading someone to think you agree with him when you don't (p. 229)
Working game—borrow money with no intention of repaying (p. 229)

HOW TO STOP THE GAME

Reacting strongly is playing the game, so the best way to stop is by ignoring it. When the teacher isn't shocked, the student isn't encouraged, and the game is extinguished. The way you ignore the game is important, however. To pretend you haven't noticed the behavior is sheer folly; the student will repeat the outrageous behavior until he gets some kind of reaction. Therefore, you can use several relatively low profile techniques to recognize that the behavior occurred, and to demonstrate that you are not shocked:

"Well, Andy, I hope you're all finished with that for now — no other surprises for us, eh? — because I'd like you to turn to page...."

"I'm flattered that you think I am worthy of your efforts to shock me, but really now — how old do you think I am? OK, now I think it's time to get back to...."

There is no easy way to desensitize a teacher's cultural or moral responses to foul language and gestures. We can merely suggest that teachers make simple forthright statements of the "I don't play that game" variety. They can also talk privately with offenders who consistently disregard others' sensibilities or seem unaware of how certain words affect people because of their culture, race, religion, or position.

I Gotta Go[6]   S–7

KEY WORDS

"Can I go to the bathroom?"
"Can I have a hall pass?"
"Can I get a drink of water?"
"I gotta go to my locker."
"I gotta go see the nurse."

Functional Routine Legitimate requests deserve reasonable and caring responses. People get thirsty, restless, and forget things. Occasionally a need becomes severe, as in the case of a bladder disorder.

Sometimes needs are not what they are stated to be; real needs are present but hidden, and this is when the games begin.

Dysfunctional Game Actually, the student's need is real and serious. He may need to leave the room, or to get a drink. He invents escape games when the teacher does not honor his real reasons for leaving. The teacher plays the game by responding to the fake reason as if the real reason did not exist. The teacher has two possible moves; part of the student's fun is predicting which the teacher will make:

1 Agree to the student's request. Many teachers habitually make a preliminary move even before they agree; it adds an extra measure of fun for the student, because it is a cat-and-mouse game the student always wins, a signal of ultimate success. The teacher cross-examines the student:

> TEACHER: Are you sure you have to go?
> STUDENT: Yes.
> TEACHER: Well, OK, but just this once.

Of course the student's answer is always yes, but the teacher asks the question anyway, wasting time in the process, and the request is granted as a foregone conclusion. The student often grins at a fellow student as he exits.

2   Deny the request. In playing this game, the teacher makes the denial curt, thus giving the student a reason to pout or sulk or complain. To play the game further, the teacher responds to the student's complaint:

> STUDENT: Can I....?
> TEACHER: No, sit down.
> STUDENT: Awww, why...?
> TEACHER: Because I said so.
> STUDENT: (Long, slow return to her seat, where she may break immediately into animated conversation with a fellow student.)

The danger in this game, as every substitute teacher knows, is that regardless of which move the teacher makes, the first student is only one of several (or many) who will make the same or similar requests so they can play the game, too.

HOW TO STOP THE GAME

Like most dysfunctional games, it is best to stop this one before it begins. If the teacher establishes reasonable rules and procedures, preferably with student input and participation, to govern movement around the room and building, most need for game playing disappears.

When the game does occur, however, it should be handled in a way that avoids confrontation and distracting other students' attention. The teacher makes two moves at the same time: acknowledging the student's unspoken need and focusing the student on the task:

"I can appreciate your discomfort, but I'd also appreciate your waiting until [10:00] [the end of the hour] [after this part of the lesson is over]. How far are you into the assignment now?"

"You seem to be feeling desperate to get out of the room, but before you do so, I want you to bring your book here so I can review with you...."

"I am concerned about your continually asking.... You interfere with your learning and my teaching when you do this. Let's find out what the problem is right now." [Begin choice counseling.]

To control this game, as in most others, notice the importance of turning the student's attention back to specific content, not simply back to the task of studying.

S—8   **Time For The Bell**[7]

KEY WORDS

"Is it time to go yet?"

"Hey, the bell's gonna ring!"
"Isn't it time to go yet?"

Functional Routine   Any organization that runs by the clock must serve and heed the clock. Teachers and students plan and manage their time by the clock, and talk about time all the time: "Hurry up, there's not much time left," and "I didn't have enough time." The end of a class hour can be a legitimate topic of conversation.

A functional teacher-student interaction can occur even when a student complains about time. A student who is bored with a lesson asks innocently, "When does the bell ring?" The teacher's functional reply would be, "You're getting tired, aren't you? Let's finish this up and then stop." In other words, the teacher uses the student's question as a cue to the student's learning.

Dysfunctional Game   Students also use "When does the bell ring?" as a device to disrupt the lesson, to bug the teacher, and to call attention to themselves. The teacher joins the game with replies like these:
"You know as well as I when the bell rings."
"It rings when it rings."
"Shut up."
The irritation of this game far exceeds its short duration.

HOW TO STOP THE GAME

The teacher stops the game in two stages: first, at the student's interruption; second, in private conversation afterwards (follow up). In class, she says, "At ten o'clock, Phyllis." As follow up, she says, "You may not have realized, Phyllis, that your questions about when the class is over distract other people in the class and interfere with the timing of my lesson. I wish you'd stop."

Helpless[8]   S—9

KEY WORDS

"I can't."
"I don't know how."
"I'm too dumb."

Functional Routine   The teacher must show students how to seek help actively rather than passively. "I can't" is often a legitimate learning behavior.

In a functional transaction, the student's complaint is legitimate, and the teacher responds with assistance. A novice teacher sometimes rushes in with a naive solution or question before fully understanding the problem; for example:

STUDENT: I can't do this.
TEACHER: Well, try again.
STUDENT: But I can't do it!

> STUDENT: I can't do this.
> TEACHER: Why can't you do it?
> STUDENT: I don't know. I just can't.

> STUDENT: I can't do this.
> TEACHER: Well, what about it can't you do? What don't you understand?
> STUDENT: I don't know. That's why I called you to help!

These teacher responses waste time by asking the student to do precisely what he says he cannot do! Nevertheless, we must consider these teacher-student interaction patterns routine because they contain no deception or ruse.

In contrast, the skilled teacher often asks diagnostic questions that clarify the difficulty and sometimes solve the problem at the same time:[11]

> STUDENT: I can't do this.
> TEACHER: Well, let's go back a step or two. Do you remember... and can you.... So now can you do it?
> STUDENT: OK, I see it now.

The key words "I'm too dumb," when legitimate, reflect either a temporary or a persistent feeling; in either case, several teacher options make the transaction functional rather than wasteful:

"I know how you feel. I sometimes feel dumb too when I can't do something the first time. So give yourself a chance, try it again."

"This is not easy, it's true, but you'll feel good when you know how. Look at it another way...."

"Are you saying this because you want to give up? I don't think you should, because you'll be catching on very shortly, I can tell. Here, try it again this way."

"I don't think you are dumb, but I do think you're tired, and tired smart people can feel dumb sometimes. Let's work on this later."

Dysfunctional Game   "I Can't" is often a cop-out, a use of lazy lower-level thinking in place of higher-level thinking. For example:

Low level thinking: "I can't do this."

High level thinking: "I understand this part, and I see how these two things go together, but I can't see what to do next."

The teacher falls into the student's lazy game by responding with a well meaning suggestion such as, "Why don't you...?" which invites the lazy rejoinder, "Yes, but...." or "I still can't."

"I Can't" is also a game of diversion. The student plays a helpless and defeated dummy who couldn't do the task even if she wanted to. The teacher plays a helpful omniscient who tries to persuade the student she really isn't dumb at all. For example, Helpless complains ("This book is torn," "It's too hot in here," "I'm hungry"). Helper responds helpfully to each complaint whether legitimate or not. When Helper gives up, Helpless wins the game!

HOW TO STOP THE GAME

When the key words are "I can't," the teacher has several options:

1 To treat the student question as if it were routine and legitimate, and respond not with a suggested remedy but rather with incisive diagnostic questions.
2 To respond with a knowing smile that silently says, "I know that old game," while saying aloud, "I really think I've helped enough. It's time for you to do your part."
3 To follow up difficult cases, again with a smile: "I think you're playing a 'helpless' game with me, right? I don't want to play any more. Let's see you do it now."

The last two options signal that the teacher is aware of the con. Exposing the con takes the fun away and ends the game.

Sometimes the student desperately needs personal attention from the teacher, and the con may or may not be conscious and deliberate. (This need is not limited to younger students; high school students occasionally manifest it too.) To stop the game, the teacher must somehow meet the student's need — time, energy, and propriety permitting. Here is one example: "Know what I'd like to do? I'd like to spend some time with you (at noon) (after school) (after class), just to talk, just you and I; right now I'd like to see how well you can do this all by yourself."

When the key words are "I'm too dumb," the teacher has several options:

1 To treat the complaint as if it were legitimate and respond with diagnostic questions.
2 To respond with a smile, "OK. I think you've played dumb enough for now" and follow immediately with a content-oriented question or directions.
3 To follow up with a conference, if the game is recurring and persistent, to find out why the student needs so desperately to play the game that he does so even when the teacher is aware of it. There are almost certainly deeper problems working that should be brought out in the open. The student will probably appreciate the teacher's concern, even if the behavior does not change.

Why Do We Have To?   S–10

KEY WORDS

"Why are we doing this?"
"What good is this to me?"
"Is this really relevant?"
"Do we *have* to do this?"

Functional Routine Although many teachers do not interpret them as such, these words usually communicate the message that the student doesn't know what he is supposed to do, or why he is supposed to do it. If he were more sophisticated, he might say instead:

"I really don't see any coherent logic in what we're doing."

"I really don't see any relationship between what we're doing and anything else significant in my life."

"I'd really rather be doing something else right now."

In other words, the questions simply ask the teacher's purpose and objectives and why the objectives were established for this class. If the question is usually legitimate, why don't all teachers simply answer the question honestly? If the teacher did so, the interaction would be beneficial to learning. Unfortunately, some teachers haven't thought much about an answer ahead of time. Also, many teachers do not recognize the question as legitimate because students don't ask the question in a reasonable way; for one thing, they whine. A third reason, infrequent but nevertheless significant, is that students are objecting to busywork, and the teacher does not want to admit it to herself or to her students.

"Why" questions are limitless, but a few can be anticipated at least once a year:

"Why can't we hold class outside today?"

"Why do we have to write this — why can't we just say it?"

"Why do we have to do this dumb stuff?"

"Why did you give me a B instead of an A?"

"Why did he get a higher grade than me?"

"Do we have to answer all the questions?"

Dysfunctional Game　Of all questions students ask, "Why do we have to" is most likely to irritate. By treating the question as the opening move in a game, teachers indicate that they consider the question a rude challenge to their dignity, expertise, worth, and authority. Consequently, the most common teacher reply is "Because I say so!" — the most defensive of all authoritarian answers and the classic move in the "Why" game. Here is another example:

> **STUDENT:**　Why do we have to use pens? Can't I use my little pencil right here?
>
> **TEACHER:**　I've told you why! Now you just get busy there and quit asking such questions.
>
> **STUDENT:**　(Smiles).

HOW TO STOP THE GAME

The teacher who tries hard to give a thoughtful answer to "Why do we have to" need not worry about students playing the why game very often; other students will silence the faker fast because they don't want to hear the teacher's long-winded answer again!

When a student does not respond to honest answers, however, and clearly tries to con the teacher, the teacher can handle the game directly.

1　Smile, ignore, and continue the lesson. [Level 2]

2　(Privately) "Billy, you seem to wonder a lot lately why we are doing what we are doing. But your questions sound to me less like questions and more like complaints. Want to talk about it?" [Level 4]

3 "Billy, I answered that a little earlier; perhaps you didn't hear. I'll be glad to tell you later; in the meantime, I'd like you to think about...." [Level 5]

4 "Let me talk with you about your question after (the test) (class), Billy. In the meantime...." [Level 6]

5 "I guess that's enough, Bill." [Level 7]

Try never to turn off a legitimate "why" question with a curt reply, because the teacher who does so loses stature. Always give a thoughtful answer whenever there is the slightest doubt as to the legitimacy of the question.

The danger in the other direction is even more terrifying to any teacher who has been led astray by a skillful class. Whole lessons have been subverted, assignments aborted, and examinations delayed while teachers tried to explain the reasons for a scheduled activity. It pays to have thought about the reasons beforehand and to provide time for them as part of the activity.

Why Don't We Ever Have Any Fun?　　　　S–11

KEY WORDS

"Why can't we do something fun?"
"Why does the other class get to... and we don't?"
"This is a dumb way to do it."
"Why did you give him a higher grade than you gave me?"

Functional Routine While the "why do we have to" pattern is routinely a legitimate question about classroom *purposes,* this "why don't we ever" pattern is usually a legitimate question about teaching *methods.* Assuming that there are two ways to present a lesson—boringly or interestingly—the question asks why the boring method was chosen rather than the interesting one.

Perhaps teachers are so often irritated by the question because students don't know how to ask it properly; they whine, insult the teacher, and act spoiled. Still, the teacher can avoid playing games by using the question to gain information about students' feelings and to gain their trust and confidence—and even to train the students to ask questions more skillfully. Consider these teacher responses:

"Well, what did you have in mind?"
"Are you saying that you would like to...?"
"Do you mean that what we have been doing has not been fun, or do you mean that we have been doing it too long?"
"How else could you ask that same question without making me feel insulted? I don't feel insulted, but I *could.*"

Dysfunctional Game "Why don't we ever have any fun" can be a superb game; its purpose is usually diversionary, to postpone or delay the business at hand. A teacher plays the game with the best of intentions, to accommodate students and appear concerned about their feelings and wishes. Unfortunately, if the question is calculated to interfere rather than inform, the game easily degenerates into "It's your fault" with lots of "yes but's" and even snickering.

HOW TO STOP THE GAME

There are several ways to stop the game. The teacher can say:

1   "Good question. Let's discuss it after we finish talking about..." [Level 2]
2   "OK, let's say that you are the teacher, and you are supposed to teach A, B, and C. Your students tell you to make it fun. What would you do?" Listen for good suggestions and recognize them when they come. Keep A, B, and C at the forefront of the conversation, for that is your lesson content, which you are teaching all during the discussion if you are clever and professional about it. [Level 1]

An example might sound like this:

> **TEACHER:**   OK, let's say that you are the teacher, and you are told to teach multiplication tables or lose your job. What would you do? Jamie, did you have a suggestion?
> **STUDENT:**   Go outside and teach the class out there.
> **TEACHER:**   OK, go outside. Once you were there, Jamie — or anybody else — how would you teach 6 times 7? That's a pretty hard one, isn't it, 6 times 7? What is it? 42? Good. Now how would you teach 6 times 7 equals 42 and make it fun for the kids outside?

S–12   It's Your Fault

KEY WORDS

> "You didn't tell us."
> "You didn't explain...."
> "When did you say that?"
> "See what you made me do."
> "It's your fault."

Functional Routine   Sometimes good teachers make bad assignments. Sometimes they give directions that are not clear. Sometimes they think they have said something with great emphasis when they actually haven't said it at all. And often teachers say something to the class but fail to ensure that all students are paying proper attention.

When students inform a teacher of the error, and the teacher responds reasonably, the transaction sounds like this:

> **STUDENT:**   You didn't tell us.
> **TEACHER:**   Oh, I didn't? That's odd. I thought I had, but perhaps you're right. So let me say it now. Ready?

When the student is clearly trying to blame her own mistake on the teacher, the teacher can still make the exchange functional; for example:

> **STUDENT:** It's your fault.
>
> **TEACHER:** I know you feel that way, but I honestly don't think I'm to blame. The real question is, what can you do now?

Dysfunctional Game   In order for "It's your fault" to qualify as a game, the teacher must spend time openly debating the responsibility a student has cannily transferred to the teacher. Entering into an argument is playing the game with the student, and tacitly permitting him to win.

HOW TO STOP THE GAME

How should a teacher handle a game player's outburst of "It's your fault" in the middle of class with everyone watching and listening? The game player is dangerous, because even if he begins the transaction as a put-on, he soon becomes enthralled with the battle and begins to believe his own fabrications, as does his audience. So the basic principle is to turn off the game player fast while letting him save face:

1   Treat the charge as legitimate, and respond reasonably. (Level 1)
2   Defer action and let the subject die: "I hear you, and I am willing to discuss your views with you after class. In the meantime...." [Back to lesson, especially with a diagnostic question] (Level 3 or 4)

If the student continues to press, the teacher must treat the behavior as a disruption. After trying a sequence of control techniques, the teacher may inform the student that he will have to leave if he continues.

Teach Me if You Can[9]   S–13

KEY WORDS

> "I don't wanna."
> "I don't know."
> (Nonverbal: Heavy shrug of shoulder, look away)
> (Nonverbal: Slouch down in seat, head down, look at teacher from under eyebrows)

Dysfunctional Game   I consider "Teach me if you can" a game because I assume that every student is potentially an eager learner at any moment. If he is not eager to learn at any given moment, the teacher has not been able to capture his attention.

A student who hates the lesson has three options: to run away, to sit passively, or to actively fight and disrupt the lesson. The student who elects to sit passively presents a covert challenge to the teacher, who plays the game by making one of two moves: ignoring the student, or accepting the challenge and playing into it. Accepting the challenge sounds like this:

> **TEACHER:** Ann, we haven't heard from you at all. What do you think about...?
> **STUDENT:** I don't know.
> **TEACHER:** What do you mean, you don't know?
> **STUDENT:** I don't know!
> **TEACHER:** Sit up, Ann, and look alive.
> **STUDENT:** (Almost sits up.)
> **TEACHER:** Now, I want an answer from you.
> **STUDENT:** What answer?
> **TEACHER:** To my question!
> **STUDENT:** I don't know.
> **TEACHER:** You're impossible! Dave, let's hear from you.

Sometimes uncooperative withdrawal behavior is a deeply motivated attempt to avoid pain. The student may be attempting to avoid the pain of failing a specific task—a question, an assignment, a course. Or, he may be avoiding the teacher simply because other teachers have caused him pain in the past, or because this teacher has caused him pain before or reminds him unpleasantly of someone else.

Occasionally a student plays "Teach me if you can" to gain dominance over a teacher who needs and seeks positive responses from students. Students often play the game with substitute teachers, usually to amuse their peers.

The student takes the position that he doesn't care about the class, the subject, or the teacher. He's not going to exert any effort, and he doesn't care what happens as a result. He may challenge the teacher with loud sighs and frowns of boredom; most likely he will simply volunteer nothing, not respond to teacher invitations and requests, and fail to cooperate in minor tasks.

The teacher either takes the position that the student isn't motivated and therefore not worth time and effort, or that he cares enough about the student to shake him out of his lethargy. The student wins the game if the teacher shows frustration or anger.

HOW TO STOP THE GAME

Four principles apply: the first is to avoid confrontation. A student who is pressed or pestered may readily escalate his behavior into "You can't make me," a more difficult transaction for the teacher to handle.

The second principle is to conduct business as usual, but without noticeable deference to the student. For example, avoid the student's direct requests but include him in a group: "You, you, and you, I would appreciate your erasing the board for me, please."

If only two move, ignore the third or ask:

> **TEACHER:** Sandy, aren't you going to help?
> **STUDENT:** I don't wanna.
> **TEACHER:** Then let's let Liz do it. (Move on quickly, giving no more attention to the student's reluctance.)

The third principle is to follow up with individual attention. Private conferences to explore the problem communicate concern and caring, even if they do not change the student's behavior.

The fourth principle is the remedy for almost all nonproductive student resistance. If the teacher can find a way to seize the students' attention and keep it focused on a learning activity, the "Teach me if you can" transaction will not occur. Use low profile techniques to gain any student's attention.

You Can't Make Me   S—14

KEY WORDS

"You can't make me!"
"Who do you think you are?"
"You ain't got no right to...!"
"I don't know and I don't care!"
"I won't!"

Dysfunctional Game   "You can't make me" is a game in the sense that almost every student wants the teacher to succeed, if only because the student then has a better chance of success. Students seldom delight in defeating a weak teacher, but rather develop a distaste and disgust for that teacher.

Still, for a variety of reasons, a student may challenge the teacher with "You can't make me." The student who initiates this transaction might be spoiled and indulged, or perhaps feels, rightly or wrongly, that her back is against the wall and there is nothing left to do but strike out at the oppressor. Perhaps the student knows better, but has momentarily lost control, or is deliberately testing the teacher with the ultimate challenge to authority:

STUDENT: You can't make me.
TEACHER: Yes I can.
STUDENT: No you can't.

Regardless of the student's motivation, the teacher must respond strongly and carefully.

HOW TO STOP THE TRANSACTION

The best teacher control in this situation, as in almost all others, is low profile. The teacher does not resort to open displays of strength or authority unless absolutely necessary (after a proper sequence of actions), and does not embarrass the student. Consider these sample transactions:

"My goodness, something must really be bugging you today. Want to talk about it?" (Move to private conversation.)

"I guess I'd rather not even try to make you do it, frankly. I'll come back to you when you're ready."

Many teachers feel a need to demonstrate their control and authority with the high profile techniques typical of conventional teacher behavior patterns. High profile techniques work well to enforce compliance to teacher authority, especially when a student is not a habitual challenger; however, they run the risk of distracting the student further from the business of the class:

"Sorry, Bill, but I really can ask you to do this, and I would like you to do it now, please."

"Bill, you apparently aren't aware that what you just said could get you into trouble. Maybe you'd better do as I asked you."

"Bill, I want you to go to my desk/office/principal's office and wait there until I come for you. No argument. Go."

If the teacher suspects her physical safety is jeopardized in the confrontation (particularly in secondary schools), she should remove herself from the situation in such a way that both she and the student save face. For example:

"Bill, this is a very serious matter that I'll discuss with you in private. I would like to see you (in my office) at (nine thirty) please," then exit to the company of other staff.

"Bill, I'm not going to discuss this in a crowd. I will talk with you about it privately," then walk away, never looking back to see if he's coming.

If you suspect you cannot easily free yourself from the situation (a hostile crowd is gathered around you), move so as to protect your back and wait for help. Wait patiently; don't arouse the crowd with nervous movement.

S–15   Teacher's Gone[10]

KEY WORDS

"Is she gone yet?"
"Hey, Teacher's gone!"

Dysfunctional Game   The game begins with "Hey, Teacher's gone!" and ends with "How could you students have behaved so badly and done this to me?" "Teacher's gone," the student game, is a classic prelude to the teacher games "It's your fault," "Aren't you ashamed," "Who did it," and "Isn't it awful."

Teachers have long grieved about how poorly their students behave when the teacher is not present: "You know, these kids are so irresponsible when I leave the room, no matter how much I chew them out when I come back."

Student misbehavior is probably worst where teachers teach least; that is, teachers who fail to teach students how to attend to a lesson without high profile controls are those whose students will most quickly abort the lesson when the teacher's controls are removed.

HOW TO STOP THE GAME

If we have learned anything from the open classroom approach to education, it is that the skillfully taught open classroom has little or no play of "Teacher's gone." This is not to say that students are automatically responsible in open classrooms, but it does tell us that the thrill of seeing the teacher leave the room is reduced where the teacher is, in effect, continually leaving the room. The point is that a long lecture and tirade after the game occurs does not stop the game. Effective classroom control stops it before the teacher leaves. Here are six approaches.

1   The teacher designs lessons that anticipate and provide for problems of pacing, interest, difficulty, and fatigue. [low profile]

2   The teacher perfects her mastery of in-class low profile control techniques, setting a customary tone and pattern of attention and purpose rather than a pattern of high profile distractions. The teacher's presence as a controller is subtle and, for many students, of secondary importance. Thus, when the teacher is gone, the students do not feel a new teacher presence as a radical change or a disquieting and exciting opportunity. [low profile]

3   The teacher continually counsels with individual students, particularly those who are most immature, about developing self-reliance without continual supervision. Techniques such as "contingent attention" help students develop on-task work skills; see Method Z. [mid-profile]

4   The teacher gives continuous instructions to students throughout the year as to how they are expected to proceed in the teacher's absence. Brief pep-talks may be used; for example:
    "If you are through with (X) assignment, I want you to turn to (Y), even if I am not here, because Y is important to our later study of.... Do this on your own — do not wait for me to tell you to do it or for some other teacher to remind you. Build your own reminder systems so you do not have to rely on me or another teacher to give you directions you already know. Do you understand what I'm saying?" [high profile]

5   The teacher assigns students regular responsibilities for routine classroom tasks, such as distributing materials, cleaning the classroom, setting up portions of the chalkboard, marking the attendance sheet (to be supervised later by the teacher), collecting milk money, etc. Substitute teachers then need only check to see that assigned tasks have been performed correctly. The effect of this technique, whether in elementary or secondary classrooms, is to establish familiar patterns of classroom routine that occur whether or not the teacher is present. The patterns are reassuring, settling, and reliable, and make a remarkable difference for substitute teachers. They also make a difference when the regular teacher leaves the room for only a few minutes.

6   The teacher uses regular evaluation of instruction by class members to inform her of how well students feel they are learning lesson content, how effective they consider the teacher's instructional techniques, etc. The usual purpose of such procedures is to help the teacher improve the quality of instruction and to help students introspect about their success. As a written record of each student's experiences in the classroom, the evaluation sheets are informative to the teacher, students, and parents. (low profile)

A side effect of this procedure is to add another regular and functional routine to the classroom so that a substitute teacher can rely on a sensible classroom organization that runs smoothly even in the regular teacher's absence.

In addition to competent classroom organization, the professional teacher leaves the substitute teacher a well designed lesson plan — an orientation to the class and classroom — so the substitute can do a responsible job of teaching rather than babysitting. The substitute teacher should also leave a detailed report for the regular teacher about the progress of the class. A substitute teacher who does not fulfill this function competently should not be called back.

NOTES

1   These notions are based on Sol Kimball (1972), p. 64. Also see Feshback (1971) who found that student teachers most prefer students who are conforming, orderly, and rigid, and least prefer students who are independent, active, and assertive.

2   Gordon (1957), p. 25. See also Shipman (1968), p. 47.

3   This theme is well struck by Francis V. Lloyd, Jr., former Director of Precollegiate Education, the University of Chicago.

4   Early portions of this section were suggested by Debby McCollum, Virginia Ramos, Charlene Braden and Suzie Brodie.

5   Judy Lohr and Suzie Brodie contributed to earlier versions of this section.

6   This game was observed and suggested by Michelle Scherer.

7   This game was observed and reported by Larry Fink, Karen West, and others.

8   Gary Popovitz, Carole Costick and Cindi Watts provided advice on this family of transactions.

9   Nina Coulter assisted with earlier descriptions of this transaction.

10 Debby McCollum informed my early thinking about this game.

11 See Methods Td1 and Td2.

REFERENCES

BERNE, E. *Games people play.* New York: Grove Press, 1964.

FESHBACK, N. Student teacher preferences for elementary school pupils varying in personality characteristics. In M. Silberman (Ed.), *Experience of schooling.* New York: Holt, Rinehart & Winston, 1971.

FOSTER, H. *Ribbin, jivin', and playin' the dozens.* New York: Ballinger, 1974.

GORDON, C. *The social system of the high school: A study in the sociology of adolescence.* Glencoe, Ill.: Free Press, 1957.

KIMBALL, S. Cultural influences shaping the role of the child. In R. Shinn (Ed.), *Culture and school: Sociocultural significances.* Scranton, Pa.: International Textbook, 1972.

SHIPMAN, M. *The sociology of the school.* London: Longmans, Green, 1968.

WALLER, W. *The sociology of teaching.* New York: Russell and Russell, 1961.

LOSS OF CONTROL:
GAMES TEACHERS PLAY

21

Teachers sometimes pretend they are in professional control of student attention when they really are not. Instead of professional control, they exercise pseudocontrol. Like students, teachers play games in school.

Esther Rothman (1977) describes a number of power games* teachers play throughout the entire spectrum of American education. In "The Game of Silent Sitting," for example, "teachers in search of power DEMAND SILENCE. . . . They demand constant attention. All eyes on teacher. All ears listening to teacher. Teacher is on!" (p. 104)

Rothman is writing not just about the behaviors of a few teachers but about the lapses that afflict most teachers from time to time. This chapter is intended to help teachers be more aware of their loss of control so they can stop themselves and use professional skills.

T–1   Authority

KEY WORDS

"Because I said so!"
"Do as you're told."
"I want no questions!"
"Speak when you're spoken to."

Functional Routine   The teacher is responsible for students' learning in the classroom. Sometimes students cannot fully understand beforehand what they are going to do and must therefore accept the teacher's word. And there are times when students must follow seemingly arbitrary directives without question or debate. Fire drills are no time for teacher-student debate, nor are examination periods.

Schools require a basic minimum degree of order to operate; the teacher is responsible for maintaining order, and students must learn to respect the teacher's responsibility sensibly.

> **TEACHER:**   Bill, it's your turn to read.
> **STUDENT:**   Do you want me to do the introduction?
> **TEACHER:**   No, read just the text.

Dysfunctional Games   The teacher plays the Big Baboon, or the student plays the Little Baboon. The teacher promulgates military rules to govern classroom interaction: do as you're told, don't speak till you're spoken to, do not think for yourself, do only what you're ordered to do. Sometimes the teacher even struts pompously back and forth across the front of the classroom. In response, students sit passively, following directions to the letter.

---

*While some of the games described in this chapter resemble Rothman's, the lists were developed independently; hence I encourage you to seek out Rothman's work to broaden your understanding of teacher game patterns. You may wish also to refer to Ken Ernst's *Games Students Play* (1972).

A teacher who plays Big Baboon apparently has an emotional need for compliance from other people. The Big Baboon game permits the teacher to fantasize her self-importance by playing general to a captive army.

Sometimes even teachers who disapprove of the Big Baboon game play it in a crisis. For example, when the teacher has lost control of a class or of herself, she may resort to Big Baboon to restore order or to release her tensions.

Students sometimes cooperate in the game to avoid punishment and pain. Sometimes they indulge the teacher's game because they feel compassion or even pity, and don't like to see the teacher upset. Sometimes they laugh, publicly or privately, at the teacher's posturing and then set about, through game-playing, to upset or embarrass her.

HOW TO STOP THE GAME

The teacher most easily stops when she realizes it is only a game. Students occasionally stop the game by openly refusing to play, thereby reducing the teacher to tears or getting themselves suspended from school (the stakes here are high). Once in a great while, a student with unusual maturity and courage addresses the teacher publicly or privately with the student's adult voice (see Transactional Analysis, chapter 1): "You know, Mr. Smith, you don't really have to give us orders to get us to work. Most of us will do what you want if you just ask us nicely."

Finally, a skilled supervisor, instructor, supervising teacher, or administrator who observes the teacher's classroom control (using the Observation procedures described in Appendix B) can stop the game rather easily by revealing the high profile distraction of Big Baboon.

For a teacher who really needs the game to survive classroom interaction, particularly because of low self-esteem, the chances are slim that the game will stop in any way short of therapy for the teacher. The teacher should also consider another profession where low self-esteem is not so critical to job competence.

There is danger in an observer's looking for the Big Baboon game and unjustly accusing a teacher of playing it. People sometimes confuse genuine stature with pomposity. Imagine a scholar who occasionally lectures with his eyes to the ground and his mind in the sky; to an outsider who does not understand what he is doing or talking about, he looks affected, even posturing, as he paces back and forth. But look at his audience: they are rapt as they would not be were he posturing. In ordinary circumstances, however, the danger of misjudging Big Baboon is remote. Normally, when we think a teacher is posturing, we're right.

Respect   T–2

KEY WORDS

"You watch your lip when you speak to me."
"I will not tolerate your talking to me like that."
"I demand respect!"

Functional Routine   The passive teacher lets his rights and dignity be trampled on by insensitive students. The aggressive teacher tramples on the rights and dignity of students. The assertive teacher, on the other hand, is sensitive to the rights and dignity of students and protects his own rights and dignity (see Method AA, chapter 22). Here is an assertive teacher:

> **STUDENT:** You're a S.O.B.!
> **TEACHER:** I realize you're angry with me, but I don't like your calling me names. I don't call you names, and I don't want them from you.

Dysfunctional Game   The game of "How dare you" grows naturally out of Big Baboon, with an added tone of indignant elitism that demands complete subservience:

> **TEACHER:** How dare you talk to me like that! You listen here, I demand respect! Just don't you forget that I'm the teacher around here, not you. Do you hear me?
> **STUDENT:** Yes.

This teacher sits on a throne, and is not likely to leave if allowed to stay there. It is a sad game of royalty, and the game lasts as long as students are willing to play roles of passive unquestioning subjects.

HOW TO STOP THE GAME

I have never seen students stop this game, but I think they could, in private conference with the teacher, by asserting their own rights, dignity, and sensibilities:

"Mr. Jones, you clearly think we are disrespectful to you, but you seem to talk to us sometimes as if we were dumb animals. We wish you would talk to us as if we were real people."

"Mr. Jones, we won't insult you if you don't insult us."

Because students will not stop this game, a supervisor, instructor, or administrator must. As in Big Baboon, the best antidote is classroom observation: "How dare you" almost always follows a long series of high profile and distractive teacher-student confrontations. A teacher who relies on high profile controls runs the continual risk of setting up confrontation; a skilled teacher who relies most on low profile controls reduces the risk of confrontation to a minimum.

T–3   Consequences

KEY WORDS

"If you don't..., I'm going to...."
"If you continue, I will have to...."
"Do you know what happens when...?"
"That's a good way to get yourself hurt."
"You're cruisin' for a bruisin'."

Functional Routine The teacher who keeps students aware of possible consequences and helps them think about the consequences of their decisions is teaching well. For example:

TEACHER: If you choose this way to go, you could end up OK, but you could also get fouled up. What do you think your chances are?
STUDENT: I don't know.
TEACHER: I'd guess 4 to 1 against you. And if I happen to be the one who sees you, the odds are 10 to 1 against you. Got the picture?
STUDENT: OK.

Dysfunctional Game The threat is an intrinsic part of conventional negotiation strategy. In some classrooms, as in some homes, the game of "idle threats" is played with abandon; the threatening teacher fills the air with:
"I'm going to keep you in after school."
"I'm going to tear up your paper and give you an F."
"I'm going to call your mother and tell her what you're doing."
"I'm going to paddle you good."
"I'm going to sit you in the corner the rest of the week!"
"You're not going to be allowed to go to the bathroom any more this year."
The student's response ranges from passivity to insult; as long as he does not directly challenge the teacher's threat, the game goes on and on.

In one sense, "Idle threats" is a harmless activity; no one actually gets hurt, and the game provides plenty of laughs for students: "Oh, there she goes again. She never does those things, you know, just talks about it." The problem arises when classroom behavior gets so out of hand that the teacher suddenly carries out a threat, and students feel, and say, that she is being unfair — meaning she is not playing according to the rules of the game. The students are right: the teacher's sudden change is, in a way, unethical; inconsistency damages whatever credibility she may have had.

The remedial rule of thumb is obvious: if you don't intend to carry out a threat, don't make it.

Another game seen in classrooms is "Semper threat": every instruction is accompanied by a threatened consequence, no matter how mild or innocuous.

"Open your books to page 13 and do those problems, or you'll be in trouble on the test."

"I want your section number written in the upper right hand corner, or I'll give you a red mark, you hear me? And keep those margins wide or I'll take off ten points."

"Semper threat" often sounds very much like Big Baboon; they are similar and often played simultaneously.

HOW TO STOP THE GAMES

One or more students might conceivably stop these games by speaking privately to the teacher, either during or after class, in this way: "We realize we goof off sometimes, Mr. Smith, but you really don't need to threaten us. Just tell us — we'll do it for you."

But students are rarely able or willing to say such things, so a supervisor, instructor, or administrator might have to call the teacher's attention to the high profile distraction of threats; the Observation Sheet and procedures described in Appendix B can be used.

Ideally, the teacher will realize the consequences of idle threats—wasted time and wasted attention—and resolve to stop.

T–4   Responsibility

KEY WORDS

"That's your responsibility."
"It's all your fault."
"Now you've done it!"
"See what you made me do!"

Functional Routine   The student is responsible for his own behavior, anger, and mistakes. Part of the teacher's responsibility is to help the student control his anger and profit from his mistakes. (See Method O, Message-check; also Method CC, chapter 22.)

The teacher who works skillfully with students' anger and mistakes rarely uses the key words. Instead, he acknowledges the student's anger or mistake and helps the student gain self-control. For example:

> **TEACHER:**   You sure are angry.
> **STUDENT:**   Damn right I am.
> **TEACHER:**   What can you do about it? What else could you do about it? And what else could you do...?

or

> **TEACHER:**   That's a mistake, no question about that. Now let's see if it's a good mistake for you or a bad one.

Dysfunctional Game   Teachers commonly believe that when something goes wrong in the classroom, when a mistake is made, or when something should have been done but was not, the fault automatically lies with the student. If a student fails to learn, the teacher perhaps automatically assumes he isn't motivated. But students make the game possible by passively accepting the teacher's statement or implication of fault.

The game is pathetic indeed, for not only is it played with such zest and frequency by people who should know better, but it is one of the schools' most blatant manifestations of racism and sexism. For example, when a school's racial, economic, and cultural composition shifts, older faculty members invariably bewail, even in the presence of students, the loss of the good old days, with students who could maintain high standards, etc. They complain the new students don't know how to learn, without trying to modify teaching content or methods to help the students whose experiences and skills require new approaches (see Method Aa).

HOW TO STOP THE GAME

In theory, any student who feels his attitude is unfairly ascribed may respond accordingly:

"You seem to be saying, Ms. Jackson, that I am goofing off here/that it's all my fault/that I am responsible for .... Well you may be right about (X), but I don't think that (Y) or (Z) apply to me at all."

"I am willing to be responsible for what I do, Ms. Jackson, but I don't think it's fair that.... "

In fact, some students do exactly this; in many cases, they achieve good results with an honest, balanced, thoughtful exchange. Although a teacher occasionally intensifies the game of "It's all your fault," or even shifts to "How dare you," students are generally better off with assertiveness rather than passivity.

A supervisor, instructor, or administrator finds that "It's all your fault" decreases dramatically with a training program in low profile classroom control, because control of student attention is clearly the teacher's responsibility.

Remember, of course, that schools cannot be all things to all people, and teachers cannot hope to do all they are mandated, particularly in compensating for the domestic ills students suffer in pathological or unsettled homes. But when schools and teachers protest that they have done all that can be done, they only *sometimes* tell the truth; sometimes they are actually playing games.

By defining the game, we can also forewarn ourselves of the inevitable disappointments in this profession. There is bound to be disillusionment when the teacher works hard on a lesson and students do not respond, either by learning or by participating; some disappointment is a natural part of teaching. The question is whether the teacher can handle disappointment professionally, or will need to play "It's your fault" or "Martyr" to survive.

Martyr (or "You Should be Ashamed!")[1] T–5

KEY WORDS

"Well I'm surprised at you!"
"You should be ashamed of yourself!"
"How could you?"
"You people just can't be trusted."
"Why do I do this for you!"

Functional Routine   When the teacher lets students know she esteems and trusts them and expects them to perform well, the message often comes out like "Well I'm surprised at you. That's not like you at all!" Although the tone is heavy, it is not denigrating; telling students they have not fulfilled their promises or responsibilities is a normal part of life, and important to student growth. They should hear about it when they *intentionally* fail to do as they should.

Dysfunctional Game   Teachers play this game with passive students, usually following "It's your fault" played with a tone of moral outrage. The new game assumes a number of forms:

> **TEACHER:** I was only trying to help you, and now look what you've done!
> **STUDENT:** I'm sorry.

> **TEACHER:** I try everything with you, and you just don't listen. What am I to do with you?
> **STUDENT:** I dunno.

> **TEACHER:** Look how hard I've worked for you. Aren't you ashamed?
> **STUDENT:** (Admits shame, whether felt or not, by nodding or sitting passively.)

HOW TO STOP THE GAME

It is hard to stop this game because it is tied to the teacher's need to be appreciated by students and to look good to visitors. Students sometimes aggravate the game by snickering, rather than sitting passively, and by repeating the offending behavior, both of which aggravate the teacher's sense of martyrdom. The Martyr game usually ends when the teacher decides to abandon her righteous indignation.

A wise supervisor, instructor, or administrator can help a teacher by patiently listening to complaints and then, in private consultation, asking thought-testing diagnostic questions (e.g., "You're saying they were doing it on purpose? How did you know that?"), then proceeding directly to choice counseling (e.g., "Assuming that the problem is indeed that, what might you do to prevent it from happening again?"). Nonjudgmental counseling permits the teacher to let off steam and begin to think rationally about the problem. "Martyr" is an irrational game in which the teacher deceives himself. The game stops when the teacher starts thinking.

T–6   What Do You Expect?

KEY WORDS

> "Considering his (background), that's not so surprising."
> "What do you expect?"
> "Didn't you know that...?"

This transaction occurs most often in the teachers' lounge, when teachers compare stories about students, but it also appears in the classroom, usually in private or semiprivate conversations.

Functional Routine   Young people, like adults, are intolerant of weaknesses and differences. Elementary teachers particularly must constantly explain to children why one child can't run fast or see well, or why another has slanted eyes or brown skin or freckles. Explanations are part of teaching and learning; we simply assume children will not understand, so we explain.

Dysfunctional Game   The "What do you expect" game usually features a teacher's pseudoscientific appraisals of a student's family, culture, personal habits, and prior school record as the causes of current school performance. A passive or compliant listener, or one who has his own story to tell about the student, reinforces the teacher's attitude. The attitude is subtle and insidious; the teacher forms an opinion, then screens all perceptions and data to conform to that opinion, thus achieving the Pygmalion Effect, or Self-fulfilling Prophesy (see Method Aa, chapter 3).

HOW TO STOP THE GAME

The game does not stop until the teacher's attitude changes. The unwitting student reinforces the attitude by not questioning the teacher, even when he realizes the teacher has given up on him. He probably does not realize he is the victim of an injustice; this is probably not the first time teachers have avoided him. The "loser" label sticks as the student moves on to higher grades.

The teacher needs determination to change her attitude. First, think about the classroom "action zone" (Method Na) where almost all the pupil participation occurs. Is the student in the action zone? If he is at the periphery, move him. Try giving him personal attention and compliments.

Another teacher strategy is to train the student to stop by your desk on his way into class one day and say, "I'm prepared today, so I hope you'll include me in the lesson." Make him practice this line beforehand so he gets used to saying it.

The supervisor can help by asking the teacher to rank order all students in the class by ability, then observing the students' actual behaviors and the teacher's differential treatment of "top" and "bottom" students. Then he can encourage the teacher to design a program of changing the behavior of so-called "bottom students" (see Method Z2).

Isn't it Awful   T–7

KEY WORDS

"Isn't it awful the way these kids...?"
"Isn't it awful the way the administration...?"
"Isn't it awful the way parents...?"
(Eric Berne's *Games People Play* [1964] features an "Ain't it Awful" transaction as a pastime.)

Functional Routine   As a humorous exchange between two people who know what they are doing, "Isn't it awful" (IIA) has a profound virtue, especially as a form of buffoonery. It helps put little irritants into proper perspective:

> **TEACHER:** Ain't it awful the way your teacher, Mr. T., keeps giving you homework assignments?
> **STUDENT:** Yes, and worse yet, he grades them! Can you imagine?
> **TEACHER:** My land, what this world is coming to!
> **STUDENT:** Ain't it awful? Somebody should do something about it. Maybe he should be forced to do his own homework assignments!
> **TEACHER:** Very funny, ho ho.

Dysfunctional Game For purposes of the game, two consenting participants operate as peers or co-equals—which means that teachers and students rarely play except when comparing and reinforcing mutual prejudices.

But there is no more popular activity in the teachers' lounge than "Isn't it Awful," with particular students, the "younger generation," parental neglect, administrative policies, and staff inefficiency as principal topics.

The problem with this game in the teachers' lounge, as well as in the classroom, is that new teachers take it seriously and believe what they hear.

> **TEACHER:** Isn't it terrible the way these kids take advantage of you, first thing?
> **STUDENT TEACHER:** Oh?
> **TEACHER:** Oh my yes; why, you don't want to be too friendly with them, or they'll stab you in the back!
> **STUDENT TEACHER:** Yeah, you really have to be careful.

HOW TO STOP THE GAME

This game needs a willing audience; without one, the game dies:

> **TEACHER:** Isn't it terrible the way these kids...?
> **STUDENT TEACHER:** Oh, I don't know. It seems to be human nature to test the rules; even we adults do it sometimes, don't you think? I mean, that's the whole principle behind the Supreme Court's rulings on Constitutionality, right?
> **TEACHER:** Huh?

"Isn't it Awful" players are sometimes offended when others refuse to play.

T–8   I'm Different[2]

KEY WORDS

"It's a good thing for you that I got back in time."
"I realize she does it that way, but I do it this way."
"I get so annoyed with him sometimes."

Functional Routine Teachers have differences in styles, opinions, and values that students should see and understand. The teacher's candid, objective discussion of those differences can help students learn to appreciate and tolerate teacher differences, and learn how mature adults think about and reconcile differences:

STUDENT: Mrs. Jones does it different from you.
TEACHER: That's right, and do you know why? She believes...while I believe.... Both methods work—it just depends on what you're trying to achieve.

Dysfunctional Game   The "Back-biting" game is unpleasant to watch; teachers most often play it with other teachers in the lounge, but they sometimes let it slip in the classroom as well, usually in the form of complaints: "Why does she [another teacher] always get tutor aides and student teachers assigned to her and I don't? I need an aide more than she, goodness knows, the kind of textbook teaching she does" or "You can go ahead and use this room even if it is her turn to use it. She never uses it anyhow, certainly not like I do."

"Back-biting" is hard to handle; it goes on in every school and causes awkwardness for the listener. If you agree with the teacher, you reinforce his maligning behavior, but if you show disapproval, you will seem self-righteous and prudish.

HOW TO STOP THE GAME

"I haven't heard that before. I wonder why."

"Gee, that's serious. Maybe you ought to tell somebody who can do something about it (the principal) (the supervisor)."

"Wow, do you think (subject of discussion) is aware she (does that) (affects you that way)? Maybe you should tell her."

How To Reach Them   T—9

KEY WORDS

"Civilized people don't act that way."

"I just have to do something about your accent."

"Why can't you be like me?"

"You people are so ignorant."

"How can I reach (you people) (these kids)?"

"Because of me, you will be able to appreciate poetry."

Consider, first, the "How can I reach these kids" remark or attitude in the spirit of "They are out there in that sea of ignorance, and I must throw them a lifeline and pull them to safety—to me." The spirit is patronizing, and can easily put students off, yet others may be awed by the teacher's strong spirit, and even inspired by the overwhelming concern for their welfare.

Next, consider "How can I reach these kids" in the spirit of "How can I learn what these kids can really do now and what they could do if only I could find a way?" This viewpoint is highly professional and functional.

Whether these attitudes are functional or dysfunctional seems to rest on a very pragmatic criterion: whether the teacher succeeds or fails with the "Let me save you" attitude. The teacher who fails is vulnerable to heartache and despair.

Dysfunctional Game   The savior syndrome is almost as common among new teachers as the pal syndrome, and as difficult to observe. This game typically begins with the teacher's thought, "I am the one who will make the big difference in this child's life. I realize he has parents and friends, and of course there are other helpers and influences, but I must save him from himself." This attitude goes beyond ordinary assistance; the assumptions are arrogant, and insist that the child be more like the teacher — or the teacher's vision for the child — and less like anyone else's image, including the child's.

This well-disguised tyranny conspicuously appears in language study. "His English is atrocious," says the well-meaning teacher. "We've got to do something about that." Just as language style is a cultural convention, so dress and mannerisms are aspects of culture; the savior syndrome in education works steadily to erase cultural differences and make everybody the same, usually of the same culture as the teacher. Students play the game by accepting it.

At its extreme, this game features a strong and irrational stand by a teacher who no longer tries to include the child in her argument but engages in a paranoid warfare against imagined forces intent upon subverting the teacher's authority and mission. One clue to the savior syndrome is the teacher's heavy reliance on "It's your fault" to self-justify.

HOW TO STOP THE GAME

The teacher stops the game most easily by realizing that she is not as concerned with the student as with protecting her own value system. A supervisor or even a student can also stop the game by asking assertively:

"Mr. Jones, I realize you feel strongly about . . . , but don't you think other people have the right to be different from you?"

"Your concern for (Student X) is very strong, Mrs. Jones, and that concern is important — you should keep it. But let me ask you if you are concerned that if he makes up his own mind, he will make a mistake? Are you saying he should not decide for himself?"

Teachers often overreact to the savior syndrome by refusing to establish standards and expectations for students. The unfortunate students then get intellectual and moral pablum in place of challenge and excitement. Of course, some teacher acts and judgments are legitimate. For example, the statement "He's too young to decide this for himself" may be an accurate assessment of a child's ability level, and should not be overlooked.

T–10   Compliment[3]

KEY WORDS

"That's really good!"
"You're really talented."
"You should be in movies."

Functional Routine Everyone relishes a compliment, and most students relish a teacher's honest, sincere praise. Some students never learn to understand balanced praise. If the teacher says, "I like that part of your paper very much; this part I don't," the student tends to remember what was rejected, not what was praised. And unreserved, unqualified teacher praise is nice to hear as well:

> "That's really good. I like it."
> "You did a great job on that."
> "You have real talent."

Dysfunctional Game The "Flattery game" is a pathetic classroom transaction, often backfiring on the teacher's hopes. It happens this way: the teacher wants to motivate and encourage a student who is achieving at a low level so she tells the student he is doing a good job even when he isn't. The student shows outward pleasure but says inwardly, "This teacher's an idiot; my stuff is crummy, but she says it's great anyway. Wonder what her angle is." The student continues to do poor work because he learns, as the game continues, that he doesn't have to do better. He may demand even higher grades for his mediocre work; the teacher is trapped, and the student wins.

We seldom observe this game directly, but it is commonly reported by teachers and students because the immediate parties are aware of what is happening.

HOW TO STOP THE GAME

This game is best stopped before it begins, by the teacher's striving to make compliments sincere, insightful, and frequent. The trick is to avoid personal flattery and continue on-task praise (see Methods Ya and Yb):

> "You know, I do like that. I realize it will never make the Louvre, but it appeals to *me* — that's one small audience for you!"
> "I like that much better than what you had before — that's good."

Professional criticism also helps to keep praise in perspective; a supervisor or instructor can help the teacher in this skill area. You cannot usually expect students to stop the game, but I once had a mature student stop my game because she tired of the charade: "I really don't know whether to believe you, Professor Rinne. You say it's good no matter what I do, so I'm confused." I learned.

Guess   **T–11**

KEY WORDS

> "I'm thinking of something.... Who can guess?"
> "What do you think...? No.... No.... Yes."

Functional Routine Minds must reach in order to stretch. Challenging teachers force students to reach beyond their first easy answers, pushing them for more and more answers, then more and more questions.

Socrates made an art of asking questions. Some feel he was guilty of duplicity, that he knew the answers beforehand and forced students to agree with his point of view whether they wanted to or not. I would agree that Socrates was guilty of asking "leading questions," but he did stretch his students' minds in a way that few teachers have been able to duplicate since.

Most of the content-oriented factual guessing games teachers play are probably functional, in that they support and contribute to learning:

TEACHER: What's the capital of Michigan?
STUDENT: Detroit.
STUDENT: Lansing.
TEACHER: Lansing, right. Detroit is bigger, that's true, but Lansing became the capital rather than Detroit, because....

Dysfunctional Game "Guess what teacher is thinking" is particularly popular and widely played in English, reading, and social studies classes, where interpretation is a central activity. Teachers and students are usually not aware they are playing the game, although some students may suspect they are wasting their time. The theme of the game is that the teacher's opinion is right, and all other opinions are wrong.

The teacher asks a question of opinion or interpretation (or, occasionally, of obvious fact), then moderates a guessing game to determine not who is thinking or what the best answer is, but rather who can guess the teacher's answer. The teacher believes he is helping students learn to think.

The students play along, trying to guess the answer in the hope of scoring points with the teacher when they say the right words.

TEACHER: Why do you think Tom wanted to leave the party early?
STUDENT: He wasn't feeling well.
TEACHER: Hmmm.
STUDENT$_2$: Maybe he was afraid he'd be late getting home.
TEACHER: Could be.
STUDENT$_3$: Maybe he was afraid he might meet Sylvia.
TEACHER: Right. Now what do you think Sylvia wanted?

These transactions could be functional if the teacher were concerned enough about each answer and each person's thinking about the answer to examine why an answer seems plausible or not, but the transaction is only a game when the teacher is interested only in answers, not *thinking*. The game wastes time for at least three reasons: first, after they find the teacher's answer, students stop thinking; they have reached the goal. Second, students may not retain the teacher's "correct answers" very long because they are products of random guessing rather than orderly, purposeful thought. The third and major reason is that the game has no usefulness in the world outside the school. In the real world, so-called wrong answers may be as useful as right answers, and other wrong answers vary in their value to the inquirer. So in legitimate inquiry, our job is to look for the best answers for a particular purpose, as well as to understand how less-than-best answers can also be useful.

HOW TO STOP THE GAME

We cannot expect the teacher to abandon preconceived answers and teach with a completely open mind, nor can we expect the teacher never to play "Guess what teacher is thinking" because, however inane, the game is as natural to teachers as eating. Yet, the best teachers can stop the game after it begins.

"That's an idea I hadn't thought of. Tell me about that."

"Interesting observation, Juanita. How did you come up with that? What in the reading makes you feel that way? Why does that seem reasonable to you?"

"Here's another idea nobody has mentioned yet, though you may still like your own idea better after you've heard this one...."

Any student can effectively stop the game by asking "Why are we doing this?" The necessary teacher skill is to recognize the significance of the student's question and immediately act on it.

A supervisor, instructor, or administrator can help the guessing-game teacher by asking questions: "When you had the kids guessing, why didn't you just tell them your opinion to save time? Did you have another purpose in mind that I didn't see?" If the teacher states her concern for critical thinking or inquiry skills, the supervisor can suggest some of the many skills and procedures available (see Method T, Questions). An unskilled teacher may interpret the supervisor's question as a challenge to her authority, in which case the supervisor must then begin training the teacher in skills of receiving criticism professionally (see chapter 22).

Friend   T–12

KEY WORDS

"I like you."

"I want you to like me."

"See, I'm just like you."

The teaching profession offers many opportunities to develop strong friendship ties between professional and client, providing rich returns on the teacher's investment of time and caring.

Functional Routine   A particular style of friendship works well in the classroom and maintains dignity for both teacher and student. This friendship allows exchange of personal information, but not in such a way that the teacher is later at the student's mercy. Nor is the student in the absurd position of maintaining confidences for the teacher.

Even closer friendships can develop between teacher and student, coach and athlete, advisor and advisee outside the classroom. When the relationship is compatible with the student's family life and other relationships, both teacher and student can enjoy the friendship without embarrassment or heartache.

Dysfunctional Game   The Pal Syndrome occasionally appears among new teachers who want desperately to be liked—even loved—by students. A new teacher may remember his affection for a former teacher and want to duplicate it in his own classroom. Sometimes a teacher who enters the field with a zeal for reform expects students to fall all over themselves in gratitude and love for their liberator.

The teacher typically plays the pal syndrome in two ways. First, the teacher tries to get included in "the gang," tries to dress and talk and posture like the students, tries overly hard to please them even at the cost of instruction, and sometimes even tries to get invited to their parties or games. Second, the teacher watches carefully for signs of acceptance and belonging: "It's working! They really do like me!" or "Oh dear, she frowned at me—I wonder if she's angry with me."

Students often play along with the pal-playing teacher. Sometimes they feel sorry for him; his efforts to be one of them are seen as pathetic evidence of loneliness. Other students recognize that they can gain power over the teacher by playing him along; the pay-off comes later when they want a higher grade or other favor that requires the obligations of friendship to fulfill.

HOW TO STOP THE GAME

Students often end this game either by ignoring the teacher's overtures or by overplaying, thereby signaling even the neediest teacher that he has put himself in a vulnerable position. After a teacher learns his lesson from one of these games, he returns to the classroom a stronger and more independent professional personality, or he leaves teaching because the classroom does not provide the rewards and satisfactions he needs. Either result is legitimate and dignified.

The more professional attitude accepts friendship with students as an enriching sidelight; without it, one can still be a good teacher.

Beware of cynically assuming that all student expressions of regard have ulterior motives, or that all teacher displays of friendship are signs of weakness.

T–13   Who Did it?

KEY WORDS

"Who did it?"
"Someone in here...."
"If I ever catch...!"

Functional Routine   When many people work together in a small space, management problems arise. Someone has the only chalkboard eraser, or someone spills paint on the floor. Some problems must be solved, others must be tolerated.

In a functional Who Did It transaction, the teacher asks a question and someone gives a straightforward and truthful answer, or mock anger releases tension harmlessly: "If I ever catch the person who borrowed my red pencil, I'll give him a pair of red eyes." The transaction is completed by "I'm sorry, I didn't realize..." (acknowledged by the teacher) or by smiles or by nothing at all—the teacher is as free to mumble to herself as anyone else in the room. It is natural and healthful for the teacher, as for any student, to express anger or irritation or frustration once in a while, as long as it is controlled.

Dysfunctional Game   The cat-and-mouse game generates tension and takes valuable time from studies. If a teacher likes to play detective, she will always be able to find a student who likes to play dangerous games. Student pranks become *causes célèbres*, and the contest is on. (This game complements the classic, "Who, me?")

HOW TO STOP THE GAME

Try not to start this game in the first place. Some pranks are best treated by ignoring them. Others merit an announcement: "Somebody took the pencil sharpener off the wall this morning, probably for fun. After you've had your laugh, I hope you'll return it, because it's easier for us to sharpen our pencils in the sharpener than in our ears. Thank you."

In cases of actual vandalism or severe deprivation of learning, you may want to discuss the problem as the class's problem, not as the teacher's alone. If you discuss openly only the facts, including the real consequences, in this meeting, the game cannot develop.

PERSONAL REASONS TEACHERS PLAY GAMES IN SCHOOL

Teachers often fall into game playing as a result of anxiety over control. The teacher either misunderstands what "control" really means, or is unable to exercise control. She may misunderstand the meaning of control if she has never had a real model of effective teaching control during her own schooling, or if she did not recognize truly effective low profile teaching when she saw it. Teaching looks different to students than to teachers; students may sense that a teacher has "a certain something" but not know exactly what it is. Without an understanding of professional control, the teacher can only "play teacher," which is not the same as functioning *effectively* as a teacher.

Or, the teacher may simply be unable to control even if she understands what it means. Teachers have human weaknesses, and professional classroom control requires skill and discipline.

> The exercise of control requires continual attempts to direct children in particular ways, and they can and do balk. The teacher's exasperation must somehow be contained and his anger defused; otherwise he will regret his spontaneity. (Lortie, 1975, p. 159)

Every teacher has probably said at least once, "I *knew* I shouldn't have done that, but I did it anyway! Why did I do that?"

Three personal reasons cause teachers to fall into game playing.

First, teachers try to adapt to conflict situations by reducing their personal stress. In his study of American high schools, Gordon found that teachers adapt to classroom conflict in various ways:

> ...Some typical modes of adaptation were made by teachers over a period of years, as they routinized their functions in such a way as to minimize the amount of personal stress which they experienced in a situation of continuous conflict. (1957, p. 40)

Some methods for reducing personal stress are productive, some are unproductive. A game may be one of the impulsive, unproductive methods.

Second, teachers try to strengthen their position as classroom conflicts escalate. Willard Waller (1932) argued that conflict is inevitable in the classroom because each party, teacher and student, has his own moral and ethical code and attitudes toward the other party, so the parties tend to turn into conflict groups. Many teachers implicitly accept the classroom conflict model and rush to defend their authority with threats of serious consequences and other techniques.

Third, teachers fear impending disaster. Every teacher can name a child whose absence makes life almost bearable again. But when he is present, the teacher seems obsessed with preventing disaster, and ends up playing games. One child can ruin a class, so the teacher's game is to "get him before he gets you!"

More than anything else, new teachers fear loss of control. A teacher does strange things in his zeal to protect himself from unknown peril, but usually relies on traditional methods of self-protection, productive and unproductive.

INSTITUTIONAL REASONS TEACHERS PLAY GAMES IN SCHOOLS

Teachers also fall into game playing for institutional reasons. They succumb easily to the power of the school culture. Institutional values and customs pass from one generation to another, and members of succeeding generations learn the assumptions and habits of their predecessors without thinking much about them. Each new generation learns to fit into the system:

> There is a degree of order and system that gives to the people who participate in it a certain style of life that is peculiarly their own. It is not that people sit down together and consciously plan these things. Most people accept their culture as "given" and usually they are not aware of why they do things in a particular way. (Brown, 1972, p. 33)

The traditional school culture holds amazing power to make teachers behave contrary to their own best interests as well as those of their students. Some teachers seem vulnerable to six traditional school values that prevent effective classroom control.

Six Traditional and Dysfunctional School Values[4]

We Must Have Order Above All   We can agree that learning cannot take place in chaos, but when schools add those critical words "above all," they open the floodgates to bureaucratic overorganization. The schools' highest value is order—they value quiet children above thinking children.

New teachers quickly recognize this value and find themselves subtly coerced into conforming to it:

> **Principal:**   Is everything all right in your room, Miss Washington? I was walking by last hour and wondered if things were getting out of hand.
> **Teacher:**   Oh no, Mrs. Rogers, we were having a great class discussion about what good writing looks like. My kids got very excited.
> **Principal:**   Well, you just let me know if I can be of assistance.

The pressure of this distorted value makes teachers anxious about classroom noise, even the noise of learning!

The Teacher Must Be in Absolute Control   This value statement sounds much like the first, but control means more than order. The productive concept of classroom control is that the teacher continuously helps learning to occur. The unproductive, distorted notion of absolute control suggests that the teacher's personal preferences must always be obeyed. This autocratic distortion confuses new teachers and makes them susceptible to games such as "Big baboon" and "How dare you?"

Learning Means Listening, Not Talking   Sometimes this value makes good sense, for as countless teachers say, "If I had to argue everything with my students, we'd never get anything done." And every teacher knows students often give opinions before they have information, and make assumptions rather than listen to facts. But the distortion creeps in when we deny students the right to learn by verbalizing ideas.

A corollary value is that learning means accepting, not questioning. This distortion of educational purpose permeates schools today, and makes teachers susceptible to games such as "How dare you," "Idle threats," "You should be ashamed," and the savior syndrome.

Learning is a Serious Business   Education really is a serious matter in American society, but the serious purpose becomes distorted when the school declares that enjoyment is either "extracurricular" or "recess." Laughter is only tolerated briefly in the classroom, under the assumption that one does not learn from laughter. Another assumption is that laughter is a threat to order; traditional schooling continually confuses seriousness with "order above all," causing students to find schools impersonal and hostile.[5] Overemphasis of seriousness makes teachers susceptible to the games "How dare you," the savior syndrome, and "Who did it."

To Err is Evil   Ordinary life is full of small mistakes, most of which we quickly and easily forget because society has ready and routine means to fix them. In schools, however, small errors are marked, recorded, accumulated, and announced to the general public. Student testimonies are replete with tales of "missed an A by 1 point" and "docked my grade for a misspelled word." Schools traditionally make a fetish of mistakes, and teachers are more concerned about whether students make mistakes than whether mistakes facilitate learning. We almost never hear a teacher say "That was a good mistake."

Just as students may try but dare not err, so are teachers expected to try but not fail. Parents object to their children's being used as guinea pigs; they want "tried and true" methods, whether or not the methods are effective. Thus, teachers often do not talk about their errors and/or plans that went awry except in self-justification. School culture does not encourage error and risk-taking. Such forces make teachers susceptible to games of "Big baboon," the savior syndrome, and "It's all your fault."

It's the Student's Fault/Teacher is Always Right   When something goes wrong with a student's performance, traditional school culture says the fault lies with the student, not the school. This value prevails because of educational purpose and institutional rationalization. In early days, the primary purpose of education was practical training, that is, to transmit knowledge for survival from one generation to another (including the transmission of cultural values). This value made sense then, as it closed off a student's creative or divergent responses that were simply not appropriate. In recent years, the purpose of education has broadened to include helping a new generation find its own answers, so the value of "teacher is always right" is only partly right, and sometimes wrong.

As to institutional rationalization, Katz reports that emerging American public schools in the 1870s came under attack for their poor results and high costs:

> Newly created systems of public education failed to meet the ends for which they had been established, and some explanation became necessary.... They created a defense in terms of the inferiority of their inmates. That inferiority, it was argued, was hereditary; thus, given the inferior stock with which they had to contend, what could one expect? (1971, p. 111)

This defensive response to public criticism continues today, though more subtly; rather than pleading hereditary inferiority of students, schools today plead environmental or experiential inferiority — "cultural disadvantage."

Knowing the school's determination to show something wrong with the student, not with the school or the teacher, we can appreciate the cultural forces that make teachers susceptible to games of "It's all your fault," "Isn't it awful," "What do you expect," and the savior syndrome.

The power of the school culture is strong enough to make almost every teacher fall into place without thinking much about it, even to the extent of playing dysfunctional games in the classroom.

The best way to stop games is to prevent them, by creating a classroom atmosphere in which everyone considers dysfunctional game-playing out of place and unnecessary. Consistent use of low profile classroom control is the most effective method to control game-playing.

NOTES

1   Diana Williams observed and reported this transaction.
2   Nina Coulter suggested and rendered an early description of this game.
3   Diana Williams informed my early thinking about this game.
4   See also Rothman (1977) for a similar list of what she calls "myths" of teaching.
5   Kevin Ryan's book *Don't Smile Until Christmas* (1970) tells the stories of several first year teachers, in their own words, as they struggle with schools' traditional values and students' nontraditional attitudes.

REFERENCES

BERNE, E. *Games people play.* New York: Grove Press, 1964.

BROWN, I. Man and culture. In R. Shinn (ed.), *Culture and school: Sociocultural significances.* Scranton, Pa.: International Textbook, 1972.

ERNST, K. *Games students play (and what to do about them).* Millbrae, Calif.: Celestial Arts, 1972.

GORDON, C. *The social system of the high school: A study in the sociology of adolescence.* Glencoe, Ill.: The Free Press, 1957.

KATZ, M. *Class, bureaucracy, and schools: The illusion of educational change in America.* New York: Praeger, 1971.

LORTIE, D. *Schoolteacher: A sociological study.* Chicago: University of Chicago Press, 1975.

ROTHMAN, E. *Troubled teachers.* New York: David McKay, 1977.

RYAN, K. *Don't smile until Christmas.* Chicago: University of Chicago Press, 1970.

WALLER, W. *The sociology of teaching.* New York: Russell and Russell, 1932, 1961.

NEGOTIATION AND PROBLEM RESOLUTION

22

The teacher skills in this chapter do not appear in the Taxonomy because they do not normally apply to classroom instruction per se. The best time and place for negotiation is outside instructional time, in private, or in special class meetings. Nevertheless, resolving problems and conflicts are part of a teacher's job in classroom control; the problem resolution can be done well, respecting students' worth and dignity, or badly, demeaning or insulting students. We will examine five teacher skills in negotiation and problem resolution.

METHOD AA
ASSERTIVE RESPONSES

"Find out just what any people will quietly submit to and you have found out the exact measure of injustice...which will be imposed upon them."
— Frederick Douglass

The assertive technique is amazingly simple in concept, remarkably effective in controlling tensions, and discouragingly rare. The concept is this: (1) I have an opinion, a desire or goal, a value, or a feeling — my position; (2) you also have an opinion, a desire or goal, a value, or a feeling — your position; and (3) when my position differs from yours and we have a conflict, there are three ways I can respond to you: aggressively, passively, or assertively.

Aggressively   I push my own position and ignore your position; for example, "I don't care what you want to do; I want to relax and read my paper!"

Passively   I yield to your position automatically without recognizing my own position in a forthright manner; for example, "Oh, all right (grumble, grumble), I'll do your dumb dishes!"

Assertively   I state both your position, clearly and forthrightly, and my own position, again, clearly and forthrightly; for example, "I realize you want me to do the dishes right now, but I'm tired and just want to relax for a while and read the paper. Can we work this out some other way?"

In the classroom, teachers are commonly aggressive or passive, rarely assertive. An aggressive response to a student might sound like this: "I told you before and I won't tell you again, I want you to pay attention and quit fooling around." A passive remark might be one like this: "Well, if you assign these kids homework, they don't do it anyway, so why assign it at all? I never do." *Assertive* responses, however, are a basic professional tool in several situations.

Giving Orders, Commands, Directions   "I know it's late and you'd like to get home, right? At the same time, I need to give you your assignment for tomorrow, so please muster your attention for 5 minutes more." The teacher gives nothing away by recognizing the students' position, and avoids an uncaring image by showing concern for student feelings and difficulties. This technique yields enormous potential for good will.

Releasing Anger and Frustration "Doggone it, I worked hard to put those pictures up on that bulletin board and to make this place look nice for you kids. I realize that whoever messed them up probably didn't know what he or she was doing—it might have been an accident, or maybe the person just didn't know those pictures were important to me—and you may not have wanted to hurt anything or anybody, but it really makes me mad to come in and see that board looking like that, so I hope it gets fixed up neatly right after school."

The natural outlets for anger and frustration are aggression or passivity. But the teacher cannot afford to be "natural" in many situations; the teacher must be disciplined. Assertiveness allows the teacher to release anger and frustration in a professional way.

Arguing, Debating, Disagreeing "Look, what you're saying is that I should have given you an A because you worked so hard on this project, am I understanding your point? You feel that if a person works hard on something, no matter what the job looks like, he should get an A, right? OK—you're saying there is such a thing as an "A for effort." I'm saying that the grade I assign is not for effort, but for quality; see the difference?"

The assertive technique is the teacher's most effective tool for defusing arguments, relieving tensions in disagreements, and communicating reasonableness and calm in debates. People frequently get angry during arguments because they feel they are not being heard or understood; the assertive technique provides proof that you are listening as well as talking.

PROBLEMS IN ASSERTIVENESS

Two problems arise in the practice of assertiveness. The first is that occasionally a person mistakes *acknowledgement* of his position for *agreement* with his position. For example, if you say, "So, you're saying that...," the other may say, "Exactly! I knew you'd finally see it my way." You can resolve the problem by saying, "Yes, I do understand your position, but I don't think you understand my position yet, do you? Let me say it again: you're arguing that....but I'm saying that....Do you understand my point?"

The second problem is that until we become skilled in assertive responses, we often feel psychological or even physical pain in trying to acknowledge or recognize the other's position. It hurts to have to repeat the "garbage" the other claims is a worthy argument, to actually say what we are so vehemently trying to disprove, discredit, or destroy.

Assertive skill is not easy to acquire, and difficult to apply, but it works wonders in the classroom, and elsewhere as well. Study these examples of difficult problems, with their assertive teacher responses.

1 *Student wants to cut corners:* "Phil, I realize you feel the problem should be worked this way because you think it will save you steps. What I'm saying is that in some problems you will need one of those same steps to get the right answer. See what I mean?"

2 *Students argue about class schedule:* "I can understand why you want to postpone the test until Monday—it will give you more time to study—but I've got other matters planned for Monday."

3   *Student is rude:* "I realize you're getting tired, but I don't approve of your rudeness."

4   *Student claims teacher is unfair:* "It's your right to feel I've been unfair to you, but there are good reasons for what I did, and here they are...."

5   *Student wants to leave the room:* "Sure you want to leave now—I know you want to go this instant—but before you go, it is important that you..."

6   *Student is cheating:* "You say 'It's no big deal, everybody does it.' Your position is that if everybody does it, it must be OK, right? Well I do not agree. If everyone were stealing, that still wouldn't make it right."

POWER ASSERTIVE

When basic assertive techniques do not work, it is time to move to power assertive techniques: "I know you don't want to do this, and of course you're feeling grouchy and tired—it's 3:00, and that's late, of course—but I do *not* approve of your rudeness."

The power-assertive technique requires great self-discipline because it directly opposes natural tendencies. Instead of elaborating on the teacher's own position, power assertiveness elaborates on the student's position (see Method O for paraphrase and reflect techniques). The technique has four parts, which may be stated in any order you wish.

State your own position (which you have previously stated), then state your students' position in 3 parts.

■   Part 1: Paraphrase the student's demand, argument, or viewpoint (which the student has already stated);

■   Part 2: Reflect the student's emotions, those the student has already expressed verbally or nonverbally, or emotions the student most likely feels; and

■   Part 3: Reflect the student's underlying problem, situation, values, assumption, or goal, whatever is driving the student to insist on his position in Part 2.

Power-assertiveness demonstrates that you understand the student's situation perhaps even better than he understands it himself, but with all your understanding, you still feel your position is justified: "OK, you want the test moved to Monday. You're nervous, right? now that it is so close at hand, and you all want to make good marks—they're important to you and to your parents, right? You bet! But I have other matters planned for Monday that must be done. I realize this is harder for you, but I have no other choice." In this statement, the teacher paraphrases, reflects, reflects again, then states his position. When teachers state their position as well as they can, many students will stop arguing; others will need a second strong dose of power-assertiveness, or a move to "super-power-assertive."

SUPER-POWER ASSERTIVE

Using this technique, the teacher paraphrases and reflects for both the student's position and the teacher's position.

State both your own and the student's (other) positions in three parts (any sequence):

- Part 1: State own and other's demands, arguments, viewpoint;
- Part 2: State own and other's demonstrated or probable emotions at the moment;
- Part 3: State own and other's underlying problem situation, values, assumptions, or goal, whatever is driving the person to insist on Part 1.

For example, "Look, I know you're feeling pressure and want the test on Monday, but there's something here you haven't known about. I need to give the test tomorrow rather than Monday because our last unit will require three full weeks to do well. I do not feel happy with myself when I don't teach well, so I want three full weeks — including Monday — to do a good job for you. That's important to me. That's why I teach. I know you want to make good grades and are anxious to do well on the test, so please prepare well *tonight* for the test tomorrow."

EXERCISE 1: BASIC ASSERTIVE SKILLS (20–40 minutes)

To prepare for this exercise, write a paragraph-long quotation of someone in your life who makes unfair demands on you or has at some time made an unreasonable request. For example, "Look, mister, I'm in a hurry, OK? I mean, look at all those customers over there waiting to pay and get outa here. I don't have *time* to take this order back and have her cook it some more. This is rush-hour, see?"

Your example may not be quite so obnoxious: "I don't *care* about your being late — that room has to be cleaned now...."

In your class group, one person reads his statement aloud as if it were "for real," then everyone takes 30 seconds to jot notes of a reply. Quickly move around the room with each person responding directly to the speaker; no third person statements beginning with "I would say..." are allowed. Use basic assertiveness. If the response is indeed basic assertive, the group will chorus "correct." If not, the group will chorus "problem." Quickly correct the problem and move on.

Conclusion The purpose is to come up with as many basic assertive responses as possible, to fill the air with this pattern we so rarely encounter. We want to saturate ourselves for the moment.

EXERCISE 2: POWER-ASSERTIVE (20–40 minutes)

Repeat the procedures of Exercise 1, modifying to respond with power assertive.

Conclusion The best way to do these exercises is to imagine that each situation is real, and each statement, whether it makes sense or not, is actually directed at you.

METHOD BB
PRINCIPLED NEGOTIATION*

"Isn't there a way we can discuss this matter without arguing about it?" How many times have you heard this said—or said it yourself?

Negotiation is the process of getting what you want from other people. Every time teachers are presented with demands by students, they are forced to negotiate. They *must* negotiate; the question is not whether they negotiate with students, but *how well.* The only negotiating techniques most students know are "hard bargaining" techniques and "soft bargaining" techniques.

In hard bargaining, the two parties present their positions, defend their positions against attack, and in the process, become more committed to their positions. They sometimes become so ego-involved that they feel the need to win to "save face."

A common strategy of hard bargaining is to start with an extreme position, rather than one's "real" position, and stubbornly hold onto it, deceiving the other party as to one's true views and making small concessions only as necessary to keep the bargaining going. Enormous amounts of time and energy are wasted in this ceremonial dance. Hard bargaining is actually a test of will, with each party trying to overpower the other, often through tactics such as name-calling, ultimatums, and power plays. The bitter feelings generated by such tactics can last a lifetime.

The most desirable result of hard bargaining, most people agree, is compromise—by which each party has to lose something and neither party gets what it really wants. (What an odd way to do business!)

In soft bargaining, one or both parties substitute the goal of "agreement" for the goal of "victory." When both parties sacrifice their own best interests to make an agreement possible, the agreement comes quickly and efficiently, but at least one of the parties "loses." The agreement may not be wise in the long run, because one party voluntarily "gives in" for the sake of harmony. The soft bargainer is highly vulnerable to someone who plays a hard game of bargaining. Giving in makes you a doormat to be walked on by the Hard Bargainer.

WHAT IS "PRINCIPLED NEGOTIATION?"

The Harvard Negotiation Project proposes a system of "principled negotiation"— actually *reasoned discussion* —which follows these rules[1]:

1 Separate the people from the problem.
2 Focus on interests, not on announced positions.
3 Generate several choices before deciding.
4 Use objective reasons for the final decision.

---

*The concepts and many of the text discussions in this section are drawn from GETTING TO YES by Roger Fisher and William Ury. Copyright © 1981 by Roger Fisher and William Ury. Reprinted by permission of Houghton Mifflin Company.

Separate the People from the Problem   Students are people: they get angry, frustrated, fearful, hostile, and offended. Their egos are easily threatened. And they want desperately to make *their feelings* part of the problem to be negotiated! What should teachers do?

First, allow the student to "let off steam." (Message-check here — paraphrase and reflecting are your basic tools [see Method O].) Second, gradually identify the *problem* that is causing the "people-response" (feelings) in your student. Say things like, "So what started all this was…, correct?" Try to separate the *source* of frustration from the feeling of frustration itself. (Message-check reflecting is useful here, and thought-testing is critically important.)

Focus on Interests, Not on Announced Positions   Behind each student's demand is a basic interest or need he feels compelled to satisfy. His demand may seem bizarre, but his needs are important and must be recognized as legitimate even if you are not able to meet them. What should teachers do?

First, ask "Why?" and "Why not?" "Why is this so important to you?" "Why is my suggestion not good for you?" Listen carefully to the answers and message-check them: "OK, so what you're *really* worried about is…, right?" Then, state your own interests as specifically as you possibly can so your student can see *exactly* why you feel as you do. "Look, frankly I feel nervous when you kids do that, and I don't want to live my life feeling nervous."

Generate Several Choices Before Deciding   Use negotiation to *generate* new possibilities that are not obvious and have not been considered before; brainstorm with your students. How should teachers do this?

First, look for mutual gain. Try coming up with creative solutions that satisfy the basic interests of both you and your student (no matter what the expense or other costs involved). Second, look through the eyes of different experts. Try asking, "How would a judge look at this? A minister, priest, or rabbi? A doctor? A football coach? A genius? An airline pilot? A psychiatrist?"

Use Objective Reasons for the Final Decision   Part of the negotiation process is searching for objective criteria to judge what a "fair" or "desirable" agreement might be. How might the criteria be agreed upon?

First ask, "What is *your* idea of a solution that is good for both of us?" Then, think of criteria that are commonly accepted in such cases and ask, "Why would these criteria not be acceptable to you?" Use the student's reasons to think of other criteria. If this process is followed carefully, the result should be a discussion, not an argument, and a solution in which both parties win and nobody loses.

WHEN STUDENTS USE HARD BARGAINING

Students sometimes get angry, and sometimes don't play fair. They shoot verbal bullets wildly in all directions, hoping to hit something, and they often throw bombs — ultimatums — hoping to annihilate the enemy. What should the teacher do with a hard bargainer?

First, don't attack his position; look behind it. When the student repeats his demand louder and more forcefully, don't reject it or accept it; simply treat it as one possible option: "OK, Todd, I understand that you want...[Message-check]. That's one way to go, and there may be others. Now tell me how all this came about in the first place." Then, look for the basic needs behind your student's demands. When the student repeats his demands or makes new ones, assume that every position he takes is a genuine attempt to address a real problem at hand.

Second, don't defend your own ideas; instead, invite criticism and advice. Explain that you are trying to find a good idea somewhere—from him or from you—that will be good for the both of you: "So, I have been thinking of.... What's wrong with that for you? Why isn't that good for you?" Don't hesitate to ask for advice. "You know that I want to find an answer that's good for both of us; what would you do if you were in my position?"

Third, recast an attack on you as an attack on the problem. The skill here is to refuse to take any of the hard bargaining tactics personally. Instead, sit back and allow the student to let off steam, then message-check only his problem-centered concerns and ignore the rest: "What I hear you saying is that you are seriously concerned about...I want you to know that I share your concern. My concern is that I'm not sure the proposed solution will deal with this problem....Can we find an option that achieves our goal?"

Fourth, ask questions and pause. Your two key tools in negotiating with a hard bargainer are questions and silence. "Questions offer [your student] no target to strike at, no position to attack. Questions do not criticize, they educate" (Fisher and Ury, 1981, p. 117).

Silence, too, is a powerful tool. Use it. If your student makes an unreasonable proposal or an unjustified attack on you, the best response may be to say nothing, but just look at him. Or, if you have asked an honest question to which he has provided an insufficient answer, just wait. Don't say a word. Why? Because people in our culture tend to feel uncomfortable with silence, especially if they have doubts about the wisdom or taste of something they have said. Your silence can create the impression of a stalemate which your student will feel compelled to break by answering your question again or by coming up with a new suggestion. So be quiet—don't let him off the hook by asking another question or making a comment.

STUDENT: Why can't you teachers just....[silence] Well, *I* think you should....[silence] Uh, what I mean is....

Principled Negotiation requires considerable skill; it is not at all "natural" or "instinctive" for most people. To those teachers who take time to master it, the system offers great rewards in genuine respect, in classroom harmony, and in real learning for students.

EXERCISE 1: PRINCIPLED NEGOTIATION (30 minutes)

This exercise requires prior training in Methods O, P, Q, R, S, and T.
1 Form groups of three (or four, if necessary) and designate a teacher, a student, and monitors for the first negotiation.

2 The teacher and the student will select a problem from the following sample problems list, or any other appropriate problem or topic.

3 The teacher and student negotiate for five minutes (the instructor should keep track of the time) following the four steps outlined above and on the Monitor Form I; they will strive ultimately to resolve the issue so that both parties win and nobody loses. No compromise is allowed!

4 The monitor fills out the Negotiation Monitor Form I as the negotiation goes along. If at any point the teacher or student violates the procedures for Principled Negotiation, or skips them, the Monitor must say "Please go back to...[the last correctly done step] and take it from there."

5 After the five minutes are up, the instructor should set the timer for another five minutes while the Monitor and the two parties critique the negotiation. You can use these sample problems for negotiation.

- Students want to hold class outdoors on the school lawn because it's a sunny, pleasant day. The teacher has had bad experiences with kids wasting time, fooling around, and making a picnic of such occasions.

- Students want to have a party in the classroom to celebrate George Washington's birthday. The teacher is behind in current lesson plans, and wonders about setting the precedent for Abe Lincoln's birthday, St. Patrick's Day, and so forth.

NEGOTIATION MONITOR FORM I

Name of "Teacher":_____ "Student":_____ "Monitor":_____
Directions to Monitor: Keep track of each step in the negotiation process and check it off (✔) as the Teacher does that step. If the parties skip a step, say "Please go back to...and take it from there." If the Teacher uses hard or soft bargaining tactics, say "Not allowed here."

Separate People from Problem
_____ 1. Teacher invites student to let off steam. (MC)
_____ 2. Identify student's underlying problem. (MC and TT)

Focus on Interests, Not Positions
_____ 1. Teacher asks inquiring questions ("Why is this important/troubling for you?")
_____ 2. Teacher asks inquiring questions ("Why is my suggestion not good for you?")
_____ 3. Teacher summarizes student's basic interests.
_____ 4. Teacher states own basic interests.

Generate Several Choices Before Deciding: Brainstorm
_____ 1. Create solutions for mutual gain.
_____ 2. Create options according to different experts.

Use Objective Reasons for the Final Decision
_____ 1. Both parties get what they really need.
_____ 2. Nobody loses, nobody compromises his basic interests.

■ Students complain about too much homework which interferes with after-school activities and other events. The teacher knows the assignments are well within the school district's guidelines, and that reducing homework would slow instruction dramatically and therefore not be fair to those students who do their homework regularly.

■ Students want to use class time for signing yearbooks/arranging a bake sale/planning for an assembly/or other such activity. "We can't get together after school because we all take the bus, and we all live so far away from one another," they say. The teacher knows the class is behind schedule in its academic work.

■ Students want to be able to go to the bathroom or to their lockers any time they need to without lining up/without hall passes/without specific permission from the teacher. The teacher's past experience with such procedures has been meetings of girls in the bathroom, boys' smoking in the bathroom, kids leaving class during the middle of lessons, noise in the halls, and complaints from other teachers and from the principal.

Conclusion   The main questions to discuss are: Did the teacher resort to hard bargaining power plays, name-calling, threats, ultimatums? Did the teacher really identify her own underlying interests and those of the students, or was her analysis superficial (for example, the underlying interests were seen as identical to the initial positions of the two parties)? Did both parties think creatively about choices, or did they simply settle on one or the other initial position, thus making a successful resolution—without compromise—more difficult, if not impossible?

After the five-minute conference, change roles: monitor becomes teacher, teacher becomes student, student becomes monitor.

After discussions, give your Monitor Form I to your instructor. This exercise presents some of the basic concepts of Principled Negotiation. We assumed that students would not use hard bargaining (pushy, rude, coercive) or soft bargaining (passive, giving in, quiet resignation). But students do not behave this way; the teacher's greatest discomfort comes when students play hard bargainers.

EXERCISE 2: THE HARD BARGAINER (30 minutes)

1 (Same as Exercise 1.) These groups should have different members than the former groups.

2 (Same as Exercise 1.)

3 The teacher and student will negotiate for five minutes. The student will do hard bargaining, defending his position, attacking the teacher's position, and arguing in every conceivable way. The teacher will try to use each of the skills above (and shown on Monitor Form II) and strive to get the student into a *discussion* of the basic issues, a consideration of various choices, and an agreement on criteria. The teacher's goal is a "win-win" solution, as in Exercise 1: nobody gives up, nobody compromises, both parties win.

4   The monitor fills out Negotiation Monitor Form II as the negotiation goes along. If the teacher at any time violates the four skills, the monitor will say, "Sorry, not allowed here" and enter a check mark on the proper line.

5   (Same as Exercise 1.)

6   (Same as Exercise 1.)

Conclusion   Principled Negotiation requires considerable skill and self-discipline. It is not usually natural or instinctive. After the discussion, give your Monitor Form II to your instructor.

METHOD CC
CHOICE COUNSELING[2]

Choice counseling is a procedure for helping students think through their problems, decisions, and options. When the teacher wants to help without giving advice (thereby doing the student's thinking for him), choice counseling is appropriate. Using this procedure, the teacher asks questions in five carefully designed steps:

NEGOTIATION MONITOR FORM II

Name of "Teacher":_____ "Student":_____ "Monitor":_____
Directions to Monitor: Put a check mark (✔) next to each skill as the "Teacher" demonstrates that skill. If the "Teacher" uses a Hard Bargaining tactic, say out loud, "Not allowed here."

Look Behind His Position
_____ a. Treat "Student's" demand as one possible option.
_____ b. Use Active Listening to discover basic underlying needs.
_____ c. Use Thought-Testing to test implications of "Student's" demands.

Invite Criticism and Advice
_____ a. Invite "Student's" criticism of "Teacher's" ideas.
_____ b. Ask for "Student's" advice on what "Teacher" should do.

Recast Personal Attacks
_____ a. Allow "Student" to let off steam.
_____ b. Message-Check "Student's" problem-centered concerns, ignore the rest.

Ask Questions and Pause
_____ a. Use questions, questions, questions rather than repeating statements of "Teacher's" own position.
_____ b. Use pauses, long waits as a tool.

_____ Put a check mark here each time Monitor says "Sorry, not allowed here" (or whenever teacher uses a hard bargaining tactic).

THE FIVE STEPS OF CHOICE COUNSELING

STEP 1:   How does the student perceive his problem?

STEP 2:   What is the real problem? (Is it as the student perceives it, or is it different?)

STEP 3:   What alternatives does the student have available?

STEP 4:   What are the probable/possible consequences of each alternative?

STEP 5:   What are the advantages/disadvantages of each consequence? How does the student feel about each consequence?

Here is an abbreviated example of choice counseling with a single student, although you can use the technique with groups of students and entire classes.

> **TEACHER:**   Something wrong?   (Student's perception)
> **STUDENT:**   Yeah, Bernie hit me.
> **TEACHER:**   For no reason?   (Real problem)
> **STUDENT:**   Well, I hit him a little.
> **TEACHER:**   By accident?   (Real problem)
> **STUDENT:**   No....
> **TEACHER:**   So when you lose your temper, you feel like hitting somebody.   (Real problem)
> **STUDENT:**   Yeah, and....
> **TEACHER:**   So till now you've simply done it. What else could you do? (Alternatives)
> **STUDENT:**   I don't know.
> **TEACHER:**   What does your mother suggest?   (Alternatives)
>   . . .
> **TEACHER:**   Let's go back to hitting kids. What happens when you do that? (Consequences)
>   . . .
> **TEACHER:**   And what do you think would happen if you...? (Consequences)
>   . . .
> **TEACHER:**   Now I want to know how you feel about some of the results. When kids hit you back—is that really a good thing for you?   (Student's feelings)
>   . . .
> **TEACHER:**   Well, you've done a lot of thinking about this. Let me know what you finally decide to do, OK?

When using choice counseling, the teacher never injects an idea unless the student requests it, and thus avoids giving unsolicited advice. The teacher must not permit the student to skip steps. "I suppose I could...but that's no good because...." leaps from step 3 to step 5, so the teacher should say, "Well, it might not seem good to you right now, but let's just leave it there for the moment; what else might you do?" Your job is to help the student think about alternatives and consequences he might skip over without your help. You should work all of one step before proceeding to the next.

The goal of choice counseling is thinking, not decision making. Notice how the teacher in the example refused to press the student for a decision, for the teacher's job was already done; the student had thought about his options, their probable results, and his preferences. That is enough.

EXERCISE 1: Choice Counseling Demonstration (10 minutes)

This exercise requires prior training in Methods O, P, Q, R, S, and T.

Prepare for this exercise by thinking about an unresolved problem or pending decision that confronts you now or will confront you in the future. For example: "How should I handle ____ situation?" "Should I tell him or not?" "What am I ever going to do about...?"

In your class group, your instructor will quickly demonstrate an example of choice counseling.* Practice taking Monitor notes according to the following instructions:

CHOICE COUNSELING: FORM I

Directions to Monitor: Listen to the "Teacher's" questions to the "Student" and write the first 1-6 words of *every* question the "Teacher" asks (ignore "Student" responses). Then write the proper STEP number next to each question; e.g.: _3_ What *else* [could you do?]

 If the Teacher skips a step, say, "You have not yet finished STEP...." Return this form to instructor after class.

Conclusion   Discuss any problems group members might have had in monitoring the demonstration.

EXERCISE 2: Choice Counseling Demonstration (15 minutes)

Do this exercise as you did Exercise 1, modifying as follows: group members act as teacher for the instructor, who uses a real or problem decision. The instructor can monitor all questions and make suggestions even while responding as a student. Group members act as teachers here, and do not take monitor notes.

EXERCISE 3: Choice Counseling (20–25 minutes)

Form groups of three (or four, if absolutely necessary), taking turns as teacher, student, and monitor.

---

*The simplest option: Read out loud with another person the sample script in Section CC. Or else ask someone in the group to present his problem/decision and work briefly—and *quickly*—with that.

Each choice counseling session lasts five minutes, timed by the monitor. Follow the model and Form I instructions explicitly. Move right along; do not pause, linger, or drag out questions.

Conclusion If the teacher is skilled and the student's problem or decision real, this exercise will be one of the most rewarding sessions in your training course. If the teacher does not get past step 2, the session can be very successful; simply analyzing the problem is an important thinking process.

METHOD DD
POSTPONING CONFRONTATION

Students occasionally demand confrontation, and when they do, the professional teacher must be ready. A teacher can postpone confrontation by saying, "Please see me after class" (or "...after this activity period" or even "...right after school"). This signals that the teacher is protecting the lesson from assault; that the student's behavior is unacceptable and will be dealt with; and that the teacher, not the student, is in control, regardless of what the student does or says.

The teacher should therefore use the technique sparingly. Use it privately, if possible, but if other students overhear, a public statement is appropriate.

METHOD EE
RESPONSE TO CRITICISM

Since criticism is a major factor in improving professional competence, every teacher should learn to accept and use criticism, particularly since student negotiation involves a great deal of direct or implied criticism.

The usual unprofessional response to criticism is emotional. Professional response does not deny natural emotions, but postpones them until after one thinks about the criticism. The professional response to criticism involves four steps:

STEP 1: Message-check the criticism and clarify it.

STEP 2: Compare the criticism with your own perceptions; does it match your own view? Mismatch? Maybe match?

STEP 3: Think about how you feel about the criticism. Do you feel pleased? Pained?

STEP 4: What do you intend to do about the matter? Anything?

For example:
"...So you think the test items were unfair. Which ones are you thinking of?....Well, I guess I'd have to agree—there's room for confusion there;

I'm disappointed, of course, but I'm glad you raised the issue. I'll look at those items again."

"When you observed those kids fooling around in the back row, I actually saw them too, but you're right—I did nothing about them. I was trying so hard to follow my lesson plan that I ignored them. Too bad. I guess I need to improve my ability to think about two things at one time—but right now I just have to keep thinking about my lesson plan and let the attention thing wait till later; I can only concentrate on one thing at a time right now."

WHY USE THIS PROFESSIONAL MODEL?

The most instinctive response to criticism is emotional: automatic good feelings in response to compliments, automatic bad feelings in response to negative criticism. The risk in an emotional response is that a teacher will ignore or suppress good information she needs to improve her teaching; in other words, the teacher's personal hang-ups may get in the way. All criticism, whether it matches our perceptions or not, is potentially *useful* if only to keep us informed of what our critics are thinking.

A second reason for using this model is that it makes us appear strong to the people who criticize us. We appear open, thoughtful, and in control of ourselves. So not only do we get useful information, but we present a truly professional image. Both factors are important to teachers, no matter who is criticizing us.

A third reason is that this model saves time: step 1 alone is often sufficient to (a) discover the criticism is not actually a criticism at all; (b) discover that the first-stated criticism is not the *real* criticism; or (c) the criticism is only a misunderstanding that requires a brief explanation. Imagine, in any of these cases, the time wasted by using your emotions first rather than a message-check!

EXERCISE 1: RECEIVING CRITICISM, DRILL (10–20 minutes)

In class, the instructor will say to the group, "The problem with *you* is that you are not truly dedicated to teaching; you're just loafing through this training program when you should be really applying yourself." The class will chorus back, "What do you mean by 'just loafing'?" The instructor will reply, "I mean, if you were *truly* dedicated, you would be reading three outside books every week from the bibliographies in this text. Instead, you're only doing the assigned readings and preparations."

Each group member should write his response, Steps 2 through 4, according to the professional model.

Go around the group as each member reads his response aloud. The instructor should critique.

EXERCISE 2: RECEIVING CRITICISM (10–40 minutes)

Prepare for this exercise by jotting down three criticisms made of you recently by students, colleagues, administrator, instructor, or someone else.

In the class group, turn to the person on your left and state one of the criticisms to that person by name, just as it was stated to you. That person, acting as teacher, will then respond using the 4-Step Professional Model. The instructor will moderate, breaking off the interaction when he feels the "teacher" has demonstrated mastery of the model. If you appear defensive, you have not mastered the model.

NOTES

1   The concepts and procedures in this section are drawn from or based on Fisher and Ury (1981).
2   The Choice Counseling model is an adaptation of the five-step "Free Choice Game," Strategy No. 52, in Simon, Howe, and Kirschenbaum, 1972, pp. 300-301. The model is similar also to the six-step "No-Lose Method" of Gordon, 1974, p. 193.

REFERENCES

FISHER, R., & URY, W. *Getting to yes: Negotiating agreement without giving in.* Boston: Houghton Mifflin, 1981.

GORDON, T. *T.E.T. Teacher effectiveness training.* New York: David McKay, 1974.

SIMON, S., HOWE, L., & KIRSCHENBAUM, H. *Values clarification: A handbook of practical strategies for teachers and students.* New York: Hart, 1972.

UNIVERSAL PRINCIPLES
OF CLASSROOM CONTROL

EPILOGUE

Classroom control in U.S. schools is in sad disarray. Instead of subscribing to a few sensible principles, teachers, administrators, and teacher educators mouth conflicting claims and counterclaims that make them vulnerable to the intrusion of nonprofessionals who claim, in turn, to know as much as the educators. New teachers searching for effective control methods find a haphazard assortment of testimonials and philosophical recipes. Take your pick, say members of the profession, choose the approach that feels best to you, for there is no right or wrong way to teach.

Without established principles, most teachers do the logical thing: they accept conventional wisdom and teach as best they can. The conventional wisdom of classroom control consists, in part, of six vague concepts which, though often quoted, are rarely helpful.

Conventional Concept 1: It is not good to be "too soft" or "too hard" in classroom control.

This concept implies that some kinds of control are intrinsically good, others intrinsically bad. "Be firm" say some, "be supportive" say others. In fact, no professional classroom control (as listed in the Taxonomy, for example) is intrinsically good or bad; instead, each control technique is appropriate for a particular classroom situation *somewhere.*

Notions of "hard" or "soft," "good" or "bad," "strong" or "weak" discipline are meaningless. The only meaningful notions in classroom control are "effective control" and "ineffective control."

Conventional Concept 2: The teacher should begin the year with tight discipline and control, then relax discipline and control after the class is functioning smoothly.

Kevin Ryan reports the advice sometimes given to new teachers: "Don't smile until Christmas." Experienced teachers give newcomers the same advice in various ways: "Be hard on them at first, then let up later," or "Let them know at the very start that you mean business, then after a while you can relax and show them you're human." The advice is puzzling, as the last version shows. Should the teacher relax the rules and not enforce them any more? If so, why have rules at all? Relax the body? Why make oneself tense in the first place? Relax standards and expectations? That seems unethical.

The advice intends to say that when students develop good classroom behavior habits at the beginning of the year, they are less likely to misbehave later, and that the teacher who conveys a businesslike first impression will have fewer behavior problems than a teacher whose first impression is not businesslike. This intended message is valid and helpful.

But the implicit advice is that the teacher should either begin the year with high profile control and end with low, or control all behavior at the beginning of the year and later begin to ignore certain behavior. Either way, the advice is foolish. A professional teacher uses whatever control methods are necessary regardless of the time of year.

Conventional Concept 3: The best method of discipline is prevention; a teacher should organize lessons so well that behavior problems never arise.

There is both wisdom and mischief in this pronouncement. On the side of wisdom is the fact that if the lesson is well prepared, it is indeed more likely to be successful. The converse is also true; students rebel, either consciously or unconsciously or openly or covertly, against poorly prepared lessons. The mischief of the advice is the mythical vision that students always respond ideally to well planned lessons. In reality, students of all ages sometimes get overexcited during well-planned lessons; they get restless at different rates because their heads, minds, and emotions are different. Some students invariably fail to understand the best-made point; and of course, as every teacher knows, accidents happen anytime. Students can ruin good lesson plans and learning programs any day of the week.

The fact is that effective classroom control consists of (1) fine planning, (2) fine execution of plans, (3) fine adjusting of plans, and (4) fine changing of plans. Effective teaching is not one of these, but all of them.

Conventional Concept 4: We must distinguish between maintaining order and instructing students; this distinction corresponds to students' behaving themselves vs. students' learning.

The logic here persuades almost everyone inside and outside education. In fact, educators consider the distinction between maintaining order and instructing students so important that occasionally someone calls it a basic teaching skill. Unfortunately, the distinction encourages educators to maintain order at the sacrifice of learning. Students are suspended from school because they cut class; teachers distract students' attentions from the lesson to correct inattention.

The fact is that during instruction, the distinction between "instructional" and "managerial" is irrelevant. Only high profile classroom controls make such distinction; low profile controls do not.

Conventional Concept 5: Whether classroom discipline is "hard," "soft," "firm," "relaxed," "strong," or "invisible," it should always be *positive* — to help students, not to hurt them.

"Positive" here symbolizes today's confusion over classroom control. Why should we say such a thing? Is anyone seriously proposing "negative discipline"? Or do we all have different concepts of "positive"? In any case, the term "positive discipline" is meaningless jargon. Any classroom control technique that focuses student attention on appropriate lesson content is *effective*; any technique that needlessly distracts is *not* effective. We need no more jargon than that.

In summary, classroom control in U.S. schools is in sad disarray. We are searching for sensible, universal principles to replace the popular conventional concepts that divide and confuse us. We have examined three fundamental principles of classroom control that emerge from our concern with student attention. Let us observe these same principles at work in Japanese schools.

A SEARCH FOR PRINCIPLES IN JAPANESE CLASSROOMS

In 1979, I spent five months in Japan visiting 67 elementary and secondary classrooms in 19 different schools. I wanted to see whether Japanese teachers controlled their classes differently than do teachers in the United States. I expected to find every Japanese classroom "attentive" 100 percent of the time, for I had been told that parental expectations for education, social pressure for obedience and order, competitive admissions to secondary schools and colleges, and the tight link between academic success and later job opportunities would all function to make every Japanese student pay rapt attention to his teacher. In that ideal setting, how would Japanese teachers behave?

As I sat in the backs of these classrooms, I discovered that many Japanese classes were as attentive as I had expected: students took notes, actively participated, and showed all the proper visual attention cues.

Imagine my surprise to discover that some Japanese classes showed signs of inattention during lessons, and that, in many high school classrooms, students' visual cues were frequently those of unknown attention! Motionless stares were not uncommon in high school classrooms. I realized there was something to study after all. What were the differences between the 100% attentive and the relatively inattentive or unknown attention classrooms? Did high attention teachers do things differently from the others?

Several patterns appeared in our observational data. One pattern that particularly fascinated me was the markedly greater frequency of low profile techniques in attentive classrooms than in inattentive or unknown attention classrooms; these low profile techniques were primarily the following:

- High teacher expectations   Aa1, Ab1*
- Specific learning objectives   Bb1
- Publicized learning standards   Bd1
- Scrupulous monitoring   Be1
- Thorough feedback   Bf1
- Clear statements of topic   Ca1
- Intensive use of visuals (especially elaborate chalkboards)   D1
- Auditorium seating for lectures   Fd1
- Auditorium seating for recitation   Fe3
- Resources readily available   F81
- Rapid pace (*extremely* rapid compared to U.S. schools)   Ga1
- Rapid transitions (often almost instantaneous)   Gb1
- Considerable variety in student activity   H1
- Interactive lectures, choral responses, etc.   Ia1
- Direct supervision   Jb1
- Voice animation (particularly in women)   Kb1
- Eagle eyes   L1
- Much pointing to lesson objects/chalkboard   Ma1
- Considerable touching (in elementary grades)   Mb1
- Free movement around the room   Na1

---

*These were reported to us in interviews or were apparent from the teacher's W1 pep talk comments in class.

- Designated seating   Nb1
- System of hands-raised, sometimes call on others   Ta1
- Many lower-level questions, rapid-fire   Tb1
- Constant encouragement and exhortation   W1
- Override small distractions, even large ones   Xb1

In the United States, low profile classroom control techniques correlate most closely with high student attention (see Appendix A), and high profile techniques correlate most closely with low student attention. This appears true in Japan as well. The congruity is more remarkable when we consider the radical difference between cultures and customs of Japan and the United States. If the fundamental principles of classroom control appear valid in the educational systems of these dramatically different cultures, should we not wonder whether the principles may be universal?

CRITERIA FOR UNIVERSAL PRINCIPLES OF CLASSROOM CONTROL

To consider a professional principle "universal," it must satisfy these criteria:

1 It must apply to all relevant cases in all situations with no regional exceptions.
2 It must be nonideological.
3 It must be consistent with other universal principles.

The fundamentals of classroom control can probably be considered universal principles for several reasons. First, the principles apply to all levels of schooling, all subject matter, all school settings, and probably to all cultures. Second, the principles are nonideological: they assume no one system of morality or ethics, make no interpretation of human nature or development, and do not favor any existing philosophy of teaching or learning. Finally, the principles are grounded in two universally accepted principles of schooling: (1) the primary purpose of the school is to help students learn; and (2) students must pay attention to lesson content in order to learn the content.

In searching for universal principles, we are not looking for the right way to teach, the best teaching style, the ideal teaching personality, nor for foolproof teaching methods. We seek principles, not recipes.

A FINAL PERSPECTIVE ON CLASSROOM CONTROL IN AMERICAN SCHOOLS

American teaching today is a profession in search of its principles. Teaching has few principles of professional practice to which all its members subscribe (Dreeben, 1973, p. 463). One teacher claims to teach as well as the next, despite obvious differences in their students' behavior, but the profession has no way—nor, to this point, any pronounced willingness—to refute the claim. "One's personal predispositions are not only relevant but, in fact, stand at the core of becoming a teacher," says Dan Lortie (1975, p. 79), and the lack of professional principles ill serves a profession whose practices are subject to constant criticism and reproach from its clientele.

Nowhere is teaching's lack of professional principles more evident than in classroom control. Teachers today do not have a professional base of support for controlling classrooms. They have been deprived of rigorous training in the basic skills of teaching; instead, they have been encouraged to go out and find their own methods and styles of teaching to suit their individual personalities. They have created their own ways of teaching, and many are discouraged.

During the 1960s, "fundamentals" were considered old fashioned, dull, and even repressive. The mood of the 1960s and early 1970s was to exalt narcissistic self-expression: "Do your own thing," "Be yourself," "Don't hassle me," and "I'll do it my way!" were catch phrases of the era, and nowhere were they voiced more loudly than in schools.

But the mood is changing. We are forced by the energy crisis and the sheer stress of modern living to search for the basic fundamentals in our lives: transportation without chrome, warmth in winter without waste, food without additives. In the schools, we are searching for learning without distractions. We want effective classroom control.

REFERENCES

DREEBEN, R. The school as a workplace. In R. Travers (Ed.), *Second handbook of research on teaching* (American Educational Research Association). Chicago: Rand McNally, 1973.

KOBAYASHI, TETSUYA. *Society, schools, and progress in Japan.* Oxford: Pergamon Press, 1976.

LORTIE, D. *Schoolteacher: A sociological study.* Chicago: University of Chicago Press, 1975.

RYAN, K. *Don't smile until Christmas.* Chicago: University of Chicago Press, 1970.

RESEARCH ON STUDENT ATTENTION AND LEARNING

APPENDIX

The assumption that attention is prerequisite to learning was implied by notable teachers and scholars two thousand years ago.

> Therefore a student of talents and virtue pursues his studies, withdrawn in college from all besides....
> — Confucius (c. 550–478 B. C.),
> Book XVI. −HS10 K1, or, RECORD ON THE SUBJECT OF EDUCATION, 9. (Ulich, 1954, p. 20)

> The orator must above all things devote his attention to the formation of moral character and must acquire a complete knowledge of all that is just and honorable.
> — Quintilian (c. 35–85 A. D.), Institutes of Oratory, Book XII, II. (Ulich, 1954, p. 121)

> I resolved thereupon to lend my studies towards the Holy Scriptures, that I might see what they were.
> — St. Augustine (354–430 A. D.), The Confessions, Book III, Chapter V (Ulich, 1954, p. 152)

In modern times, scholars in the field of education express the same assumption.

> However valuable may be the material which the teacher has to present, he cannot make it register with his pupils, and establish in them the learning products which he seeks, unless he can and will secure and hold their sustained attention....
> — Henry C. Morrison (1931, p. 116)

> Little is known about how children learn, but one fundamental fact we do know is that one must attend to and think about most learning tasks if he is to master them.
> — Thomas L. Good and Jere E. Brophy (1978, p. 358)

> ...Learning is likely to be greater if the students give more time and attention to the learning tasks.
> — Benjamin Bloom (1976, p. 187)

> Ms. Jones is, in large degree, correct when she tells Johnny, "Pay attention or you won't learn anything!"
> — N. L. Gage and David C. Berliner (1979, p. 305)

The assumption seems so reasonable and obvious to so many people that we might wonder why it deserves any further comment. Indeed, doesn't logic alone supplant all need to prove a link between a student's attention and his learning? Perhaps so, but in recent years educational researchers have not been satisfied with logic alone; rather, they have tried to discover whether a link can be demonstrated empirically as well as intuitively.

RESEARCH ON STUDENT ATTENTION AND STUDENT LEARNING*

1956   J. E. Morsh Study of Instruction in the U. S. A. F.
1963   C. J. Krauskopf Study of Stimulated Recall in College.

---

*I was aided in compiling this section by Lomax and Cooley's (1979) review of the literature on student achievement/instructional time, and by Jackson's review of studies of attention in *Life in Classrooms* (1968).

In 1963, Krauskopf reported his earlier study at Ohio State University of 54 college students in which he compared, among other things, the relevance of students' thoughts during a lecture with the students' scores on an achievement test. (The "students' thoughts" were obtained by asking students to report "whatever they happened to be thinking at that moment" every time the tape-recorded lecture was stopped.) He found a correlation of .60 between students' test scores and what Krauskopf called their "relevant thoughts," relevance as judged by independent raters. Actually, the "relevant thoughts" were expressions of "high attention" to the lesson content.

Also in 1963, Siegel and his associates at Miami University of Ohio reported their study of approximately 240 college students whose attention during a filmed lecture was determined in a self-report manner similar to that of Krauskopf. Their correlation of .61 between attention (termed "thinking relevance" by Siegel) and achievement on a test over the lecture material is probably suspect because they collected their student reports of thinking *after* the lecture had been completed and the achievement test taken. Still, the results here seem consistent with the general trend of earlier and later studies of attention-achievement.

In 1968, Henriette Lahaderne, then at the University of Chicago, recalled an earlier study by Joseph E. Morsh in 1958. Morsh had examined classroom behavior in an Air Force school where he found, among other things, a high negative correlation ($-.58$) between student achievement and student behavior that Morsh called "inattention."

Continuing the Morsh line of inquiry, Lahaderne conducted a study of 125 students in four sixth grade classrooms to discover the possible relationships among student attitudes (about school, teacher, and subject matter), student I. Q.'s, student attention in the classroom, and student achievement. In her report, Lahaderne concluded:

> The pupil who paid attention gained the most from his instruction. Or conversely, the data might be said to show that the pupil who was inattentive was not apt to achieve academically. (p. 324)

She found notable correlations of .39 to .51 between observed rates of attention and various achievement measures (Scott-Foresman Reading and Stanford Achievement Test on reading, arithmetic, and language).

Another major finding of Lahaderne's study was a lack of correlation between student attitudes and achievement, and a lack of correlation between student attention and student attitudes about school; she had expected, as would we all, to find that students who dislike school would be less attentive than those who like school. She was surprised to find almost no relationship between student attitudes and attention. She pondered:

> Why did students who were dissatisfied with school appear to be just as attentive as those who were satisfied? What has happened to the popular stereotype of the daydreaming malcontent?
>
> Perhaps the constraints imposed on pupils to be attentive were so strong that attitudes could not influence behavior.... One of the teacher's major functions was to preserve the classroom order. She called on the reluctant, snapped the daydreamer back to attention, reprimanded the cutup, and often reminded the pupils of the designated focus of attention. In short, pupils were coaxed and compelled to adhere to a code of conduct that supported the order of the classroom. (p. 54)

While the teachers in Lahaderne's study were probably not as effective as they should have been in classroom control, for the reasons discussed in chapter 2, they still debunked the popular myth that students with "bad attitudes" will neither pay attention nor learn in school. The teachers of this study demonstrate that teachers can override student attitudes to command attention in the classroom.

In another 1968 study which was not specifically intended to relate attention and achievement, Hall, Lund, and Jackson studied the power of elementary school teachers to modify students' nonstudy behavior; in the process, these experiments in behavior modification techniques revealed instances of improved performance and/or grades among five of the six students whose attention in class was significantly improved by the experimental techniques. (The sixth student had been a high achiever to start with, but was also disruptive.)

In 1972, Joseph A. Cobb observed 103 fourth-grade students in five classrooms of two middle-class schools for nine days during arithmetic periods, recording a number of "behavioral categories" such as attention, positive talk with the teacher, positive talk with other students ("positive" here means academically-oriented), volunteering in class, initiating requests for academic assistance, compliance with teacher instructions, etc. He predicted academic achievement on the basis of "scores" compiled over the nine observation days, then administered standardized arithmetic tests one week after completing observations. He found that "the most powerful behavioral category...was 'attending' which provided an R of .40 for School A and .47 for School B" (p. 79).

In 1973, Cobb published with Hops the results of their follow-up study on attention/achievement. The experimenters were not satisfied with a correlational link between attention and achievement; they wanted to determine if a *causal* relationship exists between the two. Using eighteen first-grade students with poor attention skills and low achievement, Cobb and Hops first obtained baseline data on the children, then trained the teachers of twelve of the children in techniques designed to improve the attention and work habits of the children— "group nonsocial reinforcement, individual and group reinforcers, vicarious reinforcement, shaping procedures, close monitoring, pairing of social and nonsocial reinforcers, and the fading out of nonsocial reinforcers as the children progressed" (116, p. 109). They then observed the children's resultant attention patterns and subsequent reading achievement scores. Cobb called the students' attending behaviors "academic survival skills," consisting of "attending to teacher, following teacher instructions, and volunteering to answer academic questions" (p. 108), all of which we call "attention" in this book. The results of the Cobb/Hops study lent strong support to a causal relationship between student attention and academic achievement in reading skills: the twelve experimental children increased their "level of survival skills" by 24 percent over their baseline level and also increased their mean standard scores in reading achievement by 28 percent; the six remaining control students increased their survival skills by 3 percent and 11 percent in reading achievement.

Lomax and Cooley (1979) report an unpublished dissertation study by E.A. Schultz of Rutgers:

> Schultz (1973) studied the attentional behavior of 81 first grade middle class pupils in instruction. Each student in the classroom was observed during ten reading periods spread out over eight weeks.... Attention was coded positively if the pupil was applying himself to both the area of focus and the prescribed activity. Following the completing of the observational period, student reading achievement was assessed by the Paragraph Meaning subtest of the SAT. At the student level, reading achievement was correlated with the percentage of time the student was attending to the appropriate instructional task. With all of the pupils included in the computation, the raw correlation was .48. (p. 9)

Rosenshine (1979) reports a study conducted by Jane Stallings and David Kaskowitz during 1972–1973 in which first- and second-grade children were observed regularly throughout the school day for "attending" behavior in reading and mathematics activities. "Attending" time correlated more closely with achievement gain than any other coded behaviors or interactions of teachers or students; for example, children in the top achievement groups spent about 50 percent more time attending to reading than children in the bottom groups.

Finally, in 1974, Samuels and Turnure published their study relating attention and reading achievements in first-grade boys and girls. They wanted to test the attention/achievement relationship prior to the effects of long-term success/failure school experiences that Samuels felt might have influenced the results of the earlier Lahaderne and Cobb studies.

Samuels observed 88 first graders in four classrooms in two middle-class schools in Minneapolis during reading instruction, in fifteen visits to each classroom during one month. He then administered a reading achievement test based on the Dolch List, a random set of 45 basic sight words. Correlations between "attention" (defined and measured in a manner similar to that of Lahaderne) and word recognition (controlled for reading readiness) were .44.

Thus, the research on attention/achievement supports, with modest correlations, the intuitive notion that the more a student attends to the lesson, the more likely he is to learn it.

RESEARCH ON TIME ON TASK/STUDENT ENGAGED TIME

A related body of research has examined time-on-task or "student engaged time"—the amount of time a student actually spends studying a lesson with a reasonably low error rate. A major purpose of this research has been to determine whether there is a significant link between the amount of time a student spends studying a lesson and the probability of his learning that lesson.

To make this research completely relevant to our topic of attention, we need only understand that "student engaged time" is the time a student actually pays attention to a lesson. Student engaged time is quite different from "teacher allocated time," which is the amount of time a teacher schedules or makes available for a lesson. Because of distractions, delays, incorrect learning, etc., a student's actual engaged time is usually less than the teacher's allocated time.

One study, the Far West Laboratory BTES (Beginning Teacher Evaluation Study), has found a strong and consistent effect of low-error/engaged-time on academic learning. As stated by Richard Marliave, one of the BTES researchers:

> Simply put, it may be concluded that students who spend more time in an instructional activity, at a relatively high level of attention, and producing a relatively low number of errors, will learn more of the content of that instructional activity. (Fisher et al., 1978, p. 19)

The BTES staff placed some qualifications on these findings: only about 10 percent of the measured learning can be accounted for by these data, given the research methods used by the BTES program. Yet Marliave argues that the explanation of one-tenth of student learning is an important factor as it stands, and in addition, the figure is probably "an underestimation" of the true effect of the low-error/engaged-time factor on achievement, due to the various kinds of measurement errors that plague so much of educational research. In reviewing other current time-on-task research studies, Lomax and Cooley agree with Marliave's point on methodology (1979, p. 16).

Finally, we must consider recent work on "mastery learning," a concept with roots in the thinking of Henry C. Morrison (1931) and John Carroll (1963), among others. For our purposes, the concept of mastery learning is best explained by John Carroll:

> Briefly, our model says that the learner will succeed in learning a given task to the extent that he spends the amount of time that he *needs* to learn the task.... "Spending time" means *actually spending time on the act of learning* .... It is the time during which he is "paying attention" and "trying to learn." (1963, p. 725)

Clearly, Carroll's emphasis is on what we call "high attention" time; therefore, if mastery learning really works, that is, if students who spend more time on the act of learning do learn more, then the link between high attention and student achievement would be demonstrated *ipso facto,* for attention is a basic tenet of mastery learning.

Benjamin Bloom (see chapter 1) has built on Carroll's concept and created an entire instructional system to individualize instruction within groups, allowing students sufficient time to master lesson content before moving on to new content. Bloom's system is called "mastery learning" or "Learning For Mastery" (LFM). At the same time Bloom formulated his first major statement on mastery learning in 1968, Professor F. S. Keller (1968) announced his Personalized System of Instruction (PSI) which, though different in origin from mastery learning, espoused similar principles and methods. Several reviews of research provide evidence that mastery learning and the Keller Plan work, that is, they increase student learning as they increase student attention and time-on-task: Bloom wrote:

> There is considerable evidence that mastery learning procedures do work well in enabling about four-fifths of students to reach a level of achievement which less than one-fifth attain under non-mastery conditions. The time costs for this are typically of the order of 10 to 20 percent additional time over the classroom scheduled time. (1976, p. 5)

In 1976, Block and Burns reviewed studies of mastery learning and observed:

> In 97 comparisons of average achievement test scores, comparisons involving various types and numbers of students and various subject matter areas, mastery-taught students scored higher than nonmastery-taught students 89% of the time, and significantly higher 61% of the time. Likewise, in 27 comparisons of average retention test scores, comparisons involving retention intervals from a few weeks to many months, mastery-taught students almost always scored higher than nonmastery-taught students, and significantly higher 63% of the time. (p. 19)

In 1979, Kulik, Kulik, and Cohen analyzed studies of Keller's PSI and found significant differences in student performance on final examinations of courses taught by means of the Keller Plan:

> PSI final examinations average about 8 percentage points higher than examinations from conventional classes.... This means that PSI raises the final examination score of a typical student in a typical class from the 50th to the 70th percentile. It also means that PSI raises the performance of typical students (with SAT scores of 500) to the level previously associated with above-average students (with SAT scores of 600). (p. 317)

Finally, in 1979, Ryan and Schmidt examined the same studies reported earlier by Block and Burns, added more studies to the list, and reached the following conclusion:

> The evidence definitely favors the mastery learning approach in the acquisition of cognitive skills in the subject areas examined. While the studies in retention and transfer of learning are few, the evidence here too favors mastery learning. (p. 56)

In this review of research, we must understand that there is no single entity called "mastery learning" per se. As Block admits, "No single type of mastery learning strategy has been used for all these subjects, classes, teachers, and schools. In fact, each has required a somewhat different type of strategy" (1976, p. 115).

In addition, mastery learning is far more than a simple formula of time plus attention; it is a system of instruction consisting of continuing diagnosis and individualized instruction. Time is not the only distinctive feature in mastery learning; Bloom controls *all* conditions of instruction.

Yet, after considering all the variations in mastery learning, we must still return to the central factor of time-plus-attention as the prerequisite for all other learning factors. Bloom seems to do this in his appraisal of L. W. Anderson's study, in which students' use of time was judged by the amount of overt attention they displayed as well as the amount of covert thinking they reported for each learning task. Anderson reported a correlation of .66 between time-on-task and final achievement. Bloom says:

> In this study there is little mystery as to why the two groups [experimental and control] show increasing differences in achievement—they are increasingly different in their involvement (time-on-task) on successive learning tasks.... Such evidence suggests the rather obvious point that learning is likely to be greater if the students give more time and attention to the learning tasks. (1976, p. 187)

Reflections on the Research   Although it is still being reviewed, evaluated, and debated by scholars of educational measurement and research design, the research in this Appendix is important to us because it consistently validates our intuition that all students need to pay attention to a lesson before they can learn the lesson. Bloom's work on mastery learning gives empirical justification to an additional obvious notion that different students require different amounts of time under different conditions in order to learn. The common requirement of all teaching—regardless of lesson content, time periods, and teaching/learning conditions—is that the student must pay attention to the lesson, a fundamental truth that should require no further debate in the teaching profession.

REFERENCES

BLOCK, J. Mastery learning: The current state of the craft. *Educational Leadership,* 1979, *37,* 114–117.

BLOCK, J., & BURNS, R. Mastery learning. In L. Schulman (ed.), *Review of research in education* (vol. 4). Itasca, Ill.: F.E. Peacock, 1976.

BLOOM, B. *Human characteristics and school learning.* New York: McGraw-Hill, 1976.

CARROLL, J. A model of school learning. *Teachers College Record,* 1963, *64,* 723–733.

COBB, J. Relationship of discrete classroom behaviors to fourth-grade academic achievement. *Journal of Educational Psychology,* 1972, *63,* 74–80.

COBB, J., & HOPS, H. Effects of academic survival skill training on low achieving first graders. *Journal of Educational Research,* 1973, *67,* 108–113.

FISHER, C., FILBY, N., MARLIAVE, R., CAHEN, L., DISHAW, M., MOORE, J., & BERLINER, D. Teaching behaviors, academic learning time, and student achievement: Final report of Phase III-B, beginning teacher evaluation study. Technical Report V-1. San Francisco: Far West Laboratory for Educational Research and Development, 1978.

GAGE, N., & BERLINER, D. *Educational psychology.* Chicago: Rand McNally, 1979.

GOOD, T., & BROPHY, J. *Looking in classrooms* (2nd ed.). New York: Harper and Row, 1978.

HALL, R., LUND, D., & JACKSON, D. Effects of teacher attention on study behavior. *Journal of Applied Behavioral Analysis,* 1968, *1,* 1–12.

JACKSON, P. *Life in classrooms.* New York: Holt, Rinehart and Winston, 1968.

KELLER, F. Good-bye teacher! *Journal of Applied Behavioral Analysis,* 1968, *1,* 79–84.

KRAUSKOPF, C. Use of written responses in the stimulated recall method. *Journal of Educational Psychology,* 1963, *54,* 172–176.

KULIK, J., KULIK, C., & COHEN, P. A meta-analysis of outcome studies of Keller's personalized system of instruction. *American Psychology,* 1979, *34,* 307–318.

LAHADERNE, H. Attitudinal and intellectual correlates of attention: A study of four sixth grade classrooms. *Journal of Educational Psychology,* 1968, *59,* 320–324.

LOMAX, R., & COOLEY, W. The student achievement-instructional time relationship. Paper presented to American Educational Research Association Annual Meeting, April 1979.

MORRISON, H. *The practice of teaching in the secondary school.* Chicago: University of Chicago Press, 1931.

ROSENSHINE, B. Content, time, and instruction. In P. Peterson and H. Walberg, Research on teaching: Concepts, findings, and implications. Berkeley, Calif.: McCutchan, 1979.

RYAN, D., & SCHMIDT, M. Mastery learning: Theory, research, and implementation. ERIC, 1979, ED 169 683.

SIEGEL, L., et al. Students' thoughts during class: A criterion for educational research. *Journal of Educational Psychology,* 1963, *54,* 45–51.

ULICH, R. (Ed.) *Three thousand years of educational wisdom.* Cambridge, Mass.: Harvard University Press, 1954.

EVALUATION CRITERIA FOR INSTRUCTORS AND SUPERVISORS

APPENDIX B

Observing teacher control is surprisingly simple for the supervisor who is trained and skilled in the Taxonomy. The materials that follow can be used at any grade level, in any kind of school, in any subject area, at any location.

The Teacher Profile Observation Sheets, Figures B-1 and B-2, record two teachers' classroom control behaviors in 10-minute segments. These segments may be tied end-to-end in a sequence (for example, a 20-minute observation period requires two Observation Sheets), or an observer may take various independent 10-minute samples, prearranged or randomly selected, from an entire class period or an entire teaching day. (In these two examples, observations are recorded every 30 seconds.) Important: the observer must know the Taxonomy in order to use this observation sheet.[1]

After the observations are recorded, evaluation can take place. Evaluation is a comparison of the observed information with some standard. Similarities and differences are noted and perhaps measured, and value judgments are made about the similarities and differences. In the case of classroom control, the standard is set by the fundamental principles presented in chapter 2.

In Figure B-1, notice how the teacher, as in the earlier example of Teacher X in chapter 2, leaps quickly to high profile at time markers 3.5 and 6, and *stays* high for more than one full minute of lesson time without apparent good reason at time markers 6 to 7.5. In contrast, the Teacher Y type of Figure B-2 exhibits a "rolling" pattern of control profiles and never leaps to mid or high profile. These teachers exhibit distinctively different patterns of classroom control, with the second conforming to the fundamental principles far better than the first.

EVALUATION OF PATTERNS

Recall the five profile patterns in chapter 2, Exercise 2. According to the fundamental principles of classroom control, control Patterns A and B are not as effective as Patterns C and D.

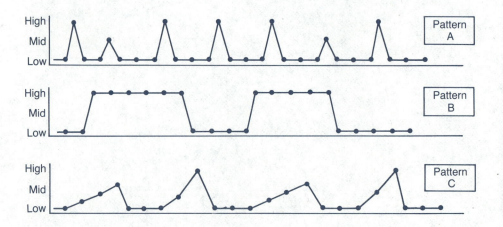

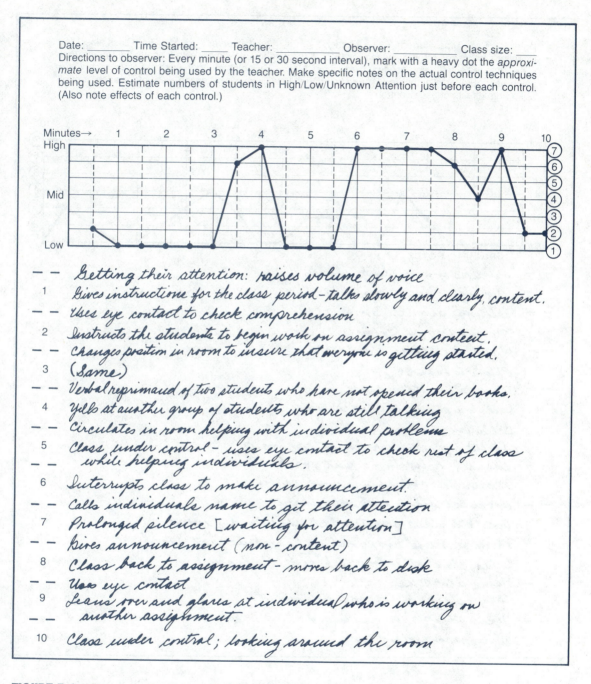

Date: _____ Time Started: _____ Teacher: _____ Observer: _____ Class size: ____
Directions to observer: Every minute (or 15 or 30 second interval), mark with a heavy dot the *approximate* level of control being used by the teacher. Make specific notes on the actual control techniques being used. Estimate numbers of students in High/Low/Unknown Attention just before each control. (Also note effects of each control.)

— — Getting their attention: raises volume of voice
1   Gives instructions for the class period – talks slowly and clearly, content.
— — Uses eye contact to check comprehension
2   Instructs the students to begin work on assignment content.
— — Changes position in room to insure that everyone is getting started.
3   (Same)
— — Verbal reprimand of two students who have not opened their books.
4   Yells at another group of students who are still talking
— — Circulates in room helping with individual problems
5   Class under control – uses eye contact to check rest of class
— —   while helping individuals.
6   Interrupts class to make announcement.
— — Calls individuals name to get their attention
7   Prolonged silence [waiting for attention]
— — Gives announcement (non - content)
8   Class back to assignment – moves back to desk
— — Uses eye contact
9   Leans over and glares at individual who is working on
— —   another assignment.
10   Class under control; looking around the room

FIGURE B-1   Classroom Control: Teacher Profile Observation Sheet (ten minutes).

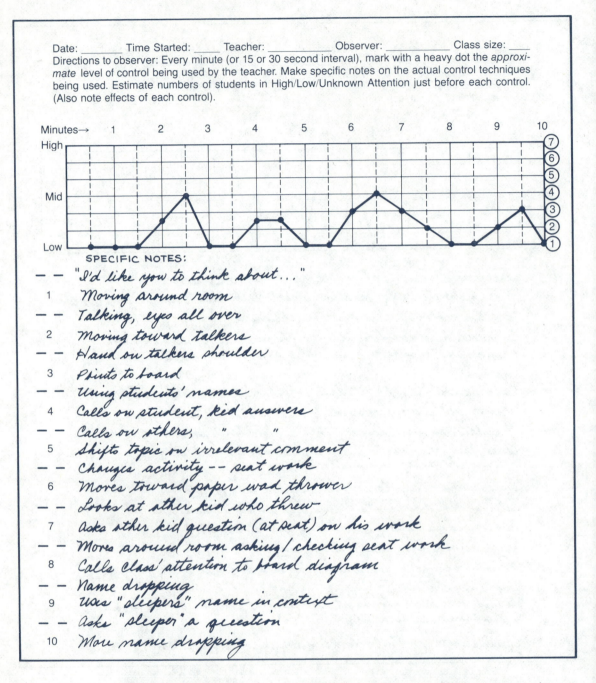

Date: _____ Time Started: _____ Teacher: _____ Observer: _____ Class size: ____
Directions to observer: Every minute (or 15 or 30 second interval), mark with a heavy dot the *approximate* level of control being used by the teacher. Make specific notes on the actual control techniques being used. Estimate numbers of students in High/Low/Unknown Attention just before each control. (Also note effects of each control).

SPECIFIC NOTES:

— — "I'd like you to think about..."
1   Moving around room
— — Talking, eyes all over
2   Moving toward talkers
— — Hand on talkers shoulder
3   Points to board
— — Using students' names
4   Calls on student, kid answers
— — Calls on others,   "   "
5   Shifts topic on irrelevant comment
— — Changes activity -- seat work
6   Moves toward paper wad thrower
— — Looks at other kid who threw
7   Asks other kid question (at seat) on his work
— — Moves around room asking / checking seat work
8   Calls class' attention to board diagram
— — Name dropping
9   Uses "sleepers" name in context
— — Asks "sleeper" a question
10   More name dropping

FIGURE B-2 Classroom Control-Teacher Profile Observation Sheet (ten minutes).

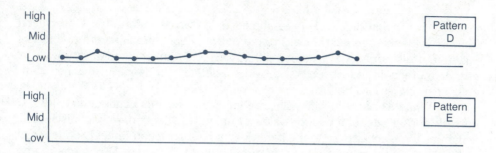

To evaluate the data displayed on a Teacher Profile Observation Sheet, compare the patterns on the Observation Sheet with Patterns A through E above. First, note any and all instances in which the teacher's control leaps to mid or high profile without adequate professional reason.[2] Then note any plateaus in which the teacher sustains mid or high profile control without adequate professional reason.[3]

Continued and consistent examples of Pattern A or Pattern B control, over time and with repeated observations by one or more qualified observers, provide strong evidence of ineffective classroom control.

In cases of Pattern A and/or B control, reports of positive student deportment or high student attention are not sufficient to refute the ineffectiveness of the patterns. For example, when an observer visits a classroom and is received with great ceremony, the situation is unreal, and everyone knows it. The students tend to be quiet and orderly even though the teacher may not demonstrate any significant classroom control skills, in either preparation or execution. The observer sees a rehearsed stage performance, not teaching; if he stays long enough, the scene will likely change — no charade can last forever.

An Observation Sheet whose pattern corresponds with Pattern C is evidence of professional classroom control. We cannot determine from the graphed profile alone whether a teacher's control techniques are artful (although comments on the sheet can provide evidence of art), but certainly we cannot question the professionalism of controls that exhibit Pattern C, with no signs of Patterns A or B, when reported by a qualified observer. A continuous record of Pattern C classroom controls, gathered over time and with repeated observations by one or more qualified observers, provides adequate evidence of teacher competence in classroom control. In cases of Pattern C control skills, reports of student deportment or attention are not adequate to refute teacher professionalism.

A Teacher Profile Observation Sheet that corresponds with Pattern D requires data on student attention before it can be evaluated for professional adequacy. The data can be based on the categories of attention discussed in chapter 2, or on any other reasonable protocol that distinguishes between student on-task and off-task behavior. If students are paying attention and the teacher is using low profile to maintain their attention, the teacher's control can be judged effective; however, if students are not paying attention and the teacher remains at low profile control, we must wonder why she does not begin sequential action to correct the problem.

When a Teacher Profile Observation Sheet exhibiting Pattern D controls, but no A or B, also reports consistent high attention student behaviors, almost no low attention behaviors, and no unabated unknown attention, that Observation Sheet is evidence of effective classroom control. A continuous record of effective Pattern D classroom control, gathered over time and with repeated observations by one or more qualified observers, provides adequate evidence of teacher competence in classroom control.

When a Teacher Profile Observation Sheet exhibits continuous Pattern D controls during extended periods of low or unknown attention, without discernible action[4] by the teacher prior to the behaviors, the Observation Sheet is evidence of ineffective classroom control. A continuous record of Pattern D controls during extended periods of low and unknown attention, gathered over time and with repeated observations by one or more qualified observers, provides strong evidence of teacher ineffectiveness in classroom control.

When a qualified observer fills out an Observation Sheet whose predominant pattern corresponds with Pattern E, the observations are evidence that instruction is not taking place under the direction of a teacher. No other conclusion can be drawn; if students are attending to a lesson during Pattern E periods, we must assume that teacher controls are not responsible for the attention.

AN EXAMPLE OF EVALUATION

When used in actual classrooms, Teacher Profile Observation Sheets usually display a variety of patterns rather than just one. For example, notice all the patterns in this sample observation sheet:

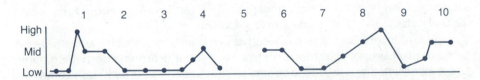

If we write the classroom control patterns directly under the graph itself, corresponding to prose statements from the Observation Sheet, we produce a picture like this:

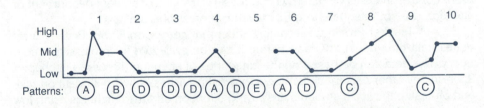

This shows a teacher whose classroom control patterns are quite varied, even erratic. There is a fair amount of Pattern D, but even one instance of Pattern A in a 10-minute segment should cause concern; three leaps are notably distracting to students. Pattern B is seen at time mark 1.5, as the teacher sustains a higher profile of control than is normally justified. (Notice, however, that if there is adequate professional reason for A and B — if, for example, time mark 1 is a safety warning following by a private conference with the negligent student — then A and B are justified.)

Next, notice that Pattern D controls between time marks 2 and 3.5 require data on student attention to show whether the teacher's control is effective during this time.

Notice, too, the hiatus of observable control at time mark 5. Prose statements should record what the teacher was or was not doing; we do not know the state of student attention during this time, but the observer reports no signs of teacher preplanning or preparation for the period. The teacher appears back on duty at about profile level 4 or 5, perhaps summoning a student to step outside the room to see a visitor, or quietly reprimanding a student who is not working on a lesson the teacher hoped would be done during the hiatus.

Finally, notice at time mark 7 how the teacher begins a Pattern C sequence ending in a high profile moment at time mark 8.5; without supporting prose we cannot know exactly what she does at 8.5 — we could imagine that she announces, "Many of you are forgetting the instructions I gave when we started, so please listen carefully now, all of you!" At time mark 9, she continues, perhaps with content-oriented low profile instructions: "Since all perspective goes to vanishing points, be sure to draw both vanishing points before you start your perspective drawing."

This teacher's classroom control is not as effective as it should be. Her observed patterns correspond with Patterns C and D little more than half the time, and her leaps to mid and high profile might indicate that she was surprised by class events she had not anticipated, such as student inattention or unruliness. It is entirely possible, even probable, that she is unaware of the distractions at time marks 1–1.5, 4, and 5.5; assuming that she wants to increase her awareness, supervision and coaching with periodic observation and conferences would help her learn and try the kinds of low profile controls she would like to use consistently.

NOTES

1   Notice the importance of specifying a qualified observer. An untrained observer might look at a beautifully controlled class of Pattern D and think it was a Pattern E. Supervisors and instructors must be aware of low profile professional control skills to observe accurately.

2   "Adequate professional reason" in Pattern A is almost always a matter of student safety, as in the example, "Don't touch that wire!" or "Careful, Jimmy, the floor is slippery there."

3   "Adequate professional reason" in Pattern B is not difficult to determine: if the teacher has been using correct sequential action, compared with Pattern C, and has arrived at Design, Level 7 or at Choice Counseling, Level 7, then we clearly have adequate professional reason for a Level 7 plateau.

4   "Discernible action," in this case, refers to a decision by the teacher — in prior consultation with a parent, supervisor, or both — to ignore certain inattention of a student or students as part of a strategic behavior modification program. (See chapter 19.) Without such prior consultation with a parent or supervisor, a teacher's "behavior modification program," announced subsequent to observation, may not be relevant to judgments of teacher professionalism or competence.

AUTHOR INDEX

SUBJECT INDEX

Boldfaced letters refer to Taxonomy method designation.

INDEX OF STUDENT GAMES

INDEX OF TEACHER GAMES

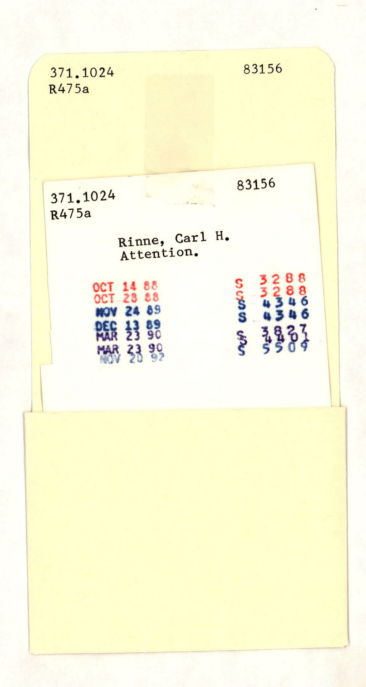